A Christian Folk-Religion in India

STUDIEN ZUR INTERKULTURELLEN GESCHICHTE DES CHRISTENTUMS
ETUDES D'HISTOIRE INTERCULTURELLE DU CHRISTIANISME
STUDIES IN THE INTERCULTURAL HISTORY OF CHRISTIANITY

begründet von / fondé par / founded by
Hans Jochen Margull †, Hamburg

herausgegeben von / édité par / edited by

Richard Friedli   Walter J. Hollenweger   Theo Sundermeier
Université de Fribourg   University of Birmingham   Universität Heidelberg

Band 40

Verlag Peter Lang
Frankfurt am Main · Bern · New York

P. Solomon Raj

A CHRISTIAN FOLK-RELIGION IN INDIA

A Study of the Small Church Movement in Andhra Pradesh, with a Special Reference to the Bible Mission of Devadas

Verlag Peter Lang
Frankfurt am Main · Bern · New York

CIP-Kurztitelaufnahme der Deutschen Bibliothek

Raj, Solomon:
A Christian folk religion in India : a study of
the small church movement in Andhra Pradesh,
with a special reference to the Bible Mission
of Devadas / Solomon Raj. - Frankfurt am Main ;
Bern ; New York : Lang, 1986.
  (Studies in the intercultural history of
  Christianity ; Bd. 40)
  ISBN 3-8204-8924-X
NE: Studien zur interkulturellen Geschichte des
Christentums

BX
6510
.B628
D487
1986

ISSN 0170-9240
ISBN 3-8204-8924-X

© Verlag Peter Lang GmbH, Frankfurt am Main 1986
Alle Rechte vorbehalten.
Nachdruck oder Vervielfältigung, auch auszugsweise, in allen Formen
wie Mikrofilm, Xerographie, Mikrofiche, Mikrocard, Offset verboten.

Druck und Bindung: Weihert-Druck GmbH, Darmstadt

PREFACE: Towards an Indigenous Christianity in India

Some thirty-five years ago a Swedish scholar, Bengt Sundkler, astonished church historians and ecumenists with his massive research on more than two thousand independent Bantu churches in South Africa.[1] Western scholars were quick to explain the proliferation of these independent churches on the basis of South African apartheid, but then similar churches emerged in other parts of Africa. Some of them, like the Kimbanguist Church,[2] joined the World Council of Churches. A number of them began mission work in Europe.

So it could no longer be denied that a revival was sweeping through Africa. But it was a revival sui generis, highly indigenized and independent. "No serious study of Christian theology in Africa can with any justification ignore these churches and their life and thought."[3] "And thought", says the author, Kwesi A. Dickson, professor in the University of Ghana.

No sooner did we get used to these independent churches in Africa than Harold W. Turner established the fact that these independent churches are not merely a local or even an African phenomenon but that they are to be found in all continents.[4] Recently David B. Barrett has furnished statistical evidence of their growth all over the world. He says: One of the more startling findings documented in this research "is the existence of a whole new bloc of global Christianity unrelated to either Western or Eastern Christendom: this is termed here Non-White Indigenous Christianity. Parts of it have been known about for many decades; but no-one realized its formidable collective zeal and its immense aggregate size - 82 million affiliated church members in 1980" and growing.[5]

Barrett and other researchers reveal such churches in places where our former statistics only mentioned the familiar mission churches. Interaction between mission churches and these newly emerging churches was lively, sometimes violent, sometimes creative.

A splendid example of such a creative interaction was published by Werner Hoerschelmann in this series,[6] the first major research on independent churches in India. He calls them "Christian Guru Churches" and presents extensive, hitherto unknown, material. In his analysis of these churches he shows their historical roots, their spirituality and their worship forms and discusses the varied influences on them – from the expatriate missionaries to pentecostal evangelists and Indian folk culture. However, he is reluctant to come to a final theological judgment stating that this task must be taken on board by Indian theologians.

Dr Solomon Raj is just such an Indian theologian. In this volume he describes the "Bible Mission" in Andhra Pradesh, a church which was founded by a former Lutheran, Mungamuri Devadas. Solomon Raj is not satisfied with the generally accepted condemnation of these churches as "sheep stealers" – although it is true that they draw many of their members not only from mission churches but also in certain cases from Europe (many Europeans travel to India in order to immerse themselves in an Indian form of Christianity). However, Raj also shows their influence on the Hindu society.

Solomon Raj sets his presentation of the Bible Mission into the debate on intercultural theology. He sees in the "Bible Mission" a contribution to an Indian Church which throws off its "Latin Captivity" (Boyd) and starts to shape its own theology, liturgy and ministry. Its theology centres on questions of inner and outer healing, on the understanding and interpretation of dreams, on an exegesis of the Bible which is less interested in its original historical meaning than in its existential application. Its liturgy borrows freely from Indian music, poetry, dance and religious heritage. Its ministry is the ministry of a Guru – either fulltime or part-time. The Guru's authority does not lie in his scholarship or ordination but in his saintliness and in his ability to help those who come to him in fear of demons, in psychological anxiety and in sickness. In short: they expect him to help them to understand and withstand the bewildering world in which they live. They expect him to make sense of a senseless world in the presence of God. Before I, as a Western theologian, criticize this unusual

approach it might be more profitable to ask myself: What other modes
of "a hermeneutics of the world" is available for people who can
barely read the Bible - and if they can read, they are neither
interested nor able to follow the Western interpretation of Scripture?
They have little understanding of the complex historical process
which shaped Western theology and in fact the biblical texts. And
why should they? They have to go on living before a coherent
Indian-Christian world-view is shaped.

One thing is sure: Neither theology nor Church History will ever be
the same again. Strange, exciting and bewildering forms of Christianity
are emerging all over the world. What will be their relationship to
our tired Western Christianity? Or will the challenge from Africa and
Asia and other parts of the world help us to sharpen our own European/
American understanding of the Gospel? Will we find a way to see the
ecumenical and missiological values of these "unauthorised" churches
who - in many places - outnumber the "authorized churches" by far?
And finally, are we able to see that at least some of the elements of
their spirituality are a bitterly needed correction to our own spirituality or lack of spirituality?

As to Dr Solomon Raj, he has returned to his native country. He is
working in a little Ashram with dance and drama groups within his own
Lutheran Church and continues to express his Indian understanding of
the Gospel in Batiks and wood-cuts. Some of them he has included in
this volume, but unfortunately only in black and white. The colour-
prints of his Batiks are available from Dr Peter Holtrop, Stadionkade
10D, Amsterdam 1076 BN, Holland. They ideally complement Solomon Raj's
scholarly work on another level.

Dr Walter J. Hollenweger
Professor of Mission

NOTES to Preface

(1) Bengt G.M. Sundkler, <u>Bantu Prophets in South Africa</u>, London (1948), 1961; see also his later work <u>Zulu Zion and Some Swazi Zionists</u>, London 1976, and the works in this series, pertaining to our topic: Erhard Kamphausen, <u>Anfänge der kirchlichen Unabhängigkeitsbewegung in Südafrika.</u> Geschichte und Theologie der äthiopischen Bewegung 1880-1910 (vol. 6 of this series, Frankfurt/Berne 1976) - Werner Korte, <u>Wir sind die Kirchen der unteren Klassen.</u> Entstehung, Organisation und gesellschaftliche Funktionen unabhängiger Kirchen in Afrika. (vol. 15 of this series, Frankfurt/Berne 1978) - Bingham Tembe, <u>Integrationismus und Afrikanismus.</u> Zur Rolle der kirchlichen Unabhängigkeitsbewegung in der Auseinandersetzung um die Landfrage und die Bildung der Afrikaner in Südafrika, 1880-1960.(vol. 36 of this series, Frankfurt/Berne 1985).

(2) Werner Ustorf, <u>Afrikanische Initiative. Das aktive Leiden des Propheten Simon Kimbangu.</u> (vol. 5 of this series, Frankfurt/Berne 1975).

(3) Kwesi A. Dickson, <u>Theology in Africa</u>, London 1974.

(4) H.W. Turner, <u>Religious Innovation in Africa</u>. Boston, Mass., 1979. See also W.J. Hollenweger, art. "Junge Kirchen" in <u>Theol. Realenzyklopädie</u> (Berlin, forthcoming).

(5) David B. Barrett, <u>World Christian Encyclopedia</u>, London 1982, 15.

(6) Werner Hoerschelmann, <u>Christliche Gurus.</u> Darstellung von Selbstverständnis und Funktion indigenen Christseins durch unabhängige, charismatisch geführte Gruppen in Südindien. (vol. 12 in this series, Frankfurt/Berne 1977).

Synopsis

This thesis is an attempt to analyse and interpret critically a Christian Folk Religion in India. The name is Bible Mission and the founder Mungamuri Dēvadās. The Bible Mission is an example of some folk religious trends appearing in India today.

Devadas was originally a member of the Andhra Evangelical Lutheran Church. What made him want to start a new church? How can one deal with his claim that he had a direct revelation (prathyaksha) and a call from God to do so? What are the distinctive teachings of the Bible Mission? What are its relationships with the other denominations in India and what are the points of strife?

After an introductory chapter wherein the problem is enunciated, a survey of the historical background and the life story of Devadas are attempted in two chapters of the first section. Then in a second section some of the basic theological views of Devadas are examined under four headings including a chapter on demons, spirits and miracles and healing, which mark the Bible Mission's major points of deviation from the teachings of the mainline churches.

Then in section three, four chapters deal with the Theology of Devadas in Action, with an emphasis on the oral tradition of story, song and parable and the collective archetypes of the community.

Finally, in the fourth section, an attempt is made to draw some conclusions in four chapters on the general characteristics of the so-called 'non-White Indigenous churches', a short theological debate on the concept of dreams, visions and healing, the process of indigenization with a special reference to the Indian Church and the possible future trends.

The overall objective of the research is to study the traditions and the theology of a folk Christian church in India and to try to discern some possible pointers for the total task of the church in India today.

There are appendixes with samples from Telugu poetry and songs, also photographs and art work by the author to illustrate various sections.

Acknowledgements

I owe a deep dept of gratitude to many people for their help, without which it would not have been possible for me to complete this thesis. First of all, I pay homage to the memory of that simple saintly man, who was in a way a representative of the 'folk Christian Religions' in India, Father Devadas, the founder of the Bible Mission, whose spirituality appealed to me early in my life. Recently some of his followers have helped me to know more about the man and his teachings and I thank them.

My interest in the subject of Inter-cultural Theology and the indigenous church movements was re-kindled after I came to Birmingham and sat in the seminars of my guru, Dr. W.J.Hollenweger, Professor of Mission, Birmingham University. He has kindly accepted to guide me in this research and helped me very patiently at every stage. His enthusiasm in the subject and his scholarship never failed to inspire all his students.

I thank Mrs. Joan Pears for her help, guiding me with the necessary reading materials and arranging regular tutorial sessions over a period of four years on this project.

My thanks are due to Professor Hans W. Gensichen, Professor of Missions at Heidelberg University, who was also my teacher at the Gurukul Theological College, Madras. As the president of the Deutsche Gesellschaft fur Missionswissenschaft he kindly arranged for a scholarship to cover the University Fees for this programme. I am thankful to the concerned officers of the Deutsch Gesellschaft for their kind interest in my project.

I am thankful to the Division of World Missions of the Lutheran Church in America, and the Asia Secretary of that Division, Dr. J.F. Neudoerffer, for a grant which enabled me to spend a summer vacation in the Mission Archives at the Chicago Lutheran School of Theology, looking into the documentary materials on the early history of the Andhra Evangelical Lutheran Church.

I express my deep gratitude to my colleague in the Cross Cultural Communications at Selly Oak Colleges, Rev. Denys Saunders, for his encouragement. Dr. George Mulrain, Dr. von Sicard, Dr. Harold Turner and Bishop Lesslie Newbigin have kindly read parts of my work and offered valuable suggestions, and I thank them. Dr. W. Hoerschelmann of Hamburg, Rev. Ernest Gallagher of Belfast, and Dr. David Hall of Aberdeen, all the three as former missionaries to India, have shared my concern in the subject and offered several suggestions and I acknowledge their help. (Shortly after I completed this work the Rev. Gallagher was called to eternal rest.)

Dr. Marcella Hoesel, Dean of Missions, Mr. John Ferguson, the president of the Selly Oak Colleges, and many other colleagues have given their encouragement. The librarians at the Selly Oak Colleges Central Library, the West Hill College Library, and the University Library at Birmingham gave their help, especially Miss Frances Williams of the Selly Oak Colleges Central Library. Miss Williams herself was a Missionary to India and she immediately knew my requirements for reading. I am thankful to Dr. Joel Lundeen, the Assistant Archivist at the Chicago Lutheran School of Theology, who took special interest in me and missed some of his holidays for my sake.

My son, Martin, took the photographs needed for this thesis, going on a long trip from his college to Andhra Pradesh for this project. My wife very cheerfully encouraged me all along in my work, facing many difficulties together with me. I thank her.

My father and mother, who brough us up in great reverence to the Church and in the Christian faith, have both been faithful workers in the Lutheran Church all through their life. I dedicate this work to their memory.

After the University of Birmingham has accepted this work for a Ph.D. degree, Messers Peter Lang and Company in Frankfurt have agreed to publish it. I am thankful to them. Drummond Trust in Scotland, Cadbury Trust in England and Hermannsburg Mission in West Germany have equally shared in providing the publishing grants. Without their help this project would not have been possible.

I prepared this manuscript for printing while on a teaching assignment at Bethany College, Lindsborg, Kansas, in the U.S.A., and my colleagues Dr. Delmar Holman and Dr. Vance Eckstrom have assisted me by reading the manuscript and managing the computer printing respectively. I am deeply indebted to both of them.

Loyola Gardens,
Vijayawada, Andhra Pradesh,
India.

P.Solomon Raj

TABLE OF CONTENTS

Synopsis	i
Acknowledgments	iii
Table of Contents	v
List of Illustrations	ix

INTRODUCTION

Chapter I: The Seeker and the Quest	1
1. The Church as Seeker	1
2. The Conflict between the Historic Churches and the Indigenous Churches	5
3. Some Types of Group Churches in Andhra Pradesh	7
4. The Dilemma of the Mainline Churches	9
5. The Success of the Group Churches	12
6. Three Possible Courses of Action	13
7. The Present Quest	14
8. Bible Mission - A Christian Folk Religion	17
9. Some Difficulties Faced in this Study	18
10. Scope of the Study	21

PART I: THE BACKGROUND

Chapter II: The Historical Setting	25
1. The Land and the People	25
2. Caste System and Social Conditions in Andhra	27
3. Advent of Protestant Missions in Coastal Andhra	30
4. Origins of the Lutheran Mission Work in Andhra	31
5. Growth and Consolidation	33
Chapter III: The Man Devadas and His Times	41
1. The Man Devadas	41
2. The Founder's Own Account	46
3. The Story Continues	47
4. The Teacher Gathers Some Disciples	49
5. The Growth of Bible Mission in the Life Time of Father Devadas	55
6. The End of a Great Life	56

PART II: SOME BASIC THEOLOGICAL VIEWS OF DEVADAS

Chapter IV: Experienced Religion (Faith, Demons, Spirits, Visions, Dreams and Healing)	63
1. The Cultural Background	63
2. Demons and Spirits in the Bible Mission	66
3. What are the Spirits and Where are They?	69

Table of Contents

    4. The Spirit of Devadas Speaks to the Faithful   73
    5. From Spirits to the Spirit   77
    6. Miracles and Healing   81
    7. Visions and Extra-Biblical Revelations   86

Chapter V: The Church as the Holy Bride   99
    1. Ecclesia in the New Testament - Stages of Development   99
    2. The Teachings of the Bible Mission about the Church   107
    3. A Theological Appraisal of Some of the Ecclesiastical Models   114

Chapter VI: God and Trinity in Action   121
    1. The God Who is Revealed to Us   121
    2. Devadas and the Doctrine of Trinity   124
    3. Praise God for What He Is   128
    4. God's Work in the World   129
    5. God Uses Human Instrumentality to Do His Will   130
    6. Jesus Christ Our Lord   131
    7. God the Holy Spirit   132
    8. Is Our God Dumb?   133

Chapter VII: The Imminent Second Coming of Christ   139
    1. Devadas and His Concern for Eschatology   139
    2. Some Eschatological Events   140
    3. A Redemption for the Whole World   143
    4. The Signs of the Times   145
    5. So What Shall We Do?   147
    6. Eschatology and Evangelism   149
    7. A Universal Quest   151

PART III: HIS THEOLOGY IN ACTION

Chapter VIII: The Hymns in the Bhakti Tradition   157
    1. The Singing Tradition of the Telugu Church   157
    2. Dhatu and Mathu, Music and Language of the Telugu Poetry   162
    3. Some Metrical Features of Devadas' Hymns   164
    4. Theological Content of the Hymns of Devadas   166
    5. Some New Trends in the Musical Experience of the Telugu Church   175

Chapter IX: The Pedagogical Methods in Guru Tradition   181
    1. Devadas a Born Teacher   181
    2. A People of Oral Tradition   182
    3. Story and Song in the Service of Theology   185
    4. Catechetical and Analytical Process   188
    5. Domesticating or Liberating?   190
    6. Systematic Theology versus Narrative Exegesis   193

Table of Contents vii

Chapter X: In the Presence of God (Prayer, Worship
 and Liturgy) 197
1. The Source Material 197
2. Daiva Sannidhi, the Presence of God 198
3. How to Conduct the Sannidhi Meetings 201
4. Practising the Presence of God, A Gift to the
 Bible Mission 204
5. God's Promise to Answer Prayer 207
6. Climbing the Ladder 210
7. Does God Need a Chair to Come and Sit with Us? 210
8. A Liturgy for the Folk Church 212
9. Fellowship of Saints 213
10. Prayer of the Church 214

Chapter XI: The Ethical Views - A Community Unto
 the Lord 219
1. Concept of a Holy God 219
2. The Dreadfulness of Sin 220
3. Family and Children 224

PART IV: CONCLUSION

Chapter XII: Characteristics of Non-White Indigenous
 Churches 229
1. Some Types of New Church Groups 229
2. Some Characteristics of Indigenous Non-White
 Churches 234
3. Tension with the Mission Churches 242
4. Conclusion 246

Chapter XIII: Dreams, Visions and Healing - A More
 Detailed Analysis 251
1. Introduction 251
 a) A Liberal Theology and Experience of God 253
 b) Dispensationalism 254
 c) Demythologising 255
 d) The Mediaeval Church 255
 e) Man and His Understanding of God 257
2. Dreams 258
 a) Significance of Dreams to a Christian Life 258
 b) Understanding Dreams 259
 c) Dreams are about the Dreamer 264
 d) Dreams in the Form of Poetry Song and Story 266
3. Visions 267
 a) Introduction 267
 b) Meditation and Visions 268
 c) How Exactly to Handle These Extra-Sensory
 Experiences? 271

Table of Contents

4. Healing 273
   a) What is Spiritual Healing? 273
   b) Development of the Church's View on Healing 275
   c) Spiritual Healing - The Present Understanding 279
   d) The Healing Church - The Tubingen Consultation 281
   e) Conclusion 286
5. Experience Pointing to the Beyond 288
   a) A Total Reality 288
   b) Three Kinds of Spiritual Experience 289
   c) Some Critical Comments 294

Chapter XIV: Towards Indigenization - A Prospect 299
1. What is Indigenization? 299
2. Indigenous Expression in Liturgy, Hymns and Worship 301
3. Indigenization of Life and Witness 305
4. Indigenization of Theological Thought 316
5. Adaptation 319
6. Agents for Indigenization 324
   a) Indian Writers and Thinkers 324
   b) New Religious Movements as Laboratories for Theology 327
   c) Interaction with Other Religions 328
7. Some Problems of Indigenization 329

Chapter XV: Where Do We Go from Here? 337

Bibliography 345

Appendixes
   I. Chariot Wheels of God 354
   II. (i) In Praise of Asia - G.Joshuwa 356
       (ii) A Mother's Lamentation - G.Joshuwa 357
   III. Who is the Source of My Joy? - M.Devadas 358
   IV. Notes on Poetical Structures in Telugu Language 360
   V. People Interviewed for the Research 367
   VI. Glossary 369

Table of Contents

List of Illustrations

Art Work by the Author

1. Man of Sorrows — Woodcut
2. Father M. Devadas, from a photograph in His Old Age — "
3. The World of the Angels — Linocut
4. The Church, the Holy Bride Received in Heaven — "
5. Abiding Presence, Artist's Dream — Batik
6. Adoration of Christ, The Bethany Home — Woodcut
7. Jesus the Teacher — Batik
8. We see Him as in A Dream — "
9. Christ with the Refugees — Woodcut
10. Service and Evangelism, the Mission of the Church — Batik

Photographs

1. Tablet of the Grave Stone of Devadas - To Whom God Revealed the Bible Mission
2. The Faithful Gather Around the Tomb of Devadas
3. The Sheep and the Goats (from the Dance Drama Kim Karthavyam)
4. A Seat for the Spirit of Devadas Awaiting at the Prayer Meetings
5. The Place Where They Buried Him It is a Place of Healing
6. Woman of Samaria (from the Dance Drama Kim Karthavyam)
7. Encounter with Christ (from the Dance Drama Kim Karthavyam)

Map of India

Man of Sorrows

CHAPTER I

The Seeker and the Quest

1. The Church as Seeker

'Seek and you shall find', said Jesus. All men are seekers in a way. As individuals and in communities we are seeking something all the time. A well known Catholic communicator, Father Pierre Babin, once said,

> Christians today are experiencing the pain of the collapse of structures. The traditional ideological strength has disappeared. We are beginning an age of pluralism in which every one must make a synthesis every day and must learn to discern the difference between the real and the transient[1].

Pierre Babin is, of course, talking about what he calls the new style of Christian Life which involves risks, particularly sacrificing some structures and asking for a clear vision of things. In this sense the Church today is seeking a new identity, a new vision.

This in a sense is the experience of the Church in India too in the 20th century. The old structures in the Indian Church seem to be collapsing. One sometimes gets the impression that the Church as an 'institution' is slowly receding into the background and a new concept of a community of the 'disciples' of Christ is emerging and words like 'discipling' instead of conversion, and 'disciples' or believers instead of Christians, are coming into use more and more. In other words, the churches are seeking new ways of living their faith and new ways of organizing themselves and witnessing.

At the beginning of the century the foreign missions which brought the Gospel into the country started giving way to their successor—'the churches'—and there was a new move towards nationalisation in administration and management and a new awareness of the indigenous form of worship and witness. An indigenous form of theological thought and expression started to emerge a little more clearly than before. For example, a long time after the advent of the modern missions to India the church started to get rid of the Western trimmings in its liturgy, including Western hymns and symbols, and it started using melodies of its own land and to some extent began expressing its faith in its own cultural art forms. The Latin Captivity of the Church, as R.H.S. Boyd calls it[2], seemed to be coming to an end. Slowly the Indian Christians have got rid of their hesitation to express their faith in truly indigenous forms. Boyd suggests that the main factor which has tended to discourage an Indian Christian theology so far was the 'widespread dislike among the Hindus and Christians for anything dogmatic'. The Hindus called Christianity an authoritarian religion[3].

However, David Barrett in his World Christian Encyclopedia reported that in 1958 and onwards there were many attempts towards a kind of indigenization and there was an attempt towards a 'Hindu-Christian' church affirming faith in Jesus Christ but at the same time rejecting the Western missionary control. These groups tried to retain Hindu culture within the Christian faith. The first such organisations which the World Christian Encyclopedia mentions are the following:

    1858 Hindu Church of the Lord Jesus Christ, Tinnevelly.
    1868 The proposal for a national Church of Bengal.
    1870 Chet Ramis, Punjab.
    1880 Church of the New Dispensation (Nava Vidhana), Calcutta.
    1886 National Church of Madras.
    1887 Calcutta Christo Samāj.
    1893 The proposal for an all-embracing National Church of India.

Others followed in 1920, 1921, 1933 (Fellowship of the Followers of Jesus, begun by Kandiswamy Chetty in Madras in 1942), and the largest still existing in 1975, the Subba Rao movement[4]. The Encyclopedia reports that altogether 'from 1858 to 1975 there have been over 150 such indigenous Hindu-Christian movements or churches in India'.

Within the historical mainline churches also there has always been an attempt at indigenization. M.M. Thomas, in his introduction to Boyd's book mentioned above, makes a reference to a certain 'continuity of the hidden stream of living theology which has been flowing in India'[5]. This theology, which has not as yet been expressed in any systems, is, according to Thomas, a living theology.

The collapse of 'structures' mentioned earlier can be observed in other areas of the church and its witness also. There was a great awakening in this period for church unity and a desire to break away from the old 'parent mission' labels and a longing towards a truly indigenous form and expression. R.H.S. Boyd has also drawn our attention to two important events which occurred in the beginning of the 20th century--the formation of the South India United Church, a union of Presbyterians and Congregationalists in 1908, and the establishment of the United Theological College in Bangalore in 1910, both of which helped the spirit of ecumenism and cooperation among different denominations.

At about the same time the National Missionary Society formed to reach the remote parts of India was born in 1905 and the National Missionary Council came into existence in 1914, which became the National Council of Churches in India in 1923.

Nearly 200 years after the advent of the modern missions to India there appeared a new revival movement and a new evangelical zeal. Many of the older practices and values, even the old formal type of Christianity, began to come under scrutiny. The cool formality of the old church worship and its liturgy has been severely criticized in some quarters. The Indian Christian writers and poets have started writing new 'bhakti' songs in the truly Indian melodies in various languages and these slowly started to replace the Western hymns.

The church in India also started growing in size, and as it grew more preachers and teachers were needed, and not enough theologically trained ministers were available for the teaching and preaching tasks of the church. Much of the work in the field of education and evangelism has become the responsibility of the lay preacher. Many of the simple village Christians, especially in South India, showed a great hunger for a simple and deeply satisfying form of religion and worship with cymbals and drums and clapping of hands and with all the India 'colour and odour'.

In India there has always been in people's minds a positive attitude for mystery and wonder and an eagerness for the miraculous. People look for miracles to happen and all along we see that a form of prayer healing was practised in the name of Jesus Christ, although the mainline churches have not taken too much interest in this type of ministry. One can understand the hesitation of the historic churches toward prayer healing. The fear of superstitious beliefs and the danger of magic and demon worship and ritual scared the earlier missionaries away from the practice of prayer healing and instead the earlier missions have practised and promoted hospital work and medical training for health workers. Instead of holding a holistic idea of life, the mission churches have concentrated on treating the body in sickness. Now, of course, the situation in this respect has changed and there is an appreciation of prayer healing on a larger scale in the churches.

The Indian masses have always been attracted to miracles. In one of the Thomas churches in Kerala I saw an old draw well outside the church which is believed to be part of an old temple tank where the Brahmins used to have their ritual bathing in the mornings and prayed to the sun god. Christians in this area believe that St. Thomas the apostle one day had challenged the Brahmin priests to throw the water up in the name of their sun god and make it stand there in the air. The Brahmins could not do that and then St. Thomas, it is believed, prayed to Christ and threw the water up with his hands and it stayed there for a moment for the Brahmins to see in wonder. Thus, the Christians in this village called Parur claim that many people were converted to Christianity and the church took root in that area. Ever since, the waters of that tank which later became a draw well attained miraculous healing powers. There are many stories like this attributing miraculous powers to places and people. Miracle healing in a country like India is part of people's religious experience.

The village Christians believed in these prayer healings, but they have experienced healing power not generally in the mission churches but in the charismatic prayer groups. This attraction to prayer healing has started almost a new kind of Christianity which is different from the one preached in the majority of the mission churches.

In the matter of church leadership also there was a new quest in these years. The Western missionary who brought the Gospel continued for a long time to be the sole leader and care-taker of the souls and bodies of the new believers. The white man was considered to have powers and gifts. But in the new dispensation, the Indian Christians were encouraged to take the leadership role, and in some cases the indigenous leaders started their own groups and their own movements. Harold Turner, in his study of the Primal Religions of Africa, indicates a similar phenomenon where the native leaders wanted to inherit the same kind of 'powers' as they saw in the white man.

As part of the revival and the new life movement which had started in India in the early decades of this century Indian saints like Sadhu Sundar Singh have appeared on the scene with their visionary powers and miracles through prayer. Sundar Singh became a well-known preacher and he visited several parts of the country with his message. He also became very controversial among missionaries. Since then there have been other Indian Christian gurus. Dr. W. Hoerschelmann has produced a monumental work on the gurus of the Indian Christian church and he documented the work of many of these gurus and their theology in detail[6].

One of the better known revival preachers today is Brother Bhakta Singh, who started several ashram type of believers' groups in Hyderabad, Madras, and other places in South India. These groups and fellowships have provided a different kind of religious experience to people, a kind which was not commonly found in the 'mission compound' Christianity, and some Christians from the mainline churches, while keeping their membership in their respective churches, have joined these prayer groups and ashrams and house-churches, for special fellowship and prayer. Many of these people have even tithed to these groups regularly from their meagre incomes. The groups fared better financially than the major churches sometimes. The groups managed their work without any foreign aid.

2. The Conflict between the Historic Churches and the Indigenous Churches

In the early days the church groups or the charismatic groups were harshly condemned by the major churches. Sometimes these small groups were called the 'splinter groups', or 'sheep stealers', etc., because many of the followers of these new groups, as already mentioned, originally belonged to the mission churches and then left their churches for various reasons to join the new groups.

An example of the attitude of the older churches and their leaders towards these groups can be gathered from a pamphlet produced by an old Lutheran missionary in Andhra Pradesh several years ago. The title of this hand-out can be translated as <u>The Story of the Thieves.</u> The thieves one day came to the hillside where some farmers had laboured hard for several years before and cultivated the waste land and brought it to a fruit-yielding stage. The thieves wanted to work in the same field but those farmers who were already there asked them to go and start in the other big waste land still available on the other side of the hill. But the 'thieves' insisted on their right to occupy the same land that the farmers had brought into cultivation.

The moral is clear. The reference of course is to the small group church people who came into the area of the existing older missions and wanted to convert the 'already converted'. In the state of Andhra Pradesh, India, in the parts then known as Andhra Desa, there was much floor-crossing and 'sheep stealing' going on in the denominational churches. It is true that the revival groups did not intend to start separate churches in the beginning. All that they wanted was to bring some 'spirit' into the churches and to encourage their followers to continue to stay in their own denominations as witnessing Christians. The aim then was to bring a little fire into the churches' preaching and a little light into their singing.

There is yet another incident I remember which may further illustrate how denominational churches have treated the members of the group movements. This happened when I was a seminary student in 1953. I was attending a big church Council meeting in our town Lutheran church. The meeting was convened mainly to deal with the question of some Lutheran members drifting away into the independent church groups which operated in that area in those days. Some such members were holding teaching jobs, etc., in the Lutheran Church and they were asked to explain why they were going to the groups' meetings and whether it would not amount to being unfaithful to their own Church. One of them, a graduate school teacher who wanted to make a statement, stood up and said that he was still a faithful member of the Lutheran Church but the group meetings he was attending were like a little 'wine' to cheer him up and so he could not resist it. (The poor palm wine shops well-known in the area are not such 'respectable places' even if the wine is attractive and hence the metaphor). Then the Chairman of the church Council, a senior pastor who never liked the group movements, retorted: "No, you do not have to miss your wine we are only asking you to come to our shop. You will get the same wine here. Why should you go to the other shop?" Many people laughed but the point was made and clearly understood.

3. Some Types of Group Churches in Andhra Prades

The independent group churches in Andhra Pradesh can be grouped into three categories. First of all, there are the so-called revival groups seeking to remain in the denominational churches. They did not want to start any churches of their own in the beginning, as we have already mentioned. But these soon developed their own structures and administrative machinery like any other older denominational church. They also started administering the sacraments and performing Christian marriages although they clearly stated in the earlier days that it was not their responsibility to do these and they left them to the major church bodies. So these in effect considered themselves as charismatic groups within the major church bodies.

Then there are other groups which did not remain as revival groups within the churches but which broke away from the main line churches and became a kind of dissident body which worked independently outside the major churches seriously differing with them sometimes on some matters of faith and practice. Some such movements have become strong and made converts from other religions and co-existed with the major denominational churches.

There is still a third type, small in number, which from the very beginning remained outside the major churches sometimes as open rivals to them. Highly critical of the historic churches, these groups never had any real dialogue or fellowship with the latter. They do not have much fellowship with the other indigenous groups either. The movement around Subba Rao of Munipalle of

Andhra Pradesh, sometimes called the 'Hindu-Christian' movement, is one such. Subba Rao had never been baptised but he claimed to be the follower of Christ by direct call[7]. Subba Rao revolted against a type of institutionalised Christianity which he saw around him and he rejected even the sacrament of Baptism which he considered as a superficial and unnecessary practice insisted on by the Western Padre and blindly followed by the Indian Christians. According to Subba Rao, to become a disciple of Christ nothing was needed, like church membership, or any kind of labels, not even prayer because once a person is united with Christ, even prayer becomes unnecessary. 'To whom does such a person pray? To himself?' asks Subba Rao[8]. But this is an example of the extreme form of Christianity. Yet it should be noted that the type of discipleship which Subba Rao had advocated appeals to many Hindus most probably because it does not require membership in any organised church and one can remain in his own social matrix with all the comforts which his social community provided while at the same time aspiring to the miraculous powers which Subba Rao had promised in the name of Christ[9].

This phenomenon is not peculiar to India alone. Reporting on similar developments in primal societies in Africa, Dr. Harold Turner says:

> The tribal people have been producing an unexpected and often unrecognised response through new religious movements of their own creation. Some of these are sufficiently Christian to be independent churches, even if some of their ways of being Christian are different from the churches developed from the missions. Others may be anti-Christian but at the same time may reveal some important transformation of the old primal religion towards a more biblical position[10].

Turner also says:

> While the founders of each of these movements had belonged to a local Christian community, their lives have moved into another orbit and the movements they created were very different from the churches they had left. Whatever their Christian content, whether

orthodox or unorthodox, this was now expressed in forms deeply rooted in the local tribal culture. This was a tremendous achievement, something that missions set as part of their goal[11].

Although the indigenous church groups which we are talking about in India are different in some ways from the new tribal religions in Africa, yet there are enough similarities between the two, and what Turner says here about the former is true of the latter.

4. The Dilemma of the Mainline Churches

Thus the mainline churches in India and in the state of Andhra Pradesh had a somewhat unprecedented problem of coping with some independent movements within and without. Some areas in the state of Andhra Pradesh have become breeding grounds for several small group churches. In a small town on the banks of the River Godavary, for example, one can count several small independent churches operating. In one family a former member of the Lutheran Church became a bishop of a certain Church of God of Witness in India, his son became the leader of a big Brethren Mission group with many workers under him, and the son-in-law became the Bishop of some other new church group, all operating in one and the same area, and all doing well.

About the situation in Andhra Pradesh, a recent issue of <u>Religion and Society</u> reports editorially:

> There are more than sixty Christian sects in Andhra Pradesh. Some are very well established. Some spread into other parts of India. For more than a decade some Bishops and other heads of churches in our CISRS (Christian Institute for Study of Religion and Society) movement--some of them foreign missionaries--have been urging us to study these sectarian movements in South India. The churches have felt threatened. Probably they still do. As interested researchers have appeared we have encouraged them in this direction. What, exactly, is going on in this very large movement towards sectarianism? Lionel Caplan (<u>Towards a Sociology of Christianity in</u>

South India, in the Anne Besant lectureship of Madras University) finds that other Christians have three main kinds of explanation:

1) A cynical minority suggests that American Religious Imperialism with its vast resources is at least partly responsible.

2) A larger pious group see the Holy Spirit at work.

3) But the majority have a more pragmatic explanation--the failure of the mainline Protestant churches to meet the spiritual needs of the ordinary Christian.

Probably this is so. Our own reading of the studies made so far leads us to conclude that not only do the mainline Protestant churches often fail to meet felt spiritual needs but also that the leaders of the churches--often on the basis of received foreign missionary patterns--have tended too readily to drive the sectarians out of the churches on the grounds of discipline and orthodoxy. This seems too bad. No doubt new Christians may need clear restraints against 'backsliding'--this may be what some of the 'hard sayings' of our Lord are about. But such patterns may no longer be appropriate for persons born into the Christian community several generations later. These patterns may also be seen as inappropriate if used largely to enforce the authority of those presently in charge of received power of the church and mission.

Bhakti movements throughout Indian history have sometimes challenged entrenched and powerful structures. We suppose that it is possible that that may be part of what is happening in the Christian community in Adhra Pradesh today. Be that as it may, in Andhra Pradesh Christian Bhakti has creatively influenced theological thought as well as spirituality[12].

Some of these group churches, like the various pentecostal groups, came from outside the country, and others sprang from out of the existing churches and denominations.

The suspicion and hesitancy with which the historic churches have reacted towards these new movements have already been mentioned. The reasons for this reaction, which often had led to a certain amount of tension and conflict with the indigenous groups, lie in the thinking of the mainline churches along the following lines:

1) These groups are new; they do not have the long history coming from the apostolic church and so these groups are man-made.

2) Their teachings are confusing; they subject the Bible to private interpretation. (The implication is that they do not go along with the widely accepted church authority in the matter of interpretation of the Scriptures. But it is interesting to note that even among the major denominations there is a wide difference on some doctrinal matters.)

3) These groups are overly emotional and the enthusiasm often cools off as quickly as it started. The followers of these do not have sound doctrine and they are just 'holy rollers'.

4) They also practise sheep-stealing instead of making converts from other religions.

Still to be explained are some of the criticisms and their validity as well as the precise points of strife and even some much deeper causes of conflict. But it is enough to say at this stage that the members of the older established churches are sometimes strictly warned against the so-called danger of these groups. Until very recently, those of us who belonged to the denominational churches had a very guilty feeling if we had anything to do with these groups. Even sitting in their prayer meetings was sometimes considered to be an act of unfaithfulness to one's own church.

5. The success of the Group Churches

In spite of all the hesitation and condemnation coming from the historic churches, the group churches continued to attract followers. Their success may be attributed at least in part to the following reasons:

1) All these small groups emphasised individual and group prayer much more than the mainline churches, which in many cases stopped with the Sunday morning worship. In the groups there are whole-night prayers, fasting prayers, house meetings, and individual waiting prayers. In the Lutheran church, for example, all this would sometimes be called 'synergism' and man-centred religion rather than God-centred faith.

2) The structure of these indigenous church groups has always been very simple without any ordained priests, without any vestments or administrative machinery, and without any councils or committees or constitutions so that they had all the time for the 'spiritual' side of life.

3) They always emphasised the charismatic gifts, especially the gift of healing, which the Indian people would quickly acknowledge as the manifestation of God's power today. The simple people of India would willingly accept a God who is concerned for them and their daily needs in this way.

4) The preachers in these groups had always preached simply and directly from the Bible, and their followers believed that they spoke 'from the power of the Spirit' and not from the commentaries. These groups also believed that any study of doctrine or theology was a hindrance to the faith. They had no seminaries, and most of their preachers had a greater credibility among their followers because they came from the working class section of the community.

5) All the members of the group churches, even the poorer among them, often gave tithes so that many of these groups did not carry the 'stigma' of receiving money from abroad; this tithing was considered to be a great witness wherever it was practised. (But there are glaring exceptions to this because in

recent times there was almost a big racket among some independent groups that sprang up to solicit money from the sympathetic 'brethren' in the more affluent lands.)

In any case, because of some of these differences, the indigenous church groups in India attracted many followers, and they grew in numbers.

6. Three Possible Courses of Action

Under these circumstances the mainline churches could take three possible courses of action vis-a-vis these group movements.

1) Condemnation of the groups as heretical and continued disregard of their existence. This approach, of course, is not in the interest of the mission churches, especially if they want to project a good image to the non-Christian neighbours outside. The Hindus always find the denominational divisions among the churches a great hinderence.

2) Acceptance of all groups and their teachings as 'roads' leading to Christ. This attitude many Christians find hard to take with good conscience. It is not easy to take this view also because of the additional problem that these small groups do not always agree among themselves in their teaching.

3) A kind of dialogue with the group churches, which the Indian churches today are largely seeking as a middle way. Truth, after all, is not one-eyed, as Bishop J.A.T. Robinson reminds us.[13] There may be something which the older churches in India may be able to learn from the new groups. Maybe God is speaking to the mission churches through these 'latter day saints'. At any rate, as Robin Boyd has rightly pointed out, within the coming Indian church there must be room for much diversity, and there is a pattern to be followed[14].

Boyd also strongly advises the Indian church to break away the bonds of 'communalism'. He says that this does not mean that we reject the historic church. But it does mean a readiness to criticise and if necessary to abandon historical structures which have ceased to be helpful and a readiness to return to the pattern of the fellowship groups of people who have direct experience of God in Christ; who have received the power of the Holy Spirit; who are committed to one another, but committed also to live not for themselves but for others and for God. The church, far too long, has been so busy saving its life that it has come perilously near to losing it[15].

7. The Present Quest

In such a spirit of research I started the study of the indigenous church groups in Andhra Pradesh. Is there a possibility of understanding and learning from the simple ways, so that a new and more vital form of Christianity may emerge in India? Is there a possibility for a useful dialogue between the historic churches and the group movements along the lines which J.A.T. Robinson suggests in his book, already cited[16]?

My quest into the problem of sectarian movements, as they were called, started in the year 1956, when I was first appointed as students' chaplain, after my ordination in a small town called Guntur in Andhra Pradesh. In Guntur and surrounding places, at that time, the group church movement was very active. Brother Bhakta Singh, a convert from Sikhism, had started several big groups, including, among others, those called Elim and Jehova-shama, and many young and old people from my own church, the Lutheran Church, began to join his fellowship. The local pastors of the mainline churches were very much concerned for the losses in their ranks. Also about that time the now well-known Hindu-Christian guru Subba-Rao, working in the same area, started bitterly criticising the older churches and their Western practices.

I was very much hurt, as a young minister, when I read one of Subba Rao's earliest booklets in Telugu, the title of which can be translated as Padre Go Back Home[17]. In this booklet Subba Rao attacked Baptism as a mistaken, out-dated, and unnecessary practice, which, in his opinion, the Indian Christians have blindly copied from the equally mistaken Western preachers[18].

Even stronger motivation to study the younger church groups came to me from the fact that Mungamuri Devadas, the founder of the Bible Mission, was living in Guntur at that time; a good old man--very few of his followers knew his real age. He was conducting meetings in the house of one of his followers, constantly teaching and preaching. I had heard about this man much earlier in my student days, and we all called him Father Devadas as a mark of respect for his saintly life. I had met some of his followers earlier. Here there was an opportunity for me, during a period of four years, to observe critically the work of Father Devadas, attending his prayer meetings as an interested outsider.

Guntur has always been the official headquarters of my church, the Andhra Evangelical Lutheran Church, which is one of the older Christian denominations in Andhra. Devadas lived in the house of Rao Sahib J. Raja Rao, a rich Christian in Guntur town, who himself was a member of the local Lutheran Church before he became a follower of Devadas. Since Father Devadas was never married and had no family, he lived in this house in his old age and carried out his work in the later part of his life until he died in 1960.

The pastors of the major church bodies used to discuss actively the teachings of Devadas; there were many shades of opinion among my colleagues about his theology. We were all keen to see how the work of these groups related to the historic churches, and how it affected the Christian cause in general. We were somewhat apprehensive.

In many ways, however, the Bible Mission started by Devadas seemed somewhat different from many splinter groups, as they were sometimes called. We shall see some of the differences and similarities as we go along. It may be sufficient to say here that Father M. Devadas was a widely honoured man both in the Bible Mission and also to some extent outside his own circles in that part of Andhra Pradesh. He denied himself many worldly comforts, including a married life and family. He did not have any material possessions and carried out his ministry living a simple life in the homes of his faithful followers, who most willingly provided him with shelter. Thus, Father Devadas, to me, was a seeker after things divine.

Over the years, the Bible Mission grew in numbers and in strength[19]. The lay ministry pattern, the simple narrative preaching methods of the followers of this mission, the emphasis on prayer life and healing ministry, their practice of including dreams and visions as channels of sharing the group's experience and its archetypes, the great tolerance of the founder Devadas towards the other Christians, the brotherly love which he advocated towards people of other religions—some of these characteristics of the Bible Mission attracted the attention of many people around, and I was deeply interested to know more about this church and its message to the major denominations, if there was any. The Bible Mission, which was started by a Lutheran, Father Devadas, is no longer considered as a breakaway group that can simply be ignored and forgotten. It is a reality to be recognised and it deserves the study and understanding which may help in the long run. A dialogue and fellowship between the Bible Mission and the major churches may prove mutually beneficial.

The Bible Mission today is not just another church. It is a movement. Like the other small groups it is not even a member of the regional Christian Councils nor of the National Council of Churches in India. It has no theological schools to train its pastors, but there are enough workers for them to take care of evangelism and pastoral needs. In some places it is growing faster than the mainline denominational churches.

Is there anything which the major churches can learn from the Bible Mission and other such small groups? Can there be real fellowship and partnership between the two? What are the factors that divide these bodies in India and what is it that can unite them? What is the future of these groups in India and what is the future of the Western mission type churches?

I propose to study some of these questions in this research. In the process I am studying the teachings of the Bible Mission and its founder Devadas. Of special interest to me is the 'bhakti', the devotional life of the followers of this group and the theology which does not easily fit into the existing moulds or systematic structures. Perhaps such a study will help us to find more of what M.M. Thomas calls the living theology—and this may even pave a new way of understanding the Bible, a way which is different from what the Western missions have bequeathed to the Indian church[20].

As I go along with the quest I cannot overlook the problems which the Bible Mission and other indigenous groups are facing. They have to pay a price for their staying aloof from the fellowship of the other church bodies. It may be that their theological assumptions and their world view have never been questioned and consequently their thinking did not show much growth. These aspects too will have to be studied critically. But the Bible Mission is only a kind of parable for me, an example in the context of which I shall try to examine wider issues affecting the whole church.

8. Bible Misssion—A Christian Folk Religion

I look at the Bible Mission as one of the Christian folk religions of India. A folk religion has its own strengths and weaknesses. As a folk religion it is distinct from the mission churches in the following respects:

1) It was not started by foreigners but was the dream of an Indian Christian--it sings the native melodies.

2) Its theology is of grass-roots type. It is the people who make the theology. Devadas himself had not been to any theological college, although he knew some Western theological models from his early training in the Lutheran mission. The leaders of the Bible Mission like those in any other non-White indigenous churches in India[21] make a selective use of the theological teachings they have learnt from the West.

3) It is people's religion also in the sense that it makes use of oral tradition and folk communication methods. It 'spontaneously uses forms of thought and modes of action natural and familiar in its own environment'[22].

4) It makes use of a more personal approach through an intimate and supportive community life of its followers. It provides the poor and neglected section of society with the comfort of prayer healing and an opportunity to share through dreams, visions and myths.

5) Its authority is based on personal relationships, style of life and powers of communication, but not mainly on status in society at large or on theological education or rank in an organisational set-up.

9. Some Difficulties faced in This Study

First of all, one should start with the fact that Father Devadas was not a theologian; he was only an evangelist, a seer and a preacher. He had very little seminary training. So one does not look for any theological formulations in his writings. But he is indeed a great thinker and a poet too. Secondly, a major part of his sermons and expositions and teachings were never committed to writing. Even among those booklets available in print there are only very few which he wrote in his own hand. Others have been compiled from notes taken by his followers. But since his followers were very careful to write down everything he taught, and since he always preached at the normal dictation speed, fortunately many of the sermons and teachings of Father Devadas are today preserved in the Telugu language.

For the present project I could gather a total of 28 booklets containing the teachings of Devadas, all except two in Telugu[23], and the total length of these writings exceeds 1500 pages in print.

Included in this list of 28 booklets is one book of songs which Devadas wrote. A great deal of the theology of this saintly man can be gathered from these songs. They are all set to simple Indian melodies, they express a deep feeling of devotion, and they have a message of proclamation. Only two out of the 122 songs in this book are translations or adaptations of Western hymns which Devadas had learnt in his early life. The rest are all his original creation.

We may get an idea of the wide range of subject matter on which Devadas wrote as we look at the titles of the booklets available.

1. Telugu Kraishtava kīrthanalu (Telugu Christian Hymns)
2. Saithānu'nedirinchuta (Resisting Satan)
3. Vāgdāna Manjari (A Row of Promises)
4. Prārdhana Metlu (Steps in Prayer)
5. Upavāsa Prārdhana Dīksha (A Vow of Fasting Prayer)
6. Upavāsa Prārdhana Prakaranamu (A Chapter on Fasting Prayer)
7. Samarpana Prārdhana (Prayer of Surrender)
8. Rākada Prārdhana Sthuthulu (Prayers and Praises for the Second Coming)

9. Rākada Prārdhana Sthuthulu, Part II
10. Sannidhi Sampada (The Treasure of God's Presence)
11. God's Presence
12. Parama Githārdhamu (Exposition of the Song of Songs)
13. Yeptha Vindu Varthamānamulu (Jepthah Feast Messages)
14. Woe Unto You
15. Prakatana Grandha Vivaramu (An Exposition of the Book of Revelation)
16. Mithra (The Friend)
17. Krismasu Varthamanamulu (Christmas Messages)
18. Mahima Varthavali (The Glorious News)
19. Abhayāni (The Apologetic)
20. Rakshana Padyamulu (Salvation Poetry)
21. Daiva Lakshanamula Sthuthi (Praise in the Attributes of God)
22. Shrama kālapu Gudāramu (The Passion Season Tabernacle)
23. Dēvudu Enduku Ūrakunnādu (Why Is God Tarrying)
24. Daiva Sānnidhyamu (The Presence of God)
25. Mounzi (Girdle)
26. Kristhu Mahimābhivridhi Pathrika (A Pamphlet on the Glory of Christ)
27. Varabōdhini (The Blessed Instructor)
28. Satyāmsa Nirūpana (The Proof of the Truth)

All these booklets contain the teachings of Devadas as we have already mentioned; most of them are his dictated notes to his followers as they were writing as he spoke. Very little did he write in his own hand--maybe a few pamphlets in the early ministry. One booklet in the above list is claimed to be his message after his death as he spoke through a medium (Yeptha Vindu Varthamānamulu, No. 13).

In the process of writing from dictation, in many places in the script, the actual words of Devadas were reported sometimes as the writer's words, and at other times the interpretations of the scribe were recorded as though they were the actual words of Devadas. One problem in the Telugu language is that there are no quotation marks in the script. Where they are used now rarely, they are a recent innovation borrowed from the English writing tradition. There are, however, other ways of introducing direct speech which have not always been used by these people writing for Devadas. Another problem is that Father Devadas sometimes repeated the themes and often there are variations in what he said in different places where the same subject was discussed. Then in the different manuscripts kept by the followers of Devadas there are some variations. Indeed, these problems are not unlike the textual problems of the New Testament texts. In the printed versions of the booklets those who were responsible for editing them called themselves the 'publishers'. To them the publisher is the one who reports—or the one who makes it 'public'. So when someone has his name printed on the cover page of a booklet as the publisher it does not always mean that he is what we call the publisher of books. It only means that he is the one reporting or proclaiming the teachings of Devadas.

In addition to the printed sources mentioned above, I interviewed several of the living leaders of the Bible Mission for this study, some of whom were trained by Father Devadas himself. One saintly lady living in our town and providing leadership to the believers in that area was known to me for several years. I prayed with the local group of the Bible Mission several times and I was called to preach and to serve at the communion table. Several pastors of the mission have helped me to know more about Devadas and his teachings. I visited several times, with great interest and a feeling of respect, the healing campaigns at Kakani, a small place outside Guntur. Hundreds of people, mostly Hindus, come there on every Friday from long distances around seeking prayer healing for various ailments and asking for the demons to be cast out. Father Devadas, when he died, was buried in a mango grove in this place and this grove was donated by his host, Raja Rao.

Thus my source of information for this study is both written and oral. The songs written by Devadas now live in the memories and lives of many Christians in Andhra; people of all denominations sing them, and sixteen of them have found their way into the approved common book of worship used by the Church of South India and all the other denominations in Telugu language area. The other booklets of Devadas have never been translated into any other language so the readership to date has been entirely Telugu.

10. Scope of the Study

In this investigation I propose to introduce the subject by tracing the historical background of the Bible Mission and the history briefly of its parent body, the Lutheran Mission, as well as that mission's successor, the Andhra Evangelical Lutheran Church. An attempt will also be made to reconstruct the life story of the founder Mungamuri Devadas, who will also be referred to here as Father Devadas. A biography of the man had never been written; since Devadas, by nature a very shy man, never allowed any publicity about himself, I had to gather bits and pieces from several sources for this story. One of these sources is a recently published article in <u>Religion and Society</u>, Bangalore, by Dr. K. Devasahayam, a former President of the Andhra Evangelical Lutheran Church, on the subject of the Bible Mission. Dr. Devasahayam had consulted documents and several persons for material in this article. I have used some information gathered by Devasahayam with acknowledgements to him and the publication.

In the second section I examine the theological views of Devadas, found mostly in the published booklets listed above. In part three we see the theology of Devadas in action. His hymns, his teaching methods, his prayer life, and his practice of the presence of God will be examined in this section. The hymns are one major source for the theological thought of Devadas; in them he expressed a profound bhakti and an understanding of Christian teaching. Then in the final section I shall draw my conclusions and shall see the possible implications of the Bible Mission and many such indigenous church groups to the mainline mission churches. What is the message of these groups to the Lutheran Church? What can the small groups and the major churches learn from each other? On the other hand I think it is also important to see in what direction these independent churches in India are travelling. What is their role in Indian society and what are the strengths which they provide for the church at large, for its life and witness?

I am only trying to interpret the situation, and the Bible Mission is only a model to help us to understand deeper matters of the Church, which is the body of Christ in India. A real dialogue between these two parts of the Indian church will be needed, for example, if the church in India has to fulfil its missionary and prophetic task to the millions of non-Christians in India.

I am including in this book some of my wood block prints and reproductions of my batiks on various themes to try to catch some of the spirit of the 'dreams' and visions I am talking about. In these, as in the various other ways I want to understand the message of the folk religious forms, my quest continues.

We are all trying to express our Christian faith and preach a Gospel which is both relevant and contextual. This study is an attempt at the understanding of the message God is giving to the churches in India today through the Bible Mission and through many other similar indigenous groups. We are not, of course, saying that God speaks only or even mainly through Devadas. We are only saying that Devadas and the Bible Mission with other folk Christian religious groups in India have started a process which deserves serious consideration.

CHAPTER I: Notes

1. Babin, Pierre, (ed.) The Audio Visual Man, Pflaum Dayton, Ohio, 1970.

2. Boyd, R.H.S., India and the Latin Captivity of the Church, Cambridge University Press, 1974.

3. Boyd, R.H.S., An Introduction to Indian Christian Theology, Christian Literature Society, Madras, 1963, p. 3.

4. Barrett, David B., (ed.) The World Christian Encyclopedia, Nairobi, 1982.

5. Boyd, R.H.S., Introduction to Indian Christian Theology, op.cit., p.iii.

6. Hoerschelmann, W., Christliche Gurus, Peter Lang, Las Vegas, 1977.

7. Baago, Kaj A., Movement around Subba Rao, CLS, Madras, 1969.

8. Songs of Subba Rao No.23, Translated from: M. Subrahmanyam, Sri Kalagara Geethabhashyam (Telugu), Vijayawada, 1980.

9. There are some other Christian thinkers who hold this view, that one can be a Hindu and be at the same time a follower of Christ. Robin Boyd tells us that as far back as 1898 Brahma Bandhav Upadhyaya, a Bengali Christian, came to the conclusion that there is no reason why a man should not be a Hindu and a Christian at the same time. See Robin Boyd, Indian Christian Theology, p. 83.

10. Turner, Harold W., Mission Focus, September 1981, Vol. 9. No. 3, p. 46.

11. Loc. cit.

12. Religion and Society, Vol. XXIX, No. 1, Bangalore, March 1982.

13. Robinson, John A.T., Truth is Two Eyed, S.C.M.Press, 1979.

14. Boyd, R.H.S., Indian Christian Theology, p. 106.

15. Boyd, R.H.S., India and The Latin Captivity of the Church, Cambridge University Press, 1974, p. 134.

16. Robinson, John A.T., op.cit.

17. Subba Rao, Thaggu Pādiri, Thaggu. A Telugu booklet, place and date not indicated, Baago suggests Munipalle, 1940. See Baago, K.A. (ed.) Library of Indian Christian Theology, A Bibliography, C.L.S., 1969, p. 37.

18. Since the publication of the booklet mentioned above, Subba Rao's teachings are more widely known and his followers are increasing in number. See Baago,

op. cit; Hoerschelmann, op. cit.

19. David Barrett in his World Christian Encyclopedia gives the present membership of the Bible Mission as 10,000 adults and 15,000 affiliated.

20. In 1938, when the Bible Mission was formed out of the Lutheran denomination, the latter was still called the Lutheran Mission. It subsequently became the Andhra Evangelical Lutheran Church in 1927 but people still referred to it loosely as the Lutheran Mission. When Devadas formed his own group he simply called it the Bible Mission and he used the word "mission" in the sense of a denomination and claimed that his mission was not named after any man but after the Word of God, the Bible.

21. I borrowed this term 'non-White Indigenous Churches' from the World Christian Encyclopedia of David Barrett. Although the attribute 'non-white' is more relevant to the African situation we are using this term to refer to all the indigenous church groups in India in the sense of 'non-mission' churches.

22. Madras Series, Vol. II, p. 276.

23. Only two booklets of the Bible Mission are found in English, Booklet No. 11, God's Presence, and Booklet No. 14, Woe Unto You.

24. Devasahayam, K., The Bible Mission, Religion and Society, Vol. XXIX, No. 1, March, 1982.

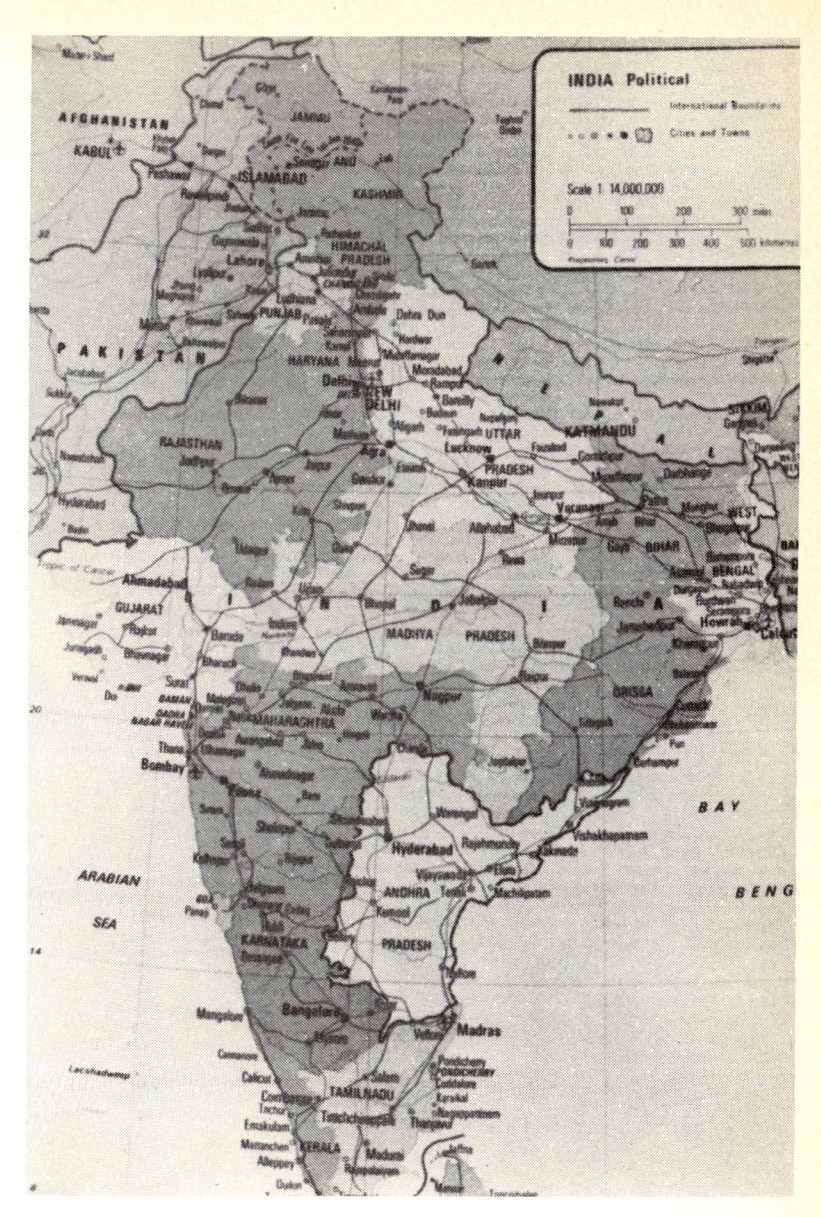

Map of India

CHAPTER II

The Historical Setting

1. The Land And The People

Āndhra Pradesh, the Land of the Āndhra People, is the present name of a linguistic, administrative province on the east coast of South India[1]. The language and the race in the region bear the same name, Āndhra. Telugu is another name for this language. So too is Tenugu, meaning "sweet as honey" (tēne = honey, agu = is)[2]. Rabindranāth Tāgore, the great poet of India, had once called Telugu the Italian of the East because of its melodious tone[3]. Āndhra Pradesh now spreads over an area of 22 thousand square miles with Orissa and Madhya Pradesh in the north, Tāmilnadu in the south and Mahārāshtra and Karnātaka in the west.

The present Andhra Pradesh was formed as a result of the linguistic re-mapping of India after independence with the Telugu speaking region of the former Madrās Presidency and some Districts from the erstwhile Nizam's Dominions. Andhra Pradesh has three distinct cultural regions:

a) The Circār Districts, or the coastal Districts of Srikākulam, Vishākapatnam, East Godāvary, West Godāvary, Kristna, Guntūr, Ongōle, and Nellōre.

b) Rāyalaseema, so named after the great Telugu emperor Kristna Dēvarāya of the 16th century, consisting of Kurnool, Cuddappah, Chittoor and Anatapūr Districts. These are also called the Ceded Districts because the Nizām of Hyderābād in 1800 had ceded them to the British East India Company.

c) The Telangāna Districts, which belonged to the Nizām of Hyderābād until after the independence of India. They are the Khammam, Nalgonda, Warangal, Karimnagar, Medak, Nizāmabād, Adilābād, Mahabūbnagar and Hyderābād Districts.

There is some truth in Dr. C.R. Reddy's description of the Circar Districts as 'Āryanised' and the Ceded Districts as 'Dravidian'[4]. A knowledge of these regions and their geographic locations and an acquaintance with some of the cultural distinctions will be useful when we consider the advent of the Christian Missions into this area and trace the spread of these missions.

The people of Andhra Pradesh are primarily agriculturists. Two of the great rivers of India, the Kristna and the Godāvary, flow through this region into the Bay of Bengal, and the coastal Andhra with two crops a year is called the Rice Bowl of India.

Andhra Pradesh today has a population of 43,394,951, of which 85.3% speak Telugu. Out of the total population in every hundred there are 87.63 Hindus, 8.09 Muslims, 4.19 Christians and 0.09 others. The 1,823,456 Christians in the Andhra Pradesh constitute 19.50 per cent of the total Christian population of the country according to 1971 census[5].

In the 1830s after a disastrous famine struck this area, Sir Arthur Cotton, the famous British army engineer, had built a huge dam across the River Godavary near the city of Rājahmundry, and the dam stands intact even today. With the construction of this dam the whole delta became a fertile agricultural land. In the recent years one of the biggest earthen dams in India has also been built across the River Kristna, and thousands of hectares of land have been brought under cultivation in Kristna regions. Rice, sugar cane and some commercial crops like cotton and tobacco are grown in Andhra Pradesh. The major religion in Andhra is Hinduism with some Muslims scattered especially in the former Nizām's dominions and a small minority of Christians as we have seen from the statistics above.

Andhra people are very simple folk and very hospitable. At the turn of the Christian era this land was very much influenced by Mahayana Buddhism. The famous University of Nāgārjuna, which attracted scholars from many parts of the world, was in this region at the mouth of the River Kristna. People in Andhra live very much in close communities and the population is mostly rural. Only in the recent years have more urbanisation and the accompanying problems appeared.

2. Caste System and Social conditions in Andhra

Here, as anywhere else in India, there are four major castes among Hindus. The caste system is particularly strong here although any discrimination on the basis of caste is prohibited by law. Section 17 of the Fundamental Rights of the Constitution of India reads:

> Untouchability is abolished and its practice in any form is forbidden. The enforcement of any disability arising out of untouchability shall be an offence punishable in accordance with the law[6].

This does not mean caste will disappear from India but it only means that discrimination on the basis of caste, especially the tragedy of untouchability, is discouraged.

The Brahmin caste in Hindu society has been for a long time, and still is to a large extent, at the top of the social rung, with monopoly on education and power. And then comes in succession the ruler caste of Kshathriyas, the merchant caste of Vaishyas and the agricultural caste of Sudras. Outside these four major castes of Hinduism is the panchama, or the fifth caste. The people belonging to this caste were considered as untouchables until Gandhi started a campaign on their behalf and worked for their uplift, calling them Harijans--God's people. For thousands of years, generation after generation of these poor people suffered cruel suppression by the higher castes and lived as virtual slaves under them. Till the time of Gandhi and his Harijan Movement very little had been done within the Hindu society to help these people within Hinduism, although some attempts were evident here and there to awaken social concern for the lower castes.

When Christian missionaries started work in Andhra Desa they concentrated their attention on these poor 'untouchables' and the missionaries felt that it was part and parcel of their mission to work for these neglected sections of the society. It is a well known fact that the panchamas, or outcastes, who received the Gospel first, did so because they found a message of hope and redemption in the Christian gospel, a relief from the social injustice to which they were subjected for such a long time. And the fact that in the early history of the Christian missions the Christian church was called the outcastes' church had its effects on the image and the witness of the church, effects which were both positive and negative. However, in the later generations William Stewart reports instances of 'groups of caste Hindus seeking baptism in Andhra Pradesh who were first drawn to the Gospel by what they saw of a transformed fellowship among the outcaste converts'7.

There were, however, some exceptions here and there to this general observation and some attempts have been made in the early history of the Lutheran missions to reach the upper classes. Dolbeer reports, for example, the story of how a Lutheran missionary, Dahl of the Hermansburg Mission, in 1868 made friends with the Rājah of Venkatagiri, who had held the richest Jamindāri (rulership) in the Madras Presidency. The Rājah became very favourably disposed to Christianity. But we are told that 'what progress Dahl might have made in the Rājah's court was cut short by Dahl's dismissal in 1873 over the caste problem. He was accused of allowing caste to exist in the mission and spending more time with the upper caste people to the neglect of the lower'8. Thus on the issue of caste the church's attitude and opinion was never consistent, as we shall see later on.

Andhra people are well known for their arts and crafts and for their great literary achievements. Telugu literature had blossomed to a high degree of beauty long ago. In the 11th century A.D. there appeared the first extant major poetical work in Telugu in the royal court of the King Rāja Rāja Narēndra of Rājamahēndravaram (the present Rājahmundry). The great literary genius Nannayabhattu (1022-63) had translated the first three cantos of the Mahā Bhāratha from Sanskrit into classical Telugu poetry, and that had set a style and structure for all the best poetical works that followed. Nannaya became known as vāgānushāsana, or the legislator of the language9. But already some generations before that, we can trace a rich folk literature in oral tradition like the songs of the boat people and the fishermen, the simple rhymes of the hill tribes and forest dwellers, the love songs and the work songs of the simple agricultural folk, and the old ballads and musical stories of heroes and heroines of the land.

Andhra land also has an age old drama, dance and folk theatre tradition. Many old palm leaf manuscripts of song dramas are now preserved in the

Saraswathi Grandhālaya library in Tānjore in Tamilnādu. Worth mentioning is the Kūchipūdi Dance Drama named after the village of that name on the banks of River Kristna and initiated in the 17th century by a Brahmin ācharya named Siddhēndra Yōgi. Siddhēndra instituted the practice that every male member of the Brahmin families in that village had to learn classical dance peculiar to that area (very similar to Bharata Nātyam) and tell the stories of Bhāgavatha Purāna[10] to the villagers all around. This style of dance peculiar to this area is now well known all over as Kūchipūdi Natya. During the centuries which followed Kūchipūdi dance had become a very popular form of dance drama and one of its stories, the Bhāmā Kalāpam[11], had been played in countless places during this period until the present day. Yaksha gāna is a more inclusive name for these rural musical and dance plays of that age[12].

There are other forms of popular entertainment like the veedhi nātakam, the street drama, the leather puppet play, the burrakatha[13] and the Harikatha[14]. Many of these performing art forms have enjoyed the patronage of the rulers of the area and of the landlords generation after generation. The Andhra people are sensitive, art loving and proverbially emotional. Their feasts and festivals are colourful. They live very intimately with nature, laughing and weeping with the vagaries of the climate and the seasons which played with their fortune generation after generation. The harvest festival[15] which comes in the month of January; the Telugu New Year's day[16] at the beginning of the spring season in April; the Divāli, the famous lights' festival of India; and many other special days in Andhra land make life here very joyous. Incidentally these are the folk institutions which provide constant social interaction in the home and in the community. Andhras have a strong herd instinct and many things happen in communities. Later on when we study the advent of the Christian gospel into this area we shall see how much this fact influenced the village Christians. It has affected the pattern of conversion, and the church made use of some of these elements of the culture in spite of the lurking fear of syncretism in some quarters. For example, very early in the history of the Christian missions the Christian hymns which the early converts wrote to classical Telugu tunes became well known as literary pieces[17].

3. Advent of Protestant Missions in the Coastal Andhra

For the purpose of our study we limit our investigation to the Christian missions which came into the coastal Andhra since only this section was called Andhra or <u>Andhra dēsa</u> in the 19th century when the Christian missions came into this area. This will also help us to view in the proper context the birth and growth of the Bible Mission, which is our main interest in this book. It was in the cradle of the Lutheran Mission that the Bible Mission started originally, and the founder, Mr. Mungamuri Devadas[18], was baptised in the Andhra Evangelical Lutheran Mission and for a long time worked in the Mission.

More than a hundred years before the Lutheran Mission came to Andhra the first Protestant missionaries came to India. They were also Lutherans who came to a place call Trānquebār on the east coast of India south of Madras. The two Missionaries, Ziegenbalg and Plütschau of the Danish Halle Mission, came in 1705. Under the tutelage of Francke the pietist leader in Germany, Ziegenbalg and Plütschau answered the appeal of King Frederick of Denmark to serve as missionaries in the Danish East India Company at Trānquebār[19]. (The Tamil name means "the Song of the Waves".) Not too long after the pioneering work of the Tranquebar Mission the area came into the ministry of the Anglican Missionaries in the Tinnevelly area and by the time of Missionary Rhenius, a Lutheran working with the Church Missionary Society in the Tinnevelly area, things began to change. He and the other Lutheran missionaries working under the English Missions found themselves in a difficult situation. Martin Luther Dolbeer quotes documentary evidence to show several successive stages of deteriorating relationships between the Lutheran missionaries and the Anglican Missionary Societies in Tinnevelly. We are told that 'with the establishment of the Bishopric in Madras in 1833 and the control of societies coming to some extent under the Bishop's supervision the break between Rhenius and the Anglican Church was inevitable'[20].

The policy of the English Societies ever since the time of Ziegenbalg and Plütschau was to employ German missionaries educated at Halle, Basel and Berlin, accepting their Lutheran ordination as valid and allowing them to preach the Lutheran doctrine, use the Lutheran liturgies and ordain native pastors. But gradually modifications started to appear in 1818. Next the Anglican form of worship service was insisted on in all stations and the Lutheran missionaries were asked to be re-ordained. Some Lutheran missionaries complied with this also. But finally they were asked to renounce the rights to confirm and to ordain ministers in favour of the prior rights of the Bishops. Men like Rhenius refused to comply[21]. The Missionaries working in the Tinnevelly area felt that work should soon start among the Telugus but it took some time before the first Lutheran Mission came into Andhra area.

However, there were some other Protestant missions working in parts of Andhra already. Dolbeer reports that the first Protestant missionaries who came to Andhra were the London Missionary Society men who arrived in India in 1804. They started work in the Northern part of the Andhra coast at Vishakapatnam. These early missionaries and their followers pioneered in translating the Bible into the Telugu language[22]. After the first thirty years of labour the London Missionary Society had made the first convert in the person of the gifted poet Purushotham Chowdury[23], whose hymns in Telugu have become very famous in church use and whose contribution to Christian literature had hardly ever been surpassed.

On the other side of Andhra two missionaries of the Plymouth Brethren established a station in 1836 at a place called Narsapur in the delta of the Godavary river[24]. And 'still other voices were raised in calling Americans and Europeans to the great needs of the Telugu area', and 1836, the same year as the Plymouth Brethren started their work, the Rev. Samuel Day of the American Baptists arrived in India to serve the Telugus. At about the same time as John Christian Frederick Heyer, the first Lutheran Missionary to India, was starting from Boston, the Rev. Robert T. Noble of the Church Missionary Society began his work in Machilipatnam in 1842 next door to the Lutheran area of Guntur.

4. Origins of the Lutheran Mission Work in Andhra

The 31st of July every year is observed as the Mission Founder's day in Guntur, the centre of the Andhra Evangelical Lutheran Church as it is known today. Special prayers are offered that day and Lutheran Christians of the town go out in procession starting from a simple monument in the old church compound which commemorates the coming of the first Lutheran Missionary to Andhra from America, Father John Christian Frederick Heyer. He arrived in Guntur in 1842 and by then the Church Missionary Society was working in Machilipatnam as we have already seen, the American Baptist Mission was working in Nellōre area, and the Plymouth Brethren in Narasapūr.

Heyer started school work in Guntur with the help of the English Collector and conducted prayers and Sunday services for the household of the collector and the English residents of the town with the help of interpreters. We are told that three adults were baptised in Gunfūr by the year 1843.

The story of Heyer's missionary labours makes very interesting reading and there is a great wealth of documentation on Heyer's work in the mission archives in the Lutheran School of Theology at Chicago, where I had the privilege of seeing some of it. Several books have been written on the history of the Lutheran Mission in Andhra of that period[25]. Very soon other missionaries from America and Germany joined Heyer in his labours and with the coming of L.P. Menno Valett from the North German Missionary Society, who joined Heyer in 1844, the work spread to the Rajahmundry area in the north-east on the banks of the River Godāvary. And the Rev. Walter Gunn came to assist Heyer in the Guntūr mission field.

In the Rājahmundry area, the centre of Telugu culture, the irrigation dam referred to above was in progress at that time, and the missionaries here as everywhere at that period enjoyed some support and patronage of the English civil officers. Many labourers working in the project heard the Gospel and we are told that the good news spread in several directions as the labourers scattered in different directions after the work was completed.

Heyer went home suddenly after four years of work in Guntūr area; during that period he completed his studies for a medical degree and returned to India as a medical doctor after an absence of about one year. The work continued to grow and there were more baptisms. During the Civil War in America no new missionaries were able to come to India, so the work suffered for lack of workers.

5. Growth and Consolidation

One of the Guntur missionaries, the Rev. Groening, wrote letters to his relatives in Hamburg suggesting that more missionaries should be sent to Andhra. Eventually the Hermansburg Mission in Germany became interested in the work and sent Augustus Myleius, who arrived in India in 1865. But he moved to the southern parts of Andhra area on the advice of the Guntur missionaries and started a new field in the Gudur area, where the work continued separately under the German missions until today.

Guntur missionaries, especially Heyer, worked mostly among the outcastes in the Guntur and Palnad areas but in the Nayudupet and Gudur areas the German missions were fortunate to enter the upper caste societies here and there. The Hermansburg Mission had reported at least two Brahmin converts as early as 1874[26].

The upper class Sudra castes and the Brahmins first opposed the Christian mission work mainly because of their age-old interest in retaining power and influence in the villages. But the schools which the missionaries had started slowly but early attracted these upper castes and broke the resistance to some extent because education helped the people get good jobs. Wherever sudra priests or brahmins became Christians they were very useful to the mission as teachers and preachers. They held great influence on the community because of their role in their pre-Christian days. The followers of the great Hindu saint Rāmānuja, whose teachings had spread in Andhra much earlier, were seekers after truth and believed in the incarnation of God, emphasised the merits of a pure life and believed that caste did not matter in the sight of God. Some of the teachings of this Hindu sect made it easier for their followers to accept the Christian Gospel[27]. And these former gurus and leaders of the community, when they became Christians, assumed responsibility to propagate the Gospel to their own people. As gurus they converted the 'uninitiated'. Dolbeer reports:

> It is quite apparent from the early history of the Lutheran Missions that without these religious leaders the success of the work would have amounted to almost nothing. They were the key to opening the hearts of the common people in the villages[28].

Similarly, A.T. Fishman, a senior missionary of the Baptist Mission in Andhra, speaks about a certain social value of the caste system:

> Caste has a social value. A Mādiga preacher (Mādiga is an outcaste of cobbler trade which is considered low) when in Cuddapah (the neighbouring town) on one occasion alone went into a non-Christian Madiga palem but was received very coldly until he sat down at one of the houses and began to help with the leather work. This revealed his caste and immediatley the village of cool strangers became cordial friends giving him food, drink and forcing upon him all the hospitality they could command.

Dr. Fishman adds:

> This solidarity of caste groups which survives changes of religion even, has its social value but the kindness and consideration shown in in-group relations is often accompanied by cruelty towards those of the out-groups[29].

Because of some of these considerations, the early missionaries could not come to a uniform opinion on the question of the Christian attitude to caste. The missionaries were divided in their understanding of the situation and they were uncertain of the best policy. Sometimes caste among the converts was strictly and openly prohibited under penalty of excommunication and at other times it was simply overlooked. A few believed that 'they have no part in a mission which allowed caste to remain or allowed the missionaries to do as they wanted in regard to it'[30]. Some new converts from the higher castes found it difficult to cope with the caste problem. A few had to slip back into Hinduism because, coming from a higher caste, they could not accept a situation where they had to eat and take communion with a Christian of the lower caste. Of course some of those who thus went away have later repented and asked for forgiveness. Sometimes for the sake of these converts the missionaries had to overlook the caste system and make some adjustment taking the counsel of Indian Christians like Satthianādham of Madras who said that 'any harsh measure (against caste) will tend not only to wound the feelings and give umbrage but it may also defeat the object which we seek to accomplish'31.

Education and literacy had also engaged the attention of the missionaries from the beginning. The missionaries were keen to make the new converts and the catecumens literate so that they might learn to read the word of God in their own language. The schools which the missionaries started helped the children to read the word of God in Scripture portions and to learn the prayers and they in turn shared these with their parents at home. Martin Luther's catechism was translated by Heyer into Telugu as early as 1851. Some British civil servants who were interested in the mission work and who had been in the country long enough to know the language helped in translating some tracts and in compiling simple books for the people. Assistant Collector Newill of Guntur had translated several tracts for the Guntur missionaries. Among Heyer's work there was also a Telugu church book, a translated version of the American Lutheran church book. The Madras Auxiliary of the Bible Society (1918) had supplied portions of the Telugu Bible to be distributed and the Religious Tract and Book Society formed in 1812 printed some Telugu tracts. The full Bible was translated into Telugu by 1850 and the revision process took another 25 years with the missionaries in the Telugu area actively participating in this work. By the year 1879 the South Andhra Mission (The Hermansburg Mission) had edited and translated their own Telugu song book with 128 hymns. We also hear of a book on dogmatics entitled The First Milk, which was produced in the Hermansburg Mission for catechetical instruction and for the new converts.

The Guntur mission from the very beginning published the Mission News magazine, renamed in 1916 as the Telugu Lutheran and again renamed in 1919 as the Andhra Lutheran. It is still in circulation under the same title. (The present writer edited it for some years during the 1950s.)

Today for the several Lutheran Churches in India there is a federal magazine in English called the Gospel Witness, which started in 1905.

The schools which the earliest missionaries had established grew into high schools and some new schools also began to function. The Andhra Christian College in Guntur, the Andhra Lutheran College of Education, the theological seminaries of the various missions and recently a United Theological College for Andhra have served generations of Andhra young men and women.

Over these many years several of the Indian Christians were trained for leadership and ministry in the Church. From the very beginning the Lutheran missionaries have trained Indian men from the converts to become teachers and evangelists. The first Indian Lutheran pastor is reported to have been ordained in the Hermansburg Mission as early as 1878 and in the Guntur mission two evangelists were ordained as pastors in 1877. These were the first national pastors and there were no more ordinations for another 26 years. But slowly the church grew in numbers and more ministers and more lay workers rose up to take important positions, and hence indigenous leadership has become adequately available. In 1927 the former Lutheran Mission became the Andhra Evangelical Lutheran Church and the first Indian president of the Church was elected in 1944 in the person of the Rev. Dr.E. Prakasam.

Progress was neither easy nor smooth. Missionaries differed on giving leadership to the Indian colleagues. Some missionaries, like Rev. Scriba of the Hermansburg mission in 1887, showed a great hesitation to give responsibility to Indians saying that

> the Indians were too poor, uneducated and weak in faith to take on the responsibility[32].

Therefore, he felt that the missionary should continue to handle and to run everything. But the situation soon changed for the better.

From 1881 single women missionaries started coming and their work among women, the programme of caste Hindu girls' schools, the medical colonies of mercy, the craft schools for widows and handicapped women and several other forms of work have yielded lasting fruits for the Mission and the Church. Dr. Anna Kugler, for example, who arrived in 1883, was an evangelistic lady missionary but later in 1895 obtained permission to start a medical mission in Guntur. The hospital which bears her name now has rendered great service to Telugu people over many years. Many Hindus came to know the love of God and the Gospel of Christ through Dr. Kugler's work[33].

This, briefly, is the story of the Lutheran Mission work in Andhra which should set the scene for our study of the Bible Mission. The so-called Bible Mission was born in this historical setting and it inherited some of the traditions of its parent church but soon made its own mark as a small and simple independent, indigenous church.

CHAPTER II: Notes

1. For more information cf. Rama Raju, B., *Folklore of Andhra Pradesh*, Delhi: National Book Trust of India, 1978.

2. Chenchian and Rajah Bhujanga Rao, *A History of Telugu Literature*, London: Oxford University Press, Calcutta: Associated Press, n.d.

3. Dolbeer, Dr. Martin Luther, *A History of Lutheranism in Andhra Desa 1842-1920*, Board of Foreign Missions, the United Lutheran Church in America, New York, 1959, p. 33.

4. Chenchiah, P., op. cit., p. 7.

5. Prabhakar, M.E., *Religion and Society*, Vol. XXIX No. 1, March 1982, p. 4.

6. Stewart, William, *Indian Religious Frontier--Christian Presence Amid Modern Hinduism*, London: SCM Press, 1964, p. 27.

7. Ibid., p. 122.

8. Dolbeer, op. cit., p. 37.

9. Chenchiah, op. cit., p. 37.

10. Bhagavatha Purana contains the stories of Kristna (Bhagavan, God) and especially of his leela, the play with the milk maids. In Vaishanava Bhakti tradition devotion to Kristna became a big cult. For an interesting account of Kristna Bhakti see Klaus Klostermaier, *Hindu and Christian in Vrindavan*, SCM Press, 1969.

11. Bhama Kalapam, the Lore of Bhama, one of the two wives of Kristna. Kalapam or Kalapa as a literary style in Telugu has become well known in the 17th and the 18th centuries. As a vehicle for imparting simple wisdom to the masses, as an entertaining performance style, and as a source of godly devotion these Kalapas have served generation after generation of Telugu people. One of these, a certain Golla Kalapam, the Shepherd's lore, is a virtual wealth of simple instruction on concerns of everyday life, including the birth of a baby.

12. Yaksha Gaana is a more sophisticated dance-song drama form than Kalapa. At one time Yakshagaanas were written and produced in royal courts of Telugu Kings. It is not known how exactly the name came to be associated with these plays because Yaksha means both the wandering singing group and also the mythological heavenly (angelic) singer. The church in some places is making use of this medium for Christian instruction and evangelism. The present author had written and produced Bible Yakshagaanas and his Bible play Kim Karthavyam had been played by trained dancers in several places in India for packed audiences, mostly Hindus. For a full treatment of Telugu Yakshagaanas: Jogarao, Dr. S.V., *Yaksha Gaana Charithra*, Andhra University Ph.D. dissertation, Waltair, Andhra Pradesh.

13. Burra Katha, so called because of burras, the small drums used in the performance, is really a song story told by three people. One narrator in the middle leads the story narration with a stringed instrument as drone and metal cymbals on fingers. The other two on either side of him will follow with their little drums as they sing the chorus. As the story progresses the narrator steps forwards and backwards and his partners also with him. In this type there is extempore humour and conversation in which the audience are naturally made to join.

14. Harikatha, meaning the story of Hari=God, is a one man performance in story and song known to the Telugu people for a long long time. Most of the stories of Harikatha used to be stories from Puranas and Epics of India much embellished with humour, deep wisdom and common sense. More recently both Burra Kathas and Harikathas have been adapted to social and educational themes. There are several Bible Harikathas or Kalakshepams as they are also called.

15. Sankranthi, which comes in the month of January is the harvest festival of the Telugu people. With the grain coming from the fields many homes are happy and joyful and the professional beggars, the singers and the Sadhus will have their heyday. This is the time when the newly married couples receive presents and almost everyone gets new clothes and there is feasting in every home.

16. The Telugu New Year's Day festival, or Ugaadi, which comes in the month of April, at the beginning of the spring season, is another important festival of the Andhras. One concomitant feature of Ugaadi is a cool drink made with herbs and flowers of six tastes (shad-rasas) as a symbol of man's life, a mixture of several tastes.

17. Purushotham Chowdury, a caste Hindu convert from Vishakapatnam area, had accepted Christ in about 1830 in response to the preaching of the Church Missionary Society in that area. He was a gifted poet and as he suffered persecution at the hands of his orthodox Hindu family people including his wife he sang out his heart to Christ and praised Him. His hymns are now sung all over in the churches in Andhra Pradesh.

18. Mungamuri is the surname, or the house name of Devadas. Andhra people have a house name before the given name and many of these house names come from the villages from where the family originally came. But there are house names with other kinds of origins like "old caste" or "trade" etc. A woman when she is married will get her husband's house name. See also ch. III of this book.

19. Dolbeer, op.cit., p. 5.   20. Ibid., pp. 22, 23.

21. Pettitt, George, Tinnevelly Mission of the Church Missionary Society, London: 1851. Quoted by Dolbeer. Cf. Dolbeer, op.cit., fn. 46, ch. I.

22. Missionaries Gordon and Pritchett of the London Missionary Society completed the translation of the Old and New Testaments by 1823 although the

Madras Bible Society did not finish revision and printing of the whole Telugu Bible until the 1850s. Cf. Dolbeer, op. cit., p. 21. I had seen parts of an earlier translation done by William Carey, but the Telugu is very archaic and almost unintelligible today.

23. See footnote 17 above.

24. Dolbeer, op.cit., pp. 38, 39, 40.

25. Cf., Bachman, E. Theodore: They Called Him Father, the Life Story of John Christian Frederick Heyer, Philadelphia: Muhlenburg, 1942; Swavely, Clarence H. (ed.), One Hundred Years in the Andhra Country: A History of the India Mission of the United Lutheran Church in America 1842-1942, Madras: Diocesan Press, 1942; Swavely, Clarence H: The Lutheran Enterprise in India, Madras: Federation of Evangelical Lutheran Churches in India, 1952; Sheatsley, C.V: Our Mission Field in India, Lutheran Book Concern, 1921; Wolf, L.B: After Fifty Years or an Historical Sketch of the Guntur Mission of the Evangelical Lutheran Church of the General Synod in the U.S.A., Philadelphia: Lutheran Publishing Society, 1896.

26. Dolbeer, op. cit., p. 75.

27. Estborn, S; The Church among Tamils and Telugus, National Christian Council of India, 1961, p. 5.

28. Dolbeer, op. cit., p. 102.

29. Fishman, A.T., Cultural Change and the Underprivileged, Madras: Christian Literature Society, 1941, p. 150.

30. Dolbeer, op. cit., P. 127.

31. Estborn, S., op. cit.   32. Dolbeer, op. cit., p. 121

33. Ibid., p. 167, quoting from Woerlein Vierzig Johre in India, 1913 p. 144.

34. Andhra people know a neighbouring Rājah who was greatly influenced by the medical services of Dr. Kugler. We quote the story as found in Dolbeer, op.cit., p. 450. P.E.Kretzmann, Glimpses of the Lives of Great Missionary Women, St. Louis, 1930, p. 85, states that this Rājah was M. Bhujanga Rao Bahadur of Ellore. Dr. Kugler had restored his wife and saved the life of his son and heir. He built a rest home for relatives of patients out of gratitude to her. He was interested in the secret of Dr. Kugler's power, so she gave him a New Testament, which he translated into Telugu poetry "which brahmans and all educated Telugus would delight to read. When the new rest home was dedicated, he gave away five hundred copies of his translation to the guests. His younger child is named Annamma (Anna) in honour of the Doctor. On his very letterhead this Brahman Rājah had printed a picture of Christ whom he now regards as the hope of India and whom, as he says in the preface to his translation, he first saw reflected in the pure and beautiful life of this American doctor".

Father M. Devadas
(From a Photograph in His Old Age)

CHAPTER III

The Man Devadas and His Times

1. The Man Devadas

Mungamūri Dēvadās, founder of the Bible Mission, was generally known as 'Father Devadas to whom God has Revealed the Bible Mission'. All the booklets published with his name give him this title. The expression 'Father' refers to no ecclesiastical office but is just a prefix indicating respect given to elders and holy men in India. Telugu language structure lends itself conveniently to this expression because the word 'ayya' which literally means father comes at the end of the name and makes a combination showning respect, e.g., Devadas-ayya.

Mungamūri is the 'house' name in the genitive case, meaning "from (the village of) Mungamūru." Many Indian and certainly Telugu people have house names that come before their given names. All the male members of the family carry the house name from father to son and the women take their husband's house name when they marry.

The origin of these house names in each case is not easy to ascertain. Some of them come from the ancestoral village, as possibly in the case of Devadas. Some others indicate the trade or occupation of the family in the distant past like Karanam Subbaiah, (the village head man Subbaiah) or Talari Rāmayya (the village messenger Ramayya), etc. Yet other house names are somewhat forgotten and transformed caste names, like Peddakāpu Rangaiah in which peddakāpu is a caste indicative prefix. Some house names are of unknown origin and sometimes they do not mean anything specific but all house names help distinguish one person from another with the same given name.

In the case of Devadas there is a village called Mungamūru[1] in the Godavary Delta area but we do not know certainly that his ancestors came from Mungamūr, or Mungamūru. He was, in fact, born in a village which bears another name, Jēgūrpād, which is about ten miles east of the well known town

Rajahmundry in the East Godāvary District. His father was Mungamūri Jonah and his mother Satyavathamma.

Jēgūrpād, incidentally, is said to have played a significant role in the history of the Andhra Evangelical Lutheran Church to which Devadas originally belonged. It was the chief centre for evangelistic work in the East Godavary District of the Rajahmundry Mission[2]. Father Heyer, the founder of the Lutheran Mission, visited Jēgūrpād for the first time in 1870 and he found that there were six Christian families and 24 children in the Mission school[3].

There is very little written material available on the life of Devadas. Like many Indian sādhus[4] he preferred to remain unrecorded in biographies. The short research article, already mentioned, by Dr. K. Dēvasahāyam, a former president of the Andhra Evangelical Lutheran Church (Convention), published in a recent issue of Religion and Society[5], is about the only published source of documentary evidence on the early life of Father Devadas. Dēvasahāyam consulted several documents and interviewed some people who knew Devadas for this research work.

The other source material used for this book comes from a short biographical sketch provided by the editors (or the publishers, as these scribes sometimes call themselves) in the introductory pages of the booklet called God's Presence[6]. This booklet is in English and the main contents must have been from the pen of Devadas himself. We reproduce the biographical note as it is found since it is not too long:

> Saint M. Devadas was a man of God, mightily used in the fullness of the Holy Spirit. The word Dēva means God and Dās means servant--that is, God's servant. This saint Devadas was born in about 1840 in a small village called Jēgūrpād near Rajahmundry. He lived a consecrated, unblemished bachelor life in communion with God, remained untouched by Mammon and lived for about a century. He was originally a Lutheran Christian and served in the Lutheran Mission until his 90th year in perfect obedience to his authorities. On the 31st January 1938 in bright day light God wrote two word--Bible Mission--in the air and showed to him. And the Lord called him by name and asked him "to come out as a prince of an

army". At that time he was 90 years old, sick and had no money in his hands. He obeyed God's word and established his Bible Mission and confessed that the founder of the Mission was Jesus Christ but not himself. The message of his mission to the whole world is that God appears and speaks to all people who dwell at his feet[7].

With all his humble origins he was a chosen vessel inspired and gifted by God. He is well known to all our country men and is certainly not a stranger to most of the missionaries and foreigners. He trod the inroads of the spiritual realm and touched the eternal purposes of God. His prayer songs, messages and every word he spelt out were the direct revelation from God. He is known as the pioneer in the field of the "Holy Spirit Revival" during the 20th century in Andhra Pradesh. Many a servant of God traces his origin of blessing with his (Devadas') touch and thus he had been a blessing to many souls. He was a good teacher as he learnt at the Master's feet and taught a variety of methods and clues of spiritual life. He fought a victorious battle with Satan and taught how to resist the Devil. That India will become a centre for spreading the Gospel message to the whole world is one of his imminent prophecies. He started divine healing centres wherein many were healed of disease, relieved of distress and also delivered from the powers of darkness all through these years. He believed and declared that God of the Bible would do here and now wonders and miracles through the church when and where these (miracles) are necessary. As a herald of His coming he exposed the Book of Revelation and the song of Solomon and especially the subject of God's presence and the glory of the Bride, the Church. It is not an exaggeration that what all we say of him fell short of reality. Maranatha. [sic]

From this account we can gather some useful information. First of all, to be fair to the followers of Devadas, one should remember that they had only a working knowledge of English and they were not attempting a precise or scholarly presentation of his life or his teachings. Most of them were only oral tradition people. So sometimes the words they use in these notes are not very clear but one can get some general idea of what the writer was trying to say here.

The followers of Devadas clearly believed that he was born about 1840. This, as we shall see later on from recorded evidence, is a gross estimate. In rural India in those days the civil records of birth and death were not so carefully kept and even if these events are reported and recorded somewhere, it is not always easy to retrieve such information after the lapse of some years. For all practical purposes people remembered dates in association with some well known events of local history. For example, it is common in Andhra Pradesh in the Godavary river area to say that such and such a thing happened before the great dam was built, or so-and-so lived before the great famine, etc.

The year 1842 is a well known landmark for the Christians in that area, because as we have already seen, this was the year in which the first Lutheran missionary from America arrived in Andhra. So the writer of this note, not unlike many other followers of Devadas, wants to believe that Devadas was born before there was a Lutheran Mission in Andhra. If this reckoning were to be true Father Devadas would be 98 years when he broke off from the Lutheran Church and 120 years when he died in 1960.

But Dr. Dēvasahāyam has done some investigation into the family history of Devadas and reported the results of his research[8]. According to the church records, Dr. Dēvasahāyam says that Father Devadas was 53 years old in 1938 when he resigned his membership in the Lutheran Church[9]. On the basis of the information gathered from the students of Father Devadas, some of whom are living today, it is reliably learnt that Devadas used to tell them that he and his father were baptised the same day when he himself was five years old. An extract from the baptismal register issued by the archivist of the Andhra Evangelical Lutheran Church for Godavary Districts situated in Luthergiri, Rajahmundry, dated the 25th September 1974, records the following information:

> 1) Mr. Devadas and his father Jonah were baptised at the same time on the same day, viz. 14-11-1880.

2) Mr. Devadas was five years old when he was baptised although the date of his birth was not entered in the register since it was not the practice to do so.

Therefore Devadas must have been born in 1875 and lived for 85 years when he died on the 9th February 1960. So he was not 120 years old when he died as his followers got it inscribed on his tombstone. It may be of further interest to note from the records, however, that the very first baptism recorded in Jegurpad was in the year 1869 of a woman called Hanna Meka on the 17th of January that year by a Lutheran missionary, named Canon Frederick William Naraal Alexander (1832-1910)[10]. Thus we are on firmer ground about the date of birth of Devadas from this documentary evidence available now[11].

In the biographical note mentioned above, from the Bible Mission booklet, we also see a reference to 'God writing in the air in the broad daylight' the name of the church which He wanted Devadas to start. This was mentioned often by Davadas himself and there was no difficulty for people to believe this as some kind of direct revelation in a vision. The reference to daylight is a way of emphasising that this was not a mere dream or a hallucination. Devadas himself said that if anyone had a doubt about this he should ask God whether this was true and God would answer[12].

Another point which may be of some interest to our study is the reference made to Devadas as a 'consecrated, unblemished bachelor'. Sanyāsa, or celibacy, is held in high esteem in Indian spirituality and the Protestant church in India has not produced many Christian sanyāsis like Sādhu Sundar Singh. Some fallen sanyāsis are also not unknown in that part of the world and hence a clear 'unblemished' bachelorhood was ascribed to Father Devadas almost as a mark of holiness[13]. Money is derogatorily called 'mammon'. We see many times in the teachings of Devadas that he gave a great importance to the ideal of poverty. He advocated self-supporting churches. Even today the Bible Mission pastors live by the offerings brought by the worshippers to the church, and my informants among the pastors have told me that they generally get all that they need for their daily life in the form of rice, fruits and vegetables and in small coins which the worshippers offer in the prayer meetings and at the healing campaigns. The Bible Mission has no central funds of any kind and their pastors do not get any salaries.

About the name of the mission, Devadas and his followers have always been careful to make it clear that their organization was not named after any human being as in the case of the Lutheran Mission or the Wesleyan Mission, etc., but it was named only after the word of God, the Bible. Concerning the programme of the Bible Mission this passage makes a reference to 'spiritual revival', to 'fullness of the holy spirit' and to the teaching and learning aspects as exemplified by their founder, Devadas. All these have become the hallmarks of the Bible Mission in the following years and Devadas himself had emphasised these aspects of the ministry in his teachings.

Finally, this passage ends with a simple assertion that 'what all we say of him (Devadas) fell short of reality'—meaning thereby that whatever great things they said about him they are not adequate to fully describe his merits. Devadas was held in such a high esteem by his followers.

2. The Founder's Own Account

In the inner title page of Bible Mission Booklet No. 14, entitled Woe Unto You, Devadas himself tells about the birth of the Bible Mission. This is what he writes there:

> Brief history of Bible Mission: In the year 1938 in bright day light God wrote two words "Bible Mission" in the air and showed to me. So the Bible Mission was established accordingly. He commanded me to hold it high. The world should ask God why He had revealed it to me this unworthy man belonging to the Andhra Evangelical Lutheran Church, Rajahmundry, Andhra Pradesh when there are so many more highly educated rich and young people. I believe and hope that the Bible Mission would go to every place in which the wind blows. It is definite that one day or other all the missions should come together and move [sic] friendly with each other. Hatred among the missions

should be removed and doctrinal differences should not hinder the harmony and peace of the religion.

> Maranatha
> M.Devadas
> To whom God revealed the Bible Mission.

3. The story continues

In the same booklet the editor also adds his own version of the story as follows:

> Mr. M.Devadas worked as a touring evangelist for 46 years in the American Evangelical Lutheran Mission[14] at Rajahmundry, Andhra state, South India taking after his Godly parents in the same line. His Lutheran pastors did not believe in the gifts of the Holy Spirit as recorded in I Cor 14:21, "With men of other tongues and other lips I shall speak unto this people; yet for all that, they will not hear me - saith the Lord". They (the pastors) called them (the gifts) devilish and they are contrary to the Lutherans and asked him (Devadas) to stop his revival meetings. After waiting upon the Lord as to what to do he saw the Lord write the words 'Bible Mission' in the air in his room in gold coloured letters in his mother tongue, Telugu. This was in January 1938. The writings in the air continued. "Resign from the Lutheran Mission", "Come out as the prince of an army", "Lift up and show the Bible Mission and its message that God appears and speaks to people and that the miracles of the Bible times are possible even today". That is why Father Devadas told me (Gnanamani, the editor of this booklet, that is) that he signs on his tracts as—M.Devadas, <u>to Whom God Revealed the Bible Mission</u> which addition I thought was monotonous and unnecessary and I told him so. [sic]

Thus we see the story of the vision was faithfully passed on from mouth to mouth among the followers of Devadas and it was accepted without any question. It became even more detailed and more colourful as it was handed down the line. The somewhat sad side of the actual controversies and the rift between the pastors and the missionaries of the Lutheran Church on the one hand and Devadas on the other is not available in record. The present investigator gathered a somewhat hazy picture from various sources, some documented and some oral. Its gist briefly is this:

Devadas was known for his proficiency in English. He even wrote a text book to teach English grammar which was used in schools in those days. He was employed as a teacher and he was always preferred as translator and as interpreter to missionaries. He was the interpreter for Sādhu Sundar Singh when the sādhu visited South India in 1919[15]. Dēvasahayam mentioned five names of former students of Devadas whom Dēvasahayam interviewed, and some of them are still living. In 1911 a call came to Devadas to be ordained but he told the church convention that he did not feel called. Later on he claimed that God himself had ordained him in a vision in 1918. While working as a teacher in the mission school and later in the seminary in Rajahmundry, Devadas was attracting some young men to his revival meetings and he was talking about visions and healing miracles. At this time it also happened that Apostle P.M. Samuel of Vijayawada, now the president of the Ceylon Pentecostal Church, came to Rajahmundry to conduct a series of meetings on the gifts of the Holy Spirit. Devadas was attending these meetings (1934) and he said openly in one of the meetings that 'he was experiencing all these even from much earlier times'[16]. It is further documented that in a sermon delivered by Devadas at an ordination service in 1945 he declared 'I have received and am experiencing the full revelation and the complete presence of our Lord already since August 21, 1901' but Devadas said he had not revealed it to anyone[17].

Father Devadas also used to recall a vision which a Pentecostal preacher from the west once narrated in a campaign in the town of Elur. In that vision the Pentecostal preacher had seen that God was going to raise a 'prophet like Moses' very soon in India and he said it was Father Devadas who was thus chosen to spread the Bible Mission[18].

Thus, as Devadas started talking about his visions and dreams the pastors of the Lutheran Church expressed some concern about his teachings, holding the view that these teachings were not widely accepted doctrines of the Church. But the general interest of people in these teachings increased. At last, after several arguments and warnings, Devadas was one day asked to resign from his job in the Lutheran Church. His services were officially terminated from March 1, 1938, as per the report of Dēvasahāyam[19]. On January 31, 1938, Devadas announced that God had shown him the name of the Bible Mission in a vision. On Sunday the 24th April as he attended the communion service in the Lutheran church the local pastor asked him not to come to the communion rail. Devadas that day stayed behind in the pews and prayed. He said later, that the Lord himself appeared to him then and personally administered communion to him. This is how Devadas himself narrates the incident:

> I tendered my resignation to the membership of the Lutheran Mission in February 1938. Since then the church officers did not reply to my resignation letter. I went to the church service in the following April prepared to receive the Lord's supper. On that day they were celebrating the Holy Communion in that service. But they did not allow me to receive the communion. I was not ashamed. I was sitting in my pew. The Lord himself came and administered the bread and wine to me[20].

4. The Teacher Gathers some Disciples

After Devadas came out of the Lutheran Church and became an independent preacher he lived in several places in succession in the Andhra Districts, preaching and teaching and gathering followers. Some of his students in the seminary and his younger colleagues are living today[21].

Mr. Vijaya Ratnam, who helped the present investigator as an informat, is now living in Rajahmundry[22]. On Thursday, May 15th, 1938, Devadas officially established the Bible Mission in what was called the Sharon House in

Rajahmundry and ordained Vijaya Ratnam on the same day and appointed him as the president of the governing body. On Wednesday, December 7, 1938, the Mission was registered at the District Registrar's Office as the India Bible Mission under Act No. XXI of the 1860 Societies Registration Act[23].

In a booklet under the title Abhayāni[24] Vijaya Ratnam made a strong appeal to the opponents of the Bible Mission, especially to the pastors and the missionaries of the Lutheran Church and to the public in general, asking them to make a dispassionate examination of the claims of the Bible Mission. It is a long discourse but the main line of argument of Vijaya Ratnam may be summarised in his own words as follows:

> Some people have heard our teachings and they have opposed us because these are not in accordance with their church teachings even if they are biblical. It is not fair to reject the teachings because they are not convenient to some people. It may be wiser to see if these teachings are scriptural, reasonable and acceptable to human conscience. Also it may be useful to wait in the presence of God till they get an answer from Him about what they should do with these teachings of ours. The Lord himself will let them know His will if they would ask Him and He will tell them with what motives we are teaching these things. The Lord Himself will let them know His will if they ask Him. We plead that people should not see our weaknesses but should objectively examine our doctrines. If the pastors think that we are in the wrong then it is proper for the pastors to come and show to us our mistakes.

Here Vijaya Ratnam cites Scripture passages from the 18th Chapter of the Gospel according to St. Matthew about the procedure the Lord had enjoined to deal with an erring brother and suggests five steps, the last one being the final excommunication. Then Vijaya Ratnam outlines the sevenfold doctrine of the Bible Mission and the gist of these seven points is as follows:

> 1) The Baptism of the Holy Spirit is essential: It is scriptural. (Several Scripture passages were cited, e.g., Acts 1.5; 2.33;

8.14-17; and 2.39; including the story of the heathen who received the baptism of the Holy Spirit before they received the Christian Baptism, Acts 10.44-48.)

2) The gift of speaking in tongues is essential: This is both necessary and possible. (St. Paul was quoted and St. Mark Ch. 16 cited.)

3) Visions and dreams are manifestations of God's kingdom here and now.

4) Divine healing should be claimed and received. (Several Scripture verses quoted.)

5) The gift of casting out of devils is real.

6) The imminent coming of our Lord into this world is real.

7) Waiting in the presence of the Lord should become a regular practice of the Christians.

After this list of the doctrines of the Bible Mission, Vijaya Ratnam recalls several incidents preceding the actual birth of the Bible Mission and makes an appeal to the readers to examine the credentials of the organisation. This is what he says in brief:

1) In 1934 during the season of Pentecost, Father Devadas preached for ten days in open air meetings convened by the Lutheran Church (name of the place mentioned) on the subject of the Holy Spirit.

2) In 1935 in another Lutheran church at the time of the festival of Pentecost, Father Devadas similarly taught for ten days on the subject of the Holy Spirit (the place and pastor mentioned by name.)

3) The same thing had happened in two other towns in 1936 and 1937.

4) In 1936, I (Vijaya Ratnam) preached in a similar convention in St. Matthew's Lutheran Church in Guntur on the request of the pastor (named) and on the invitation of the church council. At

the end of the Pentecost season many people joined in a day of fasting prayer and some of them received the baptism of the Holy Spirit.

5) In 1936, I (Vijaya Ratnam) published a booklet on the threefold intercession (Thrividha Vignāpana) and distributed copies.

6) In October 1936, I wrote to the president of the Andhra Evangelical Lutheran Church (the name of the missionary president mentioned) explaining our faith.

7) Three responsible members of the Lutheran Church who were also delegates to the convention at that time publicly expressed solidarity with us.

8) At that time I had printed a pamphlet on the baptism of the Holy Spirit and distributed to the members of the Lutheran Church.

9) In 1936, I printed a booklet on the subject of 'The Good Things' and distributed to the Lutherans[25].

10) In 1936, in the month of November according to the church calendar in the advent season I published a booklet on the second coming of the Lord (Dwitheey'agamanamu) and distributed it.

11) In December 1937 we held a four day prayer meeting and as we taught the important doctrines of our faith two of the ministers of the Lutheran seminary at Luthergiri attended these meetings[26].

12) In June 1937 we published a booklet called the Outpouring of the Holy Spirit (Vimalāthma Prōkshanam) and distributed it to the church leaders.

13) We wrote to the president of the Lutheran Convention the seven points of our doctrine asking him to see that they be carefully examined and adopted into the teachings of the Lutheran Church.

14) We then wrote to the principal of the Lutheran seminary Dr. E.Neudoerffer suggesting that the pastors in training may not be

15) Lastly this present booklet Abhayāni also provides an opportunity for anyone who wants to see our view point and if the church leaders still do not want to see it, then we are not to blame. Until these teachings are thus carefully examined, until God's will is known about these teachings, and until His guidance is asked for, it is not fair to threaten us that we will be sent away from our jobs. If we are excommunicated, we will be sent out from the organization but not from the household of God. We followed the word of God as recorded in I Timothy 4.6 which reads, "If you give these good instructions to the brothers you will be a good servant of Jesus as you feed yourself spiritually on the words of faith and of the true teaching which you have followed".

One may note from these writings of Vijaya Ratnam that much of the teaching of the Bible Mission in those days sounded like the Pentecostal teaching.

In the final sections of the booklet, Vijaya Ratnam makes a strong plea saying,

All along in the history of the Christian church even in the days of our Lord's earthly ministry it was no one but the religious leaders who opposed the truth. It was first the scribes and pharisees who rejected our Lord's teaching. They did not even consider to give him a hearing and consequently they did not find the truth. The Lord rebuked religious leaders in the 23rd Chapter of St. Matthew. Later, in the times of the Apostles it was no one but the religious leaders who opposed the Gospel. So the disciples had to ask: Is it right to hear your word rather than God's word?

At the time of the Reformation also it was the same story. It was the leaders of the church who opposed the new teaching. The same history is repeating today.

Listen, you our dear missionaries who are in authority. Many people who belong to your churches are desiring the baptism of the Holy Spirit but they are afraid of you and so they are not able to come forward. Many people have told us this. We therefore beg you to see that the words of our Lord recorded in Matthew 23.13 do not apply to you.

In this tone Vijaya Ratnam pleaded with the church authorities in those days on behalf of the Bible Mission and on behalf of Father Devadas. It was a long-drawn-out struggle for these people before they finally left the Lutheran Church in 1938. In this apologetic Vijaya Ratnam even quoted from a famous Telugu poet Vemana who said:

> If some one said something
> It is good to hear, who ever it is who said it.
> Having heard,
> It is necessary to stop and think.
> He who thus discriminates good from evil
> from what he has heard,
> Only he is the wise man and no one else[28].

We can gather some information about this man Vijaya Ratnam himself from a letter he addressed to the Rev. J. Roy Strock, the president of the Lutheran Church at that time.

We learn that Vijaya Ratnam had his Bible Training in the Lutheran seminary in the year 1931 under the missionary principal Dr. E. Neudoerffer, whom he considered as his spiritual father[29]. He was first a school teacher and then became an evangelist. During those days he stayed with Father Devadas for some days and attended his prayer meetings. He heard the teachings of Devadas on the Holy Spirit. Then Vijaya Ratnam left the church job and became an independent preacher. And we have seen that Devadas later ordained Vijaya Ratman as a minister of the Bible Mission.

After this autobiographical note, Vijaya Ratnam gives a summary of his own teachings in several places and declares that the Lord had healed many sick people in answer to his prayers and many demons were exorcised. Finally, he asks the president of the Lutheran Church and all those who are in authority to pray to God for guidance and do 'whatsoever he tells you', another phrase which Devadas and his followers always used.

Thus, Vijaya Ratnam played an important role in the early history of the Bible Mission. But after several years he moved away and started his own group and even became the Bishop of his own organisation, which received financial support from other countries. But he always held Father Devadas in high esteem. It is sometimes said that every Luther needs a Melanchthon and that what Melanchthon was to Luther, Vijaya Ratnam was to Devadas. The Bible Mission owes a great deal to the clear thinking and the pen of Vijaya Ratnam in those days[30].

5. The Growth of Bible Mission in the Lifetime of Father Devadas

Once Father Devadas came out of the Lutheran Church in 1938 he started travelling to several places in Andhra, preaching and gathering groups of followers. In each place he went he stayed in the homes of his followers in the New Testament way and his followers loved him and encouraged him in his ministry[31]. In each of these centres a small prayer group was formed and these groups started growing in size. Special Bible conventions and healing campaigns became popular and some more Lutheran Christians had joined these Devadas groups. Devadas had never even hinted a re-baptism for those who are already baptised in their own churches. This made it considerably easier for Christians from other churches to join the Bible Mission fellowship. A formal change of membership was not important for the Bible Mission but all that was expected was fellowship in prayer and an assent to the teaching.

A few years before his death Father Devadas came to Guntur to the house of his faithful follower, Rao Sahib J. Raja Rao, who was a well-to-do man in the community. Raja Rao owned a spacious house and a wide open area around, which accommodated good size groups for meetings conducted by Father Devadas. Raja Rao offered hospitality to his spiritual guru and fully supported his ministry. He had a mango grove outside Guntur in a village called Kākāni and he donated it for the big healing campaigns conducted every week. Large palm leaf sheds are now constructed in that garden and hundreds of people, mostly Hindus, come there once a week seeking prayer healing and deliverance from demon possession. A team of pastors trained by Father Devadas administer these healing prayers at Kākāni gardens and I have seen these meetings several times which start in the morning and last until late in the night on a Friday. It is a strenuous work including spoken prayers with every patient after an exposition of the word of God. The cases of demon possession take even a longer time with several preachers praying together and laying hands on the person. The demons are rebuked loudly and in the name of Christ they are commanded to leave. Many times the demons are asked to tell their names and how they came to trouble the particular person, and generally the demons answer these questions.

This is a supportive community; all the members of the group and those trying to pray for them have a real mutual concern and fellowship. The touch of the hands, the personal concern shown in different ways, the oil that is blessed and used for anointing which people can take home with them--all these make it an experience which is impossible to get in any hospital much less so in India with its big masses where a personal touch is so much needed but not easily available.

Father Devadas himself was old and feeble when these meetings became popular and he could not go to Kākāni although he firmly believed and assured his followers that his spirit was present with them and praying with them.

6. The End of a Great Life

After an eventful life, Father Devadas to whom God had revealed the Bible Mission died on Tuesday, February 9th, 1960, at 7 p.m. in Rao Bahadur Raja Rao's house[32]. Many of his trusted followers came from many places for the funeral and mourned his death. His mortal remains were buried in a grave in the Kākāni Gardens, the very place set aside for the weekly healing campaigns. Now that place is considered a kind of pilgrim centre for many faithful people.

But something more happened when Devadas died which may throw some light on the beliefs of the Bible Mission people. Devadas in his lifetime spoke often about Sādhu Sundar Singh and the Kailāsh Maharshi, the great old Christian hermit whom Sundar Singh is reported to have seen somewhere in the Himalayas. In the year 1919 when Sundar Singh came to South India many Christians of that generation had seen him and heard him and many people remembered the impact of his visit to those parts of the country. In the booklet Mithra[33] Devadas mentioned the visit of Sādhu Sundar Singh to Andhra. Sundar Singh's spirituality had made a great impact on Devadas which remained all his lifetime. On the basis of what he must have heard from Sundar Singh and read from his books and biography, Devadas believed that the spirit of Kailash Maharshi and all other saints can wander around at will to be with people of God in prayer in any place. In another booklet Sannidhi Sampada[34] Devadas speaks of the saintly spirits thus wandering all over the earth appearing to God's people in visions and prayers.

The followers of Devadas remembered all this and when he died a rumour went around among his followers that Devadas would appear and speak to them soon and some people even believed that he would rise again on the third day. He was 'the beloved disciple' and do they not read that the Lord said, 'If I want him to live until I come, what is it to you?' Is it not possible that the Lord will keep some of his saints like Devadas and Kailāsh Maharshi alive till he returns to the earth[35]?

But Devadas himself in his lifetime had never even suggested anything which would give this kind of hope to his followers. He did say that spirits of saints both living and dead may come to us in prayer as God would send them and may speak to us. However, he never said he would not die or would rise again the third day. So he is buried and his remains lie now in his tomb in the garden of Kākāni.

But the Bible Mission people still believe and strongly desire the constant fellowship of the spirit of Devadas. So today wherever they meet for prayer they keep an empty chair carefully covered with white linen in a corner for

Tablet of the Grave Stone of Devadas
"To Whom God Revealed the Bible Mission"

The Faithful Gather Around the Tomb of Devadas

the spirit of Devadas to come and sit with them. This, to them, is the real 'fellowship of the saints'.

Thus, not only the teachings but the very life of this saintly man has deeply influenced his followers in India. The marks of that influence and its effects on the quality of life and the witness of the Indian church are something we will study in the following chapters. One of the great Lutheran missionaries who worked with Devadas has this to say about him:

> Mr. Devadas is given by God as a special gift to the Christians in Andhra[36].

CHAPTER III: Notes

1. All place names in Telugu like all other nouns end with a vowel and hence, Mungamūru, Guntūru, Jēgūrupādu etc. But when writing in English the last vowel is generally omitted, hence they become Mungamūr, Guntūr and Jēgūrpād etc. This is to provide facility of reading the English text with these names. In the genitive case, the final 'u' changes into 'i' so that Mungamūri means 'of or coming from Mungamūru' etc. Mungamūri Devadas is the name of a Devadas who must have come from a place called Mungamūr.

2. Dēvasahāyam K., The Bible Mission, Religion and Society, Vol. XXIX No. 1. March 1982, p. 55.

3. Drach, George and Kuder, Calvin F., The Telugu Mission of the General Synod of the Evangelical Lutheran Church in North America, Philadelphia Pub. House, 1914, p. 144ff. Quoted by Devasahayam op.cit., p. 56.

4. Sadhu here is used in the general meaning of a saintly person.

5. Dēvasahāyam, Religion and Society, op.cit., pp. 55-89.

6. No. 11 of my list of the Bible Mission publications in Chapter I of this book.

7. This is how the Bible Mission people express their practice of silent waiting prayer. Devadas has brought this practice into active usage in Andhra area.

8. See note 2, above.

9. Minutes of the Executive Committee of the Andhra Evangelical Lutheran Church No. 9, 1936-38, p. 3. Dated February 25, 1938 quoted by Devasahayam, op.cit., p. 55.

10. Dēvasahāyam, op.cit., p. 56.

11. In a personal letter written in 1980 by Mr. Vijaya Ratnam to the present investigator, Vijaya Ratnam also expressed what he thinks about the claims about this date of birth. This is what Vijaya Ratnam says:

> Father Devadas was born in Rajahmundry Taluk, East Godavary. It is not true that he lived for 120 years. He studied in Rajahmundry Lutheran School and worked in the Luthergiri Theological College and in the Lutheran Sanatorium as Evangelist. He also worked as a teacher and as a Munshi (language teacher to Missionaries) and also a Bible teacher at Luthergiri seminary. He was for some time at Prathipadu (a village) in the West Godavary District. At Elur he stayed at the house of Kandavalli Prasada Rao. He was also at Vijayawada and Guntur. He retired from the Lutheran Mission Service in 1935. He died in 1960. He was never married. He suffered from Asthma. He started the Bible Mission in 1938. He had no temptation for money or women.

12. Cf., Bible Mission Booklet No. 14, Woe Unto You. On the title page of this booklet this advice is printed which Devadas had always given to his followers: Hate no man, and no religion: Ask God and find out.

13. Devasahayam reports from reliable evidence obtained from some informants that marriage was proposed to Devadas twice and both times he turned it down. And the girls proposed to him were married to other men and he maintained a cordial and affectionate relationship with those families.

14. There was no consistency in those days in the way people referred to the Lutheran Church in Andhra. First it began as Mission of the Lutheran Church in America and therefore for a long time it was called the Andhra Evangelical Lutheran Mission or American Lutheran Mission. Then with the amalgamation of two Lutheran bodies in America the mission in Andhra was renamed as the United Lutheran Church Mission (ULCM). And then in 1927 in the general transition from the missions to the churches, it became the Andhra Evangelical Lutheran Church which official name it bears today. But in the minds of some of the Telugu Christians these names are all mixed up sometimes.

15. Devasahayam, op.cit., p. 59.

16. Ibid., p. 62.

17. Rev. B.Elisha, President of the Bible Mission in a brief Biographical Note of Father Devadas MS in Telugu dated 28.3.70 referred to by Devasahayam, op.cit., p. 62.

18. Devadas M., Satyāmsa Nirūpana Booklet No. 28 in my list quoted by Devasahayam, op.cit., p. 75.

19. Devasahayam, ibid., p. 66.

20. Devadas M., Kristu Mathābhivriddhi Pathrika, p. 8, No. 20, quoted by Devasahayam, ibid., p. 74.

21. One of the senior pastors of the Lutheran church who went into the Bible Mission hearing the call of Devadas was Rev. P. Benjamin. He was an experienced pastor when he joined Devadas and he lived and served the Bible Mission for several years. A son-in-law of Rev. Benjamin has been serving the Bible Mission as pastor for several years now and one of his grandsons was recently ordained with a B.D. Degree to the Lutheran ministry.

22. See note 11 above.

23. Devasahayam, op.cit., p. 67.

24. Bible Mission Booklets No. 19.

25. The contents of this publication are not available.

26. There is a small hillock outside the city of Rajahmundry where the Lutheran seminary was established. That hill is known today as Luthergiri, the hill of Luther.

27. Cf., Abhayāni, Apologetic, Bible Mission Booklet No. 19, p. 24. A copy of the letter written to Dr. Neudoerffer and signed by Vijaya Ratnam reads as follows:
Dear Sir,
   Our Lord commanded his disciples not to leave Jerusalem before they get the Spirit Baptism. Students in theological institutions should not leave their classrooms unless they have the baptism of the Holy Ghost. Covering the course and counting the attendance are not more important than receiving the baptism of the Spirit. Practice is more important than theory. If any of the students of the pastors' class goes out without the baptism of the Holy Spirit, his congregation will be full of quarrels, disorders and failures in work. There will be no increase of spiritual life. Pastors will not be accepted by their congregations. The method of teaching here should be changed. I am speaking from my own experience in Luthergiri. [sic]

Yours in His service,
K. Vijaya Ratnam
Independent preacher.

28. Vemana of the late 15th century according to Chenchiah (see note 2, Chapter 2 of this book) was a great sage of Andhra who wrote a hundred short and simple four-footed metrical verses on every-day morals. These works of Vemana and other poets like him became famous as sathakas because they are in groups of hundred pieces, from the word satha, meaning a hundred.

29. Dr. E. Neudoerffer, also known as the Elder Neudoerffer because of his younger brother who was also a missionary in Andhra, was a great theologian and for a long time principal of the Luthergiri theological college, Rajahmundry. Several batches of pastors who served the Andhra Evangelical Lutheran Church were trained by Dr. Neudoerffer. Dr. Neudoerffer loved India so much that he retired and settled down and died in India.

30. About the Booklet Abhayāni itself this is what its editor has to say: In this book there are seven important doctrinal points. They are from the teachings of Father Devadas, the servant of God who taught them according to the Scriptures during 1934-37. Mr. Vijaya Ratnam had them printed in Rajahmundry in 1937. (See Abhayāni, Booklet No. 19, title page 4).

31. Vijaya Ratman's letter cited in Note 6 above.

32. Devasahayam, op.cit., p. 70.

33. Mithra, Bible Mission Booklet No. 16, p. 40.

34. In Bible Mission Booklet No. 10, Sannidhi Sampada (Treasure of Fellowship) Devadas says: When the faithful wait for the Lord in a fellowship meeting,
 1. One day Christ appears and speaks and answers their questions.
 2. Another day he sends one of the angels. That angel appears and gives a message and answers questions.
 3. Another day He would send one of the bhakthas of heaven. That bhaktha gives messages, answers questions.
 4. Another day He sends a living believer. The same thing happens.
 5. Another day He sends one of the dead from Hades. These souls are not yet in heaven, and they speak and answer our questions.
 6. He even sends a devil (He allows to come). The devil speaks and tells us things and answers our questions. But then Christ comes and comforts us, tells us that we should not believe what the devil tells us.

35. There are several instances around the world where saintly people are expected to come to life again after death and appear in the world. Hollenweger mentions the miracle healer and preacher, William Brauman who died in 1965. His followers waited for months without burying his dead body because they believed that he would rise again. See Hollenweger, W.J., Pentecostals, op.cit., p. 354.

36. Introduction to his Lenten Devotions Book: Behold the Lamb of God, Dr. E. Neudoerffer, p. vi. Quoted by Devasahayam, op.cit., p. 63.

The World of the Angels

CHAPTER IV

Experienced Religion
(Faith, Demons, Spirits, Visions, Dreams and Healing)

1. The Cultural Background

Most of the simple Christians in India live in two worlds: one, the Hindu world of the wider community around them with its festivals and feasts, social practices and cultural overtones; the other, the different world which they have inherited through their faith in Christ. One is the world in which they live with all the others in the wider society and the other is their private world confined to their homes and families and the church. Stanley Samartha rightly describes this predicament of the Indian Christian when he says that he is torn between identification with the culture of his own country and participation in the heritage of the world church; and he is struggling to bring out the distinctive meaning of Christ in the Hindu context[1].

This fact has a definite bearing on people's beliefs, attitudes and views vis-a-vis the spirits, demons, devils and other mysterious things like dreams and visions coming from Hinduism[2].

Rural folk in India hear about demons and spirits everywhere, some of them benign and some sinister, some bring disaster and disease and others just frolick and co-exist with the human beings. Some demons even protect people against other demons, and some of these protecting demons are believed to be responsible for the well-being of the village. That is why these demons are both feared and worshipped, both hated and placated. People worship demons to ward off their destructive power and to ask for their protection. In village Hindu religion prayers are offered to evil spirits to use their power against one's enemies and against wicked men rather than against the worshipper. Sometimes people believe that they need charms and talismans to protect them from the power of the evil spirits, and these magic protections are tied around their necks and arms.

Christians are taught that they should have no fear of these _galis_[3] or of the even stronger spirits called the _bhutas_[4] and _pishachis_[5], but all the same many village Christians do believe in the existence of such supernatural powers. For them it is neither easy to ignore the manifestations of the evil spirits nor to get rid of their fear. It may be useful to remember the caution so well voiced by Henry Mitchell in dealing with some of these old beliefs. Mitchell says:

> Never fight a war with or engage in frontal attack against the prevalent culture. It is not only unwise to tackle that which is so well entrenched; it is foolish and damaging to the psyche to try to destroy the world view buried so deeply in people that their identity and living wisdom are tied up in it. If and when persons are bereft of their culture, they become pathologically disoriented, in need of institutional care[6].

Apart from that, we do read about demons in the New Testament, and since Christ's ministry in no small measure included the casting out of demons, Christians find it necessary to deal with these powers even if the Western missionary has told them that this is all superstition. It may be useful to recall here that in the passages of the New Testament where Christ cast out the evil spirits we find the following features:

1) The evil spirits recognised Christ straight away (Mark 5.7).
2) They recognised him even before he revealed himself to people as Messiah. That is why he had to tell the people who were healed of the demon possession not to publish this to any one (Mark 1.34).
3) Christ directly addressed the demons in the man who was possessed and not the man who was possessed (Mark 5.9).

In addition to the demons, devils and evil spirits there are the ancestral spirits also in India, the souls of the parents and the grandparents who are very real to a Hindu. These ancestral spirits are very much around expecting an annual meal from their children which is done on the anniversary of their death. A Brahmin priest has to be called and a meal prepared under his guidance generally on the banks of a river or a canal and the spirits will thus have to be satisfied. Otherwise these ancestors will not be able to escape from a certain hell. It is the duty of their descendants to deliver these departed souls from this fate. It is also believed in some quarters of Hinduism that those who die without leaving any male progeny to perform this duty will roam around as evil spirits after their death.

The ancestral spirits sometimes appear and speak to people and convey some important messages or warn them against some impending danger or reassure them of their watchful care. We see this belief in many other cultures. In South Africa, for example in Zululand, people believe that they live in constant companionship with the ancestral spirits. Their conversion to Christianity does not affect people's belief in the ancestral spirits and their interest in the living kinsmen. Existence is a continuous process to them and there is not much difference between the pre-mortal and post-mortal stages.

What then does a village Christian in India think about these departed souls? He is not always clear. He is taught that the dead believers will rise on Judgment Day, but where are they until then? Have these Christians not heard sometimes that the departed ones are praying for them in the presence of God? Is it not a common experience that people sometimes believe that they have seen these departed ones in dreams and apparitions? What exactly is the meaning of the teaching on the 'fellowship of the living and the dead?'

The village Christians in India have also heard many stories from the Hindu Scriptures on life after death[7].

And what is the place of dreams in the life of an Indian Christian? Dreams are part of the real experience of the Indian people. They give some meaning to almost every kind of dream, some symbolism or significance which comes from generations of associations and symbols. A snake in the dream foretells some evil but if it has bitten someone in the dream and if he sees blood, that can be a good omen. If one sees in his dream that he is protected in sleep by the hood of a cobra as a shade, it augurs a great future for him. That is how some of the buddhas, the enlightened ones, saw their mission in a dream. If one sees himself in a dream with unshaven beard, it can be an indication of a coming sickness, while flying in the air in a dream is a sign of imminent success and honour. Swimming in water in a dream is good luck if the water is clean and clear, but it is a sign of trouble if the water is dirty.

Many times dreams are forgotten but the art of unravelling the meaning of dreams is very much alive in India like the art of palm-reading or the skill of fortune telling. Therefore any investigation into the church's beliefs about demons and spirits and dreams and visions will have to take into account this background since converts made in India bring a good deal of these beliefs along into the church.

2. Demons and Spirits in the Bible Mission

To Devadas, founder of the Bible Mission, Satan is very real and a power to reckon with and to resist. In most of his writings and sermons Devadas uses the biblical word 'Satan' for what the Indian people generally refer to as demon, evil spirit, Dayyam, Bhūtam, gāli, etc., Telugu words for the evil spirit depending on how powerful and big the evil spirit is. The word Satan does not appear much in non-Christian Telugu literature except in the Muslim tradition, which uses the word 'shaitān'.

Devadas believed that Satan is the opponent of God and that it is Satan who brings sin and sickness into the world. Satan and his angels, sometimes called demons, devils, or evil spirits, are the cause of all sickness and disease and trouble. Devadas believed literally the story of Lucifer, the fallen angel who with his followers has been thrown out of heaven[8]. But God sometimes sends Satan to see the faithful[9] and Devadas asks his followers not to be afraid if they see demons in their prayers because immediately after the demons leave, God himself will come and will make things clear and drive away their fears[10]. Sometimes God can even use Satan to promote His plan on the earth[11]. Devadas fully believed and taught that the departed souls of the faithful will also sometimes appear in our prayers, and in support of this view he cited the incident of the transfiguration of our Lord where Moses and Elijah appeared with Christ on the mountain. He also cited the fact that many of the dead came out of their graves in Jerusalem when Christ died on the cross and these risen spirits have appeared to many in the streets[12].

From these passages of the Bible Devadas fully believed that the departed spirits can appear to us any time they want. Not only the spirits of the departed but also the spirits of the living saints like Kailāsh Maharshi can get out of their bodies and travel around to visit us in our prayers. Devadas claimed to have spoken to many of these departed souls in his prayer, some of them known to him and some unknown coming from many ages and many lands as God permitted them.

A major part of the teachings of Devadas on demons and devils can be found in his booklet S̄athānu-nedirinchuta (Resisting Satan)[13]. This is a 76-page booklet with 108 casting-out formulae almost like exorcism spells to be used to resist the pestering devil. The theme text of this booklet is James 4.7, Resist the Devil and he will run away from you. In addition to these 108 spells directly addressed to Satan this booklet contains the following material also:

1) A sevenfold prayer to God asking him to get seven books to be written and displayed in the sky to scare away Satan.
2) A divorce letter from the believers addressed to Satan and to be delivered to him.
3) More prayers to God asking Him to drive away the evil spirits.
4) Some Bible Texts to help resist Satan.

All the 108 spells recorded in this booklet are to be used directly against Satan as one would use arrows against his opponent[14]. In the introduction to this book, the editor recalls the story of Lucifer and reminds the readers that Christ on the cross defeated Satan and Satan is therefore like a serpent 'with his head broken'. He also reminds us that the Lord has given His power to us too so that we can trample Satan under our feet and smash his head. In one of the prayers Devadas says,

> Lord, you have allowed Satan to trouble me and this is good for my strength and it is a means of winning the victory and to get the reward. Therefore I thank you[15].

Satan is seen as the anti-type of God in all respects[16] and therefore God is praised first in this booklet before Satan is rebuked. There are separate prayers making mention of all His various attributes. Ten attributes are mentioned such as Light, Love, Wisdom, etc. Sometimes these prayers are in the form of affirmations and statements to strengthen the believer in his faith. For example,

> Lord, you have commanded Satan to 'depart' from you. We also do the same thing to him. Help us to do so.
> Lord, we are saved by your grace and Satan is not saved. Help us to believe this.
> Lord, we ask you to hit Satan with your arrows in his head so that he may not send sinful thoughts into our heads.
> Hit him in his eyes with your arrows so that he does not lead us to see sinful things.
> Hit him on his feet . . . .

Thus continue these prayers asking God to hit Satan all over the body part by part so that he cannot do anything to us. While helping the believers to resist temptation and sinful thoughts these prayers are also to be used by the Bible Mission people as exorcist spells to cast out demons. Groups of the faithful sit around a person tormented by demon possession and read aloud these spells to scare away the demon. At the prayer healing meetings of the Mission, several pastors participate and use these prayers for casting out of demons and evil spirits. It may be added here that this practice of reciting manthrās (magic spells) to drive away the demons is not new to Hinduism and Gods are also praised in chain prayers with all their attributes mentioned so that they ward off the powers of the evil spirits. (Ānjanēya Dandakam is one long prayer to the monkey God to drive away demons).

3. What are the spirits and where are they?

From the reading of the prayers in this booklet of Devadas we can make the following general observations about demons and evil spirits: There are several 'worlds' for Devadas[17]--the visible world in which we live now, God's world in which He lives, the World of the Angels, the actual Heaven, the Paradise, and the World of the Space[18] where Satan and his followers and the evil spirits live. Devadas gives several Bible references indicating this Space World as the abode of the evil spirits. All these texts make mention of Satan but they do not clearly indicate the abode of the evil spirits except three passages, namely, Ephesians 2.2 where the word 'space' is used; Ephesians 6.12 where 'heavenly world' is mentioned; and II Peter 2.4 where the word 'hell' is used.

Satan and his followers are actually believed to be in bonds and God has given us strength to 'conquer' them[19].

Long ago our Lord had asked Satan[20] to 'depart' from Him and so the evil one has to depart from us if we resist him in his face. He lives in darkness but sometimes he comes like the angel of light to deceive us. He is the creator of all evil in this world[21]. The servants of Satan make false reports against us before God, but God rejects such complaints the devil and his servants make against us. When we resist Satan we are in effect resisting all his followers and they run away from us. God has already kept in bonds four devils at the River Euphrates and therefore we have to bind the devils now on earth[22].

Satan is neither a man nor a woman. He is not even a creature. We will one day become divine by the grace of God but Satan can never become even human. We can be saved even if we fall into temptation but Satan can never be saved because he will never repent. It was he who brought evil into the world and so it is he who has to perish along with the evil at the end. We are not getting visions from God sometimes because of the evil interventions of Satan. We are however strong enough to conquer him finally (Ephesians 6.10). When the Lord was on the earth he spent a major part of His ministry in casting out demons and so we too have to do the same thing now.

Satan is afraid of the Book of Deuteronomy because the Lord has used texts from this book to rebuke Satan. Just as the armies of Elijah were greater in number than the armies of his enemy, so also our armies now are greater in number than the armies of Satan. Satan has other names like 'the ancient serpent', 'the dragon', 'the false witness', 'the tempter', etc. We can know his nature and his work from these names. All sinister things happen to us because of Satan. All false visions and wrong revelations come from Satan. In our daily life several small misfortunes like the snapping of the threads in the weavers' loom are the mischief played by the devil[23]. When God's Holy Spirit comes upon us there is absolutely no power to the evil one over us.

Thus goes on the train of thought about the devil in this booklet. We see from the several passages that Devadas believes that the devil is real, personal and almost as having a body like ours although he said that the devil is not even a creature, and the followers of Devadas speak to the devil just as they would speak to any living person. He is almost chided for his foolishness sometimes, as for example when Devadas says,

> Satan, have you ever read the Small Catechism of Martin Luther? There Luther has advised us to fight with the flesh, with the world and with the devil. So we indeed will fight with you[24].

In another spell we read,

> Satan, have you not one day taken a list of sins committed by Martin Luther to show it to him and to intimidate him? Do you remember that he drove you away making an assertion that the Lord has taken away his sins for ever[25]?

Thus some of the spells in the booklet are designed to remind Satan of the several incidents from the Bible and from church history to show him that he can never win the war against us. The life and the work of the many living saints also are mentioned to the devil as manifestations of the Lord's strength against his evil deeds.

In a society which is frequently bothered with unknown evil powers as we have already seen, and in a culture which for generations has believed that sickness is caused by demons, people needed this kind of chants and spells, prayers and formulas to conquer their fears. The Hindus have similar sorts of 'manthrās' to drive away the evil spirits and to bring peace and tranquility[26].

It has already been mentioned above that there is a sevenfold prayer in this booklet asking God to cause seven books to be written to be placed publicly in the 'world of space' to scare away Satan and his followers for ever. According to this prayer the contents of these books are to be as follows[27]:

1) All the passages from this book of spells,
2) All other such prayers being offered by the angels and the Holy Saints in heaven,
3) The witness of the people who are now tempted by Satan and his followers (God is asked to send angels and collect such witness from the living beings),
4) A divorce letter which we are now giving to the devil,
5) The battle cry of Father Davadas which he raised against the devil,
6) The witness of the whole creation which is now groaning under curse because of Satan's works (Romans 1.2),
7) All the other teachings of Father Devadas which he could not yet deliver during these past forty years.

The idea is that Satan and his followers will run away when they see these books in space. Surely, in the opinion of the present writer, the Bible Mission has made the devil more real to people and the whole process of spells and exorcism has almost the flavour of cultic ritual.

It is hard to know exactly from where Father Devadas got all these complicated ideas about the devil. He was certainly influenced by the apocalyptic writings in the Bible with all the winged beasts and the flying beings. But Indian society and popular Hinduism has a great and ancient fear of devils. All sickness, and especially the dreadful epidemics which are hard to explain, are all attributed to the work of the demons. Indian literature is full of stories of 'Rākshasas', the members of the demon kingdom, as opposed to 'Dēvatas', the divine spirits. There is always a war between these two. The idea of these evil and benign spirits is so strongly rooted in Indian thinking that all wicked men and despotic rulers and murderers are associated with the demons. Therefore, much of the thinking of Devadas about the demons and devils may be coming from the surrounding non-Christian community. Professor Hollenweger rightly points out that the acceptance of thought patterns, liturgical formulations, and religious rites from paganism was an ongoing process in the Israelite religion, in the New Testament, and in European Christianity[28].

Coming now to the so-called 'divorce letter' to the Devil as mentioned above, this is how it reads:

> Satan, we do not like you and therefore we are giving you this divorce letter. This letter is valid until our Lord returns to the earth. After that we will not see you any way. Therefore it means that this letter is valid for ever[29].

Again one is reminded of the fact that in a country like India where matrimonial bonds are very strong it is not hard to imagine how bitter and shocking it is to a marriage partner to get a divorce letter. The followers of Devadas knew the seriousness of a divorce letter and they expected the devil to know that this is serious. This is an example of how an old social or cultural practice does sometimes get a new Christian interpretation. In fact this could become a powerful cultural tool for the churches to adopt for an exorcism liturgy as a symbol of denouncing the devil. In cases of demon possession people need help to get rid of their fear and anxiety. They ask for prayers. There may be some advantage in adapting something like this divorce letter as a part of a special service in the church so that people actually experience by active participation real relief from their fears. There are examples in the Indian church where people actually burned their totems and charms publicly as a symbol of their renouncing the old fears and beliefs. In recent times in regular prayer meetings people are sometimes asked to write down on pieces of paper their secret sins which they wanted to get rid of and these papers are burnt after prayer as a symbol of redemption. Such enacted parables can be very meaningful indeed.

4. The spirit of Devadas speaks to the faithful

We have already seen that Father Devadas in his lifetime firmly believed in the fellowship of the departed spirits. He told his followers many stories from his own experience where the Lord and His angels and the spirits of the departed saints had visited him many times in his prayers. Even some of the living saints, he said, have often left their bodily abode and travelled far to come to him in prayer. These apparitions and communion with the spirits and with the Lord himself were not uncommon to Devadas.

The story is told that one day before he left the Lutheran Church Devadas was to speak at a pastors' meeting in the seminary. He spent some time in private prayer and started to go to the meeting place and suddenly realised that Christ was physically walking with him and talking to him. He could clearly see the Lord but others could not see Him. Thus Devadas and the Lord walked to the place of the meeting and there was only one chair provided for the speaker. So Devadas later narrated the story and told his followers how he asked the Lord to take the seat but Christ clearly asked Devadas to take the seat and speak to the meeting as he usually did. This was a clear experience to Father Devadas and he recalled the incident years later.

Similarly the spirits of the departed saints also appeared to Father Devadas many times and he had communion with them. True to this teaching of Devadas, his followers after his death claimed that Devadas himself would come to his followers in prayer. A very important documentary evidence of this belief is available in one of the Bible Mission publications called the Jeptha Vindu Varthamānamulu[30]. A varthamānam is a message, often from a very important person or even from God. The messages preserved in this book are messages from Devadas after he died. They were delivered through the voice of a living person as the faithful waited in prayer. These messages are dated the 15th, 16th and the 17th of November 1977, nearly seventeen years after the death of Devadas. They came in succession in a prayer convention in the hearing of many who were present during those days.

The central theme of the messages is the sacrifice of the daughter of Jepthah as recorded in the Book of Judges (Chapter 11). We shall consider the contents of these messages and their spiritual significance in the chapter on the Church because, according to Devadas, the daughter of Jepthah is a symbol of the Church.

But it is important to note here the process of communication of the departed spirits because it is a common practice in the Bible Mission to receive messages from the departed souls, especially from the founder Devadas himself. I interviewed one preacher who knew Father Devadas when he was alive. This preacher's name is Ananda Rao, who, when he kneels down in prayer, often becomes a channel for Devadas to speak and to give messages to the faithful. Someone in the prayer meeting may have an important question to ask or a problem which was bothering him and Father Devadas may speak to that problem through Ananda Rao, as his channel. At such times his voice changes and many people who knew Devadas claim that they recognise his real voice through Ananda Rao. Devadas can guide his people through the medium.

So in the Jepthah Feast Messages, for three days in succession the spirit of Devadas spoke through one of the women who was in prayer and exhorted the church with his teachings.

Thus it became an accepted belief and a regular practice in the Bible Mission to receive messages from the departed saints. The founder himself vindicated this phenomenon by the fact that he himself spoke after his death, as his followers claim. It may be added here that the Lutheran Church and many other major churches have discouraged the practice of communicating with the departed. It is held that the Bible does not approve of such practices. Likewise the whole area of miracles and visions is under criticism in some quarters. But it may be adequate to note here that the criterion may not be whether it is good or bad to talk to the departed souls. The test should rather be whether these messages thus delivered and received are in accordance with the teachings of the Bible or not and whether they serve the purpose of edification of the believers or not. Father Devadas himself said on many occasions that in all these matters if we have any doubt we should 'ask God in prayer'.

The structure and the style of the Jepthah Feast Messages has a flavour of mystery. To start with, there is a prayer to God asking for His blessing on the church and for the guidance of the Holy Spirit. Then there is a short greeting to the church from Father Devadas. From this point on the message becomes a little broken up, somewhat confused. Here and there it is somewhat incoherent:

> Let four servants gather here on this side...Let seven women gather on that side...Sing from song 62 verse 132...Close the door...What is it that is new?...Do we declare the new to the old[31]? Now what should I teach you?...What message shall I deliver to you?

Thus the message comes bit by bit before it comes to the actual story of Jepthah's daughter. People gathered in the prayer meeting listen carefully as the words come through the medium. They even recognise the tone and the style of Father Devadas. Sometimes the voice addresses them by their names. All through the messages, the voice clearly identifies itself as that of Father Devadas in several ways. For example, at one stage he tells that he obeyed God's call to start the Bible Mission and that he became 'a sacrifice on the altar of God for the sake of the church'. He also expresses great sorrow for the lukewarmness which he saw creeping into the church.

After the spirit of Devadas thus speaks for three days at appointed times, then God's voice comes through the same person and people eagerly wait for His message. God's voice also starts with the story of Jepthah's daughter and at one stage God's voice says:

> Jepthah's daughter had asked for a tarrying time of two months. And my daughter the church has also asked for time to prepare herself, not two months but two thousand years. Therefore I am delaying my second coming to the world[32].

The voice of God also says:

> Like wind it blows, like fire it glows...(It is not clear here what the reference is to, maybe to the Holy Spirit) I am testing every person in the church. I came down to see how many people are walking according to my word. Read Deuteronomy 12.6 and you will find that implicit obedience is important for those who cross the river of Jordan.

Then the spirit of the daughter of Jepthah herself gives a message through the medium. In her opening words she says:

> I do not want to reveal my name but the Holy Spirit wants to make my name public any way. (Jepthah's daughter remains unnamed in the Bible). I do not have a song in my mouth. My heart is trembling. I loved the Lord. I am not yet ready to meet the Lord and so I have asked him to delay his return (here the symbolism changed to the church, the bride[33]).

She also says:

> I went into the mountains to conquer the world, to subdue my body and to get victory over sin. The one who prepared me for this is none other than your Father Devadas. He helped me to confess my sinful state. He led me to the archangel to confess by sins[34].

At this stage again the train of thought becomes somewhat misty and it looks as though the 'medium' is not able to receive the message clearly.

Thus the whole story of Jepthah's Feast Message is the story of a mysterious visitation of the Lord and the spirits heard through the voice of a living human being. The present investigator knows some of the individuals who were present when these messages were reported to have been received and these people do not know how to explain the mystery but they firmly believe that the experience is real. Those to whom the messages came were fully conscious; they felt some kind of power taking charge of them and they were led to say the things which were delivered to them.

From time to time as the messages came the voice asked the worshippers to sing a song or the verse of a hymn and thus there was full involvement and constant attention and expectation.

The practice of spirits speaking through people is not strange to Indian society. Christian churches have considered the practice of 'palukulu', or oracles, as heathen and uncivilised and irrational and unscientific. But every year in the big temple places the village goddess of that particular shrine spoke through the priest or the priestess. Sometimes the goddess is believed to talk through 'possession' and tells people all the things which were to happen that year. Sometimes some objects are thrown out from the temple and brought to the people by the priests and they are interpreted by them. A half burnt straw may indicate fire incidents in the village in summer. An ear of corn may indicate a good rice harvest and so on. In the absence of any recourse to satellite pictures and weather forecasting systems, people sometimes feel that they have to depend on temple oracles to warn them of an impending cyclone for example.

5. From the spirits to the Spirit

It is hard to explain the phenomenon of the spirit of Devadas speaking to his followers. But the transition from the spirits to the Spirit is not difficult to trace in the teachings of the Bible Mission. The Holy Spirit to Devadas and his followers is not just something mentioned in the creedal formulas. The Holy Spirit to them is a daily experience. In other words, the Holy Spirit to them is not something like 'a third horse to a coach driver, the extra one held in reserve which he hardly ever sees'[35]. Devadas clearly stated that there are two baptisms, the first one being the water baptism; and the second one being the baptism of the Holy Spirit. This is Lukan pneumatology as we see in the book of Acts. Thus in the teaching of Devadas we read:

The disciples of our Lord when they were in prayer in the upper room, the Holy Spirit descended on them and they received the power and preached the good news in many languages. By the baptism of the water which is an initiation into the church the followers of Christ become Christians. But the baptism of the Spirit of God which takes hold of the human heart is an outpouring of the Holy Spirit[36].

We have already seen in the early history of the Bible Mission when the doctrinal controversary started with the Lutheran Missionaries, Vijaya Ratnam wrote to the principal of the Lutheran seminary suggesting that the pastoral candidates should not leave their classrooms unless they received the baptism of the Holy Spirit[37]. Again, in a similar letter written by Vijaya Ratnam to the president of the Lutheran Church on the 2nd September 1937, we read:

The Book of Acts in 2.39 says that the promise of the Holy Spirit is meant for all people...How wonderful it would be if the students in the theological seminary receive first the baptism of the Holy Spirit and then enter into service. [sic]

This, as we shall clearly see later on, is Pentecostal teaching. Although the followers of Devadas claim that they have nothing to do with the Pentecostals, we see many similarities to Pentecostal teachings in the Bible Mission, especially in their understanding of the Holy Spirit and its work. To start with, much of the teaching of Devadas contains Pentecostal language. The word 'tarrying' which he so often used comes from the story of the disciples tarrying in the upper room in Jerusalem until the coming of the Holy Spirit. So the actual practice of waiting in prayer received a great emphasis in the life of the Bible Mission people--tarrying in prayer, tarrying for a vision, tarrying for the Lord to speak, and tarrying for the Holy Spirit to come. Indeed as the New Testament Church was born with the coming of the Holy Spirit, so also the Bible Mission attributes its origin to a time of prayer and tarrying and a final revelation received from God.

In fact, Father Devadas and his follower Vijaya Ratnam used to conduct a series of Pentecost Festival prayer meetings for several years at the invitation of the Lutheran Pastors in their churches in Andhra Pradesh in accordance with the dates of the church calendar until they finally were separated from the Lutherans[38]. Also from the very beginning the Bible Mission practised healing ministry as a witness to the manifestation of the work of the Holy Spirit. We do not see, however, that much importance was given to the speaking in tongues in the Bible Mission.

Thus, in the understanding of the nature and work of the Holy Spirit, the Bible Mission takes the view that the Spirit works where Christ works and that the baptism of the Spirit is a second experience which as in Acts Chs. 2, 8 and 19 is a further experience that was necessary 'in order to bring the disciples in Jerusalem, Samaria and Ephesus up to the standards of fully mature Christians'[39].

However, the position held by Devadas about the Holy Spirit does not seem to be that of 'Filioque'--proceeding from the son--which being the view of the Western churches was never accepted by the church in the East. Devadas' teaching of the Holy Spirit is nearer to the Old Testament pneumatology. In the Old Testament the Spirit of God, Ruah Yahveh, is the universal substance of power, giving life to Leviathan and the Lion, to all creatures great and small, as Professor Hollenweger has put it (Ps. 104.29-30; cf. Gen. 2.7). In several instances Devadas did not exclude areas outside the church as possible venues for the Holy Spirit to operate. For example, to receive healing by laying on of hands one need not be a Christian and the possibility of visions and speaking to God is open to any one who ardently desires such a gift, according to Devadas.

The Lutheran missionaries and pastors of that day differed from Devadas on the question of the 'free floating activities' of the Spirit which the major churches sometimes found difficult to accept in the teachings of small groups like the Bible Mission. The Lutheran Church, like all the mission churches of that day, held the view that the Spirit does not generally speak except in and through the church authority and does not work except through its ministry, and they taught that Christ works through the Holy Spirit in and through the

Gospel and the sacraments. This is more a question of Christology. This is what many Western theologians and the Western churches are asking today:

> What precisely is the funcion of the Holy Spirit which is the prisoner of the church and its interpretation of the Bible? Is he in fact superfluous? What is his function if he only glorifies, increases, actualises the work of Christ? Is the risen Christ not perfectly able to fulfil these functions without the Holy Spirit[40]?

The question remains to be answered. At any rate, the Bible Mission, like the Pentecostals, preached the second baptism of the Holy Spirit. In actual practice, in its administration of the healing ministry to non-Christians for example, and in its promise that God would speak to anyone in dreams and visions, the Bible Mission went further than the Pentecostals and mission churches. To them the Holy Spirit is the universal Ruah Yahveh, the lifegiving Spirit, or the cosmic Shakti, as some Indian theologians would put it[41]. Thus we meet many followers of the Bible Mission today who tell us that 'the reason for their conversion to Christianity was seeing a healing miracle in their own lives or in the lives of their relatives or seeing a dream or a vision or some such experience. And it is almost never because of listening to straight preaching'.

While following the Lucan pneumatology, the Bible Mission accepted the fact that the work of the Holy Spirit is possible even outside the church. In this the Bible Mission went into the area of the Old Testament pneumatology although they perhaps took the position of the later prophets in that the Holy Spirit works for 'common good' and He is not just the 'spirit vitale' but also the source of ethical and moral power.

The pneumatology of the Lutheran Church, on the other hand, tended towards the pneumatology of St. Paul. To them the Holy Spirit is not something additional to faith and the baptism of water. But the Bible Mission insisted on the new baptism of the Spirit as a mark of sanctification and a state where the people of God become the 'bride among the virgins'[42]. They separate into temporal succession things that belong together[43].

The Place Where They Buried Him
It is a Place of Healing

It is not accidental that the picture presented by Luke has been accepted as the true biblical view by people who are not capable of dialectic thought...44.

We shall consider this in the chapter on the teaching methods of Devadas.

Thus Devadas and his followers insisted on the gift of healing mainly as a manifestation of the work of the Holy Spirit. But they also expected other gifts: miraculous powers, visions, dreams and unlettered people reciting whole portions of the Scripture sometimes through the power of the Holy Spirit. In fact, the Spirit gives the power and the words to them to pray a real prayer (Mark 13.11).

6. Miracles and Healing

To Devadas God's world is basically a good world. Sickness is nothing but the work of Satan and it is the outcome of sin. God is always a God of healing and for His healing act there are no conditions. 'Whatsoever you ask' God will do for you. Since God is good He wants His children to be free from sin and sickness. In many of these teachings the Bible Mission is similar to the Pentecostals[45].

In Mahima Vārthāvali[46] under the section dealing with the certainty of God listening to our prayers, Devadas makes the following points about sickness and healing[47]:

1) There was no sickness when God created the world. Sickness came through the fall of man. God removes sickness as one removes weeds from the field.
2) God said, I am the Lord, the one who heals you. Exodus 15.26.
3) When Abraham prayed for a heathen, he and his household were healed. Gen. 20.17.
4) God once provided the brass serpent to heal and save His people from death. Num. 21.4-9.

5) Our Lord Jesus Christ in his earthly ministry had always healed the sick. Luke 6.17-19.
6) The prophet Isaiah said that the Lord bears all our sicknesses on the cross. Isa. 53.4.

Because of all this scriptural evidence Devadas strongly advocated prayer healing and the followers of the Bible Mission made prayer healing a regular part of their witness and ministry to the Hindus. In the same booklet cited above under the topic of Divine Healing Father Devadas includes a small catechism to teach some simple truths the readers should learn about healing[48]. The 25 questions and answers in this section can be summarised as follows:

> God heals us without any need for medicine if we pray to Him. This is what is called the prayer healing. This may happen in different ways: Some people read the Bible and get healing, others praise the Lord constantly and they are healed and some get relief in the act of repeating the name of Jesus constantly affirming again and again that there is no other name but that of Jesus to heal. Some may get healing by partaking in the Holy Communion and others by simply believing and walking like the paralytic in the Bible did, etc.

Here it may be interesting to see what George Bennett says about healing:

> I came to realise that as far as the Bible is concerned health and salvation are inseparable. The two go together. The phrase in St. James' epistle can be translated, 'the prayer of faith shall <u>save</u> the sick' or the prayer of faith shall heal the sick. It is we in our materialistic Western world who have separated the two. Furthermore, the Bible sees man as an essential whole. The division we have made for so long between body, mind, and spirit is not the message of the Holy Scripture. It stems from the Graeco-Roman philosophic thought on which so much of our civilisation is built[49].

Devadas suggests several other possible ways of obtaining divine healing. Seeing Jesus in a vision may bring healing, and rebuking Satan to leave can bring healing. There are today regular healing campaigns every week in the place called Kākāni in Andhra Pradesh in a garden where Father Devadas is buried and hundreds of people gather there every week for healing prayers. The preachers pray there for the sick, anointing them with oil and laying hands on them. Some receive immediate relief from their ailments, and if they come from other faiths, they believe in the Lord Jesus and accept him as saviour. Many demons are cast out and sick people take home oil blessed by the preachers.

If sickness does not leave a person after prayer, Devadas says that it may be due to lack of faith or lack of fervent prayer, or because of some unconfessed sin, or because God wants to speak to us through the sickness. In such cases we should not give up nor should we think that the Lord is not listening to us.

> God is always willing to heal and there is promise and evidence in the Scripture to this fact. God is able to heal. What the Bible says about healing is good not only for the past but it is also good for the present. God is the same yesterday, today and for ever.
>
> To get healing it is useful for the sick person to read all the teachings of the Bible Mission on the subject.
>
> God never sends any disease. The Bible tells us that he rather drives away all our sicknesses.
>
> Faith is needed for healing. But such a faith is something that God Himself will give to us. Satan is the cause for all sickness because sin comes from Satan and sickness comes from sin.
>
> All believers should ask for the gift of prayer healing but some will be granted this special gift. Everyone can get this gift through prayer.
>
> Sickness and sin are related just as healing and forgiveness are related. (James 5.14-15).

These views of Devadas on healing will have to be more carefully examined as we go along. Did every person healed by Christ in the New Testament narratives have faith in him? Devadas raises this question and gives an interesting answer:

> The blind men said openly that they believed, the dumb men walked to him in faith, the mad greeted him, many walked away taking his word and they were healed and thus faith was always present but expressed in different ways.

Devadas recognised the fact that sometimes sickness may increase in spite of prayer and that happens because God sometimes allows the devil to do this so that our faith may increase. It may be remembered that Father Devadas suffered with asthma all his life but this never discouraged him.

The followers of Bible Mission firmly believed that it was due to spiritual sloth[50] that the major churches were not seriously interested in prayer healing. As George Bennett again says:

> In these days when people are turning in all directions to find healing and peace, it is important that the Christian church should be clearly seen to be preaching a Gospel that has something very positive to say about sickness and disease[51].

The Lutheran Church has never ruled out the possibility of miraculous healing. There are some cases of prayer healing reported in the other churches also in India. But most of the time the Lutheran Church has left the matter to the individual Christians and never made prayer healing a programme of the church's ministry. Some of the reasons for this hesitation on the part of the average Lutheran pastor can be mentioned as following:

1) The whole motivation may not be right, in that people look for 'fishes and loaves' rather than for 'the kingdom of God'.
2) Those who are not healed may become very bitter and may even lose their faith. This can be disastrous.

3) In those many cases where healing is granted, often the glory is given to the miracle worker and not God to whom glory is due. Many miracle workers were led to doom by their own success.

It is this last problem which George Bennett refers to when he says:

> I never felt entirely happy whenever anyone told me they thought I had a gift of healing. Only One could heal, and that was the risen Christ. We were but instruments in His hands and channels through which His healing love could flow. I have always strongly felt that the healing ministry finds its rightful place only when it is lifted above the level of the individual 'healer' into the glory of Christ seen throughout His church. It was something that all Christian believers ought to be engaged in[52].

All these points of hesitation on the part of some mainline churches can be answered. Hollenweger rightly reminds us that the Scripture is clear in this matter[53]. However, the question is sometimes asked in some circles of Hindu mysticism whether the physical well-being is so important for the spiritual good of man. Is there not a spiritual state of perfection to them where sickness and health, poverty and riches, even outward joy and sorrow, do not make much difference? Is it true that sometimes when the body is weak the soul is at its strongest? These are questions sometimes the philosophers do ask. Hans-Ruedi Weber reminds us that:

> There has always been a tendency in Christian spirituality to despise physical health, the human body, the material things of this world, including power and riches. This tendency comes more from Greek thinking than from the Bible[54].

It has to be remembered that, to the poor man in a country like India who needs health and happiness without having to go for costly medical help, any relief from bodily suffering through prayer is a great blessing and it is to him the manifestation of God's kingdom and His concern and it is to him an evidence of God's power. The Bible Mission is never concerned with philosophical questions. Its followers are interested in man's need for his body, mind and soul and they are interested in God's redemptive power today. This may be useful to remember. But we shall return to this topic in more detail later.

7. Visions and Extra-Biblical Revelations

Father Devadas in his life time was very much preoccupied with visions, dreams and revelations as we have already seen. "Ask God and find out" was his constant advice to everyone. He taught people to pray and ask 'Lord, reveal this to me either in a dream or a vision'. The very birth of the Bible Mission was with a vision from above as Father Devadas claimed, and his followers never forgot the claim. Father Devadas himself in the later part of his life was known as the 'one to whom God had revealed the Bible Mission'. And these are the very words inscribed on the tombstone when he died. In a booklet entitled God's Presence[55] Devadas says:

> It is most ardently believed by many people that the age of direct revelation ended because they believe that all that is necessary for man is revealed and recorded in the Bible. [sic]

In answer to this contention Devadas says that we still need guidance to understand the Scriptures and we go to commentaries and exegetical works seeking such a guidance. Is it not more important then to ask God to reveal His truth from His Scriptures directly for us? Is it impossible to get such help from God if His children get together and pray? According to Devadas the Scriptures are clear that we need such help. These are the texts he cites in support of his thinking:

> Christ promised the Holy Ghost to reveal the Scriptures to us. John 14.16.

He will testify (speak about) me. John 15.26, 16.13-15.

The Spirit speaks to the churches Rev. 2.7.

Therefore to Devadas the days of direct revelation are not over and the days of messages coming from heaven have not ended. Rather these experiences were very real to him and he declared that these can be real to anyone who seeks them. Devadas in his simple narrative way tells a story in answer to those who maintain that God need not speak to us today because all His will is revealed in the Bible. This is the story as told by Devadas:

> A son returned to his mother after a long sojourn in a far off land. The mother received him with great joy. But would she ever say to him: "I read all the letters you have sent me from that distant land. Now you do not have to speak to me any more, because I have read your messages?"
>
> Similarly, do we say to the Lord if He wants to speak to us: "Lord, we read in the Bible all that you wanted to tell us and you do not have to speak to us[56]"?

The authors of the Willowbank Report ask the same question with regard to the finality of the Scriptures and the work of the Holy Spirit:

> Does our emphasis on the finality and permanent normativeness of Scripture mean that we think the Holy Spirit has now ceased to operate? No, indeed not. But the nature of His teaching ministry has changed. We believe that His work of inspiration is done in the sense that the canon of Scripture is closed but that His work of "illumination" continues both in every conversion (e.g. 2 Cor. 4.6) and in the life of the Christian and the Church. So we need constantly to pray that he will enlighten the eyes of our hearts so that we may know the fullness of God's purpose for us (Eph. 1.17ff) and may not be timorous but courageous in making decision and undertaking fresh tasks today[57].

One tends to believe that Devadas is doing exactly this, namely making courageous decisions and undertaking fresh tasks today expecting the Holy Spirit to speak to God's people. Devadas suggests six different ways in which God can speak to His children in answer to their prayers[58]:

1) Through visions of God Himself or His angels or His holy saints either singly or in groups. Sometimes through living saints in the visions.
2) Through God's voice heard in the air. The Scripture tells us that 'His sheep will hear His voice'. Sometimes the voice is of the departed saints whom God Himself will appoint[59].
3) God writing in the air. It may appear in the mid-air in some kind of golden letters and at other times a white slate or board is lowered with words written in clear language.

One may add here that there are similar kind of experiences reported in other parts of the world. Professor Hollenweger reports the case of J.B. van Kestern, a Flemish Pentecostal pastor whose father was also a pastor of the Reformed Church who

> received the fullness of the Holy Spirit, when the Lord wrote strange language for me in clear letters as a text on the wall[60].

Devadas' list continues:

4) Through Dreams. There are several instances in the Bible when God revealed His will to His people through dreams.

Devadas however was aware of the possibility of empty dreams and even some misleading visions that the devil can bring. But the children of God, he says, will easily discern which dreams and visions actually come from God.

Harold Turner, speaking about the dreams and visions in African Primal religions, makes the following observations:

Another cultural retention we find hard to take seriously is the belief in revelation from God coming through dreams and visions. For us dreams tend to be viewed either as trivial and of no great consequence or as pathological - as signs of unresolved problems and tensions in our lives, as a data for a psychoanalyst. For most non-Western cultures, dreams have always been potential means of revelation from the Spirit world, and this is clear in many African movements. The movement itself may have begun through a dream or vision of the founder, which is now the divine charter of the church as having come from God. The prophets and members lay great stress on dreams, but not, be it noted, quite uncritically. One must 'discern the spirits' and realise that not all dreams are the voice of the Holy Spirit; hence various ways of checking and interpreting dreams may be found in operation. Again, these independent churches have the Bible on their side, for dreams have played a conspicuous part as means of revealing the will of God at a large number of important junctures in the scriptural story. Perhaps we Westerners have something to learn here[61].

Most of what Harold Turner says here is true of the teachings and the history of the Bible Mission with regard to the visions and dreams and their significance.

Devadas has also included in his list

5) "Impressions received in prayer"

6) "The promptings of God" as valid ways of His revelation.

Even human wisdom guided by God's Spirit to him is a means of revelation and he cites Solomon from the Bible as an example of one who received such wisdom from God. All these to Devadas are the various ways in which God can and will speak to His children today. However, among these various ways, his followers seek the more spectacular than the ordinary. When they meet in prayer groups they like to share with each other their special experiences of revelation like voices and visions and special dreams.

At the end of all this teaching about revelation, Devadas clearly indicates that the Word of God, the Bible, is the surest guide for His children.

V.P. Thomas in an article on "Indian Christian Theology and Its Identity" says:

> Apart from the so-called spectacular we all need visions--a nation without a vision will perish. Part of our life is mystic and visionary. An artist is a visionary and a poet is a visionary. Each person can become a visionary at some time or the other[62].

Fortunately, Devadas gave the highest place to the śruti (scripture) as the supreme pramāna (revelation) although he strongly advocated anubhav (experience) following the example of people like Sādhu Sundar Singh[63].

True to the name of the Bible Mission which Devadas claimed that God Himself had given, Devadas believed in the verbal inspiration of the Scriptures and accepted it as the ultimate standard to know God's will. But nevertheless he also believed that God can use other means to speak to His people today, and such extra-biblical revelation, he maintained, should be validated by the Word of God. Avery Dulles in his book, Models of the Church, agrees with this view when he says,

> In some fashion every discovery is ultimately validated in terms of what was already given in Scriptures and tradition. But even the past would not be a revelation to us unless God were still alive and giving Himself to mankind in Jesus Christ[64].

Devadas taught his followers to clearly ask God to appear to them and to speak to them. This is the prayer he suggested:

> Almighty God, the creator of heaven and earth and of all mankind, forgive our sins and appear to us and tell us what you intend for us.

Answer our questions. Redeem us from our troubles and receive us to your heavenly abode after our death[65].

Similarly, in his hymn No. 49, which is a long teaching hymn on private prayer, Devadas exhorts the believer thus:

> If you plead with the Lord to appear to you, you will see his vision (<u>darshan</u>) and your heart will rejoice. If you cry to the Lord to speak to you, you will hear His voice (<u>swaram</u>), And whatever question you may ask, you will receive an answer from Him[66].

To describe his own visionary experience Devadas used the words of John the seer who said,

> On the Lord's day, the Spirit took control of me and I heard a loud voice that sounded like a trumpet speaking behind me (Rev. 1.10).

Commenting on these words Devadas says that in this vision John the elder was 'beyond the dictates of his body, breath and mind and beyond the dictates of this world. He was completely in the control of the Spirit'[67]. Thus Devadas lived in a world of mystery in a new universe in which he had constant fellowship with God and with His angels, speaking to them constantly and receiving spiritual strength as he claimed. To him, as to all the saints who lived through the centuries, it was not difficult to perceive spiritual things in this physical body although it is quite hard to explain, as it was to St. Paul who said,

> I do not know whether this has actually happened or whether he (Paul is speaking in the third person about himself) had a vision. Only God knows. Cor. 12.2.

One example of these extraordinary experiences from outside the Christian Church may be of some interest here. It comes from Paul Brunton in his fascinating book, <u>A Search in Secret India</u>. Brunton clearly describes a vision he had in India some years back. He had a long-awaited interview with the head of the Philosophic Hindu sect, Sri Shankarācharya of Kanchi Kāmakōti, the major Shrine of Vēdanta. That night after he returned to his lodge in Madras from Kanchipuram something very strange had happened to him, and this is how Brunton himself narrates the incident:

> The next thing of which I am aware is suddenly awakening. The room is totally dark. I feel my nerves strangely tense. The atmosphere around me seems to be like electrified air. I pull my watch from under the pillow and by the glow of its radium-lit dial, discover the time to be quarter to three. It is then that I become conscious of some bright object at the foot of the bed. I immediately sit up and look straight at it.
>
> My astonished gaze meets the face of His Holiness Shri Shankara. It is clearly and unmistakably visible. He does not appear to be some ethereal ghost, but rather a solid human being. There is a mysterious luminosity around the figure, which separates it from the surrounding darkness. Surely the vision was an impossible one? Have I not left him at Chengleput? I close my eyes tightly in an effort to test the matter. There is no difference and I see him quite plainly[68].

Thus we see that the world of visions and extraordinary experiences need not be limited to the Bible Mission nor even to the Christian Church. There is some kind of mystery and wonder in all these experiences. C.G. Jung reminds us that,

> It is important to have a secret, a premonition of things unknown. It fills life with something impersonal, a numinosum. A man who has never experienced that has missed something important. He must sense that he lives in a world which in some respects is mysterious; that things happen and can be experienced which remain inexplicable; that everything which happens can be anticipated[69].

CHAPTER IV: Notes

1. Samartha, S.J. The Unbound Christ: Towards a Christology of India Today, What Asian Christians are Thinking (ed.) Douglas J.Elwood, Quizon City: New Day Publishers, 1978, p. 238.

2. For a detailed account of village goddesses and disease-bringing demons and spirits in India see: Luke and Carman, Village Christians and Hindu Cultre, London: Lutterworth Press, 1968, pp. 33ff.

3. Gāli is a Telugu word which means wind or air. The small spirits are referred to as gāils or winds because they float around and cause mischief.

4. Bhūt, the Sanskrit word means an 'element' like the 'panch bhūt', the five elements of nature, viz., earth, air, water, fire and the ether. Demons are considered as parts of nature, the elements.

5. Pishāchi is another Indian word found in several languages which refers to a nasty kind of troublesome devil.

6. Mitchel, H.H. The Recovery of Preaching, London: Hodder and Stoughton, 1977, p. 24. See Ch. IX, note 23.

7. An interesting śloka in the Brihad Āranyaka Upanishad about the dead souls is well-known in India:

> Those who know this and those who in the forest truly
> worship in faith, pass into the flame (of the cremation
> fire); from the flame into the day,
> from the day into the half month of the waxing moon;
> into the six months during which the sun moves northwards;
> from these months into the world of the Gods (Dēvalōka)
> from the world of the Gods into the sun;
> into the lightning fire.
> A person consisting of mind goes to those regions
> of lightning and conducts them to the Brahma worlds.
> In those Brahma worlds they dwell for long extents.
> Of these there is no return.
>
> But they who by sacrificial offering, charity and austerity,
> conquer the worlds pass into the smoke, into the night;
> from the night into the half month of the waning moon;
> into the six months during which the sun moves southwards:
> from those months into the world of the fathers (Pithru lōka)
> and into the moon.
> Reaching moon they become food.
> Then they pass forth into the space;
> from space into the air;
> from air into rain;

from rain into the earth;
they cycle round again thus.

- Brihadāranyaka Upanishad 2. 15, 16. Tr. Robert Ernest Hume, London: Oxford University Press, 1921, p. 163.

8. Mithra, Friend, Bible Mission Booklet No. 16, p. 8.

9. An idea which can be clearly traced to the book of Job.

10. God's Presence, Bible Mission Booklet No. 11, p. 54.

11. Bible Mission Hymns No. 37, verse 25.

12. Bible Mission Booklet No. 16 op.cit., p. 54.

13. Sāthānunedirinchuta: (Resisting the Devil): Bible Mission Booklet No. 2.

14. The word 'arrow' referring to prayer is used first in the introduction of this booklet and then many times in the text.

15. Introduction to Booklet No. 2, op.cit., p. ii.

16. In several places in the writings of Devadas we see Satan pictured as the antitype of God. In Mithra for example, (Booklet 16) there are ten pairs of sentences contrasting God and Satan such as, Satan tempted the first man and God promised to redeem mankind etc. Also cf: ibid., p. 42, 43 and Poetry of Devadas No. 18.

17. Mahima Vārthāvali: Bible Mission Booklet No. 18, p. 4.

18. Telugu word Vāyumandala means the regions of the air or the atmosphere.

19. Bible Mission Booklet No. 2, op.cit., p. 1.

20. In most of his writings and teachings Devadas uses the biblical word Satan for what Indian people generally call demon, evil spirit, dayyam, gāli etc. The word Satan does not appear in non-Christian Telugu literature except in Muslim circles where the word used is Shaithān.

21. Booklet No. 2, op.cit., p. 3. Twenty-four sins are mentioned here including the sin of laziness as caused by Satan.

22. Rev. 16.13. Booklet No. 2, p. 7.

23. Booklet No. 2, op.cit., p. 21. It is popularly believed by Hindus that things like spoiled milk in the milk pot and the children crying without stopping are due to the pranks played by demons.

24. Ibid., p. 16.

25. Ibid., p. 32.

26. Raymando Panikkar quotes some mantras from Rig Vēda: See: Panikkar Raymando, Vēdic Experience Mantramanjari:

>All evil spirits, male and female alike,
>drive far from us, O Earth, the ones that grab
>and the ones that devour, all vampires and all
>demons drive each and every one to distant realms.
>
>>Bhūmi Sūkta, Atharva Vēda XII, i.
>
>She (Dawn, daughter of heaven) drives off wicked
>spirits and dread darkness, She awakens living creatures.
>
>>Rig Vēda VII, 75, 1 (Panikkar p. 165).
>
>Destroy with your heat the workers of magic
>destroy with your power the evil spirits;
>destroy with your flames idolatrous persons;
>burn to nothingness murderous scoundrels.
>
>Giver of salvation, Lord of the people,
>>destroyer of demon,
>>overpowerer of enemies,
>>O, powerful Lord, enjoyer of Sōma,
>>Go, before us calming our fear.
>
>>Scatter our foes, O Indra
>>subdue those who attack us.
>>Send them down to nethermost darkness
>>who seek to destroy us.
>
>There may be evil ghosts dwell
>in the house infernal
>There may be decay and every witch find an abode.
>
>>Rig Vēda X 87, 14, 20 (Panikkar p. 152)

27. Booklet No. 2, op.cit., pp. 48-50.

28. Hollenweger, W.J. All Creatures Great and Small, in Mullen, David Martin (ed.) Strange Gifts - A Guide to Charismatic Movement, Blackwell, forthcoming.

29. Booklet No. 2, op.cit., p. 51.

30. Jepthah Vindu Varthamānamulu (Jepthah Feast Messages), Bible Mission Booklet No. 13.

31. The suggestion implied here may be that the Bible Mission should show the way to the older churches.

32. Booklet No. 13, op.cit., p. 19.

33. Ibid., p. 20.

34. Loc.cit.

35. Schweizer, Eduard. The Holy Spirit, London: SCM Press, 1982, p. 2

36. Mithra, Bible Mission Booklet No. 16, p. 16.

37. Supplement to Abhayāni, Bible Mission Booklet No. 19. Cf., Vijaya Ratnam's letter to Dr. Neudoerffer, cf., also Chapter III above.

38. See Chapter III above for a detailed account of these meetings.

39. Hollenweger, W.J., All Creatures Great and Small, op.cit.

40. Ibid.

41. Dockhorn, K., Christ in Hinduism as seen in Recent Indian Theology, Religion and Society, Vol. XXI No. 4, December 1974, p. 40.

42. Bible Mission Booklet No. 13, op.cit., p. 7. Bible Mission Booklet No. 15, op.cit., p. 3.

43. Hollenweger, W.J., The Pentecostals, p. 341.

44. Loc.cit.

45. Ibid., Section on Doctrine of healing through Prayer, p. 358f.

46. Bible Mission Booklet No. 18, op.cit.

47. Ibid., p. 51.

48. Ibid., p. 69-75.

49. George Bennett, The Heart of Healing, Evesham, Worcs: Arthur James Ltd., 1971, p. 23.

50. Hollenweger, W.J., The Pentecostals, p. 353.

51. George Bennett, op.cit., p. 93.

52. Ibid., p. 35.

53. Hollenweger, W.J., The Pentecostals, p. 368.

54. Weber, Hans-Ruedi, Experiments With Bible Study, World Council of Churches, p. 105.

55. Bible Mission Booklet No. 11, p. 14.

56. Mounzi, Bible Mission Booklet No. 25, p. 14.

57. Gospel and Culture, Willowbank Report, No. 2, p. 9.

58. Types of Revival, in Booklet No. 11, p. 17.

59. Reference has already been made in this chapter to the voices of God, Devadas and the daughter of Jepthah coming to people in prayer and talking to them through a medium. See also Ch. III, note 34.

60. Hollenweger, W.J., The Pentecostals, p. 334.

61. Turner, Harold, Religious Movements in Primal Societies, Mission Focus, September 1981, Vol. IX, No. 3, p. 50.

62. Thomas, V.P. Indian Christian Theology and its Identity, Religion and Society XXV, No. 3, Bangalore, September 1978, p. 29.

63. See Appasamy, A.J., The Gospel and India's Heritage.

64. Dulles, Avery, S.J., Models of the Church, Dublin: Gill and Macmillan, 1976, p. 23.

65. Bible Mission Booklet No. 11, p. 23.

66. Bible Mission Hymns, p. 75.

67. Devadas, Commentary on Revelation, Booklet No. 15, p. 19.

68. Brunton, Paul, A Search in Secret India, London: Rider and Company, 1934, p. 133.

69. Jung, C.G., Memories, Dreams, Reflections, London: Fontana Books, 1963, p. 389.

The Church, the Holy Bride
Received in Heaven

CHAPTER V

The Church as the Holy Bride

1. Ecclesia in the New Testament - Stages of Development

Bible Mission, like many other independent churches around the world, claims that it is more similar to the New Testament Church than any of the mission churches are or can be. It is therefore necessary to study what the New Testament says about the Church and its nature before we examine the teachings of Devadas and of the Bible Mission about the church.

First of all, it must be said that the Church as we know it now did not exist until after the festival of Pentecost in Jerusalem. When the Holy Spirit descended on the disciples in Jerusalem and when Peter preached the good news to the pilgrims in that city, about three thousand people were added to the fellowship of the disciples that day (Acts 2.41). Pentecost day is generally remembered as the birthday of the Christian Church. Even then, Eduard Schweizer rightly reminds us that the band of disciples gathered around Jesus in his earthly ministry can not be really described as a 'church'.

> There is no sign to distinguish those who gathered round Jesus from the other Israelites - neither a rite such as the baptism of John, or a set creed such as that daily recited by faithful Israel (Deut. 6.4), nor a given place of assembly like the monastery of Qumran by the Dead Sea, nor a common rule such as the Manual of Discipline[1].

Whether Jesus anticipated any of these features of the Church after his resurrection is a debatable question. First of all, on the basis of a thorough examination of the existing scholarship, Eduard Schweizer comes to the conclusion that the two places where the word 'church' is used in the four gospels would not give us enough to infer the existence of a 'church' as we understand it today. Also, words like 'the people of God', 'the saints', 'Israel' etc., are not used in the first three Gospels. Only the word 'flock' however appears and it may be understood as a reference to whatever ideas one might have about the future Church but even about that we can not be very conclusive[2].

At any rate it is beyond doubt that what in the later days became the Church had started with the gathering of the believers in Jerusalem who 'spent their time in learning from the apostles, taking part in the fellowship, and sharing in the fellowship meals and the prayers'[3].

One important feature of this Jerusalem church which may have some implications for the present study is that it considered itself a kind of new Israel. The early Christians continued in the Jewish national and religious associations[4]. This means that it was not too big a break in many respects for a Jew to come into the Christian Church. There were very few things to be sacrificed for the sake of one's new faith. The Church which was predominantly Jewish at that time would not let itself be pushed away into a Galilean sect. But it considered itself as the New Israel, the real Israel. Incidentally, traces of this idea of the Church being the new Israel in a spiritual sense are also to be found in the Indian church today. For example, the 19th century Telugu poet, Purushotham Choundhury, sings in one of his famous songs,

> The Lord is surely our father
> and Jesus is our Brother.
> Even the Holy Spirit to us
> has revealed this relationship.
>
> The heavenly City is our birth place
> And the heavenly angels are our friends.
> Therefore, having seen this clearly
> We do not mind the miseries of this world.
>
> Men of faith like Abraham and David
> are the very members of our family.
> We therefore rejoice in them
> and we are never found in need.

We belong to the blessed fellowship
of Peter and the other Apostles.
Since we are in the glorious company
All honour is ours in full measure.

Our Brother gave his life for us
And our Father has forgiven our sins
The Spirit himself bears witness
And we do not mind whatever others may say.

In the Book of Life of God
Written even in the blood of JESUS
Our names shine for ever
and no one can erase them from it.

Away from the touch of our hands
and beyond the sight we can see
Is the heavenly reward waiting for us
And therefore we are not afraid of our poverty here[5].

Thus, even today, the Christian Church considers itself the successor to Israel in the sense that God Himself has chosen it as His own people to fulfil His plan for the world. Thus, expressions like the chosen race, redeemed people, the household of God, the New Jerusalem, are used also in the Telugu language and people know what they mean when they use these words.

But the first Christians in Jerusalem in a very real sense were an integral part of Israel. They still worshipped in the temple, they met in the synagogue to hear the Torah, they had their prophets, they had their pilgrimages and festivals, and they kept most of their national characteristics. This fact of history raises some interesting questions for the church in India today. In fact the so-called Rethinking Christianity group, with the lay Indian Theologian Chenchiah as their leader, has already raised these questions[6]. What happens when a community coming from Hindu religion accepts the Christian faith? Should it not do what the Jewish Christian community had done in Jerusalem?

Is there anything in the former religion of these converts which is worth preserving and adapting? Is so-called syncretism a greater sin than sectarianism? What should be done with the Hindu scriptures, which formed part of his life, when a man becomes a Christian? Can a Christian keep Hindu festivals of any kind after he becomes a Christian?

In fact Chenchiah's group suggested that an 'Indian Bible' can be re-made with the Vēdas and Hindu Scriptures replacing the Old Testament. In a sense this school of theologians in India thought that Christianity is a fulfilment of Hinduism and that Christ is present and hidden in Hinduism[7]. In an article he wrote on the subject, Chenchiah has this to say:

> One of the vexed questions of western theology arises from its tendency to regard the Old Testament as integral to Christianity. There has been a recrudescence of the primacy of the Old Testament in Christian thought of late. Western theology takes an inconsistent and untenable attitude. While holding that the other non-Christian religions do not lead to Christ, it believes that Judaism is a divinely appointed path to Jesus notwithstanding the fact that Jews rejected the Messiahship of Christ. While denying that Jesus was the fulfilment of pagan religions, they insist that he was the fulfilment of the Old Testament. The liberty that St. Paul acquired for the gentile Christians has been of a very limited nature. The theology of the western mind is still under bondage to Judaism. In fact the latest phase of Latin theology - that of Barth - is in substance a theology of Judaism into which Jesus could not easily fit[8].

Clearly this view of Chenchiah represents an extreme.

Chenchiah's concern of course was more with the using of the New Testament to 'get the raw fact of Christ', as V.P. Thomas says[9]. He makes several assumptions which may need checking. But the quotation helps us to see that there are some theologians who think that Christ can be reached without having to resort to the way of Judaism and the Old Testament. At any rate the historic fact still remains that the primitive church in Jerusalem considered itself a descendant of Israel.

An examination of the patterns of the New Testament Church and its administrative structures and their development can also yield useful results for the Church today. As we see already in the New Testament, through the writings of St. Paul and St. John, changes were coming in this regard; new relationships appeared and new questions cropped up demanding new answers as the Church grew and expanded. The structures needed change and such a change had started already in the New Testament Church. Eduard Schweizer, talking about the need to go to the New Testament source for an understanding of this issue, observes:

> a return to the source can have meaning only if what we discern there is recast in the light of the present time and situation. There is no question therefore, of a static Christianity; a mere repetition of New Testament formulae or regulations no more guarantees the church's authenticity than does the continuance of the same line of development within the same traditon[10].

Yet another fact is important to our present study, namely, the existence of the Hellenistic group of Christians even before the conversion of St. Paul. This and similar other groups had very little connection with the primitive church that had formed around the twelve apostles. Churches of the diaspora were also in Rome and Antioch before St. Paul started his missionary journeys (Phil. 1.15f; Rom. 16.7; Col 1.6). Schweizer suggests that the breach between the old and the new Israel took place amid suffering, the Church having had to remain within Israel until it was expelled. Sometimes we tend to forget that the church in Jerusalem

> did not deny that even those groups that think and act differently on important matters are members of the one church in which salvation of the last days is present, even if those groups are often only very loosely joined to it--e.g. the group round Stephen, and the Pauline Churches[11].

If Jesus was 'the fulfilment of God's whole purpose in history'[12], then this fact has implications for the Jew and the Gentile and for the Hindu and the Muslim, whoever accepts Christ. The Church cannot afford to build walls around itself. It may be dangerous, and

> it would be a wrong development wherever the church reerected the walls, even if the required righteousness based on the law were replaced by the <u>sacrificium intellectus</u> and the assent to dogmatic formulae – that is, if orthopraxy is replaced by orthodoxy[13].

Several Christian thinkers have warned against this temptation which is natural to the churches all over. For example, Stanley Samartha put it very succinctly when he said that

> in all human efforts there is the persistent temptation to succumb later to the very slavery from which man tried to free himself[14].

In the matter of administration styles and the gifts of the Spirit in the primitive Church we see a gradual development starting with a simple fellowship to a more and more structured pattern. Whatever administrative machinery we find in the Jerusalem church must be a continuation of what came from Judaism. The analogy of the priest continued to be used and the work of the prophet was carried on with a slightly changed type of ministry. St. Paul speaks of prophets and prophecy in the Church.

As for the authority in the Jerusalem church it seems to be not an authority 'provided by any formal appointment' but it was a type of authority which rested on 'either natural causes such as greater age, or association with the earthly Jesus, or on supernatural causes such as the gift of prophetic insight'[15].

From what Schweizer calls Matthew's church we can gather some facts abouts the church's administrative structures as follows:

There must have been some scribes to write down and interpret the word of God. But there was no hierarchy of any kind. Moreover the highest among them must be the one who rendered the highest service (23.11; 20.26f). The 'little ones' are the most important members of the Church (18.1f). There was no office bearer and all graduated titles are forbidden to the Church (23.8-10). (The epistle of James tells us that the problem of disparity between the rich and poor existed in the Church but the writer of the epistle pleads for unity).

In St. Luke's Gospel we see a distinctive idea of the role of the apostleship, that is, the role of a witness. These apostles were the only teachers and leaders of the Church. Then we see the emergence of the 'elders'[16]. They served the Church along with the apostles. 'But still any disciple can baptise and the laying on of hands and the imparting of the spirit is not the privilege of a special class of people'[17].

We see the office of 'elders' mentioned in the pastoral epistles (I Tim. 5.1; Titus 2.2). They were appointed for special service and received some consideration. So also we come across the office of the bishops in the pastoral epistles (Titus 1.5-7). Besides them there were deacons. The elders were probably overseers and preachers and teachers. Along with these there were widows too now as a specail group (I Tim. 5.3f) and their service was intercession.

What the office of the bishop meant precisely we do not know. G.B. Caird points out that the word bishop was used to denote a variety of persons in the Septuagint, persons in a position of authority like army officers (Num. 31.14, Judges 9.28, II Kings 11.15, 18), foremen in charge of building operations (2 Paral. 34.12, 17), business managers (Nehe. 11.9, 14, 22), city officials (Isa. 60.17), and superintendents appointed by Antiochus Epiphanes to enforce his decree against the Jewish religion (I Macc. 1.51).

The earliest use of episcopos in the New Testament is in the epistle to the Philippians which was addressed to 'God's people who live at Philippi, including episcopai and diakonai'[18].

Caird rightly observes that it is a matter of conjecture what Paul could have understood by these words in this context because there was a plurality of each type of leader in the small church at Philippi. At any rate in I Timothy the episcopos seems to be emerging the holder of a distinct office. Ignatius (c.AD 115) seems to have declared that each church ought to have an episcopos, but Caird says that even with Ignatius we are still a long way from the diocesan bishops as we know them.

Compared to the present day hierarchical systems in many churches in the world, the New Testament Church had a very simple organizational set-up and it grew up in different churches at different stages. In fact there was not a 'Church' in the New Testament, as James Dunn says; there was unity in diversity[19]. It is therefore easy for some of the group churches today in India as well as elsewhere to claim that they are more like the New Testament Church in that many of them do not have even an ordained clergy. These non-White Indigenous churches, as David Barrett calls them in the World Christian Encyclopedia[20], have a very simple way of deciding matters of common concern. At any rate only in the Letter of Clement do we read about the 'surprising innovation' of majority decisions which we never see in the New Testament. From then on, the present day mission churches have travelled a long way and they are now almost unable to administer their affairs without resorting to a complicated paraphernalia of constitutions, committee reports, minutes and resolutions and ballots. Already in the time of the Letter of Clement the process had started of 'secular and civil order coming in and overshadowing the testimony given by the church' just as in the Didache, 'pagan religious standards succeeded in entering in'[21].

No class system was approved in the churches known to St. Paul. St. Paul rebukes the church in Corinth for their internal differences (I Cor. 11.17f). There was freedom of the Spirit. Everyone had the Spirit and anyone 'who does not have the Spirit of Christ does not belong to him' (Rom. 8.9). The Spirit gives gifts to believers as he pleases (I Cor. 12.11) and the enumeration of the different kinds of gifts are quite unsystematic, with no sort of hierarchical character. There was only one standard for measuring their importance: whether they testify to Jesus as Lord or not (I Cor. 12.3)[22]. The so-called ordinary gifts of the Spirit were not to be despised. Paul includes among the gifts of grace the performance of such natural ministries as the guidance of the church, or the care of other people.

Finally, the Church of the New Testament is a suffering Church and a pilgrim Church. It is not allowed the security of becoming a great institution comfortably settled down in one place. The Book of Revelation shows the Church as a tormented woman 'who had given birth to a boy' and was persecuted by a dragon. This is the picture of a Church waiting for redemption, and it had to endure in faith (Rev. 13.10 and Ch. 2). The New Testament Church is also a scattered church. God's people are on the move again and this new Israel is passing through the wilderness once more to fulfil God's plan. The earthly Jerusalem is no longer important and is called Sodom and Egypt (Rev. 11.8).

2. The Teachings of the Bible Mission about the Church

In the light of this background picture of the New Testament Church let us study the teachings of the Bible Mission about the church. We have noted that the Bible Mission is a break-away branch from the Lutheran Church guided by the new ideals of Devadas and his followers. Devadas claimed that God Himself had asked him to start this new church. This new group has always called itself a Mission partly because in those days Devadas knew several missions working in that area. Naturally the word Mission suggested itself to Devadas when he thought of a name. Bible Mission is a mission among the missions.

In a small booklet of the Bible Mission[23] we see the statement of Devadas himself about the name and the purpose of the Bible Mission:

> Mission means task or work. Our task is threefold, namely, to preach, to give witness to Christ, and to make disciples. This is the same task as the Lord gave to his disciples. Bible Mission is a new mision and there are some new things in this mission which we do not find in other missions and they are,
> 1) the experience of God speaking to the believers,
> 2) the experience of visions,
> 3) the experience of seeing God's writings in the air to reveal His plan to us,
> 4) and the truth that God can grant us now all the miracles mentioned in the Gospels.

The name of the Bible Mission was also significant to its followers because they believed that they seek to follow the Bible which is their standard. They believed that the other churches are not following the Bible because they did not teach the possibility of miracles and the real possibility of God granting visions. Devadas was very much worried also because the Lutheran Church as he saw it then did not teach enough about the second coming of the Lord. Therefore, in his opinion, the Bible Mission was to fill the gaps left by the other missions. It should teach that God speaks to His children today, that miracles of healing and casting out of the devils are possible to God's children now and that the Lord's second coming is near and the church will be received into glory. An added emphasis is on the baptism of the Holy Spirit as a second and deeper experience for all those who seek it[24].

Thus, the Bible Mission is an indigenous independent church movement, and it is non-white[25]. It had many Pentecostal features as we have already seen. There are no centrally paid pastors in the Bible Mission. The congregations meet the needs of most of the pastors, and some preachers and evangelists live on free offerings of believers and some even earn their own living working in various small jobs. Whenever there are pastors, they are responsible only for teaching and healing, when they are not simply on their knees in prayer either alone or with other believers spending long hours waiting for a vision or a voice.

Father Devadas' idea of the church is rather simple. We can learn most about the teaching of Devadas on the church from two main sources: his exposition on the Book of Revelation (Bible Mission Booklet 15, Prakatana Grandha vivaramu) and his commentary on the Song of Songs (Bible Mission Booklet 12, Parama Geethārdhamu).

The primary model Devadas uses for the church is the model of the Bride. In his hymns and other writings we find some additional images such as the house of God, the body of Christ, and the flock[26]. Among these, the Bride imagery takes a larger share in his teaching both in the exposition of the Song of Songs and the Book of Revelation and also in the Jepthah Feast Messages to which reference has already been made in which the daughter of Jepthah is an archetype of the church.

The Bride model is rich and abundant in its creative imagery. It clearly suggests the idea of separation of the church for the Lord. Devadas talks about virgins and among the virgins he separates the bride. This is a status given only to one among the virgins. The church, like the bride, keeps herself holy and unblemished and dedicated to her beloved, the Lord. She awaits the return of her Lord and waits for the day of consummation and the heavenly feast. The church also has to become a sacrifice on the altar of God like the daughter of Jepthah, and her Lord will accept her supreme sacrifice with honour.

In his exposition on the Book of Revelation, Devadas uses the bride imagery and cites similar archetypes from the Old Testament. In the story of Rebeccah and Isaac, for example, he sees the image of the Lord and the church. The servant Eliazar is a symbol of the Holy Spirit who brings the church to the Lord. He also cites the story of Esther, Psalm 45, and the Book of Isaiah, Ch. 54, where Israel is called a 'young wife':

> Israel, you are like a young wife,
> deserted by her husband and deeply distressed,
> But the Lord calls you back to Him and says:
> For one brief moment I left you
> with deep love I will take you back.
> I turned away angry only for a moment,
> But I will show you my love for ever.
> So says the Lord who saves you[27].

A whole series of ideas sin, forgiveness, reconciliation, and eternal love--are reflected in this passage, and the rich image and evocative allegory fit quite appropriately into the relationship of God to His Church. So also the other passage in the 62nd chapter of the prophet Isaiah:

> No longer will you be called "forsaken"
> Or your land be called "The deserted wife"
> Your new name will be "God is pleased with Her"
> Your land will be called "Happily Married"

> Like a young man taking a virgin as his bride,
> He who formed you will marry you.
> As a groom is delighted with his bride,
> So your God will delight in you[28].

These symbols and images are very familiar to the people in India and Devadas has successfully used these texts and the models to show the deep relationship of God with His people.

So also he expounds the Book of Hosea and the prophet Ezekiel (16.1-14) showing the holy relationship between God and His Church. This is a mystery, said Devadas, too deep to be fully understood, as St. Paul states in Ephesians Ch. 5. God himself has chosen the Church as His bride to take her into heavenly places as Isaac took Rebeccah into his mother's tabernacle. Christ has several titles like the shepherd, the lamb, the lion, the vine, the rock, etc., but no other title is so beautiful as the title of the bridegroom.

Commenting on Ch. 1, verse 10 of the Song of Songs, Devadas makes a long list of the spiritual 'jewels' of the bride. The gifts of the Holy Spirit are like jewels for the believer. He makes a list of 21 gifts of the Spirit as jewels of the bride[29].

The image of the wedding feast, with all the colour and beauty and the joy and festivity associated with it and also the honour and glory, is a familiar image to the people in the Bible Mission. The thought of the feast in heaven and the consummation of the marriage and the uniting with the Lord--these are very beautiful thoughts to the believers. Similarly, the perfume mentioned in the Song of Solomon is a symbol of love, of a spirit of thankfulness, of praise, holiness and sacrifice, according to Devadas [30]. He cites the story of Mary Magdalene who anointed the feet of the Lord as a symbol of her love and thankfulness.

Devadas expounds at great length the symbolism of the kiss as an expression of love and affection. He tells the story of God once actually coming in a vision into a prayer meeting and kissing everyone in that meeting. The Bible enjoins the practice of kissing among the saints (I Thess. 5.26; I Pet. 5.13). The father kissed the prodigal son as he returned to him (Luke 15.20). The sinful woman washed the Lord's feet and kissed them (Luke 7.38).

Bengt Hoffman reminds us that Martin Luther sometimes used nuptial metaphors to speak about the experience of relationship with God. Hoffman says,

> The imputed justification must contain experiential insight, empirical spiritual <u>Erfahrung</u>. We have found that Luther, in order to depict this experience, frequently adopts nuptial metaphors which abound in mystical literature[31].

Quoting Martin Luther from his several writings, Hoffman says:

> Life with Christ is like a 'secret wedding'. The soul is like a bride who "with cordial trust relies on her bridegroom". "This bridegroom, Christ, must be alone with His bride in His private chamber, and all the family and the household must be shunted away". "For he who relies on Christ through faith is carried on the shoulders of Christ, and he will cross over successfully with the bride, of whom it is written that 'she comes up through the desert leaning on her beloved'"[32].

Similarly, in the Jepthah Feast Messages of Devadas[33] the same imagery of the church as the bride appears again and this time the bride becomes a sacrifice. Jepthah's daughter asked for some time before she could go to the sacrificial fire. She says to her father,

> Do this one thing for me. Leave me alone for two months so that I can go with my friends to wander and grieve that I must die a virgin[34].

Sacrifice is the symbol of acceptance by the Lord. As the daughter of Jepthah asks for time to prepare herself the church asks the Lord to tarry, not for two months but for two thousand years and the Lord grants the request[35]. In this story can be seen the symbolism of separation, the holy state of the church, preparation for the final day of the Lord's return, the self-surrender of the church and the acceptance of the Lord.

In all these writings Devadas sees a prophecy of the end of times. He writes much about the rapture. He sees three states among the believers, viz., the bride, the saved ones and the living faithful[36]. For him the nominal believers are different from the real ones, and every one can grow into the state of the bridehood. This is a kind of second stage of Christian perfection. In the Bible Mission Booklet called Mahima Varthāvali[37], Devadas mentioned three stages of Christian perfection, viz., Repented stage, Saved stage, and the Bridal stage. In support of his view Devadas cites St. Paul and the passage on the 'order of resurrection' - each one in his own order (I Cor. 15.23). God's firstborn sons (Heb. 12.21), the thrones in Heaven reserved for the apostles (Matt. 19.28) and many such images in the Bible have influenced the thinking of Devadas in this matter. He is fully convinced that there are levels of holiness among the faithful.

There is another long passage on the subject of the different classes among the believers in Booklet No. 21, Daiva Lakshanamula Sthuthi. The main teaching of the passage is: there are separate places in heaven for the churches according to the spirtual state. The seven churches in the Book of Revelation represent seven states of spiritual preparation. The church at Laodicea was the nearest to God's throne, although all the other six churches are also in heaven.

Devadas however assures that there will not be jealousy among the faithful in heaven because of their places. It is God who assigns these places and those who get higher places will be as much surprised as those who get some lower places. Devadas cites Mat. Ch. 25 in support of this[38].

All these teaching of Devadas about the places and ranks in heaven sound very strange sometimes. An interesting interpretation of Devadas of the letters to the seven churches in the Book of Revelation deserves special mention. He suggests that these seven churches are the images of the Church universal in its seven stages during the centuries. His idea of the spiritual development of the Church is tabulated as follows:

Ephesus stage	50 - 170 A.D.
Smyrna stage	170 - 312 A.D.
Pergamum stage	312 - 606 A.D.
Thyatira stage	606 - 1620 A.D.
Sardis stage	1620 - 1720 A.D.
Philadelphia stage	1720 - 1900 A.D.
Laodicea stage	1900 - until the Lord returns

It is hard to identify the source which Devadas used to make such interesting calculations. But his followers eagerly read these messages and looked in their Bibles to find out these wonderful ideas. We know however that Devadas was not the first man to try this kind of exegesis of the Book of Revelation.

May of these writings of Devadas can be considered under the category of story and allegory rather than well-informed exegetical study. These can be considered as parables and not in any sense doctrines.

When Devadas looked at the churches around the world today he saw Christ outside the church, but inside the hearts of the individual believers. He made a table to show the churches within the churches as follows[40]:

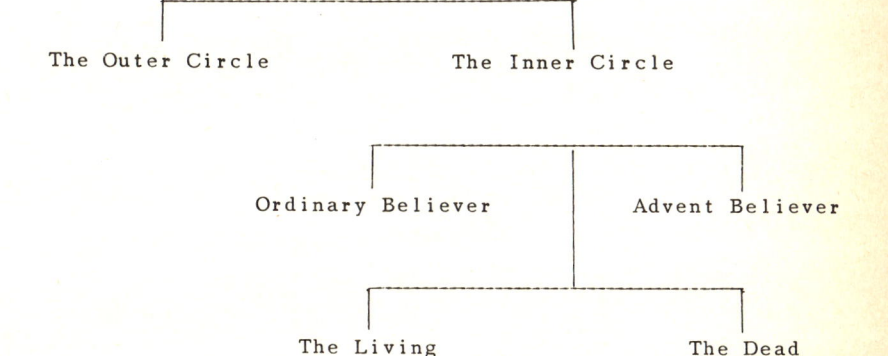

```
         ┌─────────────────┴─────────────────┐
   The Outer Circle                   The Inner Circle
                        ┌──────────────┴──────────────┐
                Ordinary Believer              Advent Believer
                                    ┌─────────┴─────────┐
                              The Living            The Dead
```

Devadas finds biblical support for this classification. George Carey, talking about the indwelling of the Spirit of God in Christians, reminds us that St. Paul himself makes this distinction between 'pneumatikoi', and the 'sarkikoi' and the 'nepioi' (the babes) in the epistle to Corinthians (I Cor. 3.1)[41]. Devadas mentioned these differences in spiritual levels among the faithful almost consistently. He considered spirit baptism higher and subsequent to water baptism. God himself separates the 'bride' group from the 'virgins' group, the advent believers from the ordinary believers. Devadas sees this process going on all along in the Bible, like the separation of God's people at the time of the flood, in the story of the calling of Abraham, at the time of Pentecost, and in future when the Lord returns to the earth at the second Advent. 'His sheep' will know His voice and He will separate the sheep from the goats.

Thus the church in the view of Devadas is very much a chosen and separated group in the world, a bride specially set apart among the virgins, purified, awaiting the return of her Lord, and kept clean from the sins of the world.

This kind of teaching had its own effects on the life of the Bible Mission Christians, some of those effects positive and some not so positive. For one thing, the Bible Mission always considered itself as a kind of other-worldly body, always looking for the future.

3. A Theological Appraisal of some of the Ecclesiastical Models

Having seen in brief the teachings of the Bible Mission on the concept of the church, we may now examine some of the other 'everlasting images in the scripture'[42]. Thus we may be able to see where Devadas and his followers stand in the total context of the biblical teaching about the Church. We have mentioned above that the New Testament uses several analogous words to describe the Church. The Church is called by several names and pictured in several types, such as the building raised by Christ, the house of God, the temple and the tabernacle of God, God's people, His flock, His vine, His field, His city, the pillar of truth, the bride of Christ, His mystical body. Avery

Dulles reminds us that the 'New Testament is extremely luxuriant in its ecclesiastical imagery'[43].

Images, however, are more than definitions. A definition is prescriptive whereas the image is evocative; definitions are closed, whereas images are open. One is meant for information and the other for meditation. Images are born in the experience of people and serve the needs of a culture at various stages of its development. They fit into the narrative communications pattern and can be very profitable for teaching. That is why Jesus Christ used images and parables, and St. Paul used several image words to describe the Church and its nature.

Therefore the image of the bride used by Devadas in his teachings is familiar to people with all its associations of purity, faithfulness, choice and separation, preparation and presentation of the Holy bride, etc. It conjures up the idea of consummation and perfect bliss. Wedding feasts are memorable and enjoyable occasions. They are primarily community affairs. There is an element of promise, of group solidarity and group commitment as may be observed in Indian marriages.

But any image has its possibilities and its limitations. Images are not formulae and by their very nature they show the direction to the truth outside themselves. Sometimes any single image is inadequate and it needs other images to illustrate a point. As Dulles puts it, any single image or paradigm, however excellent, does not solve all the problems[44]. It is quite true in the case of images used for the 'church' which is, after all, a mystery in its nature. So, St. Paul starts with the image of a building and quickly combines it with the image of the body. This is logically incoherent, but theologically apposite, as Dulles says[45].

All models have their limitations, and models used for the church are no exception. Among the several models identified by Dulles, the institution model is one of the models used in the New Testament. That is the model which we see many times in the mission churches in India with their labels and impressive names, the creeds, confessions, councils, and administrative structures, their trained ministry and all their multifarious activities and programmes. Even the names of some of the church bodies denote nothing but institutional models. Words like convention, samāvēsam (gathering) synods, sabhas, and many such terms used to identify the 'church bodies' in India suggest the institutional model. They are marks of the Gesellschaft nature of the church rather than the Gemeinschaft nature[46]. These organisations are remote control agencies, most of the time transacting business in high-powered committees to run the household of God.

Indigenous churches like the Bible Mission do not have this problem. Their model is not the institutional model. For them it is not 'those behind the air-conditioned offices of the Mission headquarters, nor those behind the pulpits who will determine the future course of the church but it is those in the pews (or those who sit on the straw mats on the floor), the ordinary laymen who live their faith in the hostile world'[47].

The training that the pastors in the Bible Mission and such other indigenous churches are getting is very non-formal through a simple oral instruction by a life lived in fellowship with godly people. It is a loving leadership, always evolved and seldom appointed. These groups are real primary groups with free to face association, an unspecified character of association, small numbers and intimately related participants.

There is also no authoritarian administrative system in these churches and among the 'leaders' there is no difference of high and low level except perhaps the difference in the fulness of the spirit and a certain difference in the 'growth in fellowship' with God [48]. They are also free from any excessive concern to do things 'aright', and face from too much preoccupation with order and discipline matters. Consequently they have all the time for spiritual care and healing, as we have seen already.

The suggestion is not to discard the Institutional Model altogether for the church nor is it to underestimate the importance of much-needed church-growth. There are some problems in the bride model also. A passing reference was already made to the spirit of exclusiveness we sometimes see in these small groups and a separatist tendency which is not helpful. There is less opportunity in the bride model for questions to be asked and answered about one's own theological understanding. There is less opportunity to test understandings and views.

It is hard to say what the future shape of the church in India is going to be. What model will be most useful to the Indian church? We can at least say that much in the inherited mission church model is not so helpful to India. It may be time now for the Indian church to re-assess its structures and patterns and even administrative methods.

It may be neither the institutional model nor the bridal model that is most useful to the church in India. It may be the model of the 'small lump that leaveneth the whole lump' model which is more relevant. It may be the mustard seed model, which helps the churches and makes them aware of their mission. It may be a matter of being more open to the Spirit of God.

CHAPTER V: Notes

1. Schweizer, Eduard, Church Order in the New Testament, London: SCM Press, 1961. p.21.

2. Ibid., p. 23.

3. Acts, 2.42.

4. Schweizer, E., op.cit., p. 35.

5. Choudhury, Purushotham, Andhra Christian Hymns, No. 435. (this is a paraphrased translation).

6. Cf., Thangasamy D.A., Theology of Chenchiah, Bangalore: YMCA, CISRS, 1966.

7. Cf., Raimundo Panikkar, The Unknown Christ of Hinduism, London: Darton Longman and Todd, 1964.

8. Thangasamy, D.A., op.cit., p. 163.

9. Thomas, V.P., "The Indian Christian Theology and Its Identity," Religion and Society, Vol. XXV No. 3, Sept., 1978, p. 29.

10. Schweizer, E., op.cit., pp. 18, 19.

11. Ibid., p. 45.

12. Ibid., p. 61.

13. Ibid., p. 46.

14. Samartha, S.J., "The Unbound Christ: Towards a Christology in India Today," What Asian Christians are Thinking, (ed) Douglas J. Wood, Quizon City: New Day Publications, 1978, p. 238.

15. Schweizer, E., op.cit., p. 50.

16. Ibid., p. 71.

17. Ibid., p. 72.

18. Caird, G.B., The Language and Imagery of the Bible, Duckworth Studies in Theology, London: Gerald Duckworth, 1980, p. 81.

19. Dunn, James D.G., Unity and Diversity in the New Testament, SCM, 1977.

20. Quoted by Hollenweger, W.J., Pentecostal and Charismatic Movements, to be published in Mircea Eliade (ed.) The Encyclopedia of Religion, New York.

21. Schweizer, E., op.cit., p. 147.

22. Ibid., p. 100.

23. Mounji, Bible Mission Booklet No. 25, p. 5.

24. Cf. Chapter III of this book on the Seven Features of the Bible Mission.

25. David Barrett includes the Bible Mission in his encyclopedia in the section on Indian churches.

26. Cf., Paramageethārdhamu, (Exposition of the Song of Songs), Bible Mission Booklet No. 12, pp. 50, 51.

27. Isa. 54.6-7.

28. Isa. 62.4-5.

29. Bible Mission Booklet No. 12 op.cit., pp. 60, 61.

30. Ibid., p. 74.

31. Hoffman, Bengt R. Luther and the Mystics, p. 155

32. Ibid., p. 156.

33. Bible Mission Booklet No. 13, Jepthah Feast Messages.

34. Judges 11.37f.

35. Bible Mission Booklet No. 13, op.cit., p. 19.

36. Here the classification is not very clear. It is not easy to say whether this is an error of the editors of the booklet or in dictation or a confusion of Father Devadas himself. In Booklet No. 16, Mithra there is another classification but that is not the same as the one we see here.

37. Bible Mission Booklet No. 18, The Glorious News, Mahima Varthavali p. 37.

38. Bible Mission Booklet No. 21, Daiva Lakshanamula Sthuthi.

39. Booklet No. 15, Prakatana Grandha Vivaramu, p. 25.

40. Booklet No. 16, op.cit., p. 41.

41. Carey, George, "The Indwelling Spirit", Theological Renewal, No. 14 Feb. 1980, p. 8.

42. Dulles, Avery, Models of the Church, Dublin: Gill and Macmillan, 1976.

43. Ibid., 17.

44. Ibid., p. 29.

45. Loc.cit.

46. Ibid., p. 43.

47. Athyal, Safir, Towards an Asian Christian Theology, What Asian Christians Are Thinking, p. 83.

48. Dulles, Avery, op.cit., p. 35.

The Abiding Presence
Artist's Dream

CHAPTER VI

God and Trinity in Action

1. The God who is Revealed to Us

Many of the Indian Christian theologians consider anubhava or anubhav (experience) as an important pramana (standard of faith). Of the three possible pramanas of Hinduism, namely sruti (that which is heard, Scripture), yukti (reason or theology) and anubhav (experience), Appasamy gives an important place to anubhav[1]. Of course Appasamy gives the first place to Scripture as the most important pramana and he adds the fourth pramana to the above three and that is the sabha or the church.

Another theologian, Chenchiah, however, gives the highest place to anubhav. Chenchiah of course is a lay theologian and he represents a certain 'Rethinking Christianity Group'. He argues that even the Scripture (sruti) is a record of the experience of someone. We read the Scripture and learn the fact that Jesus saves and then we verify that knowledge through our experience. But Chenchiah holds that in the strictest sense no question of verification arises if we start with our own direct experience (prahtyksha anubhava). So to Chenchiah it seems that the Scripture (or sruti) is an indirect experience whereas there is a direct experience possible of God. He thinks that Western theology is reducing God's personality into indirect experience.

These questions raised by Chenchiah made Appasamy study carefully the pramanas. This is how Boyd puts it:

> The question which gives rise to Appasamy's study is one put by Chenchiah: Can we have direct, unmediated knowledge of Jesus, or must such knowledge always come to us mediated by scripture and Church tradition? The query is an important one, one which, in a rather different form, was the touch-stone of the European Reformation, and it is a vital one today in any kind of dialogue with Hinduism. Appasamy affirms its importance in no uncertain fashion

when he writes that 'the primary task of Christian theology today is to settle the sources of our authority'[2].

In the teachings of Devadas about God, he tends to rely more on the experience of God's love, God's fellowship and God's revelation directly in dreams and visions and in similar experiences of the believers. This we can say is direct experience. But he also relied heavily on the Bible revelation, the witness of Scripture, to know the nature of God. Scripture to us is like a letter which God has written. But having written a letter to us God is not silent for ever. He wants to speak to us and reveal Himself to us always in prayer giving us His fellowship, His visions, and His messages. This is direct experience. Although Devadas would acknowledge that God would reveal Himself in the fellowship of believers he would not make 'the Church' as the pramana or standard as we understand the word.

Chenchiah was also critical of the way the Church tried to understand the biblical Revelation. He says,

> The Roman Catholic view is that Jesus rules through the Church, contacts through the Sacraments. The Protestant churches hold that the Word of the Lord is not so much what Jesus speaks to you today but what you read today of what Jesus said when he was on earth[3].

Devadas seems to rely on anubhava (experience) as much as on sruti, the Scripture. He pictured God in His attributes. He tried to understand what God is like from what the Bible tells us about Him. And he said that he tested these qualities of God in his own experience in his own meditation and prayer. In his commentary on the Song of Songs[4] Devadas mentions ten attributes of God and comments on them,

> a) God is love
> b) God is life
> c) God is light
> d) God is holy
> e) God is wise

f) God is just
g) God is omni-present
h) God is unseen
i) God is self-will
j) God is eternal

These attributes of God appear in other booklets and sermons of Devadas. Thus in Upavāsa Prārdhana Deeksha (Booklet No. 5, pp. 56-58) these attributes appear in several prayers, each prayer in Praise of God for one of His attributes. In Mahima Vārthāvali (Booklet No. 18, p. 1) Devadas gives these attributes with more Scripture references and he adds another attribute there, namely, that God is Spirit. In Mithra (Booklet 16, p. 7) this list appears again. This kind of thinking about God in His attributes is important to Devadas because he believed that it helps people to know God and how He acts in men's lives.

The most important thought which appears in His teachings again and again is that God is Holy. The Hindu philosopher likes to think of God as Sat-Chit-Ānand, truth, consciousness, bliss. But in the teachings of Devadas the Holiness of God is the dominant idea. To him the holiness of God is mainly moral holiness. God is sinless. He shines like a thousand suns and he cannot see sinfulness in his children. As we see in his teachings this idea of Devadas about the moral Holiness of God also includes the ritual holiness and this is evident when he talks about washing hands and feet before going to prayer, and wearing clean clothes when we come to the presence of God. But primarily to Devadas God is Holy in the sense that there is no sin in Him. In one of his hymns he sings:

> How can God who is Holy, be the cause of sin in this world?
> He who leads into sin must be a sinner himself.
> Can a mother ever lead her children to do wrong?
> How can we say that the creator would mislead His creation[5]?

This concept of a Holy God is not very common in Hinduism. The Hindu Vēdāntin tends to think God as 'nirguna' without any attributes, devoid of all qualities including holiness. That is why some followers of Vēdāntha think that sin does not touch God, that sin itself is an illusion, māya. In popular Hinduism there are gods and goddesses who are clearly immoral but that immorality is explained away in various ways, as leela, divine play, or symbolism, etc. Devadas lived in the midst of all these stories of Hindu gods and goddesses who, it is believed, do not have to be confined to any qualities, but his faith in a Holy and loving God was very strong.

Although God is so Holy, like a consuming fire, Devadas taught that God is to be loved more than He is to be feared. This is the point at which Luther also arrived in his spiritual pilgrimage after a long struggle with his concept of God as a terrible and righteous judge always condemning the sinner. Luther's struggle ended when he realised that the 'righteousness' of God means that man is 'righted' by God in Jesus Christ. Devadas says that because God became incarnate in Jesus Christ we have the freedom to approach Him and actually appropriate His love and attention to us.

2. Devadas and the Doctrine of Trinity

Devadas in his attributes of God mentions the trinitarian nature as one of the attributes[6]. In his commentary on the Song of Songs he also deals with the trinitarian nature of God. For him it is primarily a mystery and he did not try to expound the mystery but he confessed that it is not difficult for him to believe. To Devadas any concept like 'the internally constitutive unities' was not familiar but he intuitively believed that God can be One and Three at the same time. Leonard Hodgson, in his book, The Doctrine of the Trinity, says,

> By the labours of post-renaissance scientists God has familiarised our minds with the idea of internally constitutive unities, and thus opened them to receive a fuller grasp of His revelation of Himself[7].

Hodgson further draws a useful distinction between the idea of the unity of God in the sense of excluding non-multiplicty on the one hand, and the internal unity on the other. He says,

When we say that God is one, the first thing we mean is that there is none other God; we exclude multiplicity in the mathematical sense. The revision that was required by the revelation was a realisation that the internal unity of Godhead need not be, and indeed is not, definable by absence of multiplicity in the same way as unity whereby He is said to be the one and only God asserts the absence of any other Gods[8].

Devadas taught from the beginning God revealed Himself as three in one. The first person plural of Gen. 1.11 is an indication to Devadas that God is speaking in all three persons. In Genesis, it looks as though God is at work as a single person, says Devadas, but we see in the act of creation the work of Trinity. God thought that he would create, the Son spoke the word of creation and the Holy Spirit acted as the creator[9]. Here Devadas is using the classical analogy of thought, word and deed--manah, vac, karma—the well-known threefold nature of man's personality according to Hinduism.

Hodgson draws our attention to this kind of threefold activity of God in His revelation as understood by Calvin. This is what Hodgson says,

> Referring to the empirical evidence of the threefold activity of God in His historical self-manifestation, Calvin writes, and writes truly: "Ea distinctio autem est quod Patri principium agendi, rerumque omnium fons et scaturigo attribuitur: Filio sapientia, consilium, ipsaque in rebus agendis dispensatio: at Spiritui virtus et efficacia assignatur actionis".
> (There is this distinction, that to the Father is attributed the organisation of the action: He is the fount and source of all things. To the Son are assigned wisdom, counsel and the actual carrying out of the action, to the Spirit its power and efficacy)[10].

Devadas tried to see the reflections of the divine trinity in nature all around, in the nature of man and in the teaching of Scripture.

a) There is a trinity in Nature. In the sun we have the flame, the light and the heat. There are three seasons, the winter, summer and rainy season. There are three parts of the day, morning, noon and evening. All these to Devadas are reminders of the essential threefold nature of God and they are reflections of the Divine trinity.

b) Human personality reveals a trinitarian nature. In Gen. 1.26 God says, Let us make man in our image and likeness. The plural is an indication of God's trinitarian nature and that is reflected in man in that man is body, mind, and soul in one personality.

c) There is a trinity in the threefold praises of the Angels.

d) There is a trinity in the biblical blessing formulas (Num. 6.24-26, 2 Cor. 13.14, Rev. 1.4-5).

e) There is a trinity in the Old Testament stories (e.g., the three angels who visited Abraham, Gen. 18.1-3).

f) Trinity was revealed at the baptism of Jesus Christ (Matt. 93.16-17).

g) The disciples were commissioned to baptize in the name of the Father, Son and the Holy Spirit. (Matt. 28.19)[11].

Devadas used some other paradigms also to help people to mentally visualise this mystery of the Trinity. At the end of his Booklet Mithra[12], there is a short catechism dealing with several questions of faith. Included in this catechism is a question on the mystery of the Trinity. He answers this question using several well-known images which he must have learnt in the seminary earlier. One is an analogy used by St. Augustine[13], Devadas would not elaborate these points but would simply say that it is God's revelation as Father, Son, and the Holy Spirit which is the basis of the doctrine of the Holy Trinity.

Tracing the historic development of the doctrine of Trinity from the incarnate Jesus of Nazareth, Chenchiah says,

Creeds arose out of the conflict of intellectual interpretations of the fact of Jesus—arose out of the conflict of thought forms. It may be that in the apostolic age, interpretation of Jesus depended on the experience of Jesus. But in sub- and post-apostolic system it was entirely a clash of ideas—of interpretation in which experience has no part. In the formulation of the doctrine of the Trinity as crystallised in the formula "Father, Son and Holy Ghost", direct experience of Jesus and Holy Spirit might have played a part. But in the Nicene controversy it is not experience but thought forms, not psychology but ideology, that takes an important part[14].

At the end, it must be admitted in the words of V.P.Thomas that,

> The Christian doctrine of Trinity has been very difficult to understand to the non-Christian and to the Christian as well. Bhrahma Bāndhav Upādhyāya has taken the concept of Sachidānanda and found in it a useful framework to understand and expound the being of God as Trinity. Western expositions of Trinity as three persons in One has often imperilled the unity of the Godhead. In any case the Greek and the Latin expressions used to explain the Trinity and which have found their way into the creeds have no relevance to the Indian mind. Upadhyaya, using the Indian concept of Sachidānanda, preserved the unity of God and raised it to the highest level of that which is absolutely personal[15].

Similarly, Paul Althaus, quoting Martin Luther, expressed the same feeling of frustration when he said,

> Reason admittedly finds all this talk about one-ness and three-ness in God a stumbling block. But since it is based on clear Scripture, reason must be silent at this point and we must believe[16].

Devadas as we have seen, preferred to be silent on the whole about the mystery of Trinity because he considered that it is too great for the human mind to probe into.

But the more basic question now stands: How important is this doctrine today? What is its function? What role does it play in our understanding God's presence in the world today in relation to Jesus of Nazareth? These questions will have to be answered but it is not in the scope of this book to go into that area.

3. Praise God for What He is

In Booklet No. 4, Prārdhana Metlu (Steps in Prayer), Devadas included several long prayers, making mention of an attribute of God in each one and praising Him for that. One of these prayers is for God being three in one.

> Father, we thank you for the wonder of your revelation as God the Father, Son and the Holy Spirit. We joyfully thank you for the wonder and your power to reveal yourself to us as One, being in nature three. You have appeared to us as Three while you are really One. We also joyfully thank you because you have given us body, spirit and life so that we also may be a trinity as you are Trinity[17].

At the end of this prayer Devadas adds a short comment on the doctrine of Trinity again using the analogy of the sun. He says that we address God as Father, Son and the Holy Ghost but God is one. We do not have three Gods. He has helped us to know Him by revealing Himself in the Bible as these three. It is a mystery and therefore we should not strain our minds too much about it. We just accept it as something we do not understand but believe and praise Him and rejoice in Him. Here we see that Devadas is interested not in Yukti or doctrine but rather in anubhava, experiencing God's love. He used some of the old analogies of the church only to help his listeners to grasp what he is talking about.

The sun analogy, and the images of the three seasons of the year, and the parts of the day, and the three aspects of man--all these to Devadas are simple similes pointing to the mystery but not in any sense arguments for a doctrine. At the end, it is Christ, he says, who is all in all for us.

4. God's Work in the World

Devadas clearly taught that God is active in the world today, guiding his people and ruling the universe. He claimed that the visions and the miracles which God is performing in the church today are clear manifestations of God's rule and his work. These to him are the proof that God's kingdom is here. He asked his followers to pray to God to appear to them too and to answer their doubts. In fact one of the main tasks of the Bible Mission, as he claimed, was to declare that God appears to His children and speaks to them today. Listen to Him, was his message. Do whatever He tells you (John 3.5) is the motto of the Bible Mission and these words of the Scripture in Telugu script are cut out in steel and installed as the altar rail in the Bible Mission church in Vijaywada so that all the worshippers constantly see and get the message.

The concept of Divine transcendence is no problem to Devadas. God has already become man and therefore we can approach Him and we can see Him in visions as Christ the incarnate. In all the attributes of God, Devadas talks more about His immanence than His transcendence. God speaks to His people and therefore the Bible Mission strongly advocates the habit of waiting in prayer before God for Him to speak. Sometimes this waiting goes on for long hours. Although Devadas has declared that God spoke to him and that He will speak to anyone who is obedient, he never described his visions at any length. Whether he considered these experiences too difficult to describe or too holy and sacred to speak about is not clear. We are told that Martin Luther very rarely spoke about his mystical experiences[18]. Devadas, however, recognised and declared that God can speak in more than one way, including through the spirits of the departed ones, and even by showing some writing in the air. We have already mentioned Booklet 18, The Glorious News (Mahima Vārthāvali), where there is a section on how God listens to and answers prayer. Here Devadas mentions more than fifty Scripture verses in support of his conviction that God does hear our prayers and answers them and speaks to us. He, however, recognises that God sometimes may not take away our suffering in answer to our prayer. He believed that there must be some good reason which we do not know at the time but God still loves us in our suffering[19].

God can appear to us in a vision, said Devadas, and He will speak to us. Sometimes Christ and His saints or the angels will appear. But it is also possible for God to speak to us in dreams, or through guiding our thoughts in prayer. He can also speak to us from the Scripture, His word[20].

5. God Uses Human Instrumentality to Do His Will

Commenting on the Song of Songs 1.11, Devadas talks about the instruments which God can use to do His will on earth. To declare His promises to the world, He used Abraham and his race; to reveal His law, He used Moses; as the head of the earthly family of Christ, He used David; for Jesus to become incarnate, He used Mary; to be witnesses to Christ's life and His work on the earth, He used the disciples. He appointed Martin Luther to bring into light His hidden word, the Bible Society to spread the Scripture into many languages of the world, and to 'teach to the world that God appears today and speaks to His children, He chose the Bible Mission'. He chose Devadas as the founder of the Bible Mission.

Thus Devadas proclaimed that God is at work today and He will still be so until Christ returns to the earth. To Devadas, everything, including men, institutions and instruments like the printed page and the printing press, can all be used by God for His purpose.

To Devadas, the Father image of God is more important than any other image. To him God is a loving father more than a condemning judge. He has not used the judicial image of God. The righteousness of God to Devadas as to Martin Luther was that which makes mankind 'right' before God through grace. This view is more clearly evident in the sections which Devadas wrote on prayer in the prayer passages themselves. He taught that we can freely approach God and plead with Him and ask whatever we want from Him[21]. He became incarnate and since in this way he became part of mankind we can ask Him to save all mankind, not only us[22]. We are walking with Him as the disciples walked with Christ on the way to Emmaus and like them, we can raise all our doubts with Him.

Adoration of Christ, The Bethany Home

6. Jesus Christ our Lord

Devadas used the words Christ and God interchangeably. When he uses the word prabhuvu, kurios, he sometimes refers to God and sometimes to Christ, and many times he means both. In fact he never used the word Jehova although it is found in the Telugu translation of the Old Testament. He says that Jehova and God are the same and they are both included in Jesus[23]. Christ to him was the revelation of God and in a sense Christ is the continuation of God in time and space as he is the extension of God in the Holy Spirit. The Revelation is all one continuity. Therefore words and concepts like substance and persons, etc., were never necessary to Devadas. The Telugu language, in any case, has never found satisfactory dynamic equivalents to these words. Devadas has not used the avatār for Christ as some Indian writers have done.

In Booklet No. 18, Devadas has a section on the glory of the Lord Jesus Christ[24]. In this section Devadas gives 38 points with proof texts describing Christ's work including his second coming. Then there are 33 points of argument that Christ is everything to everyone and another 80 points on the attributes of Christ. Devadas has also picked up 500 title names to Christ from the Bible. And finally in this booklet we have 15 points on the kind of relationship the Lord comes into with the believers. This booklet with all the Scripture texts is very good material for the new converts.

The earthly life of Christ is very important to Devadas, and there is a big section on Christ's work in the world in another booklet, Mithra[25]. To Devadas, Christ is cosmic and eternal because he once became man like us. On the subject of the eternal existence of Christ this is what Appasamy says:

> (According to the Johannine writer), the living Christ is not a permanent extension into eternity of the historic Jesus who teaches and acts in the realms of the spirit, unhampered by the limits of space and time almost those very words and deeds which he taught and did while he was on earth. The idea of the fourth gospel of the Eternal Christ is far grander than that. He is the one who exists

> from eternity to eternity, the Creator of the worlds, the life of men[26].

So the concern of many Indian theologians is more with the cosmic and eternal Christ, not so much with the historic Jesus. Devadas considered both as important. Moreover, to Devadas the birth of Christ is as important as the death and resurrection for our salvation. It is the whole fact of Jesus, the person of Christ, that is important to Devadas.

Summarising the understanding of salvation on the part of some Indian Christian theologians, this is what Dr. V.P. Thomas, the principal of the Marthoma Theological College, Kottayam, says:

> In dealing with Christ's work in traditional doctrines of atonement, the cross has been central. All the traditional theories of atonement have been dealing with what Christ did on the cross, in terms of sacrifice, sanctificaiton, penal substitution, etc. The Indian theologians, however, have been inclined to look at the whole fact of Christ, the whole Christ event as redemptive - the incarnation, life, death, resurrection etc.[27].

To Devadas the fact of incarnation is the central part of the Christ event. In a whole booklet of Christmas messages[28] covering 68 pages in print Devadas underlines the humble birth of the Lord, the utter emptying of Himself for us men. The eternal God became man bound by time and space, the immortal became mortal and God came to live with men. This in itself is as wonderful to Devadas as the death and resurrection. This emphasis on incarnation is basic also in Sādhu Sundar Singh's teachings.

7. God the Holy Spirit

Devadas wrote little on the doctrine of the Holy Spirit. But to him the Holy Spirit is Christ in action today. The Holy Spirit is preparing the bride, the Church, to meet the Lord, the indwelling Spirit speaking to and guiding the believer, giving healing to the sick. Such aspects of the work of the Holy Spirit Devadas considered as his experience. Boyd rightly points out that,

> India is a country with strong tradition of 'spirituality' and Chenchiah seems correct in saying that the doctrine of the Holy Spirit may become the corner-stone of Indian Christian theology. The word ātman (spirit, soul) and its cognates paramātman (Supreme Spirit) and antarātman (Inner Spirit) are obviously capable of use with deep Christian content, and there are other words like antaryāmin (Inner Ruler) which are promising, as is the conception of sakti when applied - as it frequently is in everyday Christian usage - to the power of the Spirit[29].

Although Devadas has not used these words for the Spirit he knows by experience the working of the Holy Spirit, and he often talked about His sakti, the power. We certainly see in Devadas the 'tendency to blur the distinctions between the Persons of the Trinity, which Western theology defines so clearly', as Boyd puts it[30]. Like many other Christian thinkers Devadas believed that 'through the Spirit, Christ is present today as antarātman (Indwelling Spirit), and so the incarnation advances from the historical to the spiritual becoming real in our experience today'.

Although the Bible Mission advocates and encourages the second spiritual or conversion experience—that is, the coming of the Holy Spirit—speaking in tongues, however, has never been considered as a sign of this coming. Prophecy, on the other hand—seeing the future events in the Spirit—is considered by most of the Bible Mission people as the work of the Holy Spirit. That is why many saintly people who are known to see the coming events in prayer are asked to pray for special needs of the other members from time to time and they give advice after praying about those special concerns[31].

8. Is Our God Dumb?

In Bible Mission Booklet 23, Devadas deals with another important issue, namely the nature of God in relation to His creation. The title of this booklet can be translated variously as: Why is God silent? or Why is God tarrying still? etc. The question of the relationship between the creation and the Creator is an old one in Hindu philosophy. Is he the purusha (Lord) inside or outside the creation, the prakriti? Is he playing with the prakriti or is he just not concerned?

Devadas, like many others who believed in a holy God, is faced with the difficult question of God's role in the affairs of this world, His attitude to sin and suffering and the question of man's final destiny and specially the fate of those who do not believe in Christ. Devadas also asked the question of the suffering of mankind, of all mankind, because he believed in a kind and fatherly God.

First of all, Devadas firmly believed that God is Holy and His creation is holy and that sin is the cause of suffering and God is not the cause of suffering because He is not the cause of sin. Even after man fell into sin, God planned for him a way of redemption. God saw that all His creation was good. Many times we see only the dark side of the picture and miss the bright side, and so we blame God for the ills of the world and think that He is not concerned. God seems to be silent in the midst of sin and suffering, and Devadas said that the following are some of the reasons for His apparent silence[32].

1) God had sufficiently warned mankind already. First in the garden of Eden, then at the time of the flood, and always ever since, God had warned mankind and it is up to us to obey Him.

2) God made us like Himself, in His own image--body, mind, and soul. We have God's nature in us; we have a conscience to guide us. God is watching over us.

3) God gave us freedom. He will not force us to do anything against our will. He will not compel us to choose the good and eschew evil. He has told us what is right and we are free to choose. He can redeem man from sin but He does not force man from falling into sin. Deliver us from evil, should be our prayer because we want to be saved, to be delivered.

Why is God silent in our troubles and in our problems? Why does He not answer our prayers sometimes? Devadas says that God sometimes permits us to suffer that we may turn towards Him and repent of our sinful ways. Sometimes God allows death to come to His children so that they may be delivered from the sins of the world. Also He sometimes does not grant us what we ask because He knows better what is good for us and what we can properly use. Sometimes God allows suffering to come to His children because thus He will be glorified through their witness. The story of Job is cited as an example. God wants to put Satan to shame when we show our faith[33]. Men suffer because of their sins and the children of God will know through suffering how terrible sin is and they will also know how great God's grace is to forgive us. God's grace is much greater than the seriousness of sin[34]. Devadas never suggested that God will punish men with sickness and he never thought of God as a harmful power as we sometimes see in the Old Testament (Gen. 32.32, Exod. 4.24-26, 4.11, Isa. 45.7, Amos 3.6). To Devadas, sickness comes from Satan and not from God. Sickness comes from the evil spirits. In Hinduism sometimes a sickness and the spirit which is supposed to bring that sickness go by the same name. *Amma* (the mother) is name for both smallpox and the goddess that is believed to bring it. That is why for Devadas, healing the sick and casting out of evil spirits are such a vital part of God's work for us today.

God is silent also because He has revealed His will for us in the Bible, as we have already mentioned. God speaks to us today from His word, the Scripture, and we can hear His voice when we read the Bible.

God allowed His son Jesus Christ to die for us and it is part of His plan for our salvation. He revealed His plan in the resurrection of Jesus Christ and we shall one day be raised from our graves as Jesus Christ rose. All the children of God ask Him today as Habakuk did--Why are you silent? (Hab. 1.13). But God will not test us 'beyond our power to remain firm' (I Cor. 10.13). He strengthens our souls even as He allows trials and temptations to come to us. For the sake of our 'spiritual growth' and for reaching higher 'places' in heaven we need to stand the tests of this life. Therefore God is silent now while we suffer[35].

Then is He silent about the salvation of all those who die without having ever believed in Him? No, says Devadas, they are 'the sheep of the other fold' and they will also be saved so that the fold may be one as the shepherd is one. We should not be like Jonah if God changes His mind about those who do not accept Him. He has His own way of saving them too. Christ went into the underworld to preach to the imprisoned spirits (I Peter 3.19). That is, the good news is preached to the dead, to those who had been judged 'in their physical existence' (I Peter 4.6). Devadas believed that those who died without having accepted Christ thus will also be saved, somehow.

So God is not silent about even those who die without faith in Him and He can meet people anywhere (Psalm 139.7-8). Even the souls in the world 'below' will confess his name (Phil. 2.9-11). Devadas expressed the same concern and the same trust about those who do not know Jesus in his other writings. In the Prayers and Praises for the Second Coming he says,

> God will not leave anyone on the earth. The end will not come till the Gospel is preached to every person. Those who are in Hades too should hear the good news. After the second advent, along with the heavenly Bride the others also will be called to the wedding feast[36].

Therefore God is never silent, said Devadas. To summarise, Devadas tried to know God from what he learnt from the Bible about Him. He also learnt to love God and know His grace through prayer and constant fellowship with Him. He did not use Hindu philosophical models and concepts to define God. He considered the world of God as good and waiting for the final redemption. Those who do not believe in God are not lost; God will ultimately save them somehow. Devadas did not try to solve the problem of evil and the problem of human suffering, but he believed that sin is the cause of suffering. God has a plan for the redemption of the universe, so Devadas is not puzzled by the evil and the suffering he saw in the world. As Morton Kelsey says, Devadas is happy that his faith "offers him a way of handling the problem of evil instead of giving an intellectual solution to it"[37]. This is what people wanted, a way to handle their daily problems and live in faith and hope in God. No wonder the teachings of Devadas about God's love brought a new hope to the people who heard him.

CHAPTER VI: Notes

1. Cf., Boyd, R.H.S., Introduction to Indian Christian Theology pp. 135-38.

2. Ibid., p. 136.

3. Thangasamy, D.A., Theology of Chenchiah, p. 73.

4. Bible Mission Booklet No. 12. Parama Geethardham, p. 21.

5. Bible Mission Hymns No. 55. See also Chapter XI of this thesis.

6. Vāgdāna Manjari, Bible Mission Booklet No. 3, pp. 17, 18.

7. Hodgson, Leonard, The Doctrine of the Trinity, p. 175.

8. Ibid., p. 105.

9. Bible Mission Booklet No. 12, op.cit., p. 67.

10. Hodgson, Leonard, op.cit., p. 171.

11. Cf., Parma Geethārdham, Booklet No. 12, pp. 65-69.

12. Bible Mission Booklet No. 16, Mithra, p. 51.

13. For a more detailed discussion on the teaching of St. Augustine, Aquinas and Calvin on the subject of Trinity, see Hodgson, Leonard, op.cit., pp. 142-75.

14. Thangasamy, D.A., op.cit., p.73.

15. Thomas, V.P., The Indian Christian Theology and its Identity, Religion and Society, Vol. XXV, No. 3, September 1978, p. 31.

16. Althaus, Paul, Theology of Martin Luther, Philadelphia: Fortress Press, 1966. Translation, Robert C. Schultz, p. 199.

17. Bible Mission Booklet No. 4, Prārdhana Metlu, p. 30.

18. See Hoffman, Bengt, Luther and the Mystics, p. 186.

19. Bible Mission Booklet No. 18, Mahima Varthāvali, pp. 50-56.

20. Bible Mission Booklet No. 16, op.cit., p. 51.

21. Bible Mission Booklet No. 3, op.cit., p. 24.

22. Bible Mission Booklet No. 2, Saithānu nedirinchuta, p. 57.

23. Bible Mission Booklet No. 3, op.cit., p. 17.

24. Bible Mission Booklet No. 18, op.cit., pp. 25-45.

25. Bible Mission Booklet No. 16, op.cit., pp. 14, 15.

26. Appasamy, A.J., What is Moksha, p. 101.

27. Thomas, V.P., op.cit., p. 32.

28. Bible Mission Booklet No. 17, Krismasu Varthamānamulu.

29. Boyd, R.H.S., op.cit., p. 241.

30. Ibid., p. 242.

31. For a more detailed account of the teaching of the Bible Mission on the Holy Spirit see also Chapter III of this book.

32. Bible Mission Booklet No. 23, Devudu Enduku Ūrakunnādu, pp. 3-9.

33. Ibid., p. 18.

34. Ibid., p. 19.

35. Ibid., p. 33.

36. Bible Mission Booklet No. 8, Rākada Prārdhana Sthuthulu, p. 26.

37. Kelsey, Morton R., The Christian and the Supernatural, pp. 110-11.

CHAPTER VII

The Imminent Second Coming of Christ

1. Devadas and his Concern for Eschatology

What does the Bible Mission teach about the 'end things', as they are sometimes called? What did Devadas believe about the coming of Christ again to the world? It is very clear from his writings and his preachings that eschatology was the key thought of Devadas all his life. He taught that God's children should constantly look for the Lord's return into the world. That is why he sometimes called his church the Advent church. 'Waiting' is the most frequently used word in the Bible Mission. Waiting in prayer, waiting for the baptism of the Holy Spirit, waiting for the Lord to speak to us in prayer, etc., are expressions we find in the teachings of Devadas. All these in a way are reflections of the key thought of Devadas, that the Lord is coming to the earth again soon. He comes to take the church into heaven.

Among the writings of Devadas, Parama Geethārdhamu, the Commentary on the Song of Songs[1], contains the imagery of the Church as the holy bride and the Lord returning to take her home. Similarly, Jepthah Feast Messages[2] speaks about the holy virgin preparing to become a sacrifice for her Lord and to be accepted by Him. Prakatana Grandha Vivaramu (An Exposition of the Book of Revelation)[3] records much of the teaching of Devadas on the last things which would happen in heaven and on earth. In another booklet, Mithra, the Friend[4], Devadas interprets the present day history as the story of fulfilment of the signs for the Lord's return. Famines, wars, explosion of knowledge--these are merely parts of a series of events foretelling the return of Christ. In Mithra, he gives at least 25 signs which he thinks are happening today in the world. Then there is a section in the same booklet on how the believers should prepare themselves for the day. What exactly will happen when the Lord returns? Devadas seems to be very sure in his own heart about the events of that day and even of the order of the events. In Mithra he makes a list of the events of the day as follows:

2. Some Eschatological Events

i) <u>Paraousia</u>: This is the day when the living believers will meet the Lord in mid-heaven, in 'the air'. The Church, which is called the bride, will be received into the New Jerusalem.

ii) <u>The Period of Great Tribulation</u>: This, according to Devadas, happens after the 'bride' is received into heaven. God will be with His Church in the New Jerusalem. But during the period of the great tribulation He keeps coming to the earth from time to time, to receive His own, who repent from time to time on the earth during the tribulation. During this period there will be still some unrepenting Jews, the 'heathen' and the nominal Christians on the earth.

iii) <u>Anti-Christ</u>: He is an able, strong and powerful character. He has the features of the Devil. He can influence men and will have dominion over kingdoms, over trade and money. He is a very cunning person (Rev. 13.1-10).

iv) <u>The False Prophet</u>: The False prophet is also not yet present in the world now. He does not come until after the 'bride' is received into heaven. The false prophet tries to convince men that anti-Christ is the saviour of the world (Rev. 13.11).

v) <u>The Three Devils</u>: These devils perform miracles on behalf of the anti-Christ and will mislead people (Rev. 16.13).

vi) <u>The First Tribulation</u>: This is the first of the tribulations that should come to those who believe in Christ. They will not wear the mark of the anti-Christ and so they will not be able to buy any provisions. These tribulations are very tragic and unbearable, in the words of Devadas (Matt. 24.21).

vii) <u>The Second Tribulation</u>: This comes not from the anti-Christ but from natural causes. The heat of the sun, the famine and the wild beasts will bring this tribulation and suffering. Anti-Christ will have no dominion over the earth during this time. The tribulation during this period comes from the sinfulness of men. God allows these calamities to see if mankind will turn to Him and be saved.

viii) <u>The Samājam or the Community</u>: This community will evolve to turn away the living beings towards anti-Christ. The name given to this community is 'woman'. The 144,000 people who do not join her fellowship will be saved. Many Jewish people will turn to the Lord and also the heathen will believe in Him.

ix) <u>The War of Armageddon</u>: At the end of the tribulation there will be a war between Christ and the anti-Christ. At the sight of the Lord, the anti-Christ and his followers will shiver with fear. The faithful will pray to God and a deep valley formed by an earthquake will be the place of their shelter. Christ will then capture the anti-Christ and his followers and they will all be thrown into the lake of fire burning with sulphur. Satan then will be imprisoned in the bottomless abyss and will remain there for a thousand years. This is how Devadas interpreted the eschatological books of the Bible.

x) <u>The Thousand Years Rule</u>: Christ will come to the earthly Jerusalem and His angels and the Church with Him will rule the earth for a thousand years. There will be no Satan on the earth any more, neither will there be any false prophet. The unfaithful will have been destroyed and all sin will have been wiped out during this time and there will be holiness on the earth. But the sinful nature of the hearts of men will still be the same. Those coming from heaven to visit the earth will speak in all languages and so they preach the word of God to men in all the languages of the earth[5].

These visitors from heaven can go anywhere on earth because, having been given glorified bodies, they are not bound by time and space. All the shortcomings in the preaching of the word of God which exist today will disappear. The worship of God then will be most wonderful and many people go 'to Jerusalem temple' to witness this worship. Devadas thinks that this will not be difficult because 'then there will be many more aeroplanes' as he envisaged[6].

Clear water, crops and fruits and flowers will be in abundance. There will be no pests to plants and there will be no barren, unyielding land. There will be perfect friendship between men and the wild beasts and so there will be no bodily harm to men from the beasts (Isa. Ch. 11).

All quarrels and wars will end and men will live for a hundred years[7]. Deaths will be rare. People do not have to pay taxes any more. Christ is the king and so the believers and the non-believers will both be happy. Many will turn towards God (Matt. 17.24-26). Every knee will bow in Christ's name (Phil. 2.9-11). So Devadas thinks that there will not be any other religion but Christ's religion. Because the kingdom of Christ is the kingdom of righteousness and peace, the state of men and creatures will be just as it was before the Fall[8].

xi) <u>Judgement of the Living</u>: People on earth during the thousand years rule should take decisions on hearing the word of God and so it will be time now for Christ to judge mankind from a throne on this earth (Matt. 25.31-46). Christ now gets Satan released from the prison after a thousand years. Satan returns to earth with great anger and gathers his own people. The followers of Satan will not be able to tolerate the look of the earth which has been changed during the one thousand years and they will not be able to see the brightness of the saints and the beauty of worship and the glorious faith of the people of God. God allows Satan to come to the earth and join his own followers. Men have not prayed hard enough to God, Devadas thinks, to bind Satan; otherwise He would have done so.

Then a rain of fire descends on Satan and he will be ruined. Finally Christ captures him and throws him away into the lake of fire (Rev. 20.7-10).

xii) <u>The Last Judgement</u>: Christ then calls all those who are in the tombs from the beginning of creation and those who do not believe and there will be a judgement. This judgement will be at a place which is not on the earth, not in heaven, and not in Hades. Only Christ will be at this judgement and not His Church this time. This is the judgement that comes after the thousand years rule (Rev. 20.11-15).

xiii) The New Heaven and the New Earth: Then the believers who are on the earth will continue to be there and the earth will then be a part of heaven. The Church, which is the bride, will be in the New Jerusalem and the saved people will be in another world, and Christ will be present in these three worlds 'according to their respective brightness' (Rev. 21.11).

xiv) The Final Consummation: The Church, the holy bride, set apart, prepared, and led by the Holy Spirit as Rebeccah was led by the servant of Abraham, will rejoice in heaven with the Lord and there will be a great feast. In the commentary on the Song of Songs, Devadas fully develops the imagery of the bride with all the related symbolism of the jewelry, the sweet perfume, the inner chamber where the bridegroom meets the bride, etc.

3. A Redemption for the Whole World

The eschatology which Devadas envisaged was both individual and cosmological. He looked forward to a time when the earth still remained but without sin[9]. There are parallels to this forward look for a blessed time in the thinking of many Hindus who talked about Rāma-rāya, the Kingdom of God, where there is no suffering, no injustice, a time when people will be happy and peaceful. We shall come to examine this universal aspiration a little later.

For Devadas the day of the Lord is not only a fulfilment of God's promise to the whole creation but it is especially a culmination of the expectation of the Church, the bride of Christ. He did not also rule out the ultimate salvation of all mankind, even those outside the select group.

But Devadas sometimes suggested that there will be levels and ranks among those who are going to be saved. He talked about the universal salvation on the one hand and also about the elect group on the other and so he reconciled the two ideas by thinking that there are grades among the believers. There are separate places in heaven for each according to the spiritual state. In Mahima Vārthāvali[10] he says,

There are many believers but there are classes among them. As we see in the parable of the sower, there are three classes of fruit-bearing: thirty-fold, sixtyfold and hundredfold. According to the level of spiritual growth to which you have reached in this world you will have a place waiting for you. This is what St. Paul meant when he said that everyone will be resurrected in his order, "each in his own proper place" (I Cor. 15.23). This means that there are classes in heaven. In God's plan of salvation it is clear that the "bride" or the inner group of believers will be in the New Jerusalem each one wearing crowns of Gold. In another part of heaven there will be the "saved souls" who do not belong to the "bride" group. After the last judgement the remnant of believers will stay on the earth which will then be a redeemed and renewed place.

Devadas classified Christian life into three categories:

1) the forgiven stage,
2) the saved stage, and
3) the holy bridal stage[11].

He says,

The Epistle to the Hebrews mentions "the first-born sons of God". The idea of the first-born implies that there are other children who are next born. The first-born were set aside for priestly duties in the house of Levi in the Old Testament. This does not mean that the other children in the family are lost.

Christ also told us that there are thrones in heaven for the disciples. This means that some will be sitting on the thrones and others will be ordinary citizens of the heavenly kingdom (Matt. 19.28). There are therefore different places but every one will be happy in heaven.

Among the disciples of Christ too there were ranks and an inner circle, Peter, James, and John.

Abraham was called the father of the faithful. There were others who were also faithful but only Abraham among them was called the Father. There were many men who died and went to heaven but only a few like Enoch and Elijah who went to be with God in body. This is a symbol of the different spiritual state among the faithful.

In the parable of the talents each servant was given the gifts according to his own status. Their rewards also were different. So, God is not unjust if He gives us different places in heaven. The woman in the Gospel story loved more and she was forgiven more[12].

In all these examples, Devadas recognises some grades among the faithful and some kind of differences in the places allotted in heaven. This sometimes resulted in some Christians considering themselves as an elect and privileged group[13].

4. The Signs of the Times

Devadas indicated in several places in his writings that the signs for Christ's return to the earth are being fulfilled today if we can read the signs. In <u>Mahima Vārthāvali</u>[14] he gave a list of 47 signs as being fulfilled from the Bible. Some of the important signs he mentions are as follows:

> the growing unemployment in the world, Zachariah 8.10.
> the return of the Jews to Jerusalem, Eze. 36.38.
> invention of the submarine, Hab. 1.14.
> invention of the automobile, Nahum. 2.4.
> increase of money around, James 5.1-10.
> advent of the aeroplanes, Isa. 31.5.
> advent of radio, Matt. 10.27.
> trenches for air raid shelter, Isa. 2.19.
> rockets, Psalm 68.18, etc.

Devadas wanted God's children to pray for the coming of the Lord. This is a day of deliverence for them and a day of rejoicing. It is like a father taking away his daughter from the place of suffering and sin and sorrow to his own house. In his booklet on Fasting Prayer[15] Devadas has this prayer:

> Jesus, you are coming again soon to this world of ours and therefore we thank you. While you yourself are ready to come soon, we are remaining cool and life-less, forgive us. Fill all our minds with the thoughts of your second coming. Your immediate fellowship is the antidote for all our woes and worries and a strength in all our weaknesses. So help us to spend more time in your presence and to meditate on your coming. Thus prepare us to meet you when you come. We ask this prayer in the name of the same Lord who is coming on the clouds of glory to take us with Him into the New Jerusalem.

The analogy of the father taking his daughter away to his own abode comes from Samarpana Prārdhana[16]. This is how Devadas tells the story:

> Once in a village, all the people were quarrelling with each other and there was no rest. At that time a father came to that village to see his daughter who was sick. When he saw the problems and the quarrels he wanted his daughter to be delivered from all these problems and he took her away with him to his house.

This is a familiar picture to the rural folk in India. The father, after giving his daughter in marriage, comes from time to time to see her and to enquire after her welfare. If there is any trouble at any time, he asks his son-in-law to send his daughter with him and this is a happy redemption. This sounds strange to some cultures but the symbolism of the story is clear to the folk churches. Devadas says,

> So also, this world is wicked and full of dirt and disease, poisonous creatures, devils and death. God our father will not leave us to suffer here but He will one day take us to His home, the Heaven. For that He comes quickly and that is His second advent. Does the

daughter refuse to go with her father or hesitate? Should we not say, Lord, we are prepared to go to the heavenly home with you?

To Devadas, the coming of the Lord again to this world is a basic and fundamental Christian teaching. It is real and imminent to him. It is a part of his creed. This is how he puts it:

> those who believe that the Saviour's birth was promised in the Old Testament are faithful
> those who believe that the story of Jesus Christ, his life as recorded in the Gospels is true are faithful
> those who believe in his teachings are faithful
> those who believe that he died on the cross are faithful
> those who believe that he rose from the dead are faithful
> those who believe that he ascended into heaven are faithful
> and having believed all these,
> if you can not believe in the second coming of Jesus Christ, how can you belong to the group of the faithful ones of God?

One can see the similarity of this argument to the second article of the apostles' creed. It is all one gospel, all one confession as Devadas rightly suggests[17].

5. So, What Shall We Do?

There are two booklets (two parts of the same title) containing the teachings of Devadas about how God's people should prepare for the coming of the Lord[18]. In the introduction to one of these booklets, the editor says,

> Father Devadas taught extensively about the second coming of our Lord. He advised us to be prepared for that event. The prayers in this book are meant for us to use so that we get ready now for His coming. Those who use the thoughts in these prayers and pray

accordingly will be worthy to participate in the second coming of Christ. May God use this book for His glory.

In the first of these booklets there are several stories illustrating the theme of the second coming. There is the story of a man who came from a long distant land and whose people were not ready to meet him; another story is of some people getting ready to go on a long journey some of whom were ready and got on the train when it came, and others of whom, still busy with other things, were left behind. There is yet another story of a son who wrote to his parents that he was returning home from a distant land and who told them the name of the ship in which he was traveling and the time of its arrival. The parents waited for him that day but the boat was delayed. Then the parents went away and, when he came, they missed him.

Thus runs the thought in these stories. At the end of each story there is a prayer sentence such as: Lord, help us to be prepared for your coming. Or, Lord, help us so that we will not be careless in our preparation for your advent, etc.

The message of all these stories may be briefly stated thus:

Even if the Lord delayed his return we should still be waiting and watching. Only that way will we be received into heaven. Many people will go away disappointed because the Lord was delayed. We should not get too busy with the worldly avocations when the Lord comes. Those who get too involved in the things of this world will be left behind and those who watch and wait will go with Him. We do not enter into heaven if we do not have daily prayers and thoughts on the second coming of Christ. We have to make ourselves holy in the preparation for the coming of our Lord. We need also strength for our journey. So we need to feed on the Word of God for strength. We need the Sacrament of the Communion. Then we will be partners in the second coming of Christ.

In one of these booklets Devadas even refers to a popular Indian idea of 'someone who comes at the end of time to the earth to rule a thousand years with peace'. Many men look for someone who would change the course of history of the universe. Devadas asks his followers to pray to Christ and ask Him whether it is not for Him the whole world is thus waiting.

Truly it is the whole world, because according to Devadas no one will be left out when the Lord comes[19]. This is the kind of cosmological fulfilment of God's plan which Devadas awaited. His key word was, "watch and wait". Sometimes of course he was very confused in his exegesis and hazy in his understanding of the Scriptures, but his great desire for the final day of the Lord and the anticipation of the redemption of the world was never found to be weak.

6. Eschatology and Evangelism

Reading through the two parts of the booklet Advent Prayer, already mentioned, one can clearly see the emphasis Devadas laid on evangelising the whole world because of the imminent return of God to judge the world and to take His people to heaven. In his mind the Lord's second coming and the preaching of the good news were integrally connected. In fact he saw the Bible Mission as God's instrument in the last days to spread the message of Christ's return to make it known all over the world. As an independent indigenous church it was the Bible Mission and not any one of the older mission churches that will be able to evangelize the Western world, he thought.

He was looking for a time when the devout followers of Christ in the fellowship of the Bible Mission would write down the message of the fulfilment of the signs for the Lord's return. He anticipated a time when God would bless the leaflet-evangelism project so abundantly that this message of His coming, through the leaflets, would reach all the corners of the earth and the people of all nations would get ready to go with the Lord.

Devadas himself wrote down all the signs as he saw them being fulfilled. But this note-book, in which he had written these, was lost, as his followers believed. So they must be even more watchful to see. All the preachers should warn men to get ready for the coming of our Lord. So, the prayers in these booklets are offered by the followers of Devadas.

Lord, we have preached all these years according to our skills but now teach us your methods so that every person may hear the good news before you return to this world.

Lord, give us your message tomorrow in this prayer meeting so that we may write it down and send it around to all the five continents of the earth so that men of all lands may fear and tremble when they hear that you are coming. This way, they will seek you and be saved.

Lord, when men are busy in their own avocations someone shouts that a great person was coming. At once everyone stops working and looks up and listens. Similarly all men are busy with their worldly things; let us shout loudly that you are coming to save us.

Lord, there are some cannibals in some parts of the world. They have eaten up missionaries who went to preach the gospel to them. They are naked and they live in jungles and they are wanting in simple wisdom. It is hard to preach the good news to them by normal means. So, help us, Lord, to reach them miraculously. First send Kailash Maharshi to preach to them and then please send some from our own prayer group to go to them[20].

Thus prayed Devadas and asked his followers to pray. In all the 81 prayers in this booklet there is a great teaching to the followers of Devadas on the subject of the second coming of the Lord and urgency to preach the good news to all men. For Devadas, Christ's return was a joyful occasion. It would be a time when the earth rejoices and it is like a wedding between the Lord and the Church. Devadas rarely spoke about punishment to the non-believers. On the other hand he looked for a time when every human being who ever lived on this earth would be saved and gathered into the heavenly home. Some will be rescued from the great tribulation and some will even be lifted from Hades. The fire and brimstone and the bottomless pit are not for men but only for Satan and his followers and the anti-Christ.

7. A Universal Quest

We mentioned that this aspiration for a redeemer is commonly shared by people in India to some extent. A kind of eschatology appears outside the church, a sort of Rāma-Rājya, a kingdom of God. It is not in the scope of this book to go into this aspect. But it may be useful to close this chapter with a sample of that thinking we find in contemporary progressive writers in the secular Andhra Pradesh. This is eschatology too, for these writers are foreseeing a day when God's plan will be fulfilled, the poor shall be redeemed, the downtrodden will find a hope and the oppressed and the forgotten ones will rejoice.

Srirangam Srinivasa Rao, popularly known as Sri Sri, is a modern poet, and a great collection of poetic pieces in popular style came out from his pen after the second world war[21]. This is one of his poetic-songs very well known now in Andhra:

Jagannādha Radhachakrālu
(The Chariot Wheels of God)[22]

You the downtrodden
You the lost and lonely
You who are smitten by the serpent of grief
You who are caught up in the wheels of the chariot of Misfortune

You who are humble
You who are despised
You, the birds of the air without a nest
You, the wanderers without rest
Do not weep, do not weep.

Listen you, the despeised by your own
Listen you, who are forgotten by men
Listen you, the outcastes of society

The Imminent Second Coming of Christ

Listen you, the half dead
Listen and do not weep, do not weep.

Look, the wheels of the chariot of
the Lord of the Universe
are rolling, rolling, rolling
The wheels of the Lord of the Universe
are rolling.

The "Lion Hill" is moving
The "Snow Peak" is melting
The "Granite Rock" is breaking
The lion hill,
The snow peak and the granite rock
are rolling and reeling.

You were scorched and you suffered
in despair and sorrow
on the banks of the dried up river
under the shade of the wayside tree
locked in the cell
hung upon the tree
betrayed and beaten
trampled and trodden under
You do not weep, do not weep.

New cities are rising,
new hopes are blooming
with freedom as foundation
and fraternity as the base
along with equality and mercy
Peace itself will triumph
and justice will rule the universe.

Your dreams will become true,
your heaven is going to be real
Do not weep, do not weep

You who are fallen
you down trodden
You who are bitten
by the serpent of Grief
betrayed and cast out
Do not weep, do not weep.

The wheels of the chariot
of the Lord of the Universe
are rolling, rolling, rolling.

        (Translation: S. Raj)

CHAPTER VII: Notes

1. Booklet No. 12

2. Booklet No. 13

3. Booklet No. 15

4. Booklet No. 16

5. Devadas always had a great burden on his heart for the Word of God to be preached to all men in the world. Many times in his writings he expressed the great hope that somehow the word of God would be translated into all the languages of the world. He also looked forward for a time when eventually human language will no more be a barrier because then all men will speak the same language.

6. Many village Christians in India have a dream of seeing the Holy land some day. They like to make a pilgrimage like the devout Muslim makes a pilgrimage to Mecca.

7. 'May you live for a hundred years' is a blessing in Telugu language.

8. Several Bible texts are cited here by Devadas.

9. To Devadas this is a state of creation which existed before the fall of man.

10. Booklet No. 18 Glorious News, pp. 36-41.

11. Ibid., p. 37.

12. Here is some confusion because the Telugu rendering of the text (Luke 7.47) from its structure seems to suggest that the love of the sinful woman was the cause of forgiveness whereas a more helpful rendering seems to be: Her great love proves that her many sins have been forgiven (New English Bible).

13. On the subject of the several groups among God's children at different stages of spiritual growth, see also, Booklet No. 8 Prayers and Praises for the Coming of Christ, Rākada Prārdhana Sthuthulu, p. 37.

14. Booklet No. 18, The Glorious News, p. 47.

15. Booklet No. 5, Upavāsa Prārdhana Deeksha, p. 41.

16. Booklet No. 7, The Prayer of Surrender, Samarpana Prārdhana, p. 49.

17. Booklet No. 15, Mithra, The Friend, p. 24.

18. Booklet Nos. 8 and 9 Rākada Prārdhana Sthuthulu I & II.

19. Booklet No. 9 op.cit., p. 26.

20. It is possible that Devadas was thinking of the believers going around the world in spirit like Kailāsh Maharshi was believed to have done, to be with people in their prayers and when they need help.

21. P.R.P. Francis, the Head of the Telugu Department, Madras Christian College says this about Sri Sri: Sri Sri champions the cause of the hungry and the poor, the desperate and the downtrodden. His best known poem, Jagannādhuni Radhra Chakrālu, offers hope to the downtrodden.
  Francis, P.R.P., "Trends in Modern Indian Literature", in India Today (ed.) Anatha Kristna S.V., Madras: CLS 1967.

22. Srirangam Srinivasa Rao, Jagannādhuni Radha Chakrālu, (The Chariot Wheels of God), Mahāprasthānam, Sri Sri songs, Vijaywada: 1940. See p. 339 Appendix i for the Telugu Text.

CHAPTER VIII

The Hymns in the Bhakti Tradition

1. The Singing Tradition of the Telugu Church

Andhra people are music lovers and the Telugu Church is a singing church. The Andhra Christian Hymn Book, adopted by all the churches using this language, was first printed in 1893 according to the records of the publishers, the Christian Literature Society, Madras[1]. The present edition of the hymn book, which is a completely revised edition, was first printed in 1966 with several reprints since then. This book contains 626 hymns altogether, 130 of them translations of Western hymns to be sung to Western tunes and the rest original works in Telugu, set to Indian melodies and written by Indian Christian writers. In addition to these hymns in the Andhra Christian Hymn Book there are now in circulation several songs or lyrics[2] written by living writers, mostly young, and these are useful for almost every occasion, such as the church festivals, anniversaries or prayer meetings. Some of these new songs serve their purpose and then are forgotten, but some will be remembered long enough as people in the churches learn to sing them. Eventually, some of them may even find a place in the next revised edition of the hymnal.

There were predecessors to this ecumenical hymn book of 1893. Dolbeer reports that there was an earlier Lutheran Telugu Hymnal produced in the Hermansburg mission under the editorship of missionary Mylius, in a place called Nayudupet. This hymnal is said to have contained 128 hymns translated and edited in 1879[3].

To get a glimpse of the way in which Telugu Christians look at devotional music it may be useful to read what the chairman of the editorial committee says in the introduction to the present Andhra Christian Hymn Book:

> God Himself is the source of Christian singing. . . . He came into this world as a kind of musical message. That message is the song of salvation. Anyone that tastes the sweetness of that song can not but

sing praises to God like a Kōel sings[4]. Yea, he becomes a peacock to dance with joy before his God. He becomes a flower to touch God's feet in worship. He himself becomes an echo of that salvation message to proclaim it to all the world[5].

Indeed Telugu Christians would agree with the writer in this kind of feeling. In fact congregational singing in India became more popular through the churches. Otherwise the South Indian classical Karnatic[6] music is mostly kachēri type (court music) to be performed by trained solo singers for the beauty of the 'rendering'.

Karnatic music is melodic and not harmonic. That is how it had developed the 72 parent melodies (mēlakarthas or scales) from the 12 notes in the octave. From these parent or generic melodies have been derived hundreds of generated melodies (janya rāgas). As Fox-Strangways says in his scholarly work, Music of Hindostan[7], this is a melody absolutely untouched by harmony. But the great Indian musicologist Professor Sambamoorthy, while admitting that harmony in the Western sense does not exist in Indian music, contends that there is what may be styled as melodic harmony[8], which he also calls the linear harmony or horizontal harmony.

There is group singing tradition in India in the Bhakti movement[9] where devotees sit together and sing bhajans[10] to God, sometimes one person leading and the others joining in some kind of refrain. On the subject of the Bhakti movement and its relation to Christian Church Robin Boyd says:

> When we consider the features of Bhakti thought and of the suggestion of Rāmānuja which supports it, we can not be surprised at the great attraction it has held for Indian Christians. Here we are far removed from the cold world of Sankara. Here is a warmth and love and personal devotion - here is the experience of God's grace, here is the utter self-abandonment to the love and power of God which has distinguished so many Christian saints[11].

It is that warmth and love and personal devotion that the church in India is trying to reflect in its singing in particular.

Although it is sometimes said that Indian music is not suited for congregational singing, this is not always true. H.A. Popley, writing in the Indian Journal of Theology, on the subject of the use of Indian music in Christian worship, says:

> It is true that in classical music and in the singing and playing of Rāgabhāva (colour of the melody) it is the individual alone who can do it properly and so this aspect of the music will not be useful for congregational purposes. But this is only one aspect of Indian music and is no reason why in general there should not be more and more Indian music in our Christian services, as groups of singers are not expected to sing these individual extemporisations[12].

Obviously, the very first converts in Andhra must have learnt to sing Western hymns to Western tunes, although the words were in Telugu. The situation is still the same in places like Nāgāland in the north-east India in the foothills of the Himalayas where there was not much local tradition to interfere with Western music influence. People in the Nāgāland naturally have taken to harmonic singing even without the accompaniment of a Western musical instrument. But in the southern part of India there is strong Karnātic music tradition which comes from an ancient past, and except in a few towns, where there are people trained in Western music who can play Western instruments, there are very few churches now which use Western music to any large extent.

In the Andhra Church from an early date in its history, nationals among the Christians started writing hymns in the Indian tradition and set to Indian music. But the difficulty was that there were not many among the converts to Christianity who were gifted to write poetry and song. Even if there were a handful who could write the words, it was even more difficult to set them to music in the Karnātic styles. So the only way left to the early Christians was to write words of a song to a known folk melody or some simple light music style and leave the task of writing the notation and fixing the scale to someone else. People however have learnt to sing by the ear and the melodies are memorised.

But there were some exceptionally gifted writers, however few in number, among the early Telugu Christians who came from the Hindu background and who were scholars in the Telugu language. Choudury Purushōtham (1803-1890) was one of them. There were as many as 70 hymns by Choudury Purushōtham in the Andhra Christian Hymn Book. Another great hymn writer of the same age was Pulipāka Jagannādham (1826-1896), also a Hindu convert, and 29 of his hymns are to be found in the Hymn Book. Mallela David, whom the present investigator met shortly before the former died in 1958, belonged to a later generation, and he contributed 20 hymns to the hymnal. Thus very early in the Telugu church and all along, Christian writers wrote songs for the use of the church.

The subjects covered in the present hymn book are many and varied. The following classification of the contents is listed in the introductory pages:

WORSHIP
        Praises to God   40
        Morning Worship   8
        Evening Worship   8
        The Lord's Day   2
GOD THE FATHER   7
GOD THE SON
        Praises to Christ   36
        Birth of Christ   31
        Names of Jesus and his Titles   14
        Life of Jesus and his teachings 12
        Love and Grace of Jesus   16
        Passion and Death of Jesus 36
        Resurrection of Jesus   12
        Ascension   2
        Second Coming of Jesus   10

The Hymns in the Bhakti Tradition

GOD THE HOLY SPIRIT	15
THE HOLY SCRIPTURES	6
THE CHURCH	
The Church	8
Servants of the Church	5
Baptism	5
Communion	9
Mission of the Church	4
PROCLAMATION	
Proclamation of the Word	24
Repentence	24
Forgiveness of Sins	7
New Life in Christ	4
CHRISTIAN LIFE	
The Joy of Salvation	8
THE WITNESS OF A CHRISTIAN	
Temptations and Struggles	8
Prayer	16
Faith	5
Belief and Serenity	18
God's Help and Guidance	22
Fellowship	4
Holiness	3
Self Dedication	16
Service and Reward	16
Christian Pilgrimage	16
Hope and Joy	5
Death and Resurrection	8
Joy of Heaven	13
CHRISTIAN HOME	7
CHRISTIAN YOUTH	11
CHILDREN	27

SPECIAL OCCASIONS

Marriage	8
House Dedication	2
Christian Giving	8
Thanksgiving Festival	7
Dedication of a Church	4
Women's Groups	1
Sunday School	1
Creed	3
Palm Sunday	3
Feast of the Holy Cross	1
All Saints Day	1
Temperance	1
Christian Hospitals	1
The Beginning and the End of the Year	4
Farewell	4
National Festivals	2
DOXOLOGIES	12
SUPPLEMENTARY HYMNS	5

2. Dhātu and Mātu (Music and Language of the Telugu Poetry)

To appreciate a Telugu hymn it is necessary to consider its Dhātu and Mātu, the music and the language of the hymn. We have seen that to write a Telugu Bhakti hymn as in any other language and to give music to it is a work of art. Ideally one should know both the Dhātu and the Mātu, the Sangeetha and the Sāhithya, as they are known. Any gift of music is considered by the Hindus as something one gets from the fruits of one's good deeds of one's past janma (incarnation) rather than something one could learn easily in the present life. Therefore many people never hope to become poets or musicians.

Even to be able to write words of a song without the music, one must learn many complicated rules of prosody. Telugu and Sanskrit lyrical structures are strictly bound with many complicated rules of grammar. The 17th century Telugu grammarian Appakavi[13] prescribed lakshana (rules of prosody) for more than 200 different species of versification. Clearly many of the species are out of use today, and some others appear as metrical songs in dance drama and folk arts. There is an old Hindu belief, still held in some circles, that errors in a literary piece of work can bring bad luck to the writer as well as to the one to whom the work is dedicated. So people approached any literary activity rather warily and only after long years of preparation, preferably under the guidance of a Guru.

The literary rules for song writing are similar to those existing for poetry writing. Both lyrical and poetic pieces are strictly scanned. Fox-Strangways, talking about the tāla (time) aspect of music, reminds us that 'musical time in India, more obviously than anywhere else, is a development of the prosody and metres of poetry'[14].

Telugu Christian hymn writers while strictly following these rules tried to keep the structure of their songs as simple as possible to facilitate congregational singing. Most of the time they have used very simple and straight melodies without the so-called extemporisations.

In any kirthana[15] or devotional song we see three components. They are the pallavi, anupallavi whenever it occurs, and the charanam. Pallavi is the opening section of the song and it is sometimes called the makuta, the crown. It is generally made up of two or four āvrttas (musical cycles). In singing, pallavi is repeated at the end of every charanam or verse. So it can be called a kind of refrain. The purpose of the pallavi is to state the theme of the song and to reinforce it again through repetition. Sometimes the reinforcement is done by asking a question in the pallavi which is then answered in the charanams. A good example is Devadas' hymn No. 53 (Bible Mission Hymnal) which asks the question: Who is the Lord that is the author of my faith? Then each verse following seeks to elaborate the question and to answer it with an affirmation ending with: Who else, except Jesus the crucified.

Anupallavi does not always appear in songs but when it does, it is an extension of the pallavi, a kind of parenthesis to it and as such it either expands the meaning of the pallavi or reiterates it in a different set of words. Where there is no anupallavi, the song simply proceeds with the first verse after the pallavi. The dhātu (music) of the charanam is sometimes the same as that of the pallavi or the pallavi-anupallavi combination, or sometimes it may be different and one leading to the other.

Charanam is the verse or the stanza of the song and all the charanams have the same dhātu (music) repeating throughout. This is a specific quality of a song or a kirthan as different from other more complicated musical compositions. (For examples of these features in the works of Devadas, see Appendix IV.)

3. Some metrical features of Devadas' Hymns

The Bible Mission Hymn Book has 191 pages with 120 hymns, all composed by Father Devadas. Sixteen of these are incorporated into the Andhra Christian Hymnal, already mentioned above, the common book of songs for all the Christian denominations in the Telugu area. Only five of Devadas' hymns are translations from English. One of those is a very interesting paraphrase of the English hymn "Take My Life and Let It be Consecrated Lord to Thee". Devadas' version of this hymn is not a translation to be sung to English music but it is a rewriting of the message in Indian melody and metre. Devadas is one of the few Christian hymn writers who successfully tried this experiment. This particular lyric in Telugu sounds so original because of the right choice of idiom and the flow of the language. Apart from the five translations mentioned above, all the other songs in this hymn book are original writings set to Indian tunes.

There is a liturgical supplement in this hymn book which is optional for the worshippers. Only on Sundays if at all, this 'order of worship' is generally used, but at most other times the prayers of the Bible Mission people are extemporaneous and free in structure.

At the top of the hymns the name of the Indian rāga and tāla are printed in the book in most cases, but this does not mean much to the people who are not actually trained in music and so can not identify them. People memorise the tunes and all that they need is a listening ear and an awareness of a simplified beat, sometimes indicated with a pair of hand cymbals or some kind of a small drum which is used in the churches during singing. Most of the hymns of Devadas have a simple seven beat (akshara kāla) rhythm which is easy to follow. Let us take the example of a hymn,

>   Nannu diddumu - chinna prāyamu
>   Sannuthundagu - nāyanā, nīvu
>   Kanna thandri - vanuchu nēnu
>   Ninnu chērithi nāyanā

This runs in 3 + 4 rhythm and it is called the Misra Gati[16], the mixed rhythm.

In addition to writing of hymns Devadas had also composed poetry in Telugu. Very few Christian preachers have actually composed poetry because of the difficulties involved, as the metrical system of Telugu poetry is not so easy. But simple poetry in India communicates well and several teachers in the past in all religions have used poetry for instruction to the people with little education.

In a printed booklet of 88 pages, entitled Rakshana Padyamulu (Salvation Poems), I came across 203 poetic pieces of Devadas. There are two additional poems of invocation in the inner title page of the book asking for God's blessing on the listeners and readers. This, again, follows an age-old Telugu literary tradition. At the end of the second invocatory poem, Devadas has attempted a literary gimmick which the old time poets used sometimes to indicate the signature or seal of authorship in their works. The four line piece runs like this:

>   Dēva rājya vishayambulu - deena mathini
>   Varusagā nērchikonu vāri-vāri vasamu
>   Dānamulu vāri vasamaunu - gāna galugu
>   Sukhamu bhuvi mēdi sramalandu - shubhamu kalugu

Meaning:

> Those who learn daily
> With much humble mind
> The things concerning the kingdom of God
> Will inherit all blessings on earth
> And they will be delivered from all suffering

The first syllable of each line in succession of the above poem when read from top to bottom will add up to the name of the author De-va-da-su. This is a detail which Devadas however had never bothered to attempt anywhere else. To us this helps to identify the authorship of these poems.

He used only three simple metres for all the 205 pieces in this book and all the three belong to Telugu vrttas (poetic forms) as different from the more difficult vrttas of Sanskrit origin. Of course there are some prosodical errors in the poetry of Devadas but many of them may be ascribed to the lapses of the printers and editors who will not be generally expected to know all these complicated rules. One syllable too short or too long makes all the difference in this kind of writing. The authors did not always have the opportunity to see the proofs. In the case of the present work, it was printed in 1977, several years after the author's death. About the origin and the circumstances in which these poetic pieces were written, this is what the editors of the booklet say in its introduction:

> All these poems were not written at one time but during the course of his teachings Father Devadas had dictated them as the Lord had handed them over to him from time to time. They were written in a simple language so that every one who reads them may understand the message without difficulty. We are not able to describe the unparalleled experience of Father Devadas, his spiritual powers and his fellowship with Jesus which he enjoyed and the way he understood deep spiritual truths and how he received them from the Lord Himself and how he delivered them to others.
> (Translation by S. Raj)

4. Theological Contents of the Hymns of Devadas

Devadas is simply a bhakti poet. His songs are full of devotional language. Robin Boyd reminds us that

> we do not look to the bhakti poets for complex theological exposition. But we do find that it is largely through their work that the language of Christian devotion and even to some extent of technical theology has become fixed in the different Indian languages[17].

And this wealth of devotional songs is that much more important to a people who, to a large extent, belong to an oral tradition. Robin Boyd also underlines this truth when he says:

> The bhakti poets are the men who more than any others have made Christianity 'at home' in India; their songs are sung and learnt by heart by thousands who would never read a book of theology, and next to the Bible, their works have probably been the most important in helping the Christian Church to take root in Indian soil and to bear the blossoms which the richness of that soil encourages to grow in such profusion[18].

Devadas has used much biblical imagery in these songs. One of them is a faithful rendering of Psalm 103 into Indian music. Another one is a similar musical version of Psalm 23. Both these hymns[19], written in the first person, express in simple words a deep feeling of faith and devotion. The imagery of the shepherd is pleasingly poetic and interestingly familiar to the Indian mind. In the song based on the 103rd Psalm, Devadas lists several reasons one could think for praising the Lord. There are 13 verses in Psalm 23, the last one with a reference to the house of the Lord as the abode of the believer. Then Devadas adds another section of 12 verses to the hymn including there several other things the Lord will do for His children here and now - every small and practical thing like providing a shelter for His children when they travel. So, what do I lack when the Lord is my shepherd? And he adds other useful thoughts to help the devotee:

> The angels are always around me,
> The Holy Sacraments are provided for me,
> The anxieties of my heart are calmed,
> God Himself will appear to me in His body,
> So, why should I fear when the Lord is my shepherd?

To Devadas, God is not only a God of past history but He is also One who is at work in the world now.

There is one hymn which is a long piece of instruction to the Church[20]. It starts with a question: Do you know, O household of God? Devadas answers this question in 27 verses which include a great deal of teaching about the calling and the privilege of the Church. Do you know, O household of God,

> That Christ is going to be glorified by your works?
> That the word of God is going to be read in several languages of the earth?
> That you will travel all over the world?
> That you shall one day conquer sins?
> That you will fulfil God's will on earth?
> That hell will be defeated?
> That you will have a host of armies standing on your side?
> That you will cast out all sickness?
> That you shall raise the dead?
> That you shall feed the hungry ?
> That the work of your hands will bear fruit?
> That God will hear you cry and fulfil your heart's desire?
> That our God is the very God whom the Indian Scriptures have been seeking?
> That God will turn the work of Satan and the demons to the good of His people?
> Do you know?

There are several hymns in this book on the gift of healing. The story of the woman with the issue of blood provided a great theme for one of the better known hymns[21] of Devadas. The message of the hymn is the implicit faith of the woman and healing granted by the mere touch of the Lord's garment which is a manifestation of the power of God. The name of Jesus is the mantra[22] for healing, according to Devadas. Is there a name greater than the name of Jesus, he asks. Jesus who has healed the sick in the past and who can heal now--this is the burden of the next hymn (No. 41). There are at least 15 specific ailments mentioned by name in this hymn, ailments which Devadas declares that Jesus can cure. Similarly the next hymn (No. 42) is addressed to the 'Lord Jesus Christ our good teacher, the one who forgives our sins and our loving Father'. Devadas praises his Lord in this hymn and mentions 55 specific sicknesses from which the believer can be delivered through prayer. In the wide scope of this healing is included delivery from all diseases starting from sleeplessness and ending with demon possession problem that the Lord is concerned about and from which He wants His children to be freed. (The idea that labour in childbirth is a curse comes from Gen. 3:16.)

The concluding verse of this hymn speaks about the one-ness of Christ with us in incarnation and His willingness to deliver people from evil and to listen to their prayers whoever they are, or to whichever religion they belonged. Devadas many times transcends the boundaries of the institutional church when he speaks about the purview of God's redeeming action. He offers in the name of Christ the blessing of healing and the privilege of prayer for anyone and every one.

Hymn No. 53, which has already been mentioned, deserves a little closer examination because it is making a great affirmation which can be said to be the great foundation to the teachings of the Bible Mission. In fact it is a hymn with which any Telugu Christian will easily identify.

"Who is the author of my faith?' (Which Lord, literally). These are the opening words of this hymn, and Devadas answers the question immediately by saying, "Who else, except Jesus the crucified?" Then comes the bulk of the song expanding this fact. The question comes in different forms in the body of the song and each time the answer is: "No one but Jesus the crucified."

Who is the foundation of my faith?
Who has raised my voice with songs?
Who carried away the burden of my sins and
Who brought about the reconciliation at last
between God and me?

Who is the All Wise One who gives me wisdom
so that I know my duty towards God?
Who strengthens me to fulfil that duty?
Who confronted the opponent on my behalf and defeated him?
Who wiped my tears and who raised me up
when I swooned in the battle?
Who gave me rest and who healed the wounds of my heart?

Who is life in my death?
And who is death to death itself?
Who is going to establish me in the midst of the
Heavenly Angels?

Who is it who died to save me (to give me life)
And having died, who is He that lives for ever?

At the end of every question the conclusion comes again and again: No one but the Lord Jesus Christ the crucified. No wonder that generations of Telugu Christians went home with great assurance after singing this hymn of Father Devadas in their prayer meetings.

There are very few proclamation hymns written by Devadas. Although he was burning with zeal to preach the Gospel and to evangelise the whole world he expressed himself more eloquently in his hymns of praise and prayer. The prabōdha, or exhortation hymns, are few in number. In the few he wrote for exhortation, he asks the listener to meditate on the name of Jesus 'for forgiveness of sins, for sickness to be cured, for demons to be expelled, sorrows to be conquered, disappointments to be forgotten, darkness to be cast out, fears to be calmed--for all these meditate on the name of Jesus'. He declares that meditation on the name of Jesus helps to get rid of debts, to get a solution in our disputes, to overcome scandals. Devadas himself in his life was a victim of people's misunderstanding, and he derived deep comfort in his problems through prayer.

Hymn No. 59 again is presenting the Name of Jesus as the theme. "What do I need? Whom do I need?" asks this hymn--and the author answers his own question. The vision of Jesus (darshan), the sweet words of the Lord, the wonderful story of Jesus, the fellowship of the household of God, the grace of the Lord, the privilege of serving the Lord, the fellowship with the Lord Himself, and the blessed meditation on His cross--these are what the believer should desire. In the concluding lines the author says that he needs Jesus who forgives, Jesus who heals, Jesus who supports, Jesus the teacher, the Saviour, the Way.

The longest hymn in this collection in No. 62, a didactic hymn with 135 verses, each one containing a message from Christ himself to the believer. The makuta, the opening words or the crown of the hymn, can be translated like this:

>   Anxiety you will never need
>   But only thoughts of glory.
>
>   Daily I will give to my humble ones
>   Thoughts of tranquility and peace
>   Therefore, Anxiety you will never need, etc.

In this hymn Devadas is using the words of the Lord Himself to impart these teachings to his followers. We also see this style of instruction in the writings of Sādhu Sundar Singh, especially in his At the Master's Feet. Devadas prefaces this hymn with these words:

>   The message of this hymn is not only for me but it is appropriate to all believers.

A whole series of teachings are packed into this hymn. There are six sections with headings which can be translated as follows:

> Our enemies and our attitude towards them.
> Satan, what he did and what he does today.
> The ministry of the Church including the promise
>   of the gift of healing and the gift of tongues.
> Heaven.
> Things that will happen after the second coming.
> The Bible Mission and its origin and its calling.

In the 96th and 97th verses of this hymn the Lord says,

> As you think of me so shall I appear to you
> Only be pure in your heart.

The teaching of course is scriptural--"Blessed are the pure in heart, for they shall see God." But the meaning of the first line is not so clear. Devadas may be speaking about the different ways in which the Lord can give the darshan[23] to His people. In dreams, in apparitions, in the form of some departed dear ones, in bright light directly speaking to His people--in all these ways God can appear[24]. The words may also simply mean that God will appear to the believer just in answer to his prayer and his desire to see the Lord. But in the next verse the Lord also says that He will speak even to those who do not think of Him. Here is another example of the belief of Devadas that the Lord will not limit His revelation, Prathyaksha or darshan, to Christians only. God can directly speak to all those who seek Him. His Spirit is promised to be poured on 'all flesh'. This conviction of Devadas appears again and again in his teachings although he did not develop it into a theological statement anywhere.

In the Bible Mission Booklet No. 23, Why is God Tarrying[25], Devadas made an attempt to handle the question of those who have never believed in Jesus and about their salvation. He even says that many Christians will be offended by what he says. To him people who have never believed in Christ are 'the sheep that belong to the other fold'. Christ will bring even them to the 'fold'. He says it is just and right that God somehow should save them also. God will not reject them. To him there are three kinds of sheep: the living believers, the living non-believers and those who have died without knowing Christ. God is the shepherd of all these three groups of the flock.

Devadas also cites the story of Jonah in suppoprt of his view. 'How much more, then, should I have pity on Nineveh?' God asks Jonah.

Christ also went to the underworld. Just as he came to the earth to save men, he will also go into hell to save some there. What had happened on earth will also happen in hell.

On the subject of the unbound Christ and the ultimate destiny of the universe, the Indian Theologian Samuel Samartha says:

> Further, the New Testament also teaches that God's work of reconciliation and renewal extends beyond the history to the cosmos itself. He who is crucified and the risen Lord is also the agent of creation and so there is a wider range to the scope of the saving work of Christ. The recent emphasis on the "Cosmic Christ", both in Catholic and Protestant theology is an indication of the fact that the narrow view of salvation as being limited to saving man is being supplemented by a recognition of the work of the "larger Christ". The consummation of all life, the disclosure of ultimate meaning of creation, and the final destiny of nature and history must lie in the womb of the future, but he who is now acknowledged and accepted as the Lord is also the one in whom the divine activity is so focussed as to provide a clue to the future consummation. "Beloved, we are God's children now; it does not yet appear what we shall be, but we know that when he appears we shall be like him, for we shall see him as he is" (I John 3.2)[26].

Turning briefly now to the theology of the poetic pieces of Devadas to which reference has already been made in this chapter, we can learn a few things about his theological views from these poems. The booklet Rakshana Padyamulu starts with the story of creation, the Fall of man and the promise of the Saviour. Then comes the story of Jesus, his life, death and resurrection. There is a long section on eschatology, the signs that should appear before the Lord's return, the ascension of the faithful and of the 'children'. Then comes the fall of Satan, his armies, Hades, the four rivers, the seven years of tribulation, and Christ's final victory after the great war.

In these poetical pieces there is a section with the teachings of the Lord and their exposition by Devadas. Christ is protrayed as:

> The saviour who became incarnate
> The Lord who forgives sins and gives peace
> The healer who heals our inner and outer sicknesses
> The father who feeds the thousands
> Our teacher, Our example,
> And the One who died for us and who rose again.

In the story of the Fall, Devadas says that God separated Himself from the sinful world and men started worshipping idols. Man hated man and this resulted in some nations becoming caste-ridden (kulam). To Devadas the caste system in India with all the injustices and social barriers between man and man is nothing short of the fruits of sin.

In poem 9, John the Baptist is described as,

> vanavāsi - a forest dweller,
> hatasākshi - a martyr,
> ātmavasudu - subject to the Spirit,
> sabda vāhi - (the meaning is not too clear but could mean) carrier of the Voice,
> garjinchu prasangi - a thundering preacher,
> Streelu, etc. - the greatest among those born of women,
> Sākshi - a witness

In poem No. 18 we come across an interesting argument of Devadas:

> Satan tried to kill Jesus but Jesus rose again from the dead.
> Satan tried to kill the Church but it increased (spread).
> Satan caused rivalries in the Church but
> this paved the way to a more careful study of the Bible.
> Then Satan tried to hide the Bible (this may be a reference
> to the situation immediately before the Reformation)
> and this caused darkness.
> But then God brought the Bible out by showing it to
> Martin Luther.
> But people understood the Bible in different ways
> and hence there are so many denominations.

Devadas looks at the various denominations positively and sees in them God's plan to spread His word to 'all nations'[27].

In the next poem Devadas clearly foresees a time when all the different denominations will disappear and only a united and a true Church of the Lord will stand.

Thus, one man, not even highly educated, and feeble in physical health and most of the time a wandering 'sādhu', in his lifetime has done much teaching through song and poetry. His poetry was not superior, but that kind of literary excellence was not his main objective. He wanted to express his mystical experiences, he wanted his followers and he amply realised his objectives. This is what the Indian mind understands by 'anubhava', experience.

5. Some New Trends in the Musical Experience of the Telugu Church

The Telugu church will continue to be a singing church. If anything, its witness thorugh song, story, poetry and oral tradition will increase. There is less hesitation today on the part of the church to adapt and harness more secular forms of song and dance into its service. Dance, drama and the spirit of natural celebration are finding their rightful place in the life and witness of the Indian church. Popley, in the article already referred to, says that,

> in Andhra Pradesh, as one would expect among such music loving people, there is today a revival of Indian music in church worship both in the urban and in rural areas[28].

Popley also observes that,

> there are now in every regional language a large number of Indian lyrics and bhajans in Indian metres which express often very beautifully the fruits of the Gospel and the spirit of Christian teaching[29].

The Church needs songs. Christians in India celebrate every small occasion with music. At Christmas and Easter and at every other major festival of the Church, Telugu Christians sing special songs. Young people are today trying their hand at writing Christian songs. These new writers may not be men 'learned' in the art. They can learn from the secular film music; they certainly adapt the folk tunes of the country. Sometimes the church does not approve the film music styles. Some people think that the cinema is too worldly, but these critics do not know that some of the old-time church songs were written to tunes borrowed from the street dancers and spirit worshippers.

Radio and film have greatly stimulated Telugu music styles, and they are certainly having their effect on the church music also in India. Now there are more Christian songs on the gramophone discs in the Telegu language than there were ten years ago. They are produced with full orchestral background with voices of famous cine playback artistes. Two of the songs of the present writer in Telugu have been pressed on discs by Columbia Company in Madras with voice loaned by cine singer Bāla Subrahmanyam[30].

The national radio, in spite of the secular policy of the state, sets apart some time on Sundays to play Christian bhakti songs.

New songs are also written and learned at special meetings. Once every two years in summer, Christians from many parts of Andhra Pradesh gather on the sand banks of River Kristna for a week of open air worship and witness. Thousands of people live in the open palm leaf shelters, cooking their simple meals, bathing in the river and listening to the word of God as delivered by speakers. They sing. Someone writes a new song, 'the convention song', every time they meet there. At the end of that week people go back into various parts of the state with a new song they have learnt and which will be re-learnt in hundreds of villages and towns.

The old Karnātic classical tradition continues to grow in the church and the new lighter type of music will join the flow. The Telugu church is thankful to the older poets like Choudury Purushotham, Munagmuri Devadas, Pulipaka Jagannadham, Mallela David and a host of others who have blazed a trail of musical expression. A people who always have enjoyed their singing, whether it is in the paddy fields or at festivals, at home or in the wider community, will never forget their tradition, and the Telugu church shall never lag behind in singing praises to God in the cultural style.

CHAPTER VIII: Notes

1. Andhra Christian Hymnal, Madras: Christian Literature Society, 1977.

2. In this book the words song and lyric and hymn are used interchangeably.

3. Dolbeer, A History of Lutheranism in Andhra Desa, p. 123.

4. Koel is a sweet singing bird which augurs the Spring season, which is the New Year for the Telugu people. It is a migratory bird and appears only at that time every year. The resounding notes of its song are not easy to miss in the season. The flowering of the mango and the margosa tree and the song of the Koel are poetically well known in the Telugu land as symbols of new life.

5. Andhra Christian Hymnal, p. 3.

6. It is not certain how the South Indian classical music got the attribute Karnataka. Professor Sambamoorthy says: In Tamil language, Karnataka means tradition, purity, (sampradayam, sudhdham). Sambamoorthy, P., South Indian Music, Madras: the Indian Music Publishing House, 1977. Book I, p.21.

7. Fox Strangways, Music of Hindostan, Oxford: The Clarendon Press, 1914.

8. Sambamoorthy, P., op.cit., Book V, p. 161.

9. Bhakti religion was defined by Rudolf Otto as 'faith in salvation through an eternal God and through a saving fellowship with him'. Quoted by Robin Boyd, Indian Christian Theology, p. 110.

Boyd gives detailed treatment of the subject of bhakti in his chapter on Appaswamy and his book Christianity as Bhakti Marga.

Its faith in a personal God who can become incarnate, and its emphasis or personal devotion, its non-recognition of differences among human beings, its insistence on fellowship with God as different from amalgamation like in Vedanta--all these features of bhakti religion in Hinduism are more acceptable to Christian thinkers than any other form of spirituality.

10. Bhajan, a word found in many languages in India, means worship of God or adoration, generally done in groups of worshippers with some kind of singing. The word and the concept are adapted into Christianity also. It means worship in song.

11. Robin Boyd, op.cit., p. 112.

12. Popley, H.A., "The Use of Indian Music in Christian Worship", The Indian Journal of Theology, Vol. 6, 1957, p. 87.

13. Appakavi, Kakunuri (17th C.A.D.), Appakaveeyam (Telugu), Madras: Vavilla Ramaswamy Sasthrulu and Sons, 1970.

14. Fox Strangways, op.cit., p. 196. For additional notes on Telugu poetical structures, see Appendix IV.

15. Kīrthan comes from a root which means "to praise"; hence it means a song of praise to God. The object of this praise is generally, God, but there are also Kīrthans addressed to Kings etc.

16. Miśra gati, mixed beat because it is a combination of thiśra gati and the chaturaśra gati, the threefold beat and the fourfold beat. This counting of beats is an easy way of reckoning the tāla (time) without having to learn the complicated tāla system of Indian music. All the tālas are combinations or variations of the following beats:
        thiśra   three beats in a group
        chathuraśra   fourfold beat
        miśra   sevenfold beat
        khanda   fivefold beat

17. Boyd, R.H.S., op.cit., p. 118.

18. Ibid., p. 118.

19. Andhra Christian Hymnal, Nos. 12 and 14. Bible Mission Hymnal Nos. 4 and 50.

20. Bible Mission Hymnal, No. 36.

21. Hymn No. 40 in the Bible Mission Hymnal. It may not be a coincidence that Devadas takes this story from the Gospels in dealing with the question of sickness and healing by faith. In India sicknesses like irregular periods of women are associated with the work of demons and evil spirits and they need divine power to be cured. Cf. Hollenweger, W.J., The Pentecostals, L.Jeeva Ratnam quoted on this subject.

22. Mantra is a meditation formula, or a chant or a repeated prayer sometimes used to cast away fear and to obtain benefit.

23. Darshan, a vision of God. It is always a vision given or granted by God and as such it is God who acts and not the devotee who is given the darshan.

24. There are reflections of this teaching in Bhagavad Gita where Kristna tells Arjuna that He will appear to the devotee in whatever form the latter worships Him.

    Ye yathā mām prapadyanthe
    tams tathai'va bhajāmi aham
    mamā vartma'nuvartante
    manusyāh, Pārtha, sarvasāh
          - Bhagavadgita 4.11

In whatever way (devoted) men approach me, in the same way do I return their love. Whatever their occupation and whatever they may be, men follow me in my footsteps.
- R.C. Jaenner, The Bhagavadgita. OUP, 1969.

Bhajāmi means not only returning their love but also "I shall appear to them", according to the other scholars quoted by Jaehnner in his commentary on this verse.

25. Bible Mission Booklet 23, pp. 41-46.

26. Samartha, S.J. "The Unbound Christ, Towards a Christology in India Today", Douglas J.Elwood (ed.) What Asian Christians are Thinking, p. 236.

27. Cf., Mithra, Bible Mission Booklet No. 14, p. 44.

28. Popley, H.A., op.cit., p. 82.

29. Ibid., p. 86.

30. Columbia Discs, Madras, Nos. 45 GE 37588/1971 and SEDE 3831/1974.

Jesus the Teacher

CHAPTER IX

The Pedagogical Methods in the Guru Tradition

1. Devadas, A Born Teacher

Coming from the ancient past there is a tradition in India of holding a teacher in high esteem. A teacher, or guru, is the one who leads people to enlightenment and Vēdānta prescribes that a guru will be needed for anyone who seeks after spiritual reality. Father Devadas was considered a great teacher. He was a born teacher with an original gift and all his adult life he spent in one kind of teaching or other and as we have already said, he spent his old age at the twilight of his life still teaching his followers and giving his messages to those who came to him. When he became too weak to speak aloud even to a small group of listeners he spoke softly to someone sitting next to him and that person would relay his words in a loud voice word by word to the gathered assembly. People who knew the story would often say that he was like John the Elder who in Ephesus was said to have been carried in a chair to the meeting place to say a few words to the people who gathered around to hear his voice.

To start with, Father Devadas had only a high school education. He worked as a school teacher, a boys' school hostel warden, and a teacher in the seminary, holding these jobs one after the other. Although he was offered ordination to become one of the few earliest Indian ministers of the Lutheran Church, he refused to accept because he said he did not feel called for ordained ministry. But his diligent Bible study, his teaching and preaching skills and his facility in English and Telugu languages proved always a great help to him. We are told that he was the author of the earliest English language primer, the kind which in those days were used in the Anglo-Vernacular Schools for Telugu boys[1]. He was also the interpreter, as we have already mentioned, to Sāndhu Sundar Singh when the latter toured Andhra Pradesh and he similarly interpreted to the famous American preacher, Dr. E.Stanley Jones, in those days.

The services of Devadas were certainly used by the Lutheran Church in their earlier Christian Literature programme. It is believed that the early Telugu translations of the Lenten Meditation of Dr. E. Neudoerffer[2] and the commentary on Luther's Small Catechism by J. Stump[3] were done by Devadas. Both these books were printed in the Lutheran Publishing House, Guntur, more than fifty years ago and they are still used very much in Andhra. Since the translator's name was not usually acknowledged in print in those days, we do not find the name of Devadas on these books.

But there are at least 25 booklets available and examined by the present investigator[4], referred to in this work as the Bible Mission Booklets, all of which were either written or dictated by Devadas in his lifetime with one or two exceptions[5]. These exceptions are those booklets written by his followers based on his teachings. All these booklets were published by the Bible Mission in Guntur or Vijaywada.

We have already examined in considerable detail the hymns of Devadas. He was undoubtedly among the few best hymn writers of the Telugu church so far. The Bible Mission Hymn Book, which was entirely one man's work, contains 114 major hymns and a few choruses and bhajans, all of which were written by Devadas in Indian musical styles and melodies. Some of these hymns, as we have seen, have found their way into the Andhra Christian Hymnal, which is the ecumenical humn book of the Telugu speaking churches[6]. In addition to those well-known hymns there are 203 published poetic pieces of Devadas in simple prosody which Telugu literature for several centuries has used to preserve the folklore and the 'mother wit' of the land making it available to the people easily from the community memory system[7].

2. A People of Oral Tradition

Devadas used oral tradition to the best advantage of his teaching because the people he was mainly working with were not literate on the whole, much less were they used to theological or conceptual thinking. Printed books were not easily available in that area. His followers wrote down every word which Devadas spoke in his meetings. They passed on from person to person very faithfully the teachings of their guru. In fact the way his voice was relayed in his old age in the prayer meetings was considered as a kind of parable of what was to happen after his death for the propagation of his message. These messages are copied from the original dictated notes and they are preserved in several places in the country by his followers. In a way this reminds us of the New Testament times.

Hans-Reudi Weber reports an interesting experiment which he tried in Indonesia with oral tradition people trying to teach them the Bible in the very short time available. The 'most exciting discovery', says Weber, 'was a New Bible: the Bible as the story and oral tradition of God's great acts, the Bible as God's picture book, the Bible pointing to the symbols by which God both conceals and reveals Himself'[8]. This is very much like the Bible which Devadas was concerned with in his own way.

As Weber reminds us, the Bible remained a spoken word for centuries before it was committed to print. While appreciating all the advantages which the printing press has brought to the spread and study of the Bible, Weber rightly reminds us of a process which he calls 'liberating the Bible from the Gutenburg capitivity'[9]. After the invention of the printing press, far too much of the Bible study tended to remain with the literate and with the theologians. The common man, the hoi polloi and the village Christian in India, for example, still depended on oral narration. Behind the marriage between missions and schools as Weber says 'is the widespread (though seldom acknowledged) assumption that nobody can become a Christian without being literate. A strange reminder of the demand by Jewish Christians in New Testament times that Gentiles had to be circumcised before being baptized'[10]. But most of the ancient wisdom in India even today is passed on by oral tradition. The Vēdas are meant to be chanted aloud and learnt from mouth to mouth. They are śrutis, the 'heard' revelation. When one considers the common man and the ordinary wisdom of the villages, most of it is still stored in the form of simple proverbs, folklore, myths, poetry and song - a great wealth of oral tradition.

This is why in the meetings of these Indigenous non-White churches like the Bible Mission in India, people like to actually hear the message, they sing the song and celebrate with oral liturgy and body language. As the average Indian schoolboy memorises hundreds of pieces of wisdom-poetry in his childhood the village Christians learn their songs and bhajans and their bhakti chants and they repeat them over and over again with great feeling and fervour. They generally do not need a printed hymn book when they meet for worship.

Weber tells the story of the Egyptian god Teuth, the inventor of writing, as Socrates tells it in Plato's dialogue Phaedrus. According to this story, Thamus the Egyptian king said to Teuth that the invention of letters for writing might be a handicap rather than an advantage in that it would produce forgetfulness in the minds of those who learn to use it because they would not practise memory.

With Jewish people, Weber says, the oral tradition was very important.

> In Jesus' time it was strictly forbidden to transmit and publish the oral law in writing – partly to protect the special place of the written law, which was scrupulously guarded, memorised and copied, partly from the concern to safeguard the transmission and interpretation of the Biblical faith as a living process from the mouth of the teacher to the ear and heart and mind of the disciple[11].

It is precisely for this reason that the Vēdic Hymns of India are taught orally by the gurus to the disciples and thus the accuracy of the texts is believed to be maintained without interpolations and what is more, the personal impact of the guru on the chēla, or the disciple, is most effective that way. It is the same tradition that is largely retained in the methodology of Christian gurus today. The messages are believed to go straight into the hearts and minds of the people by oral teaching. The most interesting form of narrative many times in these circles is the first person story where an individual tells the saga of his conversion or narrates a vision or a dream he has had, or describes some miracle God has worked in the narrator's life.

The word witnessing is common parlance in these indigenous church groups. People are encouraged to tell the story of their conversion experience to others in their prayer meetings. This is not a recorded version nor a written account but each time it is told it comes with new detail, robed in much personal feeling, and in the process, the story gets the maximum credibility and displays great conviction. These preachers have not thrown out 'the baby of the solid content or the bath of the so-called emotion'[12]. Like the art of the black preachers the preaching of these Indian gurus like Devadas is 'not less logical, it is logical on more levels or wavelengths addressing both to the intellect and the feelings'[13].

Talking about the conversion story, or personal witnessing, as it is also called in India, Mitchell has this to say:

> The conversion story is the one story the preacher tells best because he knows it best with or without previous preparation. He tells it effectively because he has to do no research or memorisation to produce the feeling-laden graphic details that make for a meaningful experience[14].

Devadas as a born teacher used this method all his life and his followers successfully continued the tradition of oral communication.

3. Story and Song in the service of Theology

In all the several songs written by Devadas, there is a deep theology wrapped up in the story form and in a style easily understood and quickly memorised by the people. They sing the songs learning them by rote and the words come back to them in their work, in their daily life avocations and in their dreams. The imagery is rich and the pictures familiar. The assembly of believers as God's holy bride, the Heaven as the Father's home, the rejoicing of the faithful at the end as the marriage feast, and in ever so many ways the people make their own mental images and 'the Story' becomes their story in no time with these mental pictures which over the years have become the common property of the community from which each one can draw forth as he or she wants. And the stories of Devadas and the dreams and the visions he narrated to his people communicated his message clearly and imaginatively.

Samuel Rayan, a Catholic theologian from Delhi, in a recent Serampore Convocation address asked a searching question as to why our theological writings whould not speak in wonderful theatrical terms like the performances of Alec McCown at his stage recitals with the Gospel of St. Mark[15]. He insists that the vocation of theology should be the womb for Jesus to continue effectively his entry and birth into our history. But he complains that 'theology in our hands seems to have moved in an anti-incarnational direction'. In other words, the Word became words, the Word which once became flesh has in our hands become 'fleshless words'[16]. He suggests that we 'take a new look at the re-expression of biblical images in paintings and plays, in the works of Wesley, Sahi, Fonseca, Trinidad, Genevieve and others[17], in the illumination and illustration of texts (like the line drawings of the Good News Bible), in stained glass windows and carved cathedral doors no less than in Schulz's Peanut strips and short commentaries on them[18].

One tends to agree with Samuel Ryan when he says that there is a certain 'cerebral tradition to which belongs the awesome scientific apparatus of our theses with their interminable explanations and footnotes'. Explanation 'is the problem of the head', he says. 'It is as the author of the Little Prince who says that explanation is a need of the grown ups who never understand anything themselves, and it is tiresome for children to be always and forever explaining things to them'[19].

We can not do much about it as long as our theological colleges insist on training students in the present rationalistic kind of thinking which, as Samuel Rayan says, in the name of objectivity and science, tends to reduce language to the status of mere medium of information, stripping it of resonances and ambiguities, emotional undertones and historical associations. We forget that the Bible is in story and in parable and in song and image. Devadas and his followers did not go to a theological college and they were not exposed to Aristotelian thinking and so they tell the story in image and parable and poetry. Salvation in the folk tradition in India is sometimes expressed in the image of a ship, like the ships of the old days which carried their travellers to the shores of the other lands more prosperous and beautiful. The Salvation ship has a flag with the sign of the cross flying on its mast, and the boarding pass to get on to the ship is the sacrament of the Holy Baptism and Christ Himself is the captain, as the old Telugu folk song described it[20].

The society in which Devadas worked was not a classist society. So he did not need elitist language. Samuel Rayan rightly reminds us that,

> The conviction is growing that the task of theology is to facilitate the dismantling of the class structure of society since the primordial images with which theology works are those of an egalitarian Divine community (God as Trinity) and of humankind as God's family in earth (the Our Father) in which there can be no division into upper and lower classes, into privileged and underprivileged groups, into under dogs and upper dogs[21].

Devadas and many other small church group leaders may be called pioneers in this kind of egalitarian theology in India, a theology which is not confined to the scholars and to the theological colleges. Popular Hinduism outside the scholarly circles was always propagated by folk art and literary forms, by story and song and myth and imagery, and the church in India will do well to make use of these folk art forms for communication. This in any case is Christ's way of teaching. Advocating the story form as an effective vehicle to theological narration, a theologian like Sallie McFague TeSalle has this to say:

> To see belief not as a set of beliefs but as a story, an experience of coming to belief, means that theological reflection ought itself to be shaped by the story and to take to itself both in form and content, the story. Theological reflection of the sort I have in mind would be narrative and concrete, telling stories. After all, even the creeds, those monuments of doctrinal formulation, do this. From the novelist as well as from the stories in the scripture, the theologian should take courage to concentrate on experiences of coming to belief, not on the 'beliefs' themselves (the sedimentation of experiences of coming to belief). The latter job, the systematic one is necessary always, but the more crucial task for our time - the task that will help people to hear the word of God - is the more difficult one of locating, testing, and understanding of those stories - artistic,

personal, social and political which carry experiences of coming to belief[22].

I am fully convinced that this is what Devadas was doing with the story, concentrating on people's experience of coming to belief. He followed the well known and much tried cultural pattern of communication in India which may not have been accessible to many missionaries of his day. In his interesting book, The Recovery of Preaching, already mentioned above, Henry Mitchell has this advice to give:

> Never fight a war or engage in frontal attack against prevalent culture. It is not only unwise to tackle that which is so well entrenched; it is foolish and damaging to the psyche to try to destroy the world view buried so deeply in people that their identity and living wisdom are tied up in it. If and when people are stripped or bereft of their culture they become pathologically disoriented, in need of institutional care[23].

Devadas seems to have followed this principle by intuition and accepted the culture of the people although not without being critical about it. His use of the mysterious, the miracle and the healing and the dreams and the myth helped the people to relate themselves to the gospel more willingly than they would have done in response to a straight logical preaching of formal doctrine. The preaching methods of Devadas followed more of a person to person approach and he adapted the old āshram pattern to train his preachers, keeping them with him so that they live and learn from him in prayer and in Bible study until he sent them out to carry on the ministry as he himself had done.

4. Catechetical and Analytical Process

Devadas was always aware of the fact that the simple people whom he taught do not have much capacity for conceptualisation. So he used very simple 'step by step methods' of Bible teaching, many times structuring his material as short questions and answers. For example, his teachings on prayer-healing are recorded in the form of questions and answers, as we have seen in his Booklets. The prayer spells to cast out demons[24] are also short bits of prayer to be memorised and said aloud. There are sections in his booklet <u>Mithra</u>, for example[25], in the form of questions and answers, these being actual paraphrases of corresponding sections in Stump's notes on the Catechism of Martin Luther. Devadas of course has learnt this catechetical method of teaching from the study of the Small Catechism and the Large Catechism of Martin Luther in his childhood. Some early European missions in India have also published a few primary booklets in the regional languages for the new converts in catechetical form.

People remembered easily the simple steps from Devadas' catechism. They memorised parts of these texts. It was a great help for them to get the instruction in simple short steps. They recalled the message without difficulty in easy simple and short steps and repeated the same to others.

Talking about the communications value of these indigenous forms, Professor Hollenweger says,

> This is not a primitive but a highly complex mode of communication. Songs and stories, prayer for the sick, pilgrimages, exorcism, conversation with the living dead (in western parlance: ancestors), in short all the elements of oral theology function as a logistic system for passing on theological and social values and information in oral societies in a way which can be likened to a modern computer, because the individual memories can be plugged into the communal memory in such a way that although no one person actively communicates the whole tradition, in principle everybody has access to the total information of the community[26].

Bible Mission is a good example for the process highlighted in this observation. This may be partly the reason why the Bible Mission and such other charismatic groups in India develop into such close-knit communities, members of which are highly supportive of each other and live almost like a single family among a wider society which is often torn apart with caste problem and class differences.

The early missionaries, rightly in their own way, have concentrated on making people literate as part of their mission strategy. They started large scale educational programmes. The mission schools and colleges in India have become very well known like the medical schools and hospitals of the missionaries. Education is quite necessary since illiteracy breeds exploitation and poverty, as Hans-Reudi Weber points out[27]. But Devadas, like many other Indian Christian gurus, has made use of the cultural tools and images--the very icons people have used all along without having to be able to read and write-- and this method became much more meaningful for communication than anything that a book culture could have ever provided.

5. Domesticating or Liberating?

Sometimes Father Devadas is criticised for making people dependent on his teaching and on his revelation too much. The question is asked whether he was not making people 'domesticated' without realising it. Was he giving ready-made answers as his followers sat down and wrote his sermons avidly? It is true today that in Andhra Pradesh there are a handful of his followers who claim to own a faithful record of his teachings. Twenty years after his death there are some people who say that they have some 'inner teachings' of Father Devadas. Many pastors who followed him did not inherit the same charisma for biblical exegesis and for preaching. So the question sometimes is asked whether Devadas was not following the old 'banking method' of education (Paulo Freire) making small deposits, as it were, in the minds of his close followers but doing very little to help them to think for themselves and to inculcate a habit of praxis, reflection and action in them. This may be what is happening to some extent. All saintly men everywhere, and the gurus in India especially, are followed implicitly and their sayings are preserved faithfully and are passed on from generation to generation like a bank deposit. Devadas belonged to that category of leaders whose experience is unique and whose gifts are rare. So people listened to his sayings and preserved his teachings and repeated them faithfully. But how far these teachings have a liberating effect on the listeners in the sense that they could make people produce their own theology is an open question. At least Devadas has encouraged his followers to find out for themselves the answers to their spiritual questions. 'Ask God', was his constant advice both to his followers and his opponents. In another sense also his teaching methods were liberating. In the Bible Mission the preaching of the word of God is not always administered from the top down, 'from the front'. In their prayer meetings every believer is encouraged to pray and to preach, the gift of healing and exorcism is commonly shared by the members of the fellowship, and visions and dreams are claimed by many. The pastors of the Bible Mission do not wear any vestments, not even a simple cassock, and so they can literally sit with the members of their congregations.

Juan Segundo in his five volume study of a <u>Theology for Artisans of a New Humanity</u> has discussed the nature of a dialogical community in great detail, and examined the process by which communication happens in such a dialogical community. Segundo is clearly aware of the possibility of the church sometimes succumbing to 'a process of domestication which thoroughly negates its liberative commitment to the message of Christ'28.

What Segundo is particularly referrring to here is the church's use of the sacraments which sometimes are accepted as means of depositing merit in the believers; but this can also be said about the various other types of ministry in the church, including its teaching ministry. Like the sacraments which sometimes appear as the gifts which the ordained give to the unordained, the wealth of instruction 'delivered' by Father Devadas also was sometimes treated as a bank deposit and it is naturally feared that this could subject his followers to more domestication than to praxis, a creative action.

But much depends on, one would hope, the kind and quality of leadership which now emerges in the decades after the death of Devadas. Some critics have predicted that the movement of Devadas, like many other such movements, will fade out after the founder's death, for lack of leadership. Fortunately, it must be said that these indigenous church groups are not building any empires. Their continuity does not lie in the continuation of their organisational forms or in the finances and their buildings. Their continuity is in the people.

But the question is still valid, To what extent one can find liberating effects in the teaching methods of Devadas? We should admit also that there is another gap which appears in his teaching methods and that is the fact that Devadas did not seem to be much concerned with things temporal except perhaps in the area of physical healing. He did not speak much about social justice, about the problem of poverty and the suffering of the people. He was expecting the imminent return of the Lord and he spoke about the 'wedding feast' in heaven but did not do much about the hungry and the poor around. Segundo is absolutely right in his sharp criticism of this kind of attitude, which we see in the churches in general. He says,

> It would be delusion to pretend that liberation of the <u>individual from sin</u>, expanded in scale could bring about all other needed liberation in an effective, rapid, or realistic way: that there is no need to call into question the sinful socio-political structures which are responsible for the most tangible and urgent enslavements: poverty, hunger, ignorance, exploitation, etc. These can be overcome by an attack on the structure. This is to say the attack must be directed at the source from which they come[29].

To what extent does the Bible Mission prove to be a mission to the poor and the oppressed masses of India? We have yet to see this but Father Devadas, it must be admitted, did not address himself directly to these problems. He did raise questions but his questions are mainly atemporal. Probably one has to remember that Devadas was only a seer and a saint who largely renounced the world and who looked forward to the coming of the Lord to the earth soon. Segundo cautions us that the classic priestly duties, or the methodologies of the charismatic <u>gurus</u> many times, we may add, 'can no longer bring fulfilment to man's whole life if they are not integrated with specific contribution to human liberation'[30]. This is true in India as much as in Latin America.

6. Systematic Theology versus Narrative Exegesis

We said that Devadas had never studied any systematic theology. He was not exposed to the influence of theological colleges except as a language teacher in the seminary and a preacher for a few years. But what he missed in the field of systematic theology, he tried to make up with his Bible study and his interesting exegetical activities. He lived with the Bible and meditated on the biblical texts and came up with useful exegetical notes on some of the books of the Bible. For example, his exposition of the Song of Songs which we have already seen and the commentary on the Book of Revelation and his interpretations of the Book of Daniel are very interesting examples of the exegetical methods of Devadas. He gave a very picturesque interpretation to the words of the Song of Songs. In his teachings he gave interesting allegorical meanings to images such as the anointing oil, the virgin, the upper chamber, the bridal status, the bridegroom, the wine, the tabernacle, the keeper of the vineyards, the flock, and precious jewelry. With the help of profuse cross-references to the biblical texts he made these images come alive to his listeners.

The image of the Holy matrimony, the picture of the lover and the beloved, the archetype of sacrifice and God's accepting it and many such other archetypes from the Bible have been developed by Devadas in his teaching sessions. In this process he brought theology to the level of all God's people, not only of the theologians. We can safely say that 'the social and cultural incarnation of theology is clearly visible'[31] in the teachings of Devadas. His exegesis was not structured like a chain of argument but, it being a narrative exegesis, was like a rope with intertwining of various strands[32].

Devadas on the whole used Bible study methods which contained the 'language of the people', which interpreted the Scriptures in the light of their experience and in the context of their aspirations. In this way, The Story became the people's story in a real sense[33]. His was a language, and a

> word which does not veil the horror of a meaningless existence but which becomes a vehicle by which people remind each other in the

context of this world of the Good News, of the meaning of Jesus Christ for this world[34].

In this sense, when Devadas spoke, it was the grass roots speaking.

Of course Devadas did not have access to the exegetical tools which we have today. He never heard of the necessity of knowing the social setting, the <u>Sitz im Leben</u> of the biblical texts. So when he talked about the Battle of Armageddon, for example, he was not always aware of the full significance of the place Har-Megiddo and its meaning for the people of the times of the Bible. He did not know and he did not also bother, one would think, to find out the situation in which the book of Revelation was written and he was not aware of the social setting in which all the eschatological sayings of the New Testament emerged. Because of all this he tended to spiritualise everything as many preachers generally do. But at least through the imagery and the story he 'liberated the biblical message from the interpretation of a monocultural imperialism' which one mostly finds in the theological colleges and seminaries and their textbooks. His methods are truly indigenous and his pedagogy is the pedagogy of the grass roots.

CHAPTER IX: Notes

1. See Chapter III of this book, Devasahayam, K., Bible Mission.

2. Neudoerffer, E., Lokapapamulu mosikoni povu devuni gorre pilla, The Lamb of God that taketh away the Sins of the World, Guntur: Lutheran Publishing House, n.d.

3. Stump, J., Commentary on Luther's Small Catechism, (Tel).

4. Cf., The list of Bible Mission Booklets, Ch. I of this book.

5. For example, the Jepthah Feast Messages (Booklet 13) are claimed to have been received after the death of Devadas.

6. Cf., Chapter VIII of this book, Hymns in the Bhakti Tradition.

7. The whole series of Shathakas (collections of a hundred poems) is an example in Telugu literature of such a source of wisdom. Writing about Vemana, one of the shathaka writers of the 15th century, Chenchiah says that he is the greatest moral teacher of the Andhras. For well nigh five centuries his shathaka has been the the text book of morals for the Telugu boys and a better book can not be asked for. Chenchiah, P., and Rajah Bujanga Rao, A History of Telugu Literature, p. 99.

8. Weber, Hans-Reudi, Experiments with Bible Study, Geneva: WCC, 1981, p. 4.

9. Ibid., p. 10.

10. Ibid., p. 9

11. Ibid., p.13

12. Mitchell, Henry H., The Recovery of Preaching, London: Hodder and Stoughton, 1977, p. 30.

13. Ibid., p. 32.

14. Ibid., p. 38.

15. Rayan, Samuel, Theology as Art, Religion and Society, Vol. XXVI, No. 2, 1979, pp. 77-90.

16. Ibid., p. 78.

17. These are some Indian Christian artists of the present generation.

18. Rayan, Samuel, op.cit., p. 81.

19. Ibid., p. 78.

20. James Cone cites and comments on a similar song, "The Old Ship of Zion", coming from the Black cultures. Cf. Cone, James H., "Story Content of Black Theology", Theology Today, Vol. XXXII, No. 2, 1975, pp. 146-147.

21. Rayan, Samuel, op.cit., p. 82.

22. Sallie, McFague TeSalle. The Experience of Coming to Belief, Theology Today, Vol. XXXII, op.cit., p. 160.

23. Mitchell, Henry H., op.cit., p. 24. See also Chapter IV, note 6.

24. Bible Mission Booklet No. 2

25. Bible Mission Booklet No. 16

26. Hollenweger, W.J., "Pentecostal and Charismatic Movements", Mircea Eliade (ed.) The Encyclopedia of Religions, to be published.

27. Weber, Hans-Reudi, op.cit., pp. 8, 9.

28. Segundo, Juan Luis, A Theology for Artisans of a New Humanity, Maryknoll, 5 volumes, 1974, Vol. IV, p. 93.

29. Ibid., p. 107.

30. Ibid., p. 108.

31. Hollenweger, W.J., Conflict in Corinth, Memoirs of An Old Man, New York: Paulist Press, 1978. p. 66.

32. Ibid., p. 68.

33. Cf., Brown, Robert McAfee, My Story and "The Story", Theology Today, Vol. XXXII No. 2, 1975.

34. Op.cit., p. 166.

We See Him -
As in A Dream

CHAPTER X

In the Presence of God
(Prayer Worship and Liturgy)

1. The Source Material

Devadas was a man of prayer and he emphasised the importance of prayer in all his teachings. Many times he clearly stated that the special kind of prayer vigilance he was promoting was the foundation of the Bible Mission. Among the Bible Mission publications the following are based entirely on the subject of prayer or have prayer as their main emphasis.

1. Bible Mission Hymn Book, pages iii - x, which contain the order of worship
2. Prārdhana Metlu - The ladder of prayer, Booklet No. 4.
3. Upavāsa Prārdhana Deeksha (A Vow of Fasting Prayer, Booklet No. 5)
4. Upavāsa Prārdhana Prakaranamu (A Chapter on Fasting Prayer, Booklet No. 6).
5. Samarpana Prārdhana (Prayer of Surrender, Booklet No. 7)
6. Rākada Prārdhana Sthuthulu (Prayers and Blessings for the Second Coming of Christ, Booklet No. 8)
7. Rākada Prārdhana Sthuthulu, Part II, (Booklet No. 9).
8. God's Presence (Booklet No. 11)
9. Sannidhi Sampada (The Divine Presence, Booklet No. 24)

In these publications fully and in other booklets more sparingly Devadas dealt with the subject of prayer. So nearly half of whatever is available in print of the writings of Devadas is on the subject of prayer. His teaching on Divine healing, his discourses on dreams and visions and many other special features of the Bible Mission are directly related to prayer life.

2. Daiva Sannidhi, The Presence of God

Daiva Sannidhi is a well known expression which the followers of Devadas frequently use. The word sannidhi refers to both the place and the act. It is first a place, like the audience chamber of a king or the temple of God. The word comes from the biblical understanding of 'Shekina', the Presence of God, a word derived from the verb meaning 'to dwell'[1]. R.D. Immanuel reminds us that the Indian philosophy does not give a high place to the body. So the Hindu thinks that it must be silenced. In the presence of the Infinite, therefore, the individual should wait silently[2]. Therefore in the prayers of a Hindu, silence plays a great part. Mahatma Gandhi always kept every Monday as a day of silence. He never spoke to anyone on these days of silence[3].

Many Christian saints like Sādhu Sundar Singh in India practised the period of silence as a habit. A.J. Appasāmy and many other Christian leaders have advocated the practice of silent meditation for the followers of Christ. So Devadas knew what he was talking about when he promoted the practice of Sannidhi, the 'presence'. It is the practice of waiting before God in prayer. There are four kinds of sannidhi which the Bible Mission practises today and these are clearly prescribed by Devadas.

    i) Ekāntha sannidhi, the individual waiting,
    ii) Dhyāna sannidhi, meditative waiting,
    iii) Kūta sannidhi, waiting in small groups, and
    iv) Eduguri sannidhi, waiting of seven people.

Briefly we summarise here the teaching of Devadas on these four kind of 'waiting' prayer:

i) Ekāntha sannidhi:

This should be done early in the morning. Father Devadas himself observed this practice all through his life at least two hours daily (see Mark 14.37). Two hours is what Devadas advocated. While you are still in bed, make praises to God in the words of Rev. 1.6. Then wash your feet and hands and face and change your clothes and go to an appointed place and kneel down and just look at the face of the Lord in your mind. No thoughts whatsoever should be allowed to come into your mind. Simply wait and in your own mind look at the face of the Lord as you would look into the camera lens as your picture is taken[4]. Praise the Lord three times and say, Lord, show yourself to me and speak to me and also speak to all who seek you[5]. Then do not speak any more but wait. This is ēkāntha sannidhi.

Many prophets and sages have observed this practice all through the ages and the Church today has forgotten it, Devadas complained. Unless the prophets waited in God's presence thus, they would not have been able to receive God's messages. While thus the Lord gave the messages to them as they waited, they wrote them down and we have to do the same thing today, write down what the Lord gives to us as a message for the day. The followers of the Bible Mission who could read and write followed this advice. The greatest tragedy of the present-day churches according to Devadas is that the 'waiting in prayer' is no more a part of the regular programme. He thought that the church in India as a body had failed to pay much attention to this vital habit[6]. In one hour of such waiting prayer, many of your questions will be answered, said Devadas, and many doubts will be cleared.

Devadas also recommends this kind of prayer to people of all faiths, to people of 'any religion, any caste, any denomination, even people who do not have any religion can practise this waiting before God'. (Sadhu Sundar Singh was not a Christian when he first prayed and waited and God appeared to him). Devadas thought that it was a remedy for several of our spiritual problems such as:

> unwillingness to listen to the word of God,
> love of sinful life,
> inability to resist a secret sin,
> loss of desire to read the Bible,
> lack of faith or a spirit of despair,
> impatience, jealousy, finding excuses for laziness in prayer,
> misusing God's grace, etc.

Devadas comments on each of these problems and how they can hinder the spiritual life of a person and prescribes the habit of waiting on the knees as a remedy for all these ills. Those who practise the 'presence' will find their strength renewed, they will rise on wings like an eagle's, they will run and not be weary, they will walk and not grow weak (Isa. 40.30-31). They will always grow in spiritual life and waiting in prayer is like the bride's chamber where the believer prepares to meet the Lord. It is the place of the heavenly meal, a meal with honey and honey comb, a drink of wine and milk (Song of Songs 3, 4, 5). It is the garden where the Lord meets his beloved. Waiting is needed if we need an answer from our Lord. Pontius Pilate asked a question but he did not wait for the answer.

The disciples were asked to wait and watch in the garden of Gethsemane (Mark 14). They were also asked to wait in Jerusalem for the baptism of the Holy Spirit (Acts 1.4). Those who practice this kind of waiting will be prepared as Esther was prepared to meet the king (Esther 2). Christ imparts his own glorious brightness to those who wait as the sun imparts his bright colours to the flowers[7].

Devadas prescribed that the waiting in prayer should first be practised for 40 days without break after the example of Christ Himself. Christ fasted and prayed for forty days in the wilderness. If this chain of forty days is broken for some reason, the efficacy will be lost and the chain should be started again. And in this waiting we always seek God's will, we seek God's kingdom silently.

ii) Dhyāna sannidhi; Waiting in meditation:

Devadas is here referring to a practice of meditating on a Scripture passage after reading it. This practice is possible at any time of day. As one meditates on the Scripture one gets deeper messages from the word of God. It is not the intellect that is at work at such times but it is the spirit.

iii) Kūta sannidhi; The small group in waiting:

This is done by the believers in small groups. Devadas suggested odd number of people like three, five or seven to be in such prayer groups. Odd numbers are considered auspicious for any important enterprise in India. We do not know whether Devadas was influenced by this Hindu idea but this suggestion is simply accepted by the followers of Devadas. There are only three conditions prescribed for the practice of this kind of meeting.

- a) Empty your minds of all thoughts when you meet,
- b) Do not be too anxious for an 'experience' as such,
- c) Share your experience when you get it, with other members of the fellowship.

This practice of the believers waiting in prayer can lead them 'from the outer courts of the temple, through the holy place and into the Holy of the Holies'. It is like being in the company of the 24 elders mentioned in the Book of Revelation, sitting with them around the throne of God in Heaven. To come to this stage, Devadas commends dhyāna sannidhi every day. When counting the number of participants you can always count with you God, the Angels, the saints of heaven and the living saints in their spirits, said Devadas. All of these or any of them will be present with you in such a prayer. So even if you are alone you are still in company in prayer.

3. How to Conduct these Sannidhi Meetings

When you come to the kūta sannidhi, the group prayer, you should be punctual because God the Father, Father Devadas in spirit and the other spirits will arrive at the appointed time and they should not be kept waiting[8]. There should be no disorderliness or irregularity at these meetings because the heavenly beings cannot tolerate such things[9].

Michael Ramsey speaks about the fellowship between the Church on earth and the Church in heaven and the Church in Paradise all in one place in such prayers. it is a communion of earth and heaven[10]. When people come to these sannidhi meetings, Devadas prescribes the following:

a) Bodily Cleanliness: Usually there is a trough of water at the entrance of the meeting places of the Bible Mission and every person coming in will wash his feet at the entrance and then come in and squat on straw mats spread on the floor.

b) Cleanliness of Garments: People generally wash their clothes daily at home and dry them in the sun in India because it is considered improper to come to the presence of God in working clothes that have not been washed that morning. I have seen some people participating in the church service on Sunday mornings sometimes standing outside the compound wall in Ethiopia in the Orthodox Church. I am told that these people would abstain from entering the church if they were bodily 'unclean'. A woman in the menstrual period or a man who had sexual intercourse the previous night would consider themselves 'unclean' and they worshipped outside the church.

c.) Cleanliness of Food: Clean food habits as a way of life are considered necessary for those who wait in prayer. Meat is avoided as far as possible. Devadas advised that pork should be avoided but chicken is allowed, especially if it is a cock reared at home at least for one week before dressing. Certainly no alcholic drinks of any kind are considered good. Smoking and chewing betel leaves are both forbidden.

d.) Clean Place of Worship: The place of worship should not be cluttered with furniture, tools, etc. Even in small poor houses, a clean corner is set aside if at all possible swept and ready.

It is almost certain that Devadas borrowed some of these external cleanliness ideas from Hinduism. As Immanuel reminds us,

> The Hindu gives a great deal of attention to certain external details. If used with caution such external ideas are of great help in worship

experience. Before going to public places of worship, the Hindu insists on washing his mouth, cleaning his teeth, bathing the whole body and absolute abstention from any food.

Immanuel further reports that:

> this custom is honoured among the Tamil Christians. They hestitate to take even a sip of water before going to church to partake of communion[11].

Writing on the subject of Indigenization of Worship and its Psychology, S.P. Adinarayana also says,

> Preparatory purification has played an important part in the Hindu worship. We Indian Christians on the whole tended to neglect this side. The tank before the temple performs both a real and symbolic function. The Christian has somewhat been unwilling to emphasise this aspect perhaps due to unconscious fear that it may create in the minds of the worshippers the idea that they become acceptable to God through their own personal efforts[12].

Even very early in the history of the church in India we see this influence coming from Hinduism. Roberto De Nobili of the 17th century reports thus:

> It was the custom among the Gentiles to wash the body on getting up, or before meals, after marital union, and before going to the temple and this custom was, as I shall show later, kept up by the Christians[13].

In addition to these major stipulations laid down by Devadas in the matter of sannidhi there are many sundry instructions to those who want to practise this[14]. He said that the members of these prayer groups should be able to maintain confidentiality, each member should also practise ekantha sannidhi, the individual prayer life, every day before daybreak. When they assemble for group meditation, they should sit in rows, keep silent, sing quietly, make the sign of the cross on their bodies and start their own prayer first. They should then recite the prayers to dispel Satan[15], because he should not be allowed to disturb the prayer meetings. Then should follow the prayers for the second coming of the Lord[16], upon which the members of the group should pray for the whole creation. All these steps should be completed in about half an hour. (None of these prayers are intended to be used as prayers read from the book but people may memorise them or use the main thoughts from these learnt prayers).

Then the members of the group should consult among themselves if there is any concern for which they all should pray and seek an answer. They pray together about it and then wait for the answer. One member may get a vision as they wait, one may hear a voice, another may be reminded of a Scripture verse, yet another may unknowingly start singing a verse from a known song. All these responses can be meaningful for the occasion and can be the different ways God is answering that particular prayer. If there is consistency in the answers, then it may be concluded that it is God's answer to the prayer. If there is difference in the meaning they give to the message received, then the members should pray again until they get a coherent and consistent answer from God.

If possible, Devadas asks people to stay together for a full day in these prayers. They should follow six vigils as follows:

Early in the morning before sunrise
Morning after the day break
Noon time
After noon as the sun goes down
At bed time, and
Midnight[17].

4. Practising the Presence of God, a Gift to the Bible Mission

Devadas claimed that this practice of the waiting in prayer was a special revelation granted to the Church and to the world at large through the Bible

Mission. In the Booklet on practising the presence of God, mentioned above[18], there are ten sermons of Devadas recorded on the subject of prayer. Some of the main points in these messages can be briefly summarised as follows:

>God's presence comes down to us and we are also spiritually lifted into His presence.
>
>Enoch was taken up by the presence of God and he lived in fellowship with God, (Gen. 5.22).
>
>God's presence came to Noah and spoke to Him.
>
>God's presence came down to Abraham first when he was called out of his land and from his father's house. Then one day God himself received hospitality from Abraham and thus granted him His presence, under the sacred trees of Mamre.
>
>God's presence spoke to Abraham also about Sodom and Gomorrah.
>
>God visited Jacob in a dream and Jacob called the place Bethel, which means God's presence, God's house.
>
>God came down to speak to Moses in the burning bush as well as on the mount Sinai. Moses spent forty days with God on the mountain. (Again the magic number forty appears; this is a significant number for many things in the Indian way of thinking. It is called mandala, a forty day period.)

All these instances to Devadas are very real. They happened in the Bible and they can happen today too. To him the most important Old Testament story in many ways is the story of Jacob wrestling with God in the night (Gen. 32.22-30). This incident provided to Devadas a metaphor with a 'high degree of development'[19] to teach about prayer and waiting. Prayer thus is wrestling with God and not a mere passive experience to Devadas. It is prevailing upon God to ask his blessing. It is a real encounter with God and taking risks with Him (Jacob broke his hip in the process).

Devadas mentions several sannidhi groups active in his day in different parts of Andhra Pradesh.

The Eternal Life group in Guntur
The Little Virgin group in Vijayawada
The Revelation group in Elur
The Holy Presence group in Tadepalligudem
The Advent Prayer group in Kakinada

This is quite an impressive row of names with meanings. The meanings of names are significant to the Indian mind.

In Booklet 10, <u>Sannidhi Sampada</u> (The Treasure of His Presence), there is a section on the waiting hour, and Devadas writes the same things there about prayer with some additional hints. He suggests,

> After you kneel down and clear your mind of all straying thoughts, and after you confess your sins, then ask God to appear to you and speak to you. Then just wait in His presence and see what happens. He may appear to you and He will speak to you and answer your questions. Write down on a piece of paper what He tells you.
>
> Sometimes God may send His angels and they will speak to you and answer your questions. Write them down for your guidance. At other times He may send some saints from heaven. They will speak to you and answer your questions. Write their answers for your guidance.
>
> Sometimes He will send to you some living saints from somewhere on the earth. They will speak to you and answer your questions. Write what they say for your guidance.
>
> Sometimes He will send the spirits of the non-believers. They will speak to you and answer your questions. You write down what they say. Then He may send to you the spirits from the under-world. They will speak to you and answer your questions. Write down what they say.
>
> God may send Satan also to you. Satan will speak to you and he will answer your questions. Write down what he says. Then the Lord Himself will come and He will comfort you so that you are no longer afraid of the devil nor would you believe his words[20].

The whole narration runs like a song and these words are repeated by the followers of Devadas. One can see reflections of biblical narrative here, for example, Christ's prayer in the wilderness, the temptation of Satan, and the angels coming to serve him.

5. God's Promise to Answer Prayer

In Booklet No. 3, Vāgdāna Manjari[21] Devadas recalls several promises made by God to answer prayer. These are his remarks on some of them:

1. I will never turn away anyone who comes to me (John 6.37), the door is always open to anyone however sinful he may be. There is no condition to God's promise.
    It is Satan who causes hindrances and creates doubts in our hearts. When Satan shouts at us, creating fear and doubt, we should close our ears and show him the Scripture verse with our finger and thus we enter the presence of God.

This is a picture from Pilgrim's Progress which Devadas must have read many times.

This is what John Bunyan writes in Pilgrim's Progress describing how Pilgrim escapes the shouts of the tempters:

So I saw in the dream that the man began to run. Now he had not run far from his own door but his wife and children perceiving it, began to cry after him to return, but the man put his fingers in his ears and ran on, crying, Life, Life, Eternal Life. So he looked not behind him[22].

2. Ask and you shall receive: Ask and you shall receive, seek you shall find and, knock and it shall be opened to you (Mat. 7.7). You do not have what you want because you do not ask God for it (James 4.2). We must ask God and actually take what we ask from Him. This

verse does not limit what we may ask and so we can ask God for anything.

3. When you pray to God for something, believe that you have received it (Mark 11.24).

    When you pray, Go to your room, close the door, and pray to your Father, your Father will reward you (Mat. 6.6).

4. We pray night and day and God will answer (Luke 18.7).

This, to Devadas, is the meaning of pleading prayer that waits for an answer from God. All-night prayers are not unknown to the Bible Mission.

5. There is nothing difficult for God to do in answer to our prayers (Jer. 32.37).

6. If you ask me anything in my name, I will do it, said Jesus (John 14.14). Here Devadas comments on the expression 'in my name'. The name of Christ is power. All earthly obstacles will disappear when the name of Jesus is uttered. Obstacles come only from the devil. He and all the evil spirits run away when they hear the name of Jesus. Thus when the evil spirits run away, the obstacles and other psycho-somatic problems. Even as we recite the name of Jesus He will come and stand in our midst and when He comes the evil spirits cannot stand there any longer. Here we see the influence of Sundar Singh's writings on Devadas again. Sundar Singh reports many dreams in which he saw the unrepenting sinners running away from the glory of God because the brightness of the heavenly light was unbearable to their eyes.

Nāma-japa, reciting the name of gods for protection, is a Hindu practice. Simple uttering of the name of God has power and even uttering God's name unintentionally will have its effects and can take a dying man into heaven. Some of my Hindu classmates in high school used to write the name of a god 10 million times over many months in small writing in a specially ruled notebook and when the book was filled they would offer it in a holy shrine or a temple for merit.

Of course Devadas did not believe in any such automatic effects in reciting Christ's name but what he is suggesting here is an oral prayer even if the person does not get many words to utter.

In all this we can see three aspects of prayer life, as indicated in Matt. 18.19-20. First there is the fellowship of the believers, secondly there is the presence of the Lord with them, and thirdly there is the promise that the Lord would do what we ask. Devadas, however, is aware of the fact that God sometimes does not answer the prayers to do what His children ask[23]. Devadas gives some reasons for that:

> there may be hidden sin in our hearts,
> there may be doubt about God's power to answer prayer,
> there may be hesitation on our part to accept God's forgiveness after we confessed our sins,
> looking at ourselves, as Peter did, instead of looking at the Lord,
> God's answer may be delayed in reaching us because of the evil powers.

This last mentioned point is very interesting and the full comment of Devadas on this point may be useful. This is what he says:

> God's answer to prayer is sometimes naturally delayed because our prayers should pass through the second heaven into the third heaven to reach the throne of God. And God's answer on its way back should come through the second heaven, which is the home of the devils. Satan and his angels who live there will cause obstacles for God's answer to come to us. The answer to Daniel's prayer was thus delayed for three weeks because Gabriel who was bringing that answer was stopped for that length of time on the way. There was also war in heaven (Ephesians 2.2, 6.12). At that time Michael had to come and deliver Gabriel from the Persian ruler (Dan. 10.3).

Devadas knew his Bible even if his exegesis is not always very familiar to us.

6. Climbing the Ladder

Climbing the steps is a familiar image of spiritual growth in India. Many temples of the Hindu gods are on the hills and there are seven hills for some of the deities and there are also 666 steps to lead the devotees up to them. The climbing in itself is an act of worship. The Bible too talks about the ladder in the story of Jacob and the angels go up and down on this ladder. So it is not strange that Devadas used the image of the ladder and the rungs to teach about the progress in prayer life.

One of the Bible Mission Booklets has this title, The Ladder of Prayer[24]. In this, Devadas suggests a method of prayer consisting of successive steps starting with the emptying of the mind of all thoughts and leading through confession of sins, surrendering of self, petition, praise and ending with silent waiting. We do not know how far this order is generally followed by his followers but at least Devadas helped people to see what is involved in prayer and the place of each stage in the act of prayer. Devadas himself was known to have followed these steps carefully. In the last pages of this booklet he cites the names of 80 people in the Bible who prayed to God and received the answer to their prayers.

These teachings of Devadas on prayer had considerable impact on the prayer life of Christians in that area both within the Bible Mission and outside. If there was any one major point of contact between the followers of the Bible Mission and the members of the mission churches it was in the area of the prayer meetings and waiting sessions in prayer.

7. Does God need a Chair to come and Sit with Us?

Mention has already been made of a chair we sometimes see in the meeting places of the Bible Mission groups, always empty, covered with a white cloth and ready for occupancy[25]. The significance of the chair is somewhat enigmatic. Sometimes it is considered as a seat kept ready for the spirit of Devadas to come and sit in their prayer meetings. At other times it is thought that God or His saints would come and sit there. This is what a devout follower of Devadas says on the subject[26]:

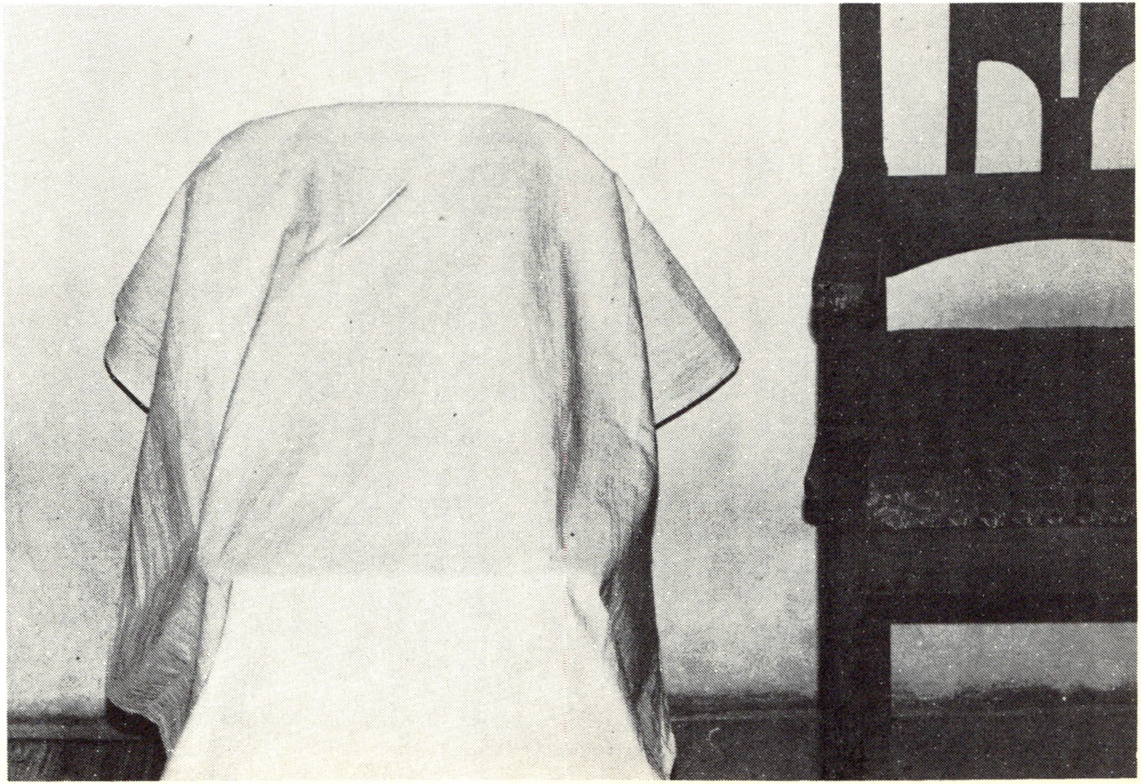

A Seat for the Spirit of Devadas Awaiting at the Prayer Meetings

We are the members of the Bible Mission wait daily for one hour in the presence of God (Mark 14.37). Father Devadas has taught us to wait thus for God's voice to be heard. He also taught us to keep a chair ready for the Lord or the saints to come and be seated. Some people have misunderstood this practice and we want to say a few things about it to dispel the misunderstandings.

1. God came to visit Abraham and Abraham gave water for Him to wash His feet and He rested under the tree (Gen. 18.1-14). This means God sat with Abraham.
2. God met Moses and spoke to him from above the lid of the arc of covenant between the two winged creatures (Ex. 25.22).
3. At Bethany, the Lord was seated to teach Mary and Mary sat at His feet (Luke 10.39).
4. The disciples brought a colt for the Lord to sit on and they spread their clothes on the colt for him to sit on (Matt. 21.7).
5. The Lord sat with the disciples for a meal in the upper room (John 13.4).
6. Today we are told that the Lord sat with Sādhu Sundar Singh to talk to him as Sundar Singh learnt at the master's feet.

So, the writer concludes,

Whenever two or three gather together in the name of the Lord, He is there with them. Therefore we keep a chair in respect for the Lord, to honour Him. It is necessary for those who love Him, thus to honour Him.

In the Old Testament, the prophets and the holy men were honoured by householders who offered them the comfort of a room to stay with a bed, a table, a chair and a lamp. When the heavenly saints come to our prayer meetings, it is but proper that we should respect them and give them a chair.

In our hymns we sing that Peter and all the apostles are the members of our assembly[27]. That means the saints sit with us in prayer.

Therefore it is perfectly proper and necessary for us, worshippers to keep a chair ready for the heavenly visitors.

8. A Liturgy for the Folk Church

The prayer meetings and the Sunday worship services of the Bible Mission are of a simple structure. It is wrong to say that they are unstructured. It is only a different kind of structure from what the mission churches are familiar with. Many times the liturgies are simple and are not committed to writing but people follow the order of worship by habit. The pastors and the preachers have not passed through any theological colleges and so they have not learnt any formal liturgical structures or rubrics. Many of the worshippers in these prayer meetings come from a Hindu background. Having become new converts they belong to a pre-literary culture and they were not used to written liturgies. They memorise Bible texts and songs and greetings and blessings which form part of their worship.

However there is a special form of worship printed in the Bible Mission Hymn Book which is believed to have been given by Devadas himself[28]. It is basically the same order of worship used by the Andhra Evangelical Lutheran Church. Starting with the Invocation and the Introit and leading through exhortation, confession and absolution and the familiar place for the Scripture lessons and the sermon, it is almost like its parent, the Lutheran order of worship. But the Bible Mission does not follow a set lectionary and they do not follow a Church year. There are three lessons generally and Devadas taught that the Old Testament lesson should be read with God the father in mind; the New Testament lesson, with God the Son; and the Epistle lesson, with God the Holy Spirit.

The creed of the Bible Mission is an elongated version of the old Apostle's creed. The eschatological section is especially lengthened by Devadas to include all his teachings about the war of Armageddon, the thousand years' rule of Christ, etc., etc.

9. Fellowship of Saints

We believe in the communion of saints--this is a key thought in the teachings of Devadas in the context of Christian worship and therefore it needs a special mention. It is not only the living saints who participate in our worship but also the departed saints, and the continued existence of these souls and their participation with us in our activities is a major tenet of the Bible Mission. This idea of the existence of spirits appears in their teaching on demons, demon possession, speaking of the spirits through the worshippers, hearing some voices in prayer, and even in visions.

This belief in spirits is not just a remnant of the old Hindu demonology but it is an inevitable result of the faith in life after death as promised in the resurrection of Jesus Christ, a part of the hope in life to come for these people. Devadas quotes St. Paul several times on this subject and especially the passage in his Corinthian letter (I Cor. Ch. 15). Therefore the fellowship of saints is an accepted idea at every prayer meeting of the Bible Mission.

Devadas did not teach much about the sacrament of the Holy Communion although it is regularly observed in the prayer meetings. On the other hand, Devadas spoke about the communion the Lord Himself will administer to his children. Twice he mentioned a vision in which he saw a table covered with a white cloth descending from heaven and the Lord Himself coming down to feed the bread and wine to him in one of these visions and at another time to a woman believer. At such times Devadas claimed to have seen the departed saints also. He sometimes spoke of the 'heavenly curtains' and those who are 'on the other side' of the curtains. At times these narratives of Devadas become vary vague and unclear.

There is one hymn among the works of Devadas on the subject of the Lord's supper. In that he suggests that participation at the Lord's table will lead to forgiveness of sins and spiritual healing, and that it will prepare the believer for the Lord's second coming.

Although Devadas believed that the departed souls and saints will be present with us in our prayers and at the Eucharist, he never suggested that they will ever be our messengers to take our prayers to God. On the other hand the spirits and the saints to him are our fellow-worshippers coming to us from God and sometimes bringing to us His messages and answering our questions and guiding us. Archbishop Michael Ramsey clearly makes a distinction between the thought that the saints are our benefactors and that of their being our fellow-worshippers. He says,

> If our prayer is shaped by our own needs and requests, then we may slip into thinking of the saints as those who answer our prayers by dispensing favours to us. If, however, our prayer is shaped by the giving of glory to God in the quest of His will and kingdom, then we may be lifted out of ourselves in the company of those who in Paradise and in heaven seek that glory and reflect it[29].

It is the latter kind of prayer and worship and the fellowship of saints which Devadas advocated and practised in his life.

10. Prayer of the Church

In the concluding general prayer of the simple liturgy suggested by Devadas, we see some interesting deviations from the usual practice. Some of the petitions in the general prayer run like this:

> Lord, reach with your good news people of all religions. Deliver us from religious strifes, and denominational quarrels, controversies, from wrong teachings, from temptation, from sin and from the fruits of sinful life. Fill your children with your spirit and prepare them for your second coming[30].

Among the intercessory prayers there are prayers for the 'families of the world, for the poor, for all the institutions of the church and specially for the Bible Society'. There is a prayer for all the trades of the world and God is asked to

> mercifully look upon all the heavenly bodies, the animals the trees and the crops of the land and all creation[31].

And finally Devadas pleads in this prayer,

> let no one blame you, Lord, that you have not blessed this or that article, or this or that living creature[32].

For Devadas, the whole creation is under God's care and there is no difference between the living creature and the non-living thing. There is also no difference to him between human beings and other creatures as far as God's care and love are concerned. God's care and love also include all those who know Him as well as those who do not know Him.

All prayers both liturgical and otherwise of the people of the Bible Mission in any situation are offered in the name of Christ. In fact the prayers are addressed to Christ. Devadas prayed to Christ and he lived in prayer and taught his followers to pray without ceasing. In fact prayer life is one of the great contributions of the Bible Mission to the simple followers. Waiting in prayer as advocated by Devadas could prove a re-discovery of the source of strength to the churches in India.

CHAPTER X: Notes

1. Caird, G.B., The Language and the Imagery of the Bible, p. 75.

2. Immanuel, R.D., Influence of Hinduism on Indian Christians, p. 50.

3. Ibid., p. 49.

4. UpavāsaPrārdhan Deeksha, Booklet No. 5, p. 4.

5. See also Booklet No. 13, Jepthah Feast Messages, p. 23.

6. God's Presence, Booklet No. 11, p. 7.

7. Booklet No. 13, op.cit., p. 24.

8. Ibid., p. 28.

9. The Telugu word 'akramamu' means simply dis-order and it refers to all kinds of disorder including untidy surroundings.

10. Ramsey, Michael, Be Still and Know, p. 114.

11. Immanuel, R.D., op.cit., p. 50.

12. Adinarayana, S.P., Indian Journal of Theology, Vol. V., No. 2, p. 29.

13. Rajamanickam, S., s.j., Roberto De Nobili on Adaptation, p. 41.

14. See Booklet No. 13, op.cit., p. 27.

15. Booklet No. 2, Sāthānu-nedirinchuta (Resisting Satan).

16. Booklets 8 and 9, Prayers and Praises for the Second Coming.

17. Booklet No. 5, Upavāsa Prārdhana Deeksha (A Vow of Fasting Prayer).

18. Booklet No. 24, Daiva Sānnidhyamu, (The Presence of God).

19. Caird, G.B., op.cit., p. 155.

20. Booklet No. 10, Sannidhi Sampada (The Treasure of God's Presence), pp. 14-16.

21. Booklet No. 3, Vāgdāna Manjari (A Row of Promises).

22. Bunyan John, Pilgrim's Progress, p. 13.

23. Booklet No. 5, op.cit., p. 34.

24. Booklet No. 4, Prārdhana Metlu (Steps in Prayer).

25. See Chapter III of this book.

26. Booklet No. 24, op.cit., pp vii, viii, Introduction by Mrs. Grace Yēsuratnam (Gresamma)

27. Andhra Christian Hymnal No. 435.

28. Booklet No. 1, Telugu Kraisthava Keerthanalu (Telugu Christian Hymns) pp iii - x.

29. Ramsey, M., Be Still and Know, p. 118.

30. Bible Mission Booklet No. 1, p. ix.

31. Loc.cit.

32. Loc.cit.

Christ With the Refugees

CHAPTER XI

The Ethical Views - A Community Unto the Lord

1. Concept of a Holy God

The foundation for all the teachings of Devadas on Christian life and witness was his understanding of God as Holy. To say that God is Holy to him was to consider Him as a consuming fire so utterly transcendent and unapproachable that even the angels cannot look at Him. He quotes Isa. 6.3, Lev. 19.2, I Pet. 1.14-16, etc., while talking about the Holy nature of God. This idea of God's Holiness appears again and again in the writings of Devadas and the thought dominates his teachings. Since God is Holy, it follows that He cannot be the cause of sin in any sense and He cannot tolerate sinfulness in His children. The word parishudha in Telugu means 'utterly clean' and in the context of God and godliness it means a moral and ethical holiness. In one of his hymns[1] Devadas sings:

> How can the Holy God ever be the cause of sin?
> If the Holy One Himself were to lead mankind into sin would He Himself not be a sinner too?
> How can a mother lead her children astray?
> How can the creator lead His own creation into sin?

On the other hand, God delivers mankind from sin and His children are advised to pray to Him daily and ask Him to lead them away from sin. They should ask Him to make a fence around them 'as He made one around His servant Job'[2].

The Holiness of God to Devadas was primarily moral holiness but it is not separated from the idea of numinous Holiness, the sheer distance and unapproachableness of God. He sometimes spoke of the veils dividing heavenly beings from him as he entered into prayer and had visionary experiences. That is why he strictly enjoined the faithful to wash their feet carefully when they came to prayer and to change their clothing. God does not come to have fellowship with His children in untidy places. Even the saints who come to us to have fellowship with us in prayer will not tolerate unclean surroundings and atmosphere[3]. Similarly in another of his Hymns, Devadas says,

> Cleanliness of body and belly
> are important when we come to God.
> But more important than these
> is the cleanliness of heart.

Thus to Devadas, God is Holy and He wants His children to be holy in body, mind and spirit. He can impart His own Holiness to His people as the sun imparts his colours to the flowers. This is the image Martin Luther also had used while talking about how God would enable His children to do His will. Paul Althaus summarises Luther's teaching on the subject in these words:

> Christ, who has fulfilled the law, dwells in the hearts of Christians and motivates and enables them to fulfill the law. The Gospel has made the law a lovely thing for man. This is the great miracle of transformation which God's spirit works in man's heart[4].

2. The Dreadfulness of Sin

Devadas considered sin very real and dreadful. In contrast to the Holiness of God is the sinful nature of man, and man needs deliverence. In another hymn which Devadas wrote[5] on the theme of the return of the Prodigal Son, he reflects the thoughts of every repenting sinner in the following words:

> There is not a single sane path in me, O Father
> I am worthy to die
> And I am deceived by the Devil
> and got lost in the world.

Sin leads to death and it is the tempter, the devil, who leads men into sin. Devadas cites Scripture verses to support this view and he asks his people to seek God's holiness:

> The heart is wicked, Jer. 17.9, Mark 7.21, 22
> Man is tempted by his own evil desires, James 1.14, 16
> We desire to do what is good but we actually do what is evil, Rom. 7. 18-19
> As God is Holy we should also be Holy, Isa. 6.3, Lev. 19.2

To Devadas, to love anything more than God is sin. The whole law to him, as it was to Martin Luther, is based on this one commandment, that we should love God with all our heart. In the Small Catechism, Martin Luther prefaced the explanation of all the commandments with a paraphrase of the first commandment--we must so love and fear God, etc. If we can love God, we can keep all the commandments[6]. In his own life, Devadas lived a simple life not cluttered with any worldly possessions because he thought that these are all obstacles which hinder us from loving God. He insisted that the faithful should lead a simple and exemplary life in this world and consider themselves as pilgrims in this life.

Idol worship is a great sin according to Devadas. It is breaking the first commandment to worship idols. Sacrifices to demons and spirits, magic and spirit worship are abominable in God's sight. In the land where Devadas lived there was worship of many sundry gods and goddesses and Devadas looked at it as a great sin which taints the soul because it is open unfaithfulness to the living God. He believed that those who worshipped idols 'will go into the lake of fire' (Rev. 21.8) and they are only 'outside the city' and hence cannot partake the heavenly glory (Rev. 22.15).

Commenting on the second commandment, Devadas suggested that quoting Scriptures irreverently is sin just as swearing by God's name is sin. To take oaths in the law courts and other public witness situations is not good for a Christian and it is sinful to be late to the worship services and to read newspapers and worldly books on Sundays. To neglect prayer in any way will constitute the breaking of the third commandment, according to Devadas. There is no doubt that some of these puritanic ideas came to Devadas from the teachings of the missionaries of those days, when schoolboys in mission schools were not allowed any but white clothes to the church on Sundays. Devadas believed that man has a responsibility before God for his own body and any neglect of the body is sinful as well as carelessness of the welfare of others is sinful. All these will amount to the breaking of the law. In his Booklet Mithra, Devadas makes a list of 41 kinds of sin and cites 28 Bible texts to illustrate his views on sin[7]. To him, sin is unclean and unethical conduct in the sight of God. He followed Martin Luther's small catechism in interpreting the Law.

On the subject of good works, Devadas however says that these are necessary for the believer but they cannot win salvation for him. Once saved through faith in Christ, man grows into the state of holiness. But many times, the followers of Devadas looked at these as temporally separated events. It is God who should protect us from sin and temptation and He has to deliver us from evil. It is He who enables us to do His will. This is how Devadas expressed this thought in another Hymn[8]:

> Who is He that gives me wisdom
> so that I may know my duty to God,
> Who is He that gives me strength
> to accomplish that duty and who
> gives me faith?

To Devadas the answer in each case is: No one but Jesus the crucified. A Holy life is impossible outside Christ. Commenting on the whole armour of God (Eph. 6.10f), Devadas clearly states that it is God's protection that can save us from temptation and not our own strength. In the process of forgiveness and what happens after that Devadas sees three categories of people: those who repent and relapse again into sin like the Pharaoh, those who never repent at all because they do not believe in God's forgiving love, like Judas Iscariot, and those who believe in Him and repent and are saved like the Apostle, Peter[9]. In this booklet on the Fasting Prayer, Devadas has written nine prayers, each one for a commandment of the decalogue, asking

God to help to obey and carry out that commandment. In each of these prayers he makes mention of our everyday problems from which God should save us. For example in the seventh prayer he says:

> God, we ask you to forgive those who give trouble to the travellers and those who rob the women of their jewelry, those who steal crops from the fields and those who break into the houses while the householders are asleep. We ask for your mercy on those who seek unlawful profit in the markets and we pray for all the merchants. Help us so that we do not misappropriate anything which is not ours through cunning or plot. Help us to use time wisely because it is your gift to us.

Devadas considered the life of a Christian a witnessing life. As forgiveness leads to sanctification the believer becomes holy in thought, word and deed. Thus he loves God more than all[10]. He mentions several small things which the believer should watch and guard against.

> God sees all your thoughts and actions.
> Do not postpone your work.
> Keep a time for every activity in your life.
> Never buy anything which you do not really need
> even if you find it cheap.

He taught that a believer has a great responsibility in his daily life to witness to God in whom he believes. This is so that 'those who see your good works may glorify your father in heaven'. When the children of God gather together, the world must be able to see their witness and thus be drawn to Christ. For example, caste is sinful to Devadas and he deeply grieved that the society he was living in was a caste-ridden society. He strictly warned his followers to guard against this evil.

3. Family and Children

Devadas remained a bachelor all his life, as we have mentioned, but he held family life in high esteem. A Christian family to him is nothing less than a holy institution. He used the man and woman analogy several times to talk about the relationship between God and the believer (Isa. 54). The state of man and woman before the Fall was absolutely holy and there was nothing in that relationship to be ashamed of. But the present state of 'carnality', he thought, was the result of the Fall. Therefore the whole imagery of the Song of Songs according to Devadas was the picture of God's relationship to His people[11]. Again, he cited the prophecy of Isaiah in chapter 62, and commenting on this passage, Devadas makes mention of seven kinds of love:

1. Love between a wife and a husband
2. Love between parents and children
3. Love between brothers and sisters
4. Love among friends
5. Love between the employees and the employer
6. Love among believers
7. Love towards all the creatures

Devadas taught that the love between man and woman is the basis for all other kinds of love and therefore it is the supreme kind of love which is the symbol of God's love towards us. This view of Devadas giving the highest place to love between the sexes follows the thinking of Martin Luther as expressed in his teachings. Paul Althaus again summarises Luther's teaching on the subject as follows:

> Luther gives a high praise to love between the sexes. Among all the forms of earthly love, it is "the greatest and the purest". He not only ranks it above "false love", which is selfish, but also above natural love between parents and children and brothers and sisters. "But over and above all these is married love, which glows like a fire and desires nothing but the husband. She says, 'It is you I want, not

what is yours. I want neither your silver nor your gold; I want neither, I want only you. I want you in entirety, or not at all'. All other kinds of love seek something other than the loved one: this kind wants only to have the beloved's own self completely. If Adam had not fallen, the love of bride and groom would have been the loveliest thing"[12].

We can see how closely Devadas followed Martin Luther in his thinking on the subject of love and the love of God to us.

Because God had used conjugal love relationship as a symbol of His own love to us and His relationship with us, Devadas considers family as a holy and divinely ordained institution. He also cites the 5th Chapter of Paul's epistle to the Ephesians to show how important it is to consider the Christian marriage as a holy bond. In a society where gods and goddesses are amoral this aspect of God's insistence on faithfulness in marital relationship is very important. In the words of St. Paul,

> I am jealous for you, just as God is; you are like pure virgin whom I have promised in marriage to one man only, Christ himself. I am afraid that your minds will be corrupted and that you will abandon your full and pure devotion to Christ in the same way that Eve was deceived by the snake's clever lies. II Cor. 11.2-3.

On the basis of the teachings of the prophet Hosea, Devadas considers the sin of unfaithfulness as the greatest of all sins. God is willing to make the fallen race of Israel holy and to receive them. So also He is willing to forgive and receive the fallen man as a husband would forgive and receive an unfaithful wife (which is difficult but God did it). So Devadas thinks that the Book of Hosea is the supreme example of God's love and forgiveness[13]. Therefore, he also concludes that there should be perfect fidelity between the married partners.

There are 11 long hymns in the Bible Mission Hymnal on the subject of Christian marriage and all of them were written by Devadas. Christian marriage is one of the few major themes in this book. The teaching contained in these hymns may be summarised as follows:

In one hymn[14] he thanks God 'for kindly granting the bride to the groom and the groom to the bride'. This idea of mutuality seems to be deliberately emphasised because many times in popular Hinduism it is just a one-sided idea: the bride is given to the man in a kanyādānam, the gift of a woman, as in the many other dānams, such as the go-dānam, bhoo-dānam (gift of a cow, gift of land, etc.). God is praised in this hymn for making the man and woman a household. A Christian marriage is always a reminder of the ideal partnership portrayed in the couples in the Bible. The whole story of Adam and Eve is recalled in another hymn[15]. The wedding in Cana is remembered and the blessings of God are solicited so that the partners in the marriage do not miss any material blessings. Christ and his disciples are sought to come to the marriage as they were present in the wedding in Cana. The honoured guests are very important in an Indian marriage and at a Christian marriage prayers are always made for Christ and his disciples and the holy saints to be present as guests.

In another hymn, which is also a prayer, Devadas remembers Adam and Eve, Abraham and Sarah, Isaac and Rebeccah, Jacob and Leah, Zachariah and Elisabeth and the un-named couple of Cana so that God may bless the partners of the marriage today as He blessed all these partners in the Bible.

Marriage is also a symbol of God's love, the assembly is a symbol of heavenly family, the marriage register to Devadas a reminder of the Book of Life in which our names are firmly inscribed, and the marriage pendals (green leaf shelters typical of Indian weddings) are symbols of God's blessing hands stretched wide. The meals served are a foretaste of the feast in Heaven, the sweet scents rising at the function are symbols of our prayers to God and the wedding cards sent around are reminders of God's call to all of us into His fellowship[16]. As we see, this is a virtual sermon very imaginatively included in this song which the Bible Mission people love to sing at their wedding services.

In another hymn Devadas praised God the Father who conceived the wedding, the Son who effected the wedding and the Holy Spirit who confirmed the wedding in the Church.

Thus Devadas used the imagery of Christian marriage to teach many things about Christian life and faith in his songs. All these teachings are skilfully wrapped up in simple songs which people could learn and sing.

To conclude this short chapter on the ethical views of Devadas we can say that his teachings are fully evangelical and true to the teachings of the Bible. This is what is needful to his people in the church and he provided a guideline for them in the matter of a witnessing Christian life. He, of course, knew that at the end it is God's grace that saves us and enables us to do His will. As Alexandar John said, commenting on an article of Russel Chandran on the Christian Style of Living,

> The new style of life of the people of God is not limited by a set of moral codes. The life of a Christian is not certainly without law or moral principles, but it is guided by much higher demands than those which contemporary society lives by. It is a life of righteousness which exceeds the righteousness of the scribes and the Pharisees (Matt. 5.48). This is primarily a promise although it is also a commandment[17].

CHAPTER XI: Notes

1. <u>Bible Mission Hymnal</u>, No. 55. See also Ch. VI of this book on God and Trinity.

2. Booklet No. 5, <u>Upavāsa Prārdhana Deeksha</u>. A Vow of Fasting Prayer, p. 4.

3. Booklet No. 6, <u>Upavāsa Prārdhana Prakaranamu</u>, A Chapter on Fasting Prayer, p, 41.

4. Althaus, Paul, <u>Ethics of Martin Luther</u>, p. 12.

5. <u>Bible Mission Hymns</u> No. 44, <u>ACC Hymnal</u>, No. 325.

6. Althaus, Paul, <u>op.cit.</u>, p. 15.

7. Booklet No. 15, <u>Mithra</u>, The Friend, p. 10.

8. <u>Bible Mission Hymns</u> 53, <u>ACC Hymnal</u> No. 348.

9. Booklet No. 5, <u>op.cit.</u>, p. 24.

10. Booklet No. 11, <u>God's Presence</u>, p. 10.

11. Booklet No. 12, <u>Parama Geethārdhamu</u>, Commentary on Song of Songs, p. 3.

12. Althaus, Paul, <u>op.cit.</u>, p. 84.

13. Booklet No. 12, <u>op.cit.</u>, p. 6.

14. <u>Bible Mission Hymns</u>, No. 81.

15. <u>Ibid.</u>, No. 86.

16. <u>Ibid.</u>, No. 86.

17. John, Alexander D., "From Insularity to a New Involvement", <u>A Vision for Man</u>, (ed.) Samuel Amirtham, Madras: CLS, 1978.

Service and Evangelism
The Mission of the Church

CHAPTER XII

Characteristics of Indigenous Non-White Churches

1. Some Types of New Church Groups

Earlier in this work a certain typology was suggested for an examination of non-mission churches in India[1]. There seem to be three types of groups emerging under this general category. First, are those small groups which started as revival groups within the major churches and remained as charismatic movements while the members retained their own denominational affinities and nominal membership in their 'mother churches'. Many of the so-called Christian guru groups which Werner Hoerschelmann is referring to in his work[2] belong to this type. Brother Bhakta Singh's group, for example, or Brother Daniel's 'fellowship' and some other groups belong to the category. These revival groups worked mostly in cooperation with the major churches although not without some critical attitude about what they called the lukewarmness and the sleeping state of the major churches which they sought to revive.

To the second category belonged those small groups which at one time differed from their mother churches on the question of a doctrinal point or on a leadership dispute or some administrative matter or even on matters of spirituality and which slowly separated themselves from their parent churches[3]. These groups eventually tried to maintain fairly cordial relations with the churches which they parted ways with and they started growing[4]. The Bible Mission is one that can be grouped in this category.

Thirdly there are some groups which started as parallel and rival bodies to the mainline churches and these are always critical and polemical and noncooperative with them. The movement around Subba Rao is an example of this kind. Subba Rao was never baptised and he never saw the need for Baptism. He taught that Baptism was an unnecessary practice ignorantly insisted on by the church. He was most critical of missionaries and pastors; in fact he was critical of many things which the church stood for[5]. These groups appeal to some caste Hindus who want to follow Christ without having to be associated with any organizational church. There are some Hindus who are willing to accept this form of Christianity because it is more convenient for them in that they do not need to make any sacrifice to become Christians. They can remain in their caste community and they can keep all their social and cultural ties; in fact some of them had inter-religious marriages with practising Hindu partners.

This three-fold classification has been suggested mainly on the basis of the origin of these groups although their different teachings and practices have something to do with it. Professor Hollenweger, in a recent article on Pentecostal and Charismatic movements[6], has suggested another classification for all these non-White Indigenous churches. This classification includes the classical Pentecostal Missions and their churches also. Actually it is more useful to look at these groups together including the classical Pentecostal churches mainly because many of these groups either had some Pentecostal connections in the beginning and were clearly influenced by some Pentecostal leader, or at any rate have some Pentecostal elements incorporated in their teachings and practices even if sometimes they deny having any links with the Pentecostals at present. Thus, for example, most of these groups insist on some kind of second spiritual experience. Similarly healing and miracles are marks of their faith and practice even if the gift of tongues is not always insisted on. Thus including the Pentecostal denominations, the following are the three categories suggested by Hollenweger:

1) The classical Pentecostal denominations,
2) The charismatic movements within all traditional churches (including their missions) and,
3) The Indigenous Non-White churches, using the name suggested by David Barrett in his World Christian Encyclopedia (Nairobi, 1982).

The classical Pentecostal churches or their adapted forms have existed in India for some time. The Ceylon Pentecostal Mission is one old branch working in several parts of India. There is one branch headed by Apostle P.M. Samuel in Andhra Pradesh. Now recently the Pentecostal Holiness group has come to Andhra and they have a big programme of evangelism and homes for orphans and other types of work. Over the past few years some of the Pentecostal groups have also joined the ecumenical bodies like the regional Christian Councils and the National Christian Council and the Bible Society, etc.

It may be noted here that after India became independent and declared itself as a secular democratic republic with freedom to religious minorities, more small groups and missions have appeared on the scene. Mostly supported by the 'powerful dollar' any enterprising preacher could start a programme with a new name and a new sign board and all the paraphernalia. It would be an interesting topic for some future researcher to study all these money raising groups and their programmes. Dr. Hoerschelmann has documented some of these movements in his work. Thus a Church of God of Witness, an Indian Christian Crusade, a Brethren Mission and many other small missions appeared in Andhra Pradesh in recent times. All this activity was not unaccompanied by its own problems. While on the one hand the major denominations have reduced the number of their missionaries coming into the country the new faith group movements mostly from the United States of America have received more missionaries and consequently a few years ago when the question was asked in the Indian Parliament about the moratorium on the incoming missionaries, the government had actually come up with facts and figures which showed an increase in the total number of missionaries in the country rather than a decrease. This was a surprise and shock to the leaders of the major churches at that time who thought that they were suffering discrimination at the hands of the government.

Considering the present trends in the growth of Christianity in the world, David Barrett has indicated that the total membership of the three streams within the indigenous churches mentioned above stands at one hundred million in the world and the outlook is that by the end of the century it would grow to 250 million. Hollenweger says that the implication is that 'in the not so distant a future, there will be more Christians belonging to this type of Christianity than the Anglican community'[7].

For India, the implications seem to be serious. For a long time the mission church has been associated with the colonial powers and their patronage and in spite of all the good work done by the missions and missionaries, the Christian enterprise in India was looked upon with a certain amount of suspicion on the part of the major religion, Hinduism. During the struggle for independence of the country, the Christian church on the whole did not know exactly how to act and it did not want to associate itself too readily in the national struggle for freedom. Except for a few individual Christian leaders who joined with Gandhiji in those days to participate in the freedom struggle, the church as a whole, for obvious reasons, did not take a stand in the matter.

This is how Dr. Eddy Asirvatham, a great Christian scholar in political science, comments on the situation at that time:

> During the days of the national struggle, the political record of Indian Christians showed marked moral weakness. Few Indian Christians put their vaunted ideas of service and self-sacrifice into operation when the testing time came between 1921 and 1945. While a scattering of high spirited ones joined the Ghandian movement and suffered imprisonment and privation, a great many elected to sit on the fence and watch, often excusing themselves saying that they were economically poor and could not therefore, indulge in such luxuries as non-violent resistance, boycott of foreign goods and the picketing of foreign cloth shops - weapons used by Gandhi and his followers in the national struggle against Britain[8].

The church's work has also been criticised in the recent times as proselytization and the welfare programmes of the church were sometimes misinterpreted, not without some justification, as inducements to convert people into Christianity taking advantage of their need and difficult situations. More than all these hurdles to the growth of the church the Hindu converts were faced with genuine problems when they came into the Christian fold in that such persons had to become cut off from their own culture and community.

There are several factors contributing to such a situation: for one thing, the old missionary thought a person's conversion should always be followed by a public denouncing of all that was past even to the extent of the person concerned becoming a stranger and an outcast among his own people in the process. It is true that this kind of thing happened in the New Testament in many cases where there was a conversion to Christian faith[9] (e.g., St. John the Baptist's call to repentance, Lk. 3.8; the story of Christ's calling the disciples, Mark 1.20; Christ's call to his people and the necessity to break with one's family, Mark 3.31; Christ's definition of the family as those who do the will of God, Mark 3.35). Paul's account of his own conversion also tells that he had to break with all that was past. But it was also true that much of the past was retained and was transformed when people accepted the new faith. The Jewish Christians observed Sabbath and kept the law and used the Old Testament Scriptures in their worship, and similarly the Hellenist converts brought their own culture into the Christian faith when they came into the Christian fold. However, insistence on the change of name, a church membership and even the rite of Baptism as it is understood in India--all these have been considered by some Hindus as too much of a burden which the church was imposing on the new converts, a burden which 'the Christians themselves were not always willing to bear'[10].

Roberto De Nobili, that great 17th century Jesuit missionary to India and a pioneer in the idea of adaptation in the context of evangelism, has much to say about this. Arguing in favour of allowing some social and religious customs to be retained when Hindus accept Christianity, De Nobili quotes a Syrian writer, Maruta, Bishop of Mipercante, one of those who attended the council of Nicea, who said,

> When the apostles started their journey to preach the Gospel of the risen Christ, they did not accompany their preaching with rules and canons; but their first care was to win the people from idolatry to the adoration of the victorious cross and only asked the new converts to shun fornication, so that they might not frighten away the gentiles, if they saw that conversion meant the imposition of new burdens on themselves or the suppression of their own way of life[11].

It was also generally thought that there was too much of Western influence on the church's public image, in its administrative system and in its liturgy, and even in the values and the world view held by the Christians[12]. In the recent years the effects of this Latin Captivity of the Church, as Boyd calls it, have become more conspicuous. Too many administrative structures, committees and councils, authority patterns, litigations and court cases, and such things have scared away many an outsider who complained that these are not in keeping with the Gospel of the Jesus of Nazareth.

Consequently there is a trend now that folk religious forms like the Bible Mission, and those that are sometimes called the Hindu-Christian groups, like the followers of the Subba Rao or an Ashram type of indigenous Christianity, and the Christian gurus like those reported in Hoerschelmann's work are gaining more followers today in India than the older mission churches.

2. Some Characteristics of Indigenous Non-White Churches

For the purpose of our study we can talk here about all the above mentioned three types together because the similarities between these types in India are more numerous than the differences. In other words, all these types together have some clear marks of distinction from the mission churches and hence they face some tensions. To the question of the tensions we shall return later in this chapter, but first the similarities among these indigenous groups may be considered here briefly.

a) Most of these groups, at least the larger ones like the Bible Mission, do not depend on outside monetary support. A few of them which first started with the overseas agencies pumping some money are now finding it very difficult to carry on as foreign support gets dried up. Many of their programmes had to be discontinued and much of the pomp and show of such groups is disappearing and consequently they are either becoming financially independent, or they are dying out.

b) Almost all these groups are self-governed; that is, their leadership is entirely indigenous.

c) All of them are trying to express their faith in indigenous forms and there is far less influence of Western theology or Western thinking in contrast with the situation in the mission churches.

d) Very few of them have top-heavy administrative structures. They do not have the time or the interest to join the councils and committees of the ecumenical nature and their ministry belongs more to the grass roots type and the grass roots type of ministry appeals to most people with an Indian type of spirituality.

e) Most of them are centred round a charismatic leader, and the idea of 'power' of the guru appeals to the people whether such a power is manifested in the acts of healing, or in dreams and visions or any such gifts.

Therefore, in spite of all the minor differences among themselves, the charismatic groups or the the Christian guru movements, or the Indigenous non-White movements in India, as they are collectively called, may be somewhat of an answer to the problems which the major denominations are facing today. It is too early to foresee exactly what the shape of the future church in India is going to be, but it is likely that many more people are willing to join indigenous groups rather than the mission churches today. The trend in this direction is likely to increase in the years immediately following the present time and it may be necessary for the mission churches to be aware of this fact.

The reasons for the fast growth of these Indigenous non-White churches are not far to seek. Hollenweger suggests some reasons for the growth of these bodies and he summarises those reasons as follows[13]:

i) Orality of Liturgy.
ii) Narrativity of Theology and Witness.
iii) Maximum participation on the level of reflection, prayer, and decision-making and therefore a form of community which is reconciliatory.
iv) Inclusion of dreams and visions into personal and public forms of worship; they function as a kind of icons for the individual and the community.

v) An understanding of the body/mind relationship which is informed by experience of correspondence between body and mind. The most striking application of this insight is the ministry of the healing prayer.

Let us now examine these factors in a little more detail with a special reference to the situation in India and in Andhra Pradesh.

i) <u>Orality of Liturgy</u>: The masses of India still belong to a pre-literary culture. One simple example is the long prayer and preaching campaigns which people like to enjoy, listening to speakers for hours at length. This is something which a Westerner or a westernised national will find very difficult to cope with. People sit for hours at length, as we said, listening to a gifted speaker as he tells the story of his own conversion, or gives his testimony of God's action in terms of miracles performed, prayers answered, and difficulties solved. For several years now the Christians of Kērala have come to a big convention in a place called Maramon on a river bed once in every two years. Crowds of people dressed in white clothes sit all the day long and late into the evening on the sand beds under temporary palm leaf shelters listening to the preachers and singing songs and celebrating their faith. This goes on for several days. World-famous evangelists like Sadhu Sundar Singh have addressed Maramon Convention at one time or the other.

Similarly, in Andhra Pradesh, in the river bed of Kristna, we have seen that people met for another mahāsabha (great convention) every two years in summer when Christians of all denominations and all creeds gather together coming from long distances staying there for several days sleeping and eating and living in palm leaf pendals (temporary structures with bamboo and palm leaf), and listen to the word of God. The only parallel which is somewhat similar to this in the West as far as I know is the Kirchentag in West Germany. But the Indian conventions are very simple and much more in the folk type.

People learn a special convention song in these meetings and at the end of the one week, this song goes back with them in all directions into the various villages and homes. People love to live like this for a few days, parents and children sleeping in the open pandals, listening to the word of God and praying together with the fellow-believers and waiting for a renewal experience. It reminds us of what we know from the Bible of the feast of the Tabernacles which the people of Israel observed in the Land of Canaan. This is an example of how the oral tradition works in actual practice in India.

ii) <u>Narrativity of Theology and Witness</u>: For those of us who are trained in the modern theological colleges it is hard to imagine how far our theology has moved us away from the womb of simple narrative thinking. We are often criticised quite rightly for becoming too academic, our approach becoming rather theoretical; our religion somewhat intellectual. Most of the seminary trained pastors in India can pour over the old commentaries and repeat them faithfully in their sermon word for word including some illustrations and anecdotes which sound irrelevant to the Indian mind and fall flat.

It is no wonder that the independent preacher who has never gone into the seminary but who preaches from the local cultural patterns and tells the simple story gathers more listeners. The reasons for popularity of such a sermon are not far to seek. 'The story evokes, informs, awakens archetypal images and allows people to identify with and experience the abstraction of truth, faithfulness and love, triumphs of the human spirit that give us heroes and saints'[14].

This does not mean that seminary training is not important nor are we suggesting that theology should just be a collection of stories. We are only saying that the narrative method of theology-making has not been explored enough in our mission churches. In fact these mission churches often shy away from folk methods and from some of the indigenous song and story and drama dismissing them as unworthy to communicate the Gospel and consequently they are not speaking the people's language any more. The preachers of the folk churches on the other hand are using the story and the song and the imagery in their communication and in doing so, they are sitting with the people and they do not have a six foot high pulpit to preach down from. So in the small churches of the Indigenous non-White type, prayer and preaching become celebration with the people.

iii) <u>Participation in the Decision making</u>: The Indigenous non-White churches feel highly fortunate that they do not have bishops or high administrative and legislative body centrally somewhere to make rules to guide their life and witness. (In some of the groups in recent times this is not quite true because sometimes the donor agencies in the Western countries helping these small groups are imposing their systems and there are bishops in some charismatic churches in India). The indigenous churches do not have to send their delegates to the inter-denominational councils and committees and they do not have to keep up with the constitutions and their amendments from time to time. Their pastors have their hands full of work preaching and praying and healing and they do not have much time for anything else. So in most cases in these churches the people collectively participate in the decision making.

Some of the problems in the church in India today are due to struggle for leadership. Churches are learning a model of competitive life from the Western world, and elections as a method of choosing church administrators has become a scandal in recent times in India. The indigenous groups on the other hand have more of a reconciliatory type of community life on the whole, and the reasons for this situation are that there are no paid jobs in these churches and few positions to be competed for and the leadership, mostly charismatic, is an evolved leadership accepted readily because of the acknowledged gifts of the leader.

Quoting from the charismatic types depicted by Max Weber, Howard Kee has this to say about the characteristics of such an ethical prophet,

> He is persuaded that he is the agent of the transcendent God, and that the precepts which he teaches are the expression of the divine will. The potency of his charismatic endowment is evident in the special gifts he possesses (such as healing and predictive capacities) and in the effectiveness of his preaching. Although the exercise of his gifts tends to confirm his authority, it is the persuasive power of the revelation which he claims has been granted him that is the ultimate ground of his effectiveness[15].

Talking about the way in which charismatic leaders are often chosen, Kee further says,

> Their assumption of their role knows nothing of an ordered procedure of an appointment or dimissal; there is no regulated career, advancement, salary or expected training, just as there is no agency of control or appeal, no delineation of jurisdiction or territory. And the enterprise gives rise directly to no permanent institution. The holder of charisma seizes the task that is adequate for him and demands obedience and a following by virtue of his mission[16].

This is almost the picture of the Indian <u>gurus</u> or the leaders of the charismatic church groups in India.

iv) <u>Dreams and Visions</u>: Many people belonging to the folk church tradition in India will be surprised if they are told that dreams and visions are not reliable and that they are not a part of religious life. We have already seen that Devadas clearly stated that dreams and visions are not superfluous to biblical revelation. It is a part of the total revelation of God even if we have to check the visionary experience with biblical revelation and with the corresponding experience of other saintly people.

Devadas knew well that Martin Luther did have psychic and spiritual experiences, and as Bengt Hoffman says in his interesting study, <u>Luther and the Mystics</u>, it is undeniable that Luther's faith was permeated with intuitions of numinous presence and experiences of the power of the supernatural forces[17]. After narrating several of the incidents from documented evidence to this fact, Hoffman concludes the chapter on Luther's experience with these words:

> No doubt, Luther had paranormal experiences. Some of them were of Pauline magnitude, both experiences of a hostile invisible world and experiences of a benign invisible world. A few of the latter sustained his faith in the same manner as St. Paul was sustained by his clairvoyant and clair-audial Damascus Experience. Without them faith would be just rational play. But Luther used these paranormal intuitions sparingly in his gospel propagation. The reason is obvious.

Homo mendax, man's mendacious, ego-involved self, tends to turn the extraordinary experience into self-glory. Besides, both scripture and Christian experience teach us that some forms of occultism can be deleterious[18].

To the people of India, as to those from many other pre-literary cultures, dreams are part of life and the interpretation of dreams is a commonly used and respected gift. Once the church denies to the people their privilege to dream dreams and once it ignores the phenomena as unimportant, the people become disoriented and they live a life in two artificial compartments as it were. Life is not holistic in that situation any more. It would not be possible for the Christian in folk culture to cope with the biblical account of dreams both in the Old Testament and in the New if their faith in dreams is knocked out. The same God who sent His angel to Mary to announce in a vision that she would bear a son had also caused a dream to Joseph to silence his doubts about Mary. Both are equally possible to God. So there is no problem to the simple Christian in India with dreams. On the other hand it would be unnatural and short of the fulfilment of one's religious life if he did not expect God to speak to him in dreams. He may have difficulty with the Trinitarian formula, for example, but he has no difficulty with the Old Testament story of Jacob's ladder, nor with the story of the vision of the dry bones (Ezekiel Ch. 37). The experience is familiar, the message is clear. The village Christian needs his gurus or his teachers to guide him by visions--he wants them to interpret his own visions and dreams for him. Most of the members of these Indigenous non-White churches live a real life of community fellowship when they share their dreams and their unusual experiences.

This disposition to dream dreams and to see visions comes to the folk-church Christians from their former religious background and their ancestral culture. An artisan sees visions, and a sculptor and an artist and even a singer and performer live with their dreams and visions. The Spirit of God works all over His creation and if these Christians do not actively seek the spiritual gift of dreams and visions they think that they are missing something very vital to their spirituality. If the churches deny a hearing to their dreams, there are some very sympathetic gurus who would listen to them.

v) <u>Body-Mind Relationship</u>: Again, coming from their Hindu religious background the members of the indigenous church groups have the firm belief that body and mind are a whole, each affecting the other intimately. It is a community experience that healthy and peaceful thoughts and understanding and loving friendship will help and protect a person from harm and evil and that poisonous thoughts and even looks can harm people. Many mothers in the village know that children can be adversely affected, even get sick, with the evil looks of a stranger. This is an example of the association people give to the body-mind relationships and health and well-being.

So when people are sick, the indigenous church groups seek healing prayer and community support. Not all diseases are easy to explain as physiological conditions. Some diseases do not respond to any medicine. There are many stories of personal witness one hears in the prayer meetings of these indigenous church groups, stories of what were considered as 'incurable' diseases having disappeared with prayer. Sometimes doctors find it hard to believe these stories. But there is living evidence in abundance attesting the cures. Only now are the mission churches seriously considering healing ministry a regular programme through prayer. In the Christian Medical college, hospital in Vellore, one finds this concern for prayer along with regular medical care and several chaplains and trained counselling staff work with the doctors. One can hope that this kind of integrated healing ministry expands in the other parts of the country in the mission churches much more[19]. At any rate, it is true that this basic understanding of the body-mind relationship as applied in the healing ministry is in no small measure resulting in the rapid growth in the Indigenous non-White churches in India. If only these churches can keep their grass-roots nature and avoid the temptation of becoming 'streamlined ecclesiastical bureaucracies' and 'fund-raising structures'[20] their credibility will continue to grow, they can attract even more people, and they can grow into very live Christian communities in India.

Their doctrinal position is much less of a problem to the mission churches today and their services of healing and their visions and their dreams and the language of these gifts appeal to people more than anything that a straight preaching of a sermon can ever do.

3. Tension with the Mission Churches

What exactly are the reasons for the tension between the mission churches and the indigenous churches? Why did the mission churches generally ignore and avoid fellowship with these new-born church bodies in the country? Why did the indigenous church groups keep a 'touch me not' attitude? It was thought that the reasons for this are theological. They are partly theological as in the case of Subbarao, who taught that no Baptism was necessary, or with some Pentecostal groups which insist that speaking in tongues is necessary as a sign of the work of the Holy Spirit in the individual. In some cases the reason for tension may be simple jealousy and rivalry among the individuals. A pastor trained in the seminary who has to work within the constraints of the church structures may feel sometimes not as free as the independent charismatic preacher who claims a personal gift to work miracles and to heal. In such cases the pastor may either simply dismiss the claims of the charismatic preacher as nonsense or call them theologically unsound.

But the real reason for tension will be found elsewhere. The strengths of the indigenous church groups are also causes of tension. We can make the following observations making use of Hollenweger's list under points of tension in the article mentioned already[21].

a) Racism versus an International Inter-Cultural Understanding of Christianity:

In the Indian context it is not racism that is a problem but there are other forms of separation in the society. The authority pattern of the mainline churches has become somewhat a real problem similar to racism compared to the informal cordial relationships generally found in the indigenous churches. Members of the indigenous church groups call each other brother and sister. Their ministers are simple people many times living on their own wages in secular jobs and serving their churches without salary. The Bible Mission has full-time pastors but they do not have salaries. They live on faith, as they say, not on any central salary fund. The offerings received at their prayer meetings are the only income for them many times.

These Indigenous non-White churches are non-racial in another sense also. Because of the mere historical reasons there are more high caste converts coming into these churches than into the mission churches. It is easier for the caste Hindus to be associated with these fellowships without generally breaking away from their own social groups and without having to be branded as a denomination. These Indigenous non-White church groups are more open in that sense. So the believers from both low caste and the high caste mix together more easily in these groups. There are stronger bonds of affinity to unite them without their having to stay in their caste clusters. In these groups they find themselves as a more closely knit family of belivers[22].

b) <u>Literacy versus Orality</u>:

We know that a man who can not read and write is not ignorant nor is he devoid of experience to which he can relate. The idea that an educated man has an advantage comes from the modern secular world and from the value system of technological societies. As Professor Hollenweger says, some of these Indigenous non-White churches will doubtless accept Western teachers and Western theology. Thus they will partake of the blessings and pitfalls of the Western culture[23]. Once they do that, they will have the same problems which the mission churches are facing in India and one hopes that it will not happen. What perhaps will be needed is not Western teachers and Western theological models but a good training for their pastors. Even there the kind of training which is given today in our seminaries and theological colleges may not be the best according to many thinkers but what will be better is a real <u>gurukul</u> type of in-service and on-going training from real life in the company of dedicated āchāryas in an āshram way of community living. But it is quite clear that one need not be literate before he becomes a follower of Christ. The more the major churches realise this fact, the less tension there will be between the indigenous church groups and the mission churches. This is not however to say that literacy is not good nor is it not desirable. This is to draw our attention to the fact that the methodology chosen by the charismatic churches at present is largely oral and not literary.

c) Abstract Concepts versus Narrativity:

Father Devadas himself was not free from thinking in abstract terms sometimes. This was probably due to his earlier training in the Lutheran schools and his work in the seminary. But whenever he tried to do this kind of thinking, he did not say anything new but he repeated what he had learnt. On the other hand, when he talked about his visions, and when he told his stories and when he expounded the Books of the Bible using the imagery, at such times his narrative genius came to light. When his followers claimed that his spirit spoke through a medium, again it is the story he told, the story of a biblical character and an imaginative new message he evolved. All this is far from any systematic theology which people read from the books. It was not logical argument but suggestive imagery in all its simplicity, not the Aristotelian straight argument but a people's language with all its open ambiguity, not an intellectual debate but an appeal to the total life touching the experience of the community. This however was not good enough for the mission churches which generally looked for authority from the teachings of the Western theologians. But the sad fact is that the average pastor today neither knows enough of the teachings of these theologians nor is he able to adequately contextualise these teachings to the life of his congregation.

Narrativity, however, is not a means of covering one's ignorance in theology. It is rather a skill to communicate theology in a non-abstract language. The Christian gurus in India have learnt this skill mainly because they had not already been conditioned by the abstract thinking habit, which is the result of modern logic which has influenced our life so much.

d) Family and Personal Relationships versus Anonymity of Bureaucratic Organisations:

We have touched this point already above briefly and more on this will come in the chapter on Indigenization. But it is necessary to mention here again that there are too many wheels within the wheels in the Indian church organisation today and it is difficult to get out of these circles of church bureaucracy. Once a presbyter is elected to the post of a bishop, for example, it is most likely that he will have no time for pastoral duties and real contact with people, which is so important. Attending all the committees and councils and the 'house keeping' he has to do will take all his time. There are bishops and presidents of churches in India today who spend half their time travelling around the globe and the other half reading reports and minutes. The Indigenous non-White churches find it difficult to wear this kind of 'armour'. Their sling and stone work better for them than all these swords and spears which, fortunately, they have never learnt to use. Hence the strife occurs sometimes.

e) <u>Medical Technology versus Holistic Understanding of Health and Sickness:</u>

Fortunately there is a better understanding today between the mission churches and the indigenous churches in the matter of health and wholeness. Today most of the charismatic groups are accepting the use of medicine along with prayer. The Bible Mission with all its healing campaigns has never discouraged people from taking medicine or from going to doctors. But they cooperate wherever possible with the medical profession, supporting it with their concern and with their prayers as a caring community. In many cases it so happens that no medicine will be needed after prayer because God, if He wants, can cure without medicine. On the other hand the mission churches are also recognising that God can break through nature and perform miracles. As Morton Kelsey says in <u>Healing and Christianity</u>,

> As more and more persons have sought psychiatric help, with others turning to drugs or violence, the awareness has grown that the modern limited view of life cuts man off from something he does need[24].

Mission churches today realise the need for praying ministry for the sick as a programme of the churches. More and more of the holistic idea of life is coming to its own and it is not difficult even for the most rational thinking person to accept that there are diseases which can not be explained and there are also cures that can not be explained. Therefore there is hope that the tension may be resolved in this area soon.

f) <u>Western Psycho-analytical Techniques versus a Group and Family Therapy</u>:

The group and family therapy which centres on human touch, prayer and informal education in dreams and visions, as Hollenweger puts it, is not a choice which the indigenous churches had to make in India. It is rather the only thing open to them. Their preachers have no knowledge of the psycho-analytical methods in any case; most of them have not even heard the name. The Bible Mission healing meetings in the grove of Kākāni, for example, are a very touching sight. People come from long distances helped by loving family members and they are received by a caring Christian community. They are touched, anointed, prayed for and they go back with a new hope and a mysterious feeling of well-being. They take home some oil that is blessed when they go and in the villages they have a story to tell and an experience to share with others. It is quite different from the situation in a city mission church at worship, where people still sit in straight pews and hardly speak to each other at the end of the service before they go home. In a small town church where I worshipped for several years, people gathered Sunday after Sunday without having to know who lives around at the church compound wall. The community a few yards all around the church was a stranger to the Christians even at festival times when people generally come together. There was no initiative by the members of the congregation and they never thought of inviting these 'outsiders' to their fellowship. This is not a stray case with the churches. But the indigenous church groups are interestingly providing this human touch and this informal education and community spirit all the time.

4. Conclusion

These are some of the important characteristics of the Indigenous non-White churches in India and the points of strife with the mission churches. On the whole the group churches have remained exclusive in their relationship with their mission counterparts. They feel separated and so their members often are self-conscious. Since there is little contact with outsiders or with the Christians of other denominations these churches are generally not open to criticism and correction and sometimes they are called a 'self-righteous' group. With more contact with the others this separatist tendency in time should disappear. The mission churches too, on their part, have not been open to the indigenous groups. This has caused some strife and bitterness. It is possible to develop cooperation between these two groups and a spirit of learning from each other and as Professor Hollenweger exhorts the mission churches,

> If the mission of the church is to be that process by which Christians from all cultures enter into a global learning process (both in the interest of the Gospel and of the world peace), then we must learn and learn fast to communicate with these emerging forms of Charismatic religion, inside and outside the Christian church[25].

This is much more true in India where a total of less than 24 million Christians are trying to witness for Christ before 600 million non-Christians.

CHAPTER XII: Notes

1. See Chapter I of this book.

2. Hoerschelmann, Christliche Gurus, Frankfurt: Peter Lang, 1977.

3. Devadas and his followers sometimes thought that by going out of the Andhra Evangelical Lutheran Church they were doing what Martin Luther himself had done when he came out of the Catholic Church.

4. Devadas always asked his followers not to criticise Christian brethren from other denominations.

5. See Baago, K.A., Movements Around Subbarao.

6. Hollenweger, W.J., Pentecostals and Charismatic Movements to be published in Mircea Eliade (ed.) The Encyclopedia of Religion, New York.

7. Ibid., p. 1.

8. Asivirtham, Eddy., Christianity in Indian Crucible, p. 25.

9. See: Kee, Howard C., Christian Origins in Social Perspective, London: SCM, 1980.

10. Cf. Subbamma B.V., New Patterns for Discipling Hindus, Pasadena: William Carey Library, 1970, pp. 33-45, where she argues that caste Hindus should not be insisted to join the outcast's churches.

11. Rajamanickam, S., s.j., Roberto De Nobili on Adaptation, p. 35.

12. People in the time of Brahma Bāndhav thought that Christians had to eat meat and drink wine. Quoting some of the scathing attacks he made on the Western trappings of that day, R.H.S. Boyd reports:

> Catholicism had donned the European garb in India. Our Hindu brethren can not see the subtlety and sanctity of our divine religion because of its hard coating of Europeanism... They can not understand how poverty can be compatible with boots, trousers and hats, with spoon and fork, meat and wine...

R.H.S.Boyd, Introduction to Indian Christian Theology, p. 83.

13. Hollenweger, W.J., op.cit., p. 4.

14. Oliphant, David, "Motives for Metaphor", to be published, Pastoral Studies, Spring School, Birmingham University, 1983.

15. Kee, Howard C., op.cit., p. 55.

16. Ibid., p. 56. The last sentence in this paragraph is a quotation from Max Weber, The Sociology of Charismatic Authority, Oxford University Press, 1958, pp. 245-46.

17. Hoffman, Bengt R., Luther and the Mystics, An Examination of Luther's Spiritual Experience and His Relationship to the Mystics, Minneapolis: Augsburg Publishing House, 1976, p. 186.

18. Ibid., p. 191.

19. In recent years there was great interest shown in prayer healing in the Western churches. The Anglican Church has a well organised hospital chaplaincy and prayer healing programme. Rev. Mark Turner of Staffordshire is engaged in healing work for several years now and he is publishing a book on the subject. Rev. Lenn Burn's anointing prayers in the hospital at Birmingham and presently in the hospitals at Bristol are well known and as a hospital chaplain he practises healing ministry through prayer.

20. Hollenweger, W.J., Pentecostal and Charismatic Movements, p. 4.

21. Ibid.

22. For example B.V.Subbamma in her book, the New Patterns for Discipling Hindus, suggests that caste converts need not be expected to join the church of the outcaste Christians. In support of her argument Subbamma quotes John Picket's Christian Mass Movements in India, (Lucknow Publishing House, 1933).

Subbamma also says that over the years many attempts made to bring two sub-groups among the outcastes have resulted in little success after their conversion to Christianity.

Subbamma quotes the president of the Andhra Evangelical Lutheran Church, who said:

> It is ideal that all believers should worship together in one place in each village. After 125 years we must realise that we are not practising this in most places. We can not expect from the Sudras (higher caste Hindu converts) this ideal which the two sub-castes among the untouchables have not been able to attain in so many generations.

(Here Schmitthenner is only citing an existing difficulty but one hopes that neither he nor Subbamma is trying to perpetuate the caste system in the church).

23. Hollenweger, W.J., Pentecostal and Charismatic Movements, p. 10.

24. Kelsey, Morton T., Healing and Christianity in Ancient Thought and Modern Times, SCM, 1973.

25. Hollenweger, W.J., Pentecostal and Charismatic Movements, p. 11.

CHAPTER XIII

Dreams, Visions and Healing - A More Detailed Analysis

1. Introduction

Dreams, visions and healing miracles have played an important role in the life of the non-White Indigenous churches everywhere and the Bible Mission and the indigenous church groups in India are no exception in this respect. To some extent a proper understanding and interpretation of these phenomena is necessary if some areas of strife between the historic churches and the charismatic groups are to be resolved.

As Morton Kelsey says about the problem of organised Christianity in coping with the situation in his well known work <u>Encounter with God</u>,

> There is trouble in institutional religions today; this much is not hard to diagnose. At the same time, enthusiasm for religion is suddenly springing up from all sides; yet organised Christianity seems unable to tap or respond to it. Why? There are several reasons each of them valid to a point[1].

This is how he explains those reasons in brief:
  a) the Church has not been consistent with its message, and the Christian Church has a very difficult message to live up to;
  b) instead of being a hospital for sinners, the Church has found itself more a museum for saints;
  c) the Church has relied on authority and doctrine, on theological understanding of experiences instead of trusting the experiences themselves. For example, in the matter of healing and disease modern thinking tends to look at some of the primitive world views as superstitious, ignorant and fear-ridden. The tendency is to think that disease must be seen as purely physiological disorder always having a detectable and explicable somatic cause; anything which can not have such a cause is always considered as pure fear and ignorance and persisting superstition. Traditional churches have sometimes

shared this view. But this is obviously an oversimplification of the issue and there is more to life than mere perceptible and repeatable reality.

The Bible, of course, is full of miracles and supernatural healings. Christ himself made healing a major part of his ministry. In fact, healing is an evidence that the Kingdom of God is here, a manifestation of the arrival of the Lord's day, as Christ himself has declared. We shall discuss this in a little more detail in this chapter.

Along with healing, the other area of our concern is visions and dreams. This visionary experience and extra-sensory perception, as psychology calls it, is not new to humanity or to the Christian Church. Kelsey cites the example of the Divine Comedy of Dante, the Stanzas of the Soul of St. John of the Cross and portions from The Hound of Heaven by Francis Thompson as fruits of visionary experience and adds,

> Such experiences also come to many ordinary people who are striving to become whole and integrate their lives around a coherent meaning. The experiences are just as valid and memorable although they are not set down with such artistic talent[2].

What is the attitude of the Church to extraordinary experiences? How does modern man react to the miracles and to the possibility of visions and signs? Kelsey reminds us that Thomas Aquinas could not deny that these unusual things had happened. It had been written in the New Testament that men had direrct contact with God and other non-physical realities in these ways.

> But he (Aquinas) did not see these happening around him very much, or else he did not notice them, just as there are so many things we do not see from our philosophic blinders[3].

Do we call this selective perception? At any rate, when modern man has experiences that seem to point to some being beyond the ordinary, he either dismisses them as insignificant, or else tries to get rid of them as symptoms of a poorly oriented psyche[4]. This is what generally is happening to the claims of dreams and visions and healing miracles in the Church today.

In addition to this, as Kelsey says:

> This new generation, both young and old, are not satisfied with authority; they want experiences of God and the Holy Spirit to verify the theology and the dogma[5].

On the subject of what he calls the Theological Blind Alley and a door out of it, Kelsey summarises the teachings of the major schools of Christian thought to see just 'what they have to say about the divine breaking into human life or into the physical world'.

a) <u>A Liberal Theology and Experience of God</u>:

Once the Enlightenment was under way in Europe, a liberal and critical tradition began to develop among Christian thinkers.

> The liberation of men's minds from the domination of authority and the development of a freer use of reason and knowledge allowed all elements of Christian life, theology and literature to be subjected to the most critical scrutiny[6].

As a result of this,

> Most of the "miraculous" elements of the Bible and of later tradition were either doubted or found to be false, because they seemed to contradict the tacitly accepted ideas of reason and natural law. God was understood as living within His creation, which he has made as self-contained and rationally explainable unit. Thus the way men could come to know God was to know themselves and the world around them, particularly through history[7].

Also,

> According to this school, the men who wrote the New Testament were informed by an incorrect world view that clouded their judgement. The job of the modern theologian is to separate the wheat from the chaff in the Biblical narrative and so reveal the gradual development of man's moral conscience and religious understanding[8].

b) <u>Dispensationalism</u>:

As against the liberal theology mentioned above, we see another line of theological thought, evangelical dispensationalism. Again, Kelsey reports,

> The natural reaction to this critical and liberal theology was to hang on to the very letter of the Bible and maintain the literal truth of the text against all comers. To do this, fundamentalism or literal theology needed to explain how there could be such a radical difference between the experiences described in the Bible and those of men today. The theory of dispensationalism provided the answer[9].

From the most liberal demythologizers to the most conservative fundamentalists, they are equally conviced that God has no contact with living individuals. Thomas Aquinas did not see miracles happening in his time though he believed that they happened in biblical times. Trying to safeguard against the liberal tendency which questioned everything, the fundamental view held to the literal interpretation of the Bible. Dispensationalism is the view largely held in the mission churches in India today. God had granted the miraculous and the mysterious in the biblical times and this is no more needed after the Bible became available. Or it is not necessary that God should speak to us today since we have all that we need to know for salvation in the Bible. This was essentially the view held by Luther and Calvin, who simply continued the Thomistic distinction between the natural and the supernatural.

c) Demythologizing:

With Bultmann, another idea quietly entered the theological thinking in the Church about the miracles,

> Bultmann started by accepting man's helplessness up against the transcendence of God, and gradually became convinced that theology needed a philosophical base to maintain such a position. This he found in the existentialism of Heidegger[10].

In the intellectual and secular society of India today, the demythologizing tendency is sometimes popular. Many people under the influence of rationalism think that the miracles of the Bible did not happen. Or if they happened, they are theologically irrelevant as Raja Ram Mohan Roy and his school of thinkers have maintained. This belief also helped them to rationalise the myths and mysteries of Hinduism. The tendency is to say that 'the writers of the New Testament' only described them as a way of speaking about the truth. Once I was asked for a local studio of the All India Radio to broadcast an Easter message. I had to submit the script for scrutiny and the concerned executive producer, an intelligent and educated Hindu, expressed surprise that I still believe that Christ rose from the grave. To him I sounded very naive to still believe that. He accepted it only as my way of saying that Christ's ideas and his teachings do live, that his memory lives and it shall live for ever, but resurrection of the body--that was an idea which he could never cope with.

d) The Mediaeval Church:

Kelsey briefly describes the situation in the mediaeval Church with regard to the supernatural. Once Latin became the language of scholarship, the knowledge of Greek was lost and with it the Greek spirit

> and also Plato's careful understanding of the human experience which had given Christians some handle on the kind of superstition that now came to pervade the entire culture.....

> It is no wonder that in the end the thinking of Aristotle completely replaced that of Plato as the basic approach to Christian ideas and experience[11].

As Kelsey says, this so-called Platonic philosophy was fine with people so long as their world was in such trouble that they were really looking for release into another world. But how long would this other-worldliness help people? How long would they be able to forget the present situation in favour of some hope for a future which they had never seen? People surely want to do something now to help their plight.

With this, scholasticism arose and dominated the scene.

> Aquinas became convinced of the truth of Aristotle's world view - particularly his view that man receives direct knowledge only through sense experience and reason - and he came to the conclusion that this was a basic truth which Christians could and must accept[12].

But Aristotle had realised that all information given by sense experience is subject to change, always uncertain, and he was looking for some access to certain knowledge. For this reason, Kelsey says, he favoured the logical certainty of deductive reasoning over the tentative character of inductive thought. One obtains knowledge not by divine inspiration but by human rational activity. In Aristotle's system there is no place for any divine revelation and Aquinas, following Aristotle, produced his 'certainty of God' logically at the same time bypassing serious consideration of dreams, visions, healing, tongues and prophecy in the present experience.

Therefore according to Aristotle and following him in the teachings of Aquinas, we see a tendency that man first obtains knowledge of the external world through sense experience. Indeed his humanness develops directly through sense experience.

> But once man has come to maturity, he can learn to use his reason, first to understand and classify his sense experience, and then to

provide direct access to logically certain knowledge. Thus knowledge is provided by reason as well as by sense experience[13].

Thus logic, rather than experience, we are told, has become the corner stone of theology of the Church through Aquinas. Churchmen turned more and more to deductive reasoning and subtle logic and dialectic that followed from it.

Martin Luther broke out of scholastic thought but without developing a system of thought in which to integrate his experience, and in the opinion of Kelsey, Calvin's view remained just as scholastic as Aquinas'.

e) Man and his Understanding of God:

Kelsey draws our attention to a certain confusion today, even despair among theologians, because people find little connection between the natural words which theology has been using all along--words such as God, soul, spirit, and mind—and their experiences of the world. This is also what Dr. Hollenweger says--that the language we need to describe man's experience of the world is different today from what it was when the New Testament was written. Not only that,

> We have also seen that modern thinkers are increasingly less sure that men can obtain any knowledge just by thinking. If the word 'God' is to have meaning, it will be the result of more than just a chain of logical thinking. If God has meaning for men's lives, this will come from a knowledge of God resulting from their experiences or encounters with the divine. Ontological analysis, deductive reasoning from first principles, or reasoning about purpose seen in the universe may support man's understanding of God but the knowledge must be first given by something that man experiences[14].

Therefore it looks important that we try to understand the language which the charismatic groups are using today about the unseen and the invisible and the extra-sensory experience. Is there a way of knowing reality other than the way of rationalism and through empirical data and repeatable experimentation?

2. Dreams

a) The Significance of Dreams to a Christian's Life:

Dreams occupy considerable space in the biblical narrative. Actually the words used for dreams and visions are interchangeable in the Bible and it is hard to tell them apart. Kelsy thinks that a dream can carry its own message and conviction: it has power. Dreams, if understood, have healing effects according to many psychologists.

The Bible records many dreams and they were sometimes considered means of God's revelation. They can be used to know God's will. But dreams often can be irrelevant, trivial, and even devastating. We can only say that it is possible that God's voice can be sometimes mediated through dreams but it is naive to think that every dream is a revelation from God. However Kelsey claims that,

> Even Christians, for nearly fiftenn hundred years, considered dreams to be a natural way in which spiritual reality reaches out and touches us. With this understanding the dream can be seen as the most natural way for God to give His revelation to people today[15].

Kelsey further states that every Church father in the early Church from Justin Martyr to Irenaeus, from Clement and Tertullian to Origen and Cyprian believed that dreams were a means of revelation.

> These men all believed that dreams gave access to the same realm of reality which one could penetrate in meditation. That realm in which God was found could be revealed either spontaneously in a dream or vision or by opening oneself consciously to it in meditation[16].

Kelsey believes from his own experience with ministers and lay people, with agnostics and confirmed believers, that dreams offer the best evidence of existence of another level of reality, as he calls it[17].

b) Understanding Dreams:

The Old Testament has many examples of people who were gifted with interpretation of dreams. Joseph in the house of the pharaohs of Egypt, Daniel in the court of Babylon and several others received the gift of interpreting dreams (Dan. 2.20). This is how Daniel acknowledges the gift:

> Blessed be God's name from age to age,
> for all wisdom and power are his.
> He changes seasons and times;
> he deposes kings and sets them up;
> he gives wisdom to the wise
> and all their store of knowledge to the men who know;
> he reveals deep mysteries;
> he knows what lies in darkness,
> and light has its dwelling with him.
> To thee, God of my fathers, I give thanks and praise,
> for thou hast given me wisdom and power;
> thou hast now revealed to me what we asked,
> and told us what the king is concerned to know.

Like dreaming of dreams and seeing of visions, interpreting dreams also was considered as a charismatic gift and it was wisdom granted to some people. But as we have mentioned above, it is futile to find meaning to every dream because some dreams are clearly meaningless and even misleading. Some are only symptoms of a disturbed mind.

As in the case of any gift there are three criteria to know whether dreaming dreams and interpreting dreams and visions are divine gifts or not. Hollenweger suggests the criteria as follows:

1) the gifts should serve the common good of God's people, help to build up the community (I Cor. 14);
2) no one can say, "Anathema Jesus", under the influence of the gifts of God. That is, the relationship to the Jesus of Nazareth, the Jesus of history is a constituent element for

Paul's spirituality. There were people in Corinth in Paul's time who said, "Christ is Lord, but Anathema Jesus."

3) in the fellowship of the believers these gifts should help the outsider to recognise the work of God among them.

Sigmund Freud suggested different ways of interpreting dreams. In what he calls the symbolic method of interpretation, the dream is considered as a whole and its content is sought to be replaced by another content which is intelligible and analogous to the original content. Joseph used this method to analyse the dream of the Egyptian pharaoh in the Old Testament. The weak cows and the strong cows are replaced by the famine years and the plentiful years in the interpretation.

In the decoding method, on the other hand, a dream is treated as a cryptograph and each sign is translated into another sign having a known meaning in accordance with a fixed key. In this case not only the dream is taken into account but also the dreamer, his character and the circumstances of the dream. That is why Freud always insisted that the dreamer should be helped to find out the meaning of his dream. In the decoding method the commonly accepted meaning of signs is important but the meanings of the signs could also change from the way the dreamer himself would interpret them.

On the general idea of dreams having some meaning in any case, Freud is very clear. He says,

> I must affirm that dreams really have a meaning and that a scientific procedure for interpreting them is possible[18].

On the matter of the dreamer's own part in the interpretation of the dream, Christopher Bryant in his interesting book <u>Jung and the Christian Way</u>[19] states that this was Jung's principle also in interpreting the dreams. This is how he summarises Jung's view:

> No interpretation, he insists, can be accepted as certainly correct unless it wins the agreement of the dreamer himself. However sure a person may be of the correctness of his interpretation he must

regard it as only a likely guess until it has won the assent of the dreamer. Even though an interpretation were, in point of fact true, it would be of no use to the dreamer unless it rang bells for him[20].

Bryant also says that,

> Unlike Freud who believed that each symbol had a fixed meaning, Jung believed that a symbol might have different meanings for different people. It is therefore important in seeking to interpret a dream to approach the task with an open mind, dismissing all preconceived notions in order to listen to what the dream is actually saying.

In the Bible there are several types of dreams from the way God's people have understood them.

i) In some dreams God's people have been warned of the coming events.
   An angel appears to Jacob to tell what was going to happen. Gen. 31.11
   God appears to Solomon in a dream. I Kings 3.15
   God says that He would reveal Himself to the Prophets in dreams. Num. 12.6.
   Joseph is warned by the angel in a dream. Mat. 1.20, 2.13, 19, 27.19.

ii) Some dreams admonished or warned people against giving trouble to God's children.
   Abimelec warned against doing harm to Sarah. Gen. 20.4.
   Laban warned against threatening Jacob. Gen. 32.34.
   Elihu tells Job that God speaks in dreams at night and men are frightened at His warnings. Job. 20.8.
   The wise men asked to go away in a different route. Mt. 2.12, 22.

iii) Some dreams foretold an impending danger,
   Pharaoh's dream about the coming famine. Gen. 41.12
   Gideon warned through the dream of a Midianite soldier. Judges 7.13.

iv) Some dreams come from worry and anxiety.
   An admonition that the more one gets worried the more likely he is to have bad dreams. Eccl. 5.3.
   Job complains that he is getting terrible dreams and visions due to worry. Job. 7.14.
   Bad dreams cause worry, and fear of God is better than dreams. Eccl. 5.7.
v) There are false dreams, misleading dreams, and dreams from the evil spirits.
   Fortune tellers and false dreamers mentioned. Zach. 10.2.
   False dreams and necromancy mentioned together and warning given against them. Jer. 27.9.
   False prophets mentioned. Jud. 8.

While admitting that many dreams are meaningless and therefore insignificant, Kelsey suggests that they can be helpful and sometimes act as therapeutic tools because of their healing power and their speaking to the immermost heart of the dreamer. This is how he describes that unusual experience:

> But then, unexpectedly a numinous experience or a powerful dream breaks in upon one and strikes at the very center of his being. His former complacency is shattered, a meaninglessness is healed, an anxiety is washed out, often a physical illness disappears; an inner confidence given, a whole direction in life becomes apparent, and a secure conviction about the nature of reality is established. In other words, there are long range, and significant results in the observable outer world[21].

In the charismatic and indigenous church groups in India dreams are often considered as God's messengers, and there are many instances where lives have been affected most deeply as a result of dreams, especially when the dreamer gives a special godly significance to the dream.

Often the dreamer himself is the best guide to interpret his own dreams. The symbols he sees in the dream and the meanings he gives to these symbols, the associations, the values and the world view--all these are his own treasure from which the dreamer brings out his own tools to interpret his dreams. It is for that reason many psychoanalysts engage the dreamer in conversation so that he may be able to interpret his own dream. Carl Gustav Jung gives many examples of this method of interpretation both from his own dreams and also from the dreams of his patients. In other words, as Kelsey reminds us,

> There is one major difference between experiences coming from this realm and those of the physical world. When a man sets out to discover the nature of the physical world, his own individual activity is of primary importance. He achieves results by directed analytical thinking. It is true that this requires the help of intuition, as so many students of philosophy of science have shown. But intuitive "inspiration" does not often come to the scientist - and it is not often used when it does come - unless he has done his homework of observing, recording, classifying, hypothesizing, analyzing and comparing. The knowledge that is given from non-physical or spiritual realm comes in quite a different way[22].

Further, Kelsey says by way of suggesting a few guidelines for this process,

> What is required of man is the openness to allow such experience a place in his life. Then one will want to see what it means to him; and to find this out, thinking is important, but even here the experience itself is the primary guide[23].

In other words, the difference between science and intuition is that one is repeatable at any time anywhere by anyone whereas the other is not so repeatable. Many things which can not be scientifically explained now we may be able to explain later when the necessary tools become available. A true scientist does not deny as untrue all that is not possible to repeat experimentally.

It is perhaps not so much the causal regularity that is important in this, as the Western man often seeks, as it is more an interest which a non-Western man shows in finding meanings in meaningful coincidences[24]. Therefore before we either dismiss dreams as meaningless stuff or romanticize them for something more than they really are, it may be useful to remember that there are levels of reality. It is true that,

> For most of us the first hurdle in understanding dreams is to lay aside our notions about them. As long as one tries to make every dream fit some particular idea, it will be difficult to make much sense of them. The idea that every dream will predict the future, or direct one's love life, makes it almost as hard to understand dreams as insisting that they are only chaotic and irrational. If one tries to find deep significance or a great revelation of God in every dream, one will end up making nonsense of most of them. The same thing is true of trying to make every dream about a familiar person reveal some fact about that individual[25].

c) <u>Dreams are About the Dreamer:</u>

The Church has never formulated a real doctrine of dreams. Dreaming has been considered as an experience purely subjective and very unreliable to use for drawing conclusions. There are dreams and revelations through dreams sometimes, of course, but these are considered extraordinary experiences not in the realm of every day Christian life like preaching the word of God for example, or prayer and meditation. To some people, experience which is not associated with intellect will have no value. But Kelsey is right when he says,

> Religious experiences do not belong just to the intelligent or the sophisticated. Quite the contrary, they are given to children and simple peasants, as well as to philosophers and theologians; they come to sinners bent on destruction, as well as to pious folk who feel they need no special help. This encounter is the real leveler of mankind[26].

What is the attitude of Christians in general about this? Kelsey thinks that a great many church people feel that these experiences, without respect for intellectual, moral and social boundaries, can have no value. This was the thinking of Aristotle again who maintained that God could not possibly speak through dreams. Kelsey summarises Aristotle's thinking on the subject thus:

> It was perfectly obvious from first principles that God would not want to communicate directly with people who were simple or stupid and depraved. Since it was equally certain that such people had just as interesting and astounding dreams as the most intellectual and morally elite, therefore, according to Aristotle's thinking God did not send these experiences[27].

Kelsey adds that modern Christianity has bought this attitude without even considering its implications. His assertion that modern religion stands isolated on this point deserves serious consideration. Kelsey maintains that there is no early culture which has not held some belief that man has direct access to gods, through spiritual reality through dreams and other extra-sensory experiences. Usually this belief has been accepted and held collectively and as long as consciousness is little developed, the experience also is usually given through collective means. It is the shaman, the seer, the prophet, or the medicine man who acts as mediator between the people and direct confrontation with these realities and he interprets the experience and its meaning into symbolic words and actions[28]. I think this is what is happening in the Bible Mission and the other charismatic groups in India today. These people who are now in the pre-literary and oral communications tradition find dreams as an important collective experience and they believe that God appears to them through the mediation of dreams and visions.

In a chapter on Luther and the Reality of the Invisible, Bengt Hoffman gives an interesting account of the Reformer's views on the subject[29]. 'Invisible' is the word used by Luther as characteristic of God's influence in our lives, perhaps because Luther found what he called mere 'historical faith' so inadequate. Luther's 'awareness of being watched, guided and used by the invisible forces' was strong. But Martin Luther very wisely was careful not to use his own revelations for the purpose of buttressing the persuasive power of his preaching. This may be the danger which many Indian Christian gurus should guard against, taking the example of Martin Luther.

Hoffman is expressing a commonly shared knowledge when he says that a personal story about psycho-spiritual experiences will soon lose its freshness and its impact both with the speaker-writer and with the hearers and the readers. To Luther even prayer sometimes became a kind of parapsychic experiece where he felt that the Holy Spirit spoke to him.

On the view of the earlier Church fathers on the subject, Kelsey reports as follows:

> It is clear that all these men held basically the same idea. There were two worlds, physical and spiritual and humanity was a bridge between them. In dreams the realities of the non-physical world were at work autonomously; acting on their own and governed by their own rules, they intruded into the ordinary lives and experience of human beings. And at times dreams were also the instrument by which God spoke to men and women[30].

But the question has to be asked, how far this view of the two worlds, one physical and the other spiritual, is biblical. The idea that the physical world is evil and sinful is basically a pagan idea and it is quite contrary to the concept of incarnation, the Word becoming flesh.

d) <u>Dreams in the form of Poetry, Song and Story</u>:

Poetry, song and story are also other forms of dreams which mankind shares. This is what Kelsey says about the part played by imagination in meditation and about story and poetry as what he calls 'maps of the inner territory'.

> In recent years a great deal has been written about the use of stories in theological study. In addition, people who are trying to describe their experiences of God have begun to find that categories

of rationalistic thought are not adequate for sharing what they have experienced, and so they turn to poetry or story, to fairy tale or fantasy. In all these ways emotions and experiences are expressed in images rather than in pure concepts[31].

As in dreams, man expresses in archetypal language some of his deep thoughts and images in poetry. Song, poetry, story and image are open, less prescriptive, and more suggestive and evocative. Through the art forms, including both performing arts like dance and drama and visual arts like painting and sculpture, man has always spoken a 'dream language' which speaks to the depths of the inner heart. All the myths and epic stories which are transmitted from generation to generation in any culture are the dreams of that culture and they are stored and used in the collective memories of the members of the community as in a modern computer system, as Hollenweger puts it. We have already seen briefly how the church in India has started to make use of these communication forms that are indigenous and imaginative, and I shall discuss this topic further when I come to consider meditation and imagination in this chapter.

But Kelsey is right when he says that in telling a story one reveals the self and not God. However he suggests that,

> Many of the great story tellers from Shakespeare and John Bunyan to Robert Louis Stevenson have been studied by individuals who work with the insights and wisdom of depth psychology. These studies show that at the deepest level a writer often reveals not only himself or herself but things about the general structure of reality itself[32].

3. Visions

a) Introduction:

The Bible makes very little distinction between visions and dreams. These two words, as I have mentioned already, are used interchangeably in the Greek and Hebrew languages. The book of the prophet Joel mentions dreams and visions together as God's gift to mankind in the last days, and Peter, quoting this text on the day of Pentecost, speaks of them as the sign of the fulfilment of God's promise to the world (Joel 2.28, Acts 2.17).

The Bible is full of visions and visionary appearances and instances when God spoke to the people in apparitions and theophanies. Post-resurrection appearances of our Lord are more than 'visions'. But one can say that it is hard to understand the post-resurrection appearances if we do not believe in visions. The disciples were very consistent in narrating these experiences and in a way these are extra-sensory experiences beyond the ordinary realm.

So many people claim that they have had visionary experiences of some kind or other and claim that God has spoken to them that it is difficult to dismiss their claims and say that these are mere imagination. Carl Jung clearly narrates a vision he had when he was critically ill. Kelsey includes three of Jung's visions in his chapter called "The Visions of the Cosmos", and these three incidents have something very much in common in all of them[33].

b) Meditation and Visions:

Many visions are connected with prayer and meditation of the visionaries. St. Peter was in prayer when he saw the vision of the heavenly sling (Acts 10.9). Sadhu Sundar Singh saw many visions in prayer and he 'spoke' to the Lord and heard many parables from the Lord. Sundar Singh says that he saw the Lord and spoke to Him. He enjoyed his fellowship. This is the meaning of expressions like, 'at the Master's feet' (Sundar Singh), 'waiting in the Presence' (Devadas), etc. Many saintly people talk about this presence in different words and in different ways. Kelsey narrates his own experience as follows:

> Several times a week I simply stop and wait before Him, sometimes picturing Him at the time of the resurrection, rising victorious from the tomb, or perhaps knocking at the door of my soul, as William Hunt's picture "The Light of the World" suggests. And then in the quiet I say, "Here I am. Tell me what you wish of me"[34].

This is what in fact many Indian Christian gurus do--imagine sitting with Christ in front of them and speak to Him and wait for messages from Him. Hours and hours sometimes pass as they wait silently in meditation in communion with Christ. And this is what Devadas had advocated as a form of fellowship with Christ--the alone with the alone, the beloved looking into the face of the Lord, his lover. This is what the Hindu sages have done in their own way for centuries. For a Hindu archaka (worshipper) it is a whole series of tender acts of adoration to the Lord starting with the offering of water to cool his feet, fruits and flowers for him to enjoy, fanning him to make him cool and comfortable, putting him to sleep and waking him up again, etc. What is it that these people meet in these imaginary acts? They meet an inner reality of themselves and it is possible but not compulsory that one would grasp the inner spiritual truth or insights about Christ through this method. It is possible for some to grasp the spiritual truths this way, just as it is possible to others through theological analysis.

So, in principle, the idea of thinking in images (imagination) in meditation should work for Christians also. Kelsey defends it in the following words,

> Christ can be approached in the same way if he is the one whom Christians say He is, the true image of the loving God. If we can communicate with other elements of the spiritual world through dream images, then we can also interact with the image of Christ and the reality which He incorporates and expresses. Of all the processes of imagination which have helped me, none has offered half as much value as this approach to Christ[35].

The experience of many of the devotees is just similar to what is described by Kelsey, a state of standing under utter underserved grace of God and tasting His love bestowed without merit on men. Kelsey says,

> Often I ask Him why He bothers to come and be with someone like me. Each time He tells me that He is Love and that it is the nature of Love to give of itself, that He cares for every human being and comes whenever we will allow Him to enter and share

Himself with us. This experience is one that is never exhausted. It returns each time as fresh and real and autonomous as a magnificent sunset or an encounter with a truly loving human being. One can never predict what the meeting will bring[36].

Many converts from Hinduism who claim that they have had this experience of fellowship with Christ in a vision always express this kind of surprise that Christ Himself had condescended to appear to them and they do not know why He gave them His darshan, vision. Kelsey confesses that from these experiences of fellowship have come to him the best ideas he has had, the most effective sermons and the best attempts to reconciliation and caring for others.

In these meetings with Love He has conversed with me and told me of His defeats in the world and His victories. Out of this sense of sharing as well as being cared for, I find encouragement to keep on trying to grow and become what He wants me to become, and I also find directions about what to do and to work on next[37].

Kelsey however is aware of the possibility of people misusing this kind of experience and sometimes telling some silly things. But those who keep at this practice will no doubt develop critical capacity. One is no longer closed to the possibility that there may be a perfectly acceptable view of the world which admits the reality of a God who cared enough to become man and dwell among us, and who still cares and communicates with us today. And in Kelsey's own words,

Like the first "giant stride" on the moon, it is then only a step to realise that one need not be gullible and uncritical about every experience that comes from across the boundary of space and time. After all, there is a view of reality that insists upon testing these experiences and demands that we bring the best of our critical and analytical abilities to these encounters[38].

c) How Exactly to Handle these Extra-Sensory Experiences:

We have already mentioned that these experiences are unusual and varied in the detail from person to person. We have not developed sufficient skill to evaluate them fully as we can do with the empirical data. In the words of Kelsey, the question is asked, How then does the mature Christian find acceptance of himself as he actually is, in relation to the world of spirit as it really exists? Kelsey like Devadas of the Bible Mission offers some basic rules to follow, such as[39]:

1) Act as if the spiritual realm exists. The man who takes the chance that the spiritual realm does exist, who acts upon that hypothesis as best he can, has every chance of finding this realm and being able to relate to it in sustained and creative way. And this is possible for all of us. Any man can enter upon this religious way no matter what he thinks or doubts.

2) Undertake the quest with serious purpose. Those who enter lightly or with idle curiosity usually end with a stomach ache wondering why the endless cotton candy turned poisonous. To some it may be a sudden illumination, for others it may be a second way of obedience to our religious heritage, persistent inner voice, listening and obeying the prick. The first was the way of St. Paul and St. Francis and the second the way of many of us.

Some enter the undertaking through despair. Finally the sensible few reflect enough to realise that all is not well with them. In all these there is one thing common--a deep inner sense that something is lacking in the searcher. The man who is perfectly adjusted to this world and completely comfortable in his 'grey flannel suit' can rarely be touched by God.

3) Seek companionship and spiritual direction--a spiritual director as an adviser, or a friend to whom we can speak. There are others in the community who are seeking this kind of fellowship.

4) Turn towards the inner world through silence and introversion. Many people find it easier to be silent in company than when

they are alone. (That is why the silent prayer groups in the Bible Mission and the practice of sharing experiences after the silence are found very rewarding to the community.)

5) Learn the value of genuine fasting. In fasting we turn our bodies away from the world. It clears the mind and heart; it opens avenues of realisation and thought which before were closed.

6) Learn to use the forgotten faculty of imagination. Remember the difference between the classical Christian meditation and the devotional practice of the major Eastern religions. In Eastern thought the individual is seen as emptying himself of all emotions and images. The goal of most Eastern meditation is union with the Godhead in which the ego is dissolved and the path towards this is suppression of images. Christian meditation is more materialistic. One's total psyche is involved and this necessarily involves the use of image and emotions.

Rational thinking, directed analytical thought, proceeding by logical reasoning from a basic concept, is one thing. But there is another kind of thinking which is equally important. That is thinking through images instead of through concepts, thinking which is passive rathter than active, which follows a meaning that seems to be independent of the rational mind.

Dreams are symbolic communications like art and music; they represent imaginative thinking, and learning to appreciate them will help to awaken the faculty of imagination.

7) Keep a journal. This helps one to reflect on the experience at a later date. A process of clarifying occurs when we write down our thoughts (Devadas had advocated this practice).

Many people keep a journal of dreams. The meaning of dreams is revealed through the same faculty which can unlock the treasures of the Bible or other works of religious devotion--the faculty of imagination.

8) Keep a record of dreams.

9) Be honest with yourself.

10) Let your life manifest genuine love.
11) Gird yourself with persistent courage.
12) Give generously of your material goods.

4. Healing

a) What is Spiritual Healing?

There has been so much written on the subject of spiritual healing recently that it is hard to summarise the thinking of Christians on the subject in a short space. But this is a very important topic which must be dealt with in this chapter because, as we have seen earlier, this is one of the major points of strife between some older denominations and the non-White Indigenous church groups. On the one hand, prayer healing is a very difficult phenomenon to understand and it is very much scriptual and quite central to the ministry of Jesus Christ as we see in the New Testament. The Church today is more alive to the recognition of the healing ministry and we interpret the healing miracles a little better than before theologically.

Douglas Webster in his interesting little booklet, What is Spiritual Healing[40], prefers not to use expressions like Faith Healing or Divine Healing but rather to use the expression, Spiritual Healing. Faith healing to him is not a helpful expression because it is not clear to whom or to what this faith is directed, and divine healing on the other hand is not a specific term according to him because in a sense all healing, including healing through modern medical techniques, is divine, just as all truth is divine. So spiritual healing is a more helpful name for the phenomenon we are now talking about.

Spiritual healing, it must be said straight away, does not discourage the use of medicine. Sometimes the healing comes through prayer of the patient, or his friends or relatives, sometimes it comes through the administration of some act like anointing and laying on of hands, and yet some other times it comes through the sacraments.

Healing is always associated with the preaching of the word of God and it is seen as a ministry to the body, mind and spirit, although this kind of trinitarian description of man is an over-simplification according to some thinkers[41] and such a concept assumes that there are definable boundaries between the three.

Webster gives us three reasons why the subject of spiritual healing deserves our utmost attention and study. I summarise his argument as follows[42].

1) There is in the human race, especially among the peoples not yet influenced by the 'scientific approach', a fundamental and absolutely right instinct that healing and religion are closely connected and that religious man, just because he is religious (whatever his religion be), has healing power. The story is told how non-medical missionaries too in India are approached by the Hindus for healing simply because they are considered to be religious men. They are believed to have power over disease because they are religious. The healing functions of the Church now cannot be handed over in toto to scientific medicine.

2) One very clear reason for the drift from the Church in our modern times, in the opinion of Webster, is that religion, even Christianity, seems irrelevant to the life of the masses. The non-Christian or the would-be Christian of the Western post-Christian society knows that there ought to be a power in Christianity, if it is what it claims to be, but he does not see the power. This is the problem of the Hindu seeker also. He has heard about the so-called spiritual powers in popular Hindu gods and goddesses. He has heard the New Testament Bible stories, and he has also heard the claims made by Christians that Jesus saves. All that matters to the sick and suffering Hindu is a manifestation of the power of Christ to heal him. The disciples of Christ did that, the New Testament Church did it and the Church today should do it, in his opinion.

3) Webster also thinks, with some justification, that the fact that the Church has neglected the healing ministry has led to a rich crop of heresies and schisms. He mentions Christian Science and Spiritualism as examples. This may be true. It is certainly true that some of the charismatic groups and the indigenous folk churches in India have claimed to possess the healing gift in the name of Christ and they despised the organised churches because, in their

opinion, these churches have lost the power to heal the sick. In the words of Webster,

> There are 1,250 different independent churches in South Africa and one of the reasons for this incredible phenomenon is our failure to proclaim and practice all that the Gospel has to say about healing[43].

b) <u>Development of the Church's view on Healing</u>:

Morton Kelsey in one of the best books on the subject[44] discusses in detail the matter of Christian healing. This is what Kelsey says,

> Most modern Christian churches believe that they have nothing to do officially with healing the sick. They do not feel that the church's actions--its religious acts--have any direct effect on human health. It is true that religious groups do build hospitals and medical centers but this does not differ from any other act of charity or compassion. Until recently many such hospitals did not even have chaplains to serve their patients. In fact it has come to be widely believed that there is no particular relation between the practice of Christianity and sound health of mind and body[45].

In fact, even the so-called spiritual healing also does not differ from any other act of charity or compassion. The prayer healing campaigns of Devadas, for example, are acts of compassion, a Christian response to the needs of the people who are suffering with disease and demons. In that sense they are also like hospitals. There are four different but overlapping views against the practice of spiritual healing:

1) The materialistic conviction that man's body can be cared for by medical and physical means alone and that religious help is superfluous.
2) The idea of sickness as God's direct and disciplinary gift to men as expressed in the English office of the Visitation to the Sick.

3) The conviction known as dispensationalism, the belief that God originally gave such ministries as healing only for the time being, in order to get the church established.
4) The theology of Bultman: the understanding that there is no supernatural agency which can break through natural law.

All the above four views have effectively influenced the major churches in India as elsewhere for a long time and to some extent even now. Modern medicine with its miraculous drugs and the many mission hospitals and the research centres have been considered adequate for the health needs of the people. And the idea of sickness as God's punishment was also very easy for the Indian Christians to believe because of the Hindu idea that any sickness, especially the more dangerous and the epidemic type, was the result of the wrath of a god or goddess on the sins of the community. There are also many stories in the Old Testament to support this view of sickness and punishment.

Although there is not much preoccupation in India with the process of demythologization, this idea of dispensationalism first preached by some Western missionaries is passionately held by some Indian pastors who do not know exactly how to handle the healing miracle stories of the New Testament. Many Christians therefore believe that the day of miracles has gone. The Reformers also seem to be clear on the question of dispensationalism. This was most probably the reason behind the hesitation on the part of the Protestant churches on the matter of spiritual healing. Kelsey says that

> Luther came to admit that no one raised the dead any more and that what passed for healing miracles seemed to him to be the devil's artifices and not miracles at all. The day of miracles has past, he concluded, and the real gift of the Holy Spirit is to enlighten Scripture, for now that the apostles have preached the Word and have given their writings, nothing more than what they had written remains to be revealed, no new and special revelation of miracle is necessary[46].

Calvin's teaching was not much different either. This is what the Swiss reformer is reported to have said:

> The gift of healing disappeared with the other miraculous powers which the Lord was pleased to give for a time that it might render the new preaching of the gospel for ever wonderful. Therefore, even were we to grant that anointing was a sacrament of those powers which were then administered by the hands of the apostles, it pertains not to us, to whom no such powers have been committed[47].

The reformers are rightly cautious about the dangers of misusing the miracles and especially healing for personal glory and exhibition of power and they are more concerned about the word of God and its power in the ordinary as well as the extra-ordinary. But this does not mean that they are dispensationalists; much less are they agnostics.

It is no wonder that the United Lutheran Church in America in 1962 took an official action and issued a statement to its members instructing them to stay clear of religious healing. This church through its appointed representatives looked at the 'religious quackery practised by certain faith healers' and declared that while God sometimes does permit miraculous cures these should not be sought since 'it can not be assumed that because of Christ's victory in their lives, Christians can expect healing effects not available to other people'. This is a very useful caution.

Also, to be fair to Martin Luther, we must say that he did believe in prayer for healing. Bengt Hoffman gave many instances in his book <u>Luther and the Mystics</u> where Luther demonstrated his faith in healing prayer. Hoffman says that,

> It would indeed have been surprising had Luther omitted charismatic healing as part of the work of salvation. His total grasp was after all based on a keen awareness of the dynamic interrelationship between body and spirit, incarnate existence and invisible grace[48].

Talking about the theory of dispensationalism which appeared under the influence of rationalism, Hoffman has this is say:

> Under the impact of rationalism the church has often relegated spiritual healing to a bygone age. Healing miracles occurred when Jesus lived in history, it has been said, but no longer. Some theologians have been known to claim that miracles (occurrences out of the ordinary, beyond the range of normal causality) perhaps never actually were historical facts but rather faith's understandable adornment of the beloved memory of the teacher. Martin Luther did not think that way, and it is futile to reconcile him with modernity in this regard, as some of his interpreters did and do. With respect to psychic force of faith in Christ his belief was not bound by his era[49].

Hoffman substantiates his view of Luther by citing examples from the Reformer's life when he expressed faith in healing prayer. After an attack of stone in 1537, in a letter which he wrote to his wife, Martin Luther said,

> However, the prayers and tears of pious men who love me have found favour before God.

After his recovery from stone about a month later a good friend asked Luther what remedy he had used. Luther replied: 'Prayer, for in all Christian congregations they fervently prayed for me according to the direction of Apostle James (5.14-15)'[50].

Hoffman in the pages that followed in this book gives many more instances where Luther expressed the same faith in healing prayer both for himself and for his friends. Hoffman reports,

> There is among Luther's letters a document which shows us beyond any doubt that he viewed spiritual healing as an integral part of the pastoral task of the church[51]. (Hoffman quotes the letter in full.)

What Luther did not do however was to make the matter of healing a subject of doctrinal discourse. As Hoffman says,

> The subject belonged to the realm of interior, mystical experience and was, as such, so personal that one could not use it in theological argumentation or in preaching[52].

Interestingly enough, in the charismatic churches like the Bible Mission in India, the healing miracles through the witness of those who received healing are shared among others, and they become instrumental for many more to believe. But this sharing is done in intimate supportive groups and not in the form of theological debates.

c) <u>Spiritual Healing: the Present Understanding</u>:

Talking about the importance of spiritual healing and the serious consideration it deserves in the churches today, Douglas Webster says,

> As in the apostolic days, healing is probably the greatest point of contact the Christian Church can have with the masses today, if only we will do as Jesus did and come to them where they are instead of expecting them to come to us where we are. Without doubt this is the aspect of the Gospel which could become most immediately relevant today almost anywhere, at home and overseas. That is why it is tragic and deplorable that so few Christians show any interest in it and so many are full of doubt. If people could be made to see that the Gospel means the whole of God being concerned with the whole of man, evangelism would enter a new and glorious chapter[53].

In another chapter in the "Theology of Healing", Webster makes five useful points with support from Scripture verses.

> 1) Disease is evil: In the story of healing miracle recorded in St. Luke 13.10-17, the Lord ascribes the tragic state of the woman

in the story to Satan's bonds. So also in the Lord's confrontation with the Pharisees on the subject of the source of his power to cast out demons (St. Mark 3.22-27). Satan is pictured as a strong man holding humanity in thrall. Jesus comes as a stronger man to bind him and set the prisoneer free.

2) Health is good: It is the creator's will that His children should be free from disease. In St. Matthew 11.2-6 we see that Christ tells the disciples of John the Baptist that the day of the Lord arrived because of the healing signs they see. The kingdom of God is that area of life where God's will is done. "If I by the Spirit of God cast out devils, then is the Kingdom of God come upon you" (Matt. 12.28). Christ gives the same authority to his disciples to heal and to cast out demons (St. Mark 16.17-18).

3) Mental attitudes do matter: Today psychosomatic has become a jargon word. Webster cites the words of Christ about what defiles man--that which proceeds from out of the heart (Mark 7.14-23). Health is something which belongs to mind as well as body. Faith is related to healing in Christ's ministry.

4) Love helps to heal: It is very important that the patient should know that God loves him and this will help him to hope and to recover. It is also important that the patient should be assured of the love of a caring community. Lambourne has this as his main thesis, the caring community, the Church in healing ministry[54].

5) The work of healing is a moral obligation: Jesus included healing as part of his work because it is part of the Gospel. Healing is not distinct from evangelism and pastoral work, it is part of both.

It is healing through religion; by faith, prayer, sacramental acts and loving service in the Name of Christ. It is healing that touches the central fibres of man's being by dealing with his "self" and not just his body. This is the kind of healing that the Church is called in every age to offer to men and women, and this ministry can never be replaced even by the most efficient and advanced medical services[55].

d) <u>The Healing Church: the Tubingen Consultation:</u>

A consultation held jointly with the representatives of the Lutheran World Federation and the World Council of Churches in Tubingen in 1964 has reported very useful insights into the subject of the healing ministry of the Church. Lesslie Newbigin in a preparatory paper outlines the relationship between the healing ministry and the mission of the Church and presents a situation where healing is seen as manifestation of the dethroning of the evil one by the coming of Christ. Newbigin says,

> This is what I have seen happening in very simple situations, where a doctor is at work in a remote village, and without any elaborate strategy healing is intimately related to the preached word. Healing illustrates, validates, the preached word, without any elaborate arrangements to make it do so. You do not have to assemble the patients to preach a sermon to them before you can treat them. The thing, as it were, authenticates itself as a visible manifestation, of what the preacher is talking about, namely that there has come into the world the kingdom of God, the reign of God by which the powers of evil are dethroned. Maybe I am oversimplifying, maybe I am romanticising, but I do not think so, for I have seen this happening in villages in South India[56].

On the question of secularization, which is the form in which the non-Western world today meets salvation history, Newbigin declares that secularization follows the Gospel. The dethroning of ancient powers becomes accepted simply as a fact apart from faith in Christ. Newbigin thinks that the whole 'business of secularization and welfare state is obviously something which could not have arisen out of the ancient pagan religions of Asia. It is the byproduct of Christianity'. However, along with modern medicine many village people in

India still believe that healing involves spiritual powers and not just physical remedies.

Picturing the great support which a healing ministry would receive in India and how the flocks of Christians would meet for mass meetings at such times, Newbigin says,

> Naturally the ordinary congregation tends to be more enthusiastic about this kind of thing than it is about the support of the mission hospital because the ordinary Christian does not see what he can do about the hospital. The mission hospital has a very big budget in relation to which the contributions of the ordinary members of the congregation would look like a drop in the bucket, whereas these healing missions are something you can do something about; you can pray, you can shout, you can sing. It seems to be linked up with the gospel to the congregations, whereas the mission hospital tends to be a place run by somebody else on a budget somebody else looks after and its only relation to the Christian congregation is that it is a place where you can get cheap treatment for yourself and your children and possibly jobs for your nephews[57].

Also the growing complexity of specialised techniques which are used in modern medicine is making the non-medical man feel that he can have very little sense of responsibility. This tends to foster non-involvement and a counter-movement towards faith healing in all its various forms. Even then the scientific forms of healing are unfortunately not the whole answer to man's sickness. As another paper at the Tubingen consultation states.

> In discussing pre-scientific forms of healing, the scientific approach can take us only part of the way. A purely scientific point of view can deal only with the observed facts and laws of nature, and when applied to the human personality, can encompass only part of human nature and not the whole. In the present state of our knowledge,

any claim that scientific method offers a totality of truth implies a pre-judged uncritical attitude on the part of the observer. When applied to pre-scientific forms of healing scientific method is apt to exhibit merely the shortcomings and lack of knowledge of these as a consequence of their being non-scientific[58].

Martin Scheel, in this paper on "Pre-Scientific Forms of Healing"[59], has reminded us that scientists of our time are aware of the fact that for its effective practice medicine can not ignore anthropological and empirical facts. Scheel is describing a situation in India in the rural areas with regard to medical services and healing and he concludes that it is probable that the same principles and motives have a wider application in Asia, though with many differences in detail. One important thing to be remembered in dealing with sickness in India is to know the beliefs and fears of the patient more than the physiological factors. This is what Scheel says,

> At the onset of illness it is first necessary to discover the cause of the disease. The patient is led to ask what special power is disturbing him, and how the balance of power could be restored. He does not trust his own ability to deal effectively with illness but seeks to add power to his natural capacities by establishing contact with the sphere of power. He therefore responds to events beyond his understanding by performing rites to make sense of them. These take the form of sacrifices offered to the gods in order to make them descend and reveal the secret[60].

The rural folk in India live in constant fear of evil spirits and powers in nature trying to harm them. They are afraid of any disturbance to the equilibrium and they depend on intermediary agencies to help them from these evil powers. Even with the available modern medical help, the patient sometimes seeks other sources of comfort and confidence. The stars of the sky, the day of the week, numbers and colours—all have some magical influences and they may affect the health and sickness of the person. All these are connected somehow with disease and cure.

> The cure or prevention of disease is achieved through rituals. There is no direct trust in God, divine power, priest, guru or himself. Intermediaries are necessary, through whom the power in which he believes and in which he trusts is able to be effective. By these means he tries to arrest threatening evil influences from the planets and also to drive out evil spirits. Many instruments and rites may be involved. Manthras are powerful compositions of words and syllables. Body and mind must be prepared by worship; the choice of the right time, right colour and right number is practised; amulets and medallions embody the deity[61].

In such a situation one effective way to help people is to create a trust in Christ as the powerful one who can conquer all evil powers, the stronger one who can bind the strong one and defeat him. This is what the Christian gurus and faith healers are doing, namely, presenting Christ as the healer who can bind the evil power of sickness and disease. It is this balance of power which Christ can restore to the sufferer. It is the Kingdom of God coming in its force. The man is at peace and the medicine now will cause the cure. The difference between the Eastern and the Western world views and their anthropologies as outlined by Scheel may be very important for the understanding of the healing process.

> The divergence of thought is believed to go back to about 500 B.C., the so-called axis time. At that time men were beginning to understand that they were different from their environment. A process of individualization went on simultaneously both in East and West. Western people tried to master the physical world by the discovery of governing principles and laws of nature in order to be able to build the world according to their wishes and needs. Eastern people saw themselves as an integral and lasting part of the total, and so subordinated themselves to the absolute in an endeavour to establish contacts with the supernatural in order to gain part of its power[62].

According to Scheel there are three types of possible reaction to modern medicine on the part of the patients with Afro-Asian background, which may be useful to note here:

1) The actions and the words of the physician may be interpreted according to the faith and understanding of the patient. The doctor is seen as a man who brings about contact with the sphere of power.
2) A second possibility may be destruction of existing faith. Since it is possible to understand Western medicine in purely technical ways, patients may think that other deeper questions are of no importance. The imminent danger in this case seems to be that either the basis for security is vanishing or another faith is appearing. Materialism may occupy the place of the former interest in religious questions and interest in communal organism may be substituted by individualism and self-interest.
3) The third reaction may be that the scientific and traditional concepts might exist side by side in the patient's mind the consequence of which would irrevocably be tension. His search for inner security, which is most important, would not come to an end, and he would probably try to find an answer to his need from other forms of healing[63].

Prayer healing in India and the healing campaigns of the non-White Indigenous church groups as we called them are serving the people in these situations. First of all, the faith healer or the praying group helping the patient is leading him to see the power of the Gospel and to believe in the redeeming work of Christ. As long as the faith healer shows himself only as mediator of God's power he can draw the man to the power of the Gospel. Secondly, since prayer healing does not destroy his concern for deeper questions, the patient does not feel deprived of his spiritual matters. His world view no doubt will be challenged and his former beliefs will be changed but what comes into its place is not a void but a rewarding experience of faith. He generally sees a need for repentance and will learn to know God and to love Him rather than living in fear of an angry god or goddess trying to destroy him.

To this extent prayer healing with or without modern medicine is helping the patient who comes from this kind of cultural and anthropological background which we have seen so far. Here is a great ministry awaiting the Christians in India today. As the Tubingen Report puts it,

> Christians thus meet a special challenge today. All the achievements of medical science are God-inspired and therefore are to be used in the service of our neighbours, but the Christian approach to human need cannot be an exclusive persistence in the scientific-technical side of healing as commonly practised today. Spiritual needs demand spiritual remedy. The world as a whole has still to make the discovery that scientific knowledge rather than superseding the Christian faith, illuminates it, and throws into sharper focus its fundamental teaching of the reality of the spiritual world, the basic unity of man, and the profound healing relationship of God to man in the person of Christ. There is challenge to every Christian to proclaim the good news in explicit and convincing terms to the sick, the despairing, and to all confronted with the barren meaninglessness of life without faith[64].

e) Conclusion[65]:

Finally, healing whether through medical treatment or prayer is a process which escapes neat explanations. It is difficult to predict exactly which medicine works in which person just as we do not know when and how prayer 'works'. Sometimes people are healed spontaneously when under observation by a medical doctor. In such cases one speaks of 'spontaneous' or 'psychogenic' healings. It is possible that human nature has healing reserves of which we are ignorant. It is therefore, at least at our present level of understanding, not demonstrable.

Therefore, phenomenologically, we can observe that,

1) There is no direct link between faith and healing. Faith is one of the factors that can help promote healing but it does not operate in cause and effect relationship. So one can say "Your faith has healed you" in a pastoral way but it cannot be considered as a kind of spiritual law. God acts according to His own free will and we cannot deal with God as we deal with a computer.

2) Healing is not limited to Christianity. There is no phenomenological difference between a Christian healing the sick with prayer and a Hindu guru healing by his own methods. All healing in fact is from God including healing with modern medicine. The difference is in interpretational framework.

So, theologically, we may conclude that,

1) Healing is a natural gift given to many human beings. This gift belongs to God's creative order, universal but not supernatural.

2) Because the Spirit of God is responsible for all life and not just for Christian life or Jewish life, or not even for religious life according to the biblical teaching, the gifts of healing may be manifested anywhere, whether we recognise these gifts as the gifts of God or not. They can be effective whether those using them are Christian or not. 'Veni Creator Spiritus', says the well-known hymn; the life-giving Spirit is active all over[66].

In practical terms, experience has suggested the following guidelines to me:

1) Healing evangelists and healing campaigns are not advisable. Healing ministry should be the ministry of the total Body of Christ. It is better that the minister does not take the healing ministry on himself but he should share it with the elders or some men and women in the church who pray with him for the sick and with the sick.

2) There should be no conditions for healing. Repentance, Baptism, even faith need not be the pre-conditions for healing. God can heal even without faith on the part of the sick person or the person praying for him. All these are good and necessary but they should not be linked with healing. It is God that heals and He does not lay any conditions to grant His healing.

3) The best way to handle the healing ministry is to integrate it into the Eucharistic liturgy of the church. Five or six people appointed from the congregation will be ready to lay hands and pray with the sick after Communion, as the sick persons come to the rail and seek the healing. The group prays. The congregation is operative and no individual is to get credit or blame. Thus the congregation will become the healing and praying community. The sick person need not tell what his or her problem is; it is enough if the sick one seeks healing by prayer and comes forward.

5. Experience Pointing to the Beyond

a) A Total Reality:

There is a reality, as we have seen above, which can be grasped through the senses and there is a reality that at present may not be experimentally perceived but has to be intuitively grasped. But the latter is just as real as the former. There is no dichotomy between the material and the non-material biblically. About the ways and means of experiencing this reality, Kelsey says,

> There is no doubt that the experience described by the advocates of Eastern meditation is a real and valid one, and we can learn much by studying those from both East and West who have experienced it. But there are other ways of experiencing the same reality, and they are just as real. Simple peasants sometimes have equally important experiences in the Eucharist or praying the rosary or repeating the Jesus prayer. Still others find by turning inward through imagination--which is one way of experiencing reality--and meeting the divine Lover who then draws them on to the deeper religious

experiences. Many people, religiously untutored, have used this imaginative method unconsciously as they conversed with God in a natural way about even the trivialities of daily living. The windows of ancient Gothic cathedrals and the icons of Eastern orthodoxy have also been launching pads for numerous individuals to enter this imaginative venture[67].

The problem with modern man is that he relies too much on the materialistic and scientific outlook. The Church also was caught up in this whirlpool of modernisation as we have seen, and consequently the Church has moved away from an immediate realisation of the beyond. We have been too much concerned with the historic Jesus and we allowed the cosmic Christ to pass by unnoticed, the Christ who acts here and now in the lives of those who follow him. Kelsey states it pointedly when he asked,

> What are the reasons for this almost total disagreement about the value and reality of mysticism? There is not much question about the main reason. The idea that one has no access to any realm of experience besides the material and rational leaves the mystic with no place for inner experience to come from. If this be so, the mystic must be suffering from delusion, or something worse. This idea itself is based upon faith—in the sense of believing something one has no evidence for--a faith that all knowledge ultimately comes from reason and sense experience. As I have shown in my book, Encounter with God, there is no good reason to maintain such a scientific faith when scientists like Oppenheimer and Heisenberg have abandoned it[68].

b) Three Kinds of Spiritual Experience:

Kelsey suggests that there are still other things to cause disagreement about religious experiences even after their validity is admitted by everyone. Religious experiences for one thing are not like peas in a pod. They are varied. There are at least three kinds of experience: the sacramental experience, the contemplative experience and that arising from meditative use of images.

i) <u>The Sacramental Experience</u>: This is a kind of religious experience in which the divine comes into focus directly through some element of the outer, physical world. Kelsey gives several examples of the sacramental experience outside the Christian Church. Within the Church, however,

> The great Christian sacraments, beginning from baptism, have offered a futher step of breaking off from one's old life and entering into a new relation with God. For Catholics and also many liturgical Protestants the Communion or the Eucharist is the continuing place of renewal where the divine touches humanity. The bread and wine become the body and the blood of Christ; in partaking of them one actually shares the life of the risen Christ. Within this tradition there are other sacramental experiences--confession and absolution, saying the rosary, the stations of the cross, the forty hours--which are alive and have power to open people up to the divine. And as Jung has shown, the dogmatic structure of the Church meets nearly all the psychological needs of those who follow its ways[69].

ii) <u>The Imageless Contemplation</u>: This kind of experience has no need for any outside elements. Physical matter, symbols, ritual are all forgotten and the only things that matter are the person and the immediate perception of the divine. Kelsey thinks that this kind of union with God which is an experience of losing one's ego gives a sense of identity, oneness and ecstasy and bliss. Commenting on this kind of experience Kelsey says,

> It is not hard to see how this idea took hold in India where human life seems to have been dominated by misery almost from the start. Detachment is probably the only attitude sensitive people can take to live alongside the hunger and poverty and sickness that are commonplace even today among masses in India. The great mystics and saints of the Middle Ages also lived with misery and dangers that are hard for us to believe. Men and women were stalked by plague

and famine and marauding hordes, and they forgot the idea of a God who came to heal and restore this life. Instead they looked for a God who would mercifully lift them out of the world into a bliss that would make up for all the misery. They turned to ascetic communities and rejected bodily life and the flesh in order to arrive at this experience of another world. Even though the great saints of this time balanced their other-worldliness by emphasizing charity and reaching out to people in the world, they were convinced that the main goal of the human soul was a blissful union with God. The point of existing was to reach a relationship with God in which nothing of this world interfered. They tried to reach a state uncluttered by emotions or images or ideas[70].

iii) <u>Meditation in Images and Symbols</u>: The third type of religious experience is found, according to Kelsey, by turning inward and using one's imagination as a tool with which to contact the reality of the spiritual world. This practice which can be learned by most people with a little determination opens up various levels and depths of reality in the inner realm that can be met and explored as one deals with the images that arise.

Symbols especially have a powerful hold on the imagination of the human psyche and they help meditation. Talking about symbols and their use, Kelsey says,

> If ordinary meadows and mountains and fairy tales can awaken repsonse from the depth of people, there is likely to be far more power in the symbols that originally come from that depth and have been hallowed by people's actions at sacred times and in holy places, by their sacraments and rituals, and in their sacred writings and religious art. Some of these symbols are well-known. We are all familiar with water that has been blessed, particularly for baptism, or with the whole image of the sacred stable at Christmas time. But when we look up at the heavens at night, how many of us stop to think that the familiar constellations of stars speak to us of the beginnings of religion? Even their names came to us from the

ancient Greeks who looked into the clear Aegean skies and peopled the heavens with gods who sent blessings or misfortunes into one's life. Out of the depths of these ancients came their deepest concerns, not very different from the way Abraham was doing farther to the East, except that the Greeks allowed these yearnings to illuminate the heavens. No wonder men are drawn by astrology. There in the stars was one of the first places that people pictured their gods[71].

There are symbols in the New Testament too, and symbols there were in the early Church. The church today will have to return to this rich heritage of symbol and imagery, and as we have seen earlier the church in India is doing so in its own way using the traditional symbols in song and story and giving them a new content, a new meaning. This is what Kelsey says about the biblical tradition of symbols and the tradition of the early Church:

> In Christianity this meaning is developed in almost a tapestry of symbols that reveal God's concern for human beings. The whole Bible is a moving story of how God works with His people and finally overcomes the evil that affects their lives. It is told mostly in images from history and in teachings that are anything but abstract. The Bible does not show to us how to put this message logically in neat propositions. Instead it is deeply concerned with giving us a picture of how we can find the reality of the victory over evil, and one way to do it is to use the images that are given[72].

But have the modern churches kept up the rich heritage as they should? Or are they becoming more and more intellectual? Kelsey thinks that they are becoming intellectual.

> The tragedy is that so many modern churches have tried to become intellectual and eliminate this rich and meaningful symbolism from their Chrisitianity. They are so worried about reaching people's minds that they leave no way to touch a person where it counts, in

the heart and soul. Of course, much of the symbolism that could reach to the depth of the psyche became surrounded by superstition, and it was sometimes expressed in atrocious art forms. But the remedy for that is to throw out the superstition and some of the art, not the symbols. Jung has pointed out in unmistakeable terms how much the stripped down Protestantism of the recent era has contributed to the neurosis of our time[73].

There are new symbols for the present age and new symbols for every age. Kelsey speaks of these new symbols,

> The best modern presentation of the central Christian idea of atonement is not found in some carefully thought-out volume of theology. It is in The Lion, the Witch, and the Wardrobe, written by C.S. Lewis for children[74].

We agree. One last word needs to be said here about imagery in song and poetry and its use in meditation, because we have dealt with that subject already when we considered the songs of Devadas. Kelsey quotes some deeply devotional poetry from the writings of St. John of the Cross and from the famous Hound of Heaven of Francis Thompson, both works already mentioned. Both of these are deeply devotional works of a high order. Both have touched the hearts of the readers because they spring from the depths of meditating hearts. Consider for example, the following lines from St. John of the Cross:

1. On a dark night, Kindled in love with yearnings--
   oh, happy chance!--
   I went forth without being observed, My house being now at rest.
2. In darkness and secure, By the secret ladder, disguised--
   oh, happy chance!--
   In darkness and in concealment, My house being now at rest.

3. In the happy night, In secret, when none saw me,
   Nor I beheld aught. Without light or guide, save that which burned in my heart.
4. This light guided me More surely than the light of noonday,
   To the place where he (well I knew who!) was awaiting me -
   A place where none appeared[75].

Or these other lines of meditative poetry from the Hound of Heaven.

I fled Him, down the nights and down the days;
I fled Him, down the arches of the years;
I fled Him, down the labyrinthine ways
   Of my own mind; and in the mist of tears
I hid from Him, and under running laughter.
   Up vistaed hopes I sped;
   And shot, precipitated,
Adown Titanic glooms of chasmed fears,
   From those strong Feet that followed, followed after.
      But with unhurrying chase,
      And unperturbed pace,
   Deliberate speed, majestic instancy,
      They beat--and a Voice beat
      More instant than the Feet--
'All things betray thee, who betrayest Me'.[76]

This kind of imagery helps meditation. It helps fellowship with God and provides the devotee a peaceful state in His presence.

c) Some Critical Comments:

All this is written from the pastoral and Eastern point of view. However, a pastoral and Eastern spirituality also can not by-pass some of the questions this kind of experience raises.

First of all, as indicated already briefly, the question should be asked: How adequate is the language which uses the categories of 'natural versus supernatural'? It seems to me the more adequate categories would be the Pauline categories of pneumatikos versus sarkikos, the categories of 'spiritual versus self-centred'.

Secondly, while Kelsey is immediately understandable to an Indian mind, he side-steps and dismisses too lightly the importance of European critical tradition. I do not believe that this is necessary. I certainly hold the view that it should be possible for a Western theologian to push the critical understanding so far that there is room for the experiences described here. However, that would be a task for the Western theologian to tackle and not for an Indian theologian.

Thirdly, and most important of all, one can say that it is doubtful whether Kelsey's insistence on a direct non-mediated encounter with God is in fact Christian. Of course an Indian Christian will immediately warm to such a proposition because of the Hindu background. But if one would follow the biblical line one would also realise that no human being can meet God directly without facing death immediately. Therefore when God speaks to men, He uses human language, He speaks through a human medium. Therefore all revelation is mediated; it comes through categories of human culture, psychology, language and biography. It follows from this that there are no categories available to the Church except human categories. We have no experience beyond the human, by definition.

However, some of our experiences point to something beyond the human, for example, some of our suffering and some of our thinking and also our dreams.

I follow the biblical line in this matter. So the whole question of encountering God through the meditation of different cultures, thought patterns and experiences is a subject for further research.

CHAPTER XIII: Notes

1. Kelsey, Morton T., Encounter with God, Minneapolis: Bethany Fellowship Inc., 1972, p. 24.

2. Kelsey, Morton T., The Christian and the Supernatural, London: Search Press, 1977, pp. 38-39.

3. Kelsey, Morton T., Encounter with God, p. 34.

4. Ibid., p. 27.

5. Ibid., p. 24.

6. Ibid., p. 28.

7. Loc.cit.

8. Ibid., p. 29.

9. Ibid., pp. 29-30.

10. Ibid., p. 31.

11. Ibid., p. 62.

12. Ibid., p. 64.

13. Ibid., p. 65.

14. Ibid., p. 143.

15. Kelsey, Morton T., The Other Side of Silence, London: SPK, 1976, p. 165.

16. Ibid., p. 168.

17. Ibid., p. 165.

18. Freud, Sigmond, The Interpretation of Dreams, p. 100.

19. Bryant, Christopher, Jung and the Christian Way, London: Darton, Longman and Todd, 1983.

20. Ibid., p. 26.

21. Kelsey, Morton T., Encounter with God, p. 145.

22. Ibid., p. 145, 146.

23. Loc.cit., p. 146.

24. Jung's idea., Kelsey, Encounter with God, p. 151.

25. Kelsey, The Other Side of Silence, p. 169.

26. Kelsey, Encounter with God, p. 148.

27. Loc.cit.

28. Loc.cit.

29. For my summary of the teachings of Luther in this paragraph, I am indebted to Hoffman, Bengt E., Luther and the Mystics, Minneapolis: Augsburg Publishing House, 1976.

30. Kelsey, The Other Side of Silence, p. 168.

31. Ibid., p. 230.

32. Ibid., p. 231.

33. Kelsey, The Christian and the Supernatural, pp. 39, 40.

34. Kelsey, The Other Side of Silence, p. 232.

35. Loc.cit.

36. Ibid., pp. 232, 233.

37. Loc.cit.

38. Loc.cit.

39. Kelsey, Encounter with God, pp. 175-209.

40. Webster, Douglas, What is Spiritual Healing?, London: The Highway Press, n.d.

41. E.g., Webster, ibid., p. 5.

42. Ibid., pp. 6-9.

43. Ibid., p. 9.

44. Kelsey, Morton T., Healing and Christianity, London: SCM, 1973.

45. Ibid., p. 8.

46. Ibid., p. 22.

47. Quoted by Kelsey, ibid., p. 23.

48. Hoffman, Bengt R., Luther and the Mystics, p. 195.

49. Loc.cit.

50. Ibid., p. 197.

51. Ibid., p. 199.

52. Ibid., p. 198.

53. Webster, Douglas, op.cit., p. 8.

54. Lambourne, R.A., Community, Church and Healing: A study of some of the corporate aspects of the Church's Ministry to the Sick, London: Darton, Longman and Todd 1963.

55. Webster, Douglas, op.cit., p. 18.

56. Newbigin, Lesslie, The Healing Ministry in the Mission of the Church, The Healing Church: Tubingen Consultation, Geneva: WCC, 1965, p. 9.

57. Ibid., p. 12.

58. Scheel, Martin, Some Comments on the Pre-Scientific Forms of Healing, The Healing Church: Tubingen Consultation, p. 24.

59. Ibid., pp. 24-28.

60. Ibid., p. 25.

61. Loc.cit.

62. Ibid., p. 26.

63. Ibid., p. 27, 28.

64. Ibid., p. 28.

65. For my summary in this section on the church's healing I am indebted to a recent lecture by Dr. Hollenweger in Selly Oak.

66. See Ch. IV, section 5 of this book for the treatment on Ruah Yahweh.

67. Kelsey, Morton T. The Other Side of Silence, p. 2.

68. Ibid., p. 128.

69. Ibid., p. 132.

70. Ibid., p. 135.

71. Ibid., pp. 187-88.

72. Ibid., p. 188.

73. Ibid., p. 188-89.

74. Ibid., p. 189.

75. St. John of the Cross, Dark Night of the Soul, trans. E. Allison Pears, Garden City, New York: Doubleday and Co. Inc., 1959, pp. 33ff.; quoted by Kelsey, The Other Side of Silence, p. 271.

76. Francis Thompson, The Hound of Heaven, Quoted by Kelsey, ibid., p. 272.

The Sheep and the Goats
(From the Author's Dance Drama, Kim Karthavyam)

CHAPTER XIV

Towards Indigenization - A Prospect

1. What is Indigenization?

What exactly is indigenization? In what areas do we see the manifestations of indigenization in the Christian Church? What is the place and purpose of indigenization? The answers to these questions are not easy. Indigenization is something which so many people in India have been talking about for so long with so many assumptions that the word sometimes becomes hazy in meaning.

Lesslie Newbigin in a recent article[1] suggests a new word, 'contextualization', in the place of indigenization or adaptation. To him adaptation and indigenization are misleading terms because the former 'implied that the message brought by the missionary is the unadapted truth unadulterated by any cultural mixture'. The latter 'tended to direct attention to the traditional elements in the receptor cultures and to seek to interpret the gospel through these often at times when the people concerned were in fact turning away from these traditions'[2]. Bishop Newbigin says that the intention of the word 'contextualization on the other hand was to point to the insertion of the Gospel into the living situation of the people concerned so that it was related to the living questions that they were asking, not so much about the past as about the future'.

This is a helpful thought. Indigenization in the broadest sense should not limit itself to the problem of the alien traditions which came with the Gospel to the receptor cultures nor should it be only busy concerning the traditional elements in the receptor culture either past or present. But even if we prefer to use the word contextualization which is much more a positive word, it is hard to forget entirely the part played by the donor cultures and the receptor cultures when we talk about indigenization. The question may further be asked whether it is necessary or wise for the receptor cultures to 'turn away' from these traditions altogether. Bishop Newbigin's observation is also true that the indigenization talk we often hear is mostly dominated by the western trained theologians of third world origin. This turning away from traditions which some suggest may not be the best solution to the problem. This is how Newbigin looks at the issue:

> The debate about contextualization among churches of the third world is understandably dominated by the struggle to break free from the embrace of western ideas. It is carried on (necessarily) by those who have themselves thoroughly mastered the western traditions in theology, having been trained in the leading universities and seminaries of the west.

Newbigin very appropriately draws our attention to another kind of Third World theology which is quite important. He says:

> There is also another kind of Third World theology--namely, that which is being continuously produced in the languages of the churches of the Third World--in the form of preaching, catechesis, song, story and drama. The volume of this material is very great, but it is rarely translated into the languages of Europe. Yet it represents the real fruit of the day-by-day struggle of the Christians of these lands to interpret the gospel to their contemporaries.

It is exactly this kind of theology of the indigenous folk-churches that the present study is aiming at. These churches are attempting the grassroots theology and they are contextualising the gospel to the masses of India through song, story, dreams and visions and through healing campaigns.

We have already mentioned Dr. Hoerschelmann's work on the <u>Christian Gurus of India</u>, Dr. Subbamma's study of the <u>New Methods of Discipling the Hindus</u>, and Rajappan D. Immanuel's <u>The Influence of Hinduism of Indian Christians</u>, wherein the last-named theologian and author discusses a whole range of topics like the Ashram movement, Yoga as a method of Christian meditation, the Bhakti, mysticism as practised by the Indian Christians, etc.

Although these authors have been trained in the Western theological institutions and have acquired the most modern tools and models, which acquisition is not a disadvantage, they are still concerned with the grass-roots Christianity of contemporary India and with a theology in its making.

In trying to interpret the teachings of the Bible Mission and Father Devadas, I have critically examined how far they made the Gospel heard as relevant, how far these teachings speak of the 'things that are real things in the lives of the hearers' and how far they begin by 'accepting their issues, using their models, and speaking their language'. But relevance is not enough, Newbigin warns us: 'The Gospel at the same time must challenge the whole world view of its hearers'.

One can look at indigenization in different aspects and at different levels, and it may be especially useful to consider the following are:
1) indigenous expression in the liturgy, in the Hymns and in the worship including the church architecture;
2) indigenous ways of life and witness;
3) indigenous thought and theology;

2. Indigenous Expression in Liturgy, Hymns and Worship

The Willowbank report of Lausanne Committee for World Evangelisation on the subject of Gospel and Culture has this to say about the place of language in culture:

> Culture is closely bound up with language, and is expressed in proverbs, myths, folk tales, and various art forms, which become part of the mental furniture of all members of the group. It governs actions undertaken in the community-acts of worship or of general welfare; laws and administration of law; social activities such as dances and games; smaller units of action such as clubs and societies, associations for an immense variety of common purposes[3].

Earlier in this work we have discussed how the churches in India in general and folk churches like the Bible Mission in particular have been using song and story and image and dreams to communicate the Gospel and to make it relevant to the contemporary situation. Such adaptation is not by any means a new phenomenon in the history of the church. The Willowbank report gives three clear examples of the way in which the Bible has made use of the then-existing cultural tools. This is how the report puts it:

> God's personal self-disclosure in the Bible was given in terms of the hearers' own culture. So we have asked ourselves what light it throws on our task of our cross-cultural communication today.
>
> The biblical writers made critical use of whatever cultural material was available to them for the expression of their message. For example the Old Testament refers several times to the Babylonian sea monster named 'Leviathan', while the form of God's covenant with his people resembles the ancient Hittite Suzerain's 'treaty' with his vassals. The writers also made incidental use of the conceptual image of the three-tiered universe though they did not thereby affirm a pre-Copernican cosmology.
>
> We do something similar when we talk about the sun 'rising' and 'setting'.

The report adds more about this process as we see in the New Testament:

> Similarly the New Testament language and thought forms are steeped in both Jewish and Hellenistic culture, and Paul seems to have drawn from the vocabulary of the Greek philosophy. But the process by which the biblical authors borrowed words and images from their cultural milieu, and used them creatively, was controlled by the Holy Spirit so that they purged them of false or evil implications and thus transformed them into vehicles of truth and goodness[4].

Bishop Newbigin also says:

> The Bible itself represents the experience of one particular culture or complex of cultures, uses the models of a particular time and place in human history. It is no Switzerland among cultures of the world,

no 'neutral zone', no 'non-aligned state'. It arises out of the experience of a people, among all the people of mankind. It is indelibly marked by their cultural peculiarities and it is embodied in their languages. How then, can it be absolutised, given an authority over the products of other cultures[5]?

It is surely indigenization that we see happening here, a contextualization of God's revelation and a process of expressing it in the existing language and thought-forms and models. The Willowbank Report further gives the example of the word avatār (descent) used in Hinduism for the so-called 'incarnations' of Visnu and applies it, with careful safeguards, to the unique incarnation of God in Jesus Christ. And many more such examples may be cited.

We are not, however, talking here about a few words here and there; rather, we are talking about a principle, about whole cultures and their possible contribution. Very little had been done, for example, in the Protestant churches in Andhra about adapting the poetical forms and the proverbs and the cultural idiom for a truly indigenous expression of the Christian faith. Fortunately we have a handful of Bhakti song writers both in Andhra and also in the other linguistic areas, some of whom we have mentioned already. Men like Choudury Purushōtham and Mungamūri Dēvadās in Telugu, Nārāyan Vāman Tilak in Marāthi, and Vēdanāyaga Sāstriyār or Kristna Pillai in Tamil, and others have done their noble part to create a Christian bhakti literature in the regional languages. But only a very few Christian writers have used the Indian poetic form, which is a powerful medium for community education and for devotional purpose. In Telugu the one major poetic work on a Christian theme which is acknowledged as of high quality, and for that reason read by many Hindus, is the Kristhu Charithra (Story of Christ) by Gurram Joshua[6]. We have seen the Father Devadas also wrote some poems for devotion among his followers.

Much less has been done for redeeming the liturgical forms from the very strange and old museum-piece type of literary structures and imagery imported long ago from the Western cloisters. There is a great deal of religious dance and drama and symbolism and a whole wealth of collective archetypes which should find their rightful place in the Indian Church liturgy. The Catholics in

India have done a few more experiments in this field. Father Proksh of Gnan Ashram in Bombay developed Christian prayer and worship in dance forms and demonstrated them in different parts of the country and abroad, and the response was good. Some of the experiments in this field from the Archdiocese of Madurai were reported at the 1956 Conference of Mission Specialists, at Fordham University[7]. How widely these forms composed and advocated by Proksh and others have been actually incorporated into the church worship and liturgy is an open question. There are experiments going on in several quarters but the main order of worship in many denominations is still what was handed down by the Western missionaries hundreds of years ago. In the matter of liturgical forms therefore the tendency to produce almost exact replicas of the so-called 'home-churches' has been perpetuated. The Willowbank Report puts it sharply and pointedly when it says:

> Gothic architecture, prayer book liturgies, clerical dress, musical instruments, hymns and tunes, decision making process, synods and committees, superintendents and archdeacons all were exported and unimaginatively introduced into the new mission-founded churches[8].

The situation is very clear. We shall come back to the question of Synods and Committees and the church authority system later in this chapter, but the authors of the Willowbank Report have no doubt about the need to redeem the worship experience from this desperate situation. They are also not oblivious to the effects of such a situation:

> If each church is to develop creatively in such a way as to find and express itself, it must be free to do so. It is its inalienable birthright. For each church is God's church. United to Christ, it is a dwelling place of God through His Spirit (Eph 2.22). Some missions and missionaries have been slow to recognise this and to accept its implications in the direction of indigenous forms and an every member ministry. This is one of the many causes which have led to the formation of independent churches, notably in Africa, which are seeking new ways of self-expression in terms of local culture.

It may be good that these independent churches are showing the way sometimes so that the mission churches may shake off their cloak of complacency in this matter.

One can look at Indian Christian art forms too. Very little indigenous art has been produced, it must be admitted, till recently in the Indian church. It is a well-known fact that India, like many other Third World countries, has its own distinctive art with all the temple carvings, rock paintings and everyday folk paintings and wall pictures, with so much symbolism and imagery coming down from past centuries; but the Christian Church was so obsessed with the fear of syncretism that it never went anywhere near this rich wealth, to explore its depths or to try to use it for the expression of its faith. The Indian church, one is constrained to say, has far too long gloried in the poor reproductions of medieval European art and imported pictures of more recent Western artists.

Only recently have we heard about A.D. Thomas, or Frank Wesley, or Jothi Sahi or Vinayak Masoji and other Indian Christian artists; and even that through the recognition they were given by the Western press and Western patrons. The Indian Christian Arts Association and the Asian Christian Arts Association now in action are doing a highly desirable and long pending service to the Indian Christian Artists. Even then, alas, it is very, very slowly that the works of these artists are finding their way, if at all, into the churches and their altars on any large scale.

3. Indigenization of Life and Witness

In addition to the language forms and the art expressions, there is also a whole range of the other aspects of life which constitutes part of its culture. R.D. Immanuel makes a reference to the festivals of India and to their role in the life of the community[9].

A) Festivals:

The life of a Hindu is centred around a number of feasts, festivals and holy days which enable him to express a group identity and help him to realise his religious aspirations in the company of his compatriots whenever there is such an occasion. It is true that for the Hindu there is very little community worship as such but community celebration there is plenty. As Immanuel reminds us, until very recently Protestant Christianity has been emphasising the much needed individual experience and conversion, but from this individual experience the converts are led rightly to the social goal, the Kingdom of God and a community which is the body of Christ. As a small minority people in India with the vast population of Hindus around, Christians many times feel isolated and suffer a deep sense of guilt when they associate themselves with the Hindus in any social function or festival. Immanuel quotes the Christian poet Narayan Vaman Tilak to show how much the Indian Christian 'resents this limitation of his freedom to absorb Indian culture'. These are the words of Tilak:

> Trampling on self you have come to us
> to bring us Christ
> For us you have given life and all things, so that
> to our debt there is no end.
> Yet will you heed one small request
> which I have still to proffer?
> You are father and mother, we helpless infants:
> enough of this relationship now.
> You have driven God afar by making yourselves gods:
> When will ye cast off this sin?
> You have set up for yourselves a kingdom of slaves:
> do not call it a kingdom of God.
> We dance as puppets while you hold the strings:
> How long shall this buffoonery endure?
> How long will you keep us dead? Hath God not eyes
> to see?
> Let us swim, let us sink or die:
> Give us at least the chance of swimming[10].

A very frustrated cry indeed but it at least expresses in a poignant way the thoughts of those who are cut off from the rest of society and from its daily life. Is this separation necessary? Is it desirable? What is the solution? Do we have any guidance in the scriptures or in church history? At least with regard to the festivals and the Indian social life and the attitude of Christians towards these, many theologians think that there should be a way out.

First of all, there is a possibility of inventing some substitute Christian festivals and myths and social functions which can take the place of the former Hindu festivals. This is already happening to some extent. Immanuel gives some instances.

a) The Chinnamalai (the small hill) festival near Madras is a festival in honour of St. Thomas. (The big hill about five miles away is the St. Thomas Mount where the Apostle is believed to have been assassinated). According to tradition current in these parts, St. Thomas was given protection at this place and received special strength before he finally became a martyr. Immanuel says:

> So on the appointed day (Sunday preceding the full moon in May) thousands of people throng to this village. Booths are erected for vendors. Merry-go-rounds and other fair attractions are arranged for; special services are held in the local Roman Catholic church. People are said to be cured of their diseases if they go to worship there. The collection received from the enormous number of pilgrims (Catholics, Hindus and even some Protestants) must be very large[11].

Immanuel mentions other festivals of even longer duration in some cases. There are many variations in these festivals, some of them associated with a legend or a myth of the place (sthala mahāthya), some purely evangelistic gatherings where Christians meet for several days to sing and listen to the word of God and to celebrate periodically with others in the community both Christian and non-Christian.

There is yet another kind of festival possible for the Christians to enjoy with their non-Christian neighbours such as the existing Christian festivals like Easter and Christmas. To some extent this is happening. In Andhra Pradesh and in fact in many parts of India Christmas is somewhat similar in its community effect and joy to the harvest festival which follows it later in January. At Christmas time, in rural Andhra, much of the joy is shared in the community. In addition to the church services and prayer meetings on Christmas eve and on the morning of Christmas day, there are celebrations at home where simple cakes are cooked carefully and shared with the neighbours. The early morning oil bath for the whole family and the wearing of new clothes, a visit to neighbours' homes in the afternoon, the home-coming of daughters and sons-in-law, especially the newly married--all these form part of Christmas festival, just like any other festival in rural Andhra. It is very helpful for the Christians to enjoy with their non-Christian friends and neighbours. Unfortunately, many times the pastors and preachers have a tendency to discourage this kind of celebration because of some puritanic considerations and for fear of syncretism, a fear of the mixing up of Christian faith with Hindu beliefs. But it is a risk worth taking. Not only Christmas and Easter and the like, but many other home festivals like the naming of a child, baptism, confirmation, occasions like the new bride coming home, the sixty years anniversary of parents (Shashti Poorthi), and scores of other times can be useful occasions which Christians can really enjoy with their non-Christian neighbours; and there is no feeling of missing the corresponding festivals of the neighbouring Hindu society. All these can be made really Christian with the necessary worship and prayer but still be social occasions for the community concerned.

We have earlier mentioned the biennial open-air, week-long evangelistic camps called mahāsabhas, on the river beds of South India in Maramon and on the Kristna River bed. Immanuel also reports a similar event in another part of the country, and it may be of some interest to note the details as Immanuel gives them:

> The Methodist Church in South India very often turns its annual conference into a sort of festival. At least, it is made like a festival in many aspects. Not only the members of the annual conference, but all, are invited to attend. By all, is meant men and women and children, Hindus, Christians and others. The place

selected is by the side of a river or a lake. Three to ten days are set apart. Those who come bring their own cooking vessels, beds and other furniture. Each family cooks its own food. Special times are set apart for music, social time, religious services, and business sessions. Thus one could find here a happy blending of Indian folkways, the appeal of camp life, and western ecclesiastical organisation[12].

Harvest Festival (this is a name given to Indian Thanksgiving Festival) is another occasion at which the services in the Indian village churches show the influence of Hindu folkways. At these harvest festivals sometimes several villages join together and each family comes to a central place for worship bringing with them their thank offerings in kind, mostly paddy from the fields and also some vegetables, fruits and chicken to be offered in the church. After the service there will be an auction of these items at which the people bid and buy. There are sales also outside the church and sweets for the children and games and fun the whole day long. It is at these festivals the latent talent among the Christian youth comes to light, as at no other time, because some boys and girls compose simple new songs just for the occasion and they get an opportunity to sing them in the festival with their friends; these creations are thrown away after the festival till others come in their place like the clay figures of the Hindu festivals which serve their purpose for celebration and then are replaced by new ones created again and again.

This way the existing Christian festivals serve the community needs where Christians and non-Christians can join together for a real fellowship. These can become channels for a true witness to the faith. Eddy Asirvatham speaks from deep conviction when he said:

> A purely rational religion, which pays no attention to the social needs of men, is in danger of atrophy. A well organised Church can serve the purpose of providing, or being a community for the Christian[13].

There is yet another way in which the Christians can express solidarity with their culture without making compromises infaith. This is by making a distinction between clearly Hindu religious festivals and the social and cultural functions leaving out the former and joining wholeheartedly in the latter. This sifting, of course, is not always easy to make, but it is not impossible. It sometimes requires imaginaiton and a little experimentation. The festival of lights (Divāli), for example, which is a big festival for all the Hindus in India, is one which, in the opinion of many Christian thinkers, can adapt itself for such an experimentation.

A Christian will give a new meaning to the lights and to the celebration, a meaning which is different from all the Hindu associations, and will celebrate it remembering Christ the Light of the World. So much has been written on the topic of adaptation of the Hindu festivals, and opinions are very much divided on the theological implications of such a process. We shall consider this a little more in detail when we come to see the work of the Jesuit missionary Roberto De Nibili, later in this chapter.

But to conclude this section, we may recapitulate the three ways open to Christians with regard to the community festivals:[14]

    a) To widen the scope of the existing Christian festivals and observe them in a typically Indian way, along with the whole community around.
    b) To invent some new festivals which will meet the needs and suit the genius of the people and to give them a Christian content.
    c) To carefully adapt, after making the necessary modifications, some of the Hindu festivals and give them a Christian meaning.

The third one is the most difficult of the three and should be carefully and cautiously done, with a real understanding of the Christian faith on the one hand, and the meaning of these Hindu festivals on the other. For, after all, there is no substitute for some of these Hindu festivals. They must be either borrowed, simply, with a bad conscience, or should be forgotten as heathen. Immanuel mentions some Hindu festivals that can be profitably adapted, like the Shārdh (the remembrance day of the death of a parent) and the Rakshbandh (the festival for brothers and sisters, to express their mutual love and affection - the sister tying a wreath of good wishes to the brother's hand,

and in return receiving a gift of a little money from him). All these have beautiful sentimental meanings attached, and Christians today are not generally allowed to participate in them because the churches have frowned upon them as 'unChristian'.

B) Āshrams Prayer and Yōga

There is a renewed interest today in the Indian Ashram or Ashrama movement, and many people around the world are looking at Ashrams and the Indian Yōga and the meditative prayer as a possible solution to some of the problems of modern society. Therefore, it may be necessary for the Indian church to take a fresh look at these ancient insitutions and tools, and revive them wherever necessary and possible, for the good of the church in the process on contextualising its faith and practice in contemporary society. Ashrams are not new to India and Christian Ashrams have taken a real root in the country for a long time now. Hindu society depended on two pillars for its structure, as Immanuel indicates[15], and these pillars were the varna (caste) and ashrama (literally meaning, the effort). The varna is now breaking down slowly, but the ashrama is still a useful institution followed in principle in its restricted meaning. It is not any more the broader classical four-fold ashrama (chatur-āshrama) in which we are interested, with its four classical stages of the Indian tradition: Brhamcharya, the learner stage, Grihastha, the householder stage, vānaprastha, the forest dweller stage and sanyāsa, the final stage of renunciation.

The Christian church adopted the vānaprastha idea for its use long ago. A simple community life, a minimum of personal needs, a life of prayer and service, obedience and discipline are some of the marks of Christian ashrams[16]. Among the better known Christian ashrams are the Kristukula Ashram (the family of Christ), Tirupattur, South India, started in 1921; Kristu Shishya Ashram (the disciples of Christ) near Coimbatore; Christu Panthi (the Fellowship of Christ), Benares; and Sat Tāl Ashram of Stanley Jones in the foothills of the Himalayas; and many others in places like Poona, Kerala, etc.

An even simpler adaptation of these is the ashram run for a week or ten days in the Lutheran Church by the Hindu convert lady B.V. Subbamma. These āshrams of Subbamma are attracting many Hindu women and new converts for a period of prayer and reflection. Among the characteristics of these āshrams, there are some which we may underline without going into detailed consideration of any of them.

a) The āshrams are non-authoritarian.
b) They are non-traditional.
c) They are non-ritualistic, unlike the Hindu ashrams which keep endless rituals at every turn.
d) They are non-denominational (most of the ashrams of the church are ecumenical and some are interfaith type).
e) They are non-sacerdotal. In many of the Christian āshrams laymen take the leadership role.
f) They are non-institutional. Some of them do not have any church support. They are started and managed by some charismatic leader.
g) The āshram life is very simple. Many of the women who attend the one-day or week-long āshrams bring their own food, cook their own meals, wash their clothes and sleep on straw mats, without any difficulty.
h) The āshram family has a kinship of spirit. All members share with each other what they have. They live, work and pray together while they are in the āshram.
i) Christian āshrams generally end up in service – they are not just idle cells of inaction. They are functional communities.
j) An āshram is not an organisation. Some of the present day āshrams do not have any permanent property of facilities. Their continuity also is not guaranteed[17].

Asirvatham observes that in modern times the Hindu āshrams have been revived on a large scale and adapted to the changing conditions and needs of the day. With Sānthinikēthan, started by Rabīndra Nāth Tāgore (1901), the āshram became an educational and cultural centre. Later, with Gandhi, the ashrams became centres of social and political action with satya and ahimsa (truth and non-violence) as their mottos[18].

Christian āshrams, as cooperative partners with the regular ordained ministry of the church, can do a great service to the witness and the life of the church. That is why there is a renewed interest in the āshram movement among the churches today. The āshram, while it is not a substitute to the ordained ministry, strengthens the spiritual life of the church in India through prayer and contemplation and through special areas of service to the community around, while the ordained minister takes care of baptisms, marriages, deaths and burials, sick visitation and the regular teaching and preaching activities in the church. He can visit the sick and the bereaved and administer the Communion. As long as āshrams do not drive people into inactivity and seclusion they are very effective places for prayer and spiritual rejuvenation; they can become strong centres of spiritual power.

Turning now to the subject of prayer and Yōga, there is a great deal that the churches in India can learn from Hindu spirituality through the concept of Yōga. It may open a whole new vision of the meaning of Christian prayer. In the Protestant churches of missionary origin there is very little emphasis on personal prayer and silent meditation. The corporate prayers in the church are formal and often impersonal. The liturgy uses book-prayers and written litanies and there is not adequate place for said prayers and for individual participation. Hinduism, on the other hand, has a long tradition of personal devotion to God and long hours of pūja (worship) expressing bhakti to God; therefore, a Christian, who is used to the Hindu form of prayer and meditation, often feels very unsatisfied in a formal church service where the major part of the time is taken by the preacher, who often talks at the congregation. That is part of the reason why the Indigenous non-White churches attract some people who find a deep satisfaction in lone prayer vigils as part of their religious experience. Devadas for example did, and the followers of the Bible Mission do wait long hours in silent meditation. Like the Hindu prayer chants and dandakams (continuous prayer chants for the use of individuals) some of the Christian prayer groups have continuous prayer sentences which they repeat in personal meditation. These, in no sense, are vain repetitions in the mind of an Indian. Silent prayer also is as important to the Indian mind as these chains of vocal prayer. Here comes the idea of Yōga into Christian spirituality.

The word yōga has several shades of meaning and often it is misunderstood and misinterpreted because of these several ideas associated with it. Immanuel, on the authority of Professor Rawson, underlines three meanings of the word from the historical development[19].

      i) Concentration
     ii) Communion
    iii) Effort

Immanuel examines the classical Yōga Sūthra-meaning of the word, which is Nirvikalpa Samādhi, a kind of hypnotic trance, as the highest stage of yōga and he discards it as unnecessary for Christian use. We agree with him wholeheartedly, for at this stage of yōga, knowledge and self-consciousness are suspended. But in the Bhagavadgita and the earlier Upanishads, a type of yōga is to be found which has many helpful suggestions for an Indian Christian, especially with a Hindu background. Immanuel quotes Bhagavadgīta VI: 10-15, which reads as follows:

> Abiding in a secret place, alone with mind and soul controlled, without craving, without possessions, a yōgin should constantly yoke his soul. Setting for himself, in a clean place, a firm seat, neither too high, nor too low, with kusa grass, a skin and a cloth spread thereon, there sitting on that couch with thought and sense restrained directing his mind he should practice yoga for cleansing of his soul. Firm, holding the body and neck erect and still, gazing at the tip of his nose, and not looking around, tranquil, free from fear and steadfast in the vow of continence, with mind controlled, thinking of me, he should sit, ever intent, only on me. Thus ever yoking his soul, the yōgin with mind restrained, attains the bliss which culminates in bliss and which abides with me[20].

This is the kind of meditation which appeals to the Indian mind and there is nothing compared to this in Protestantism. Most of the Christian Sādhus and gurus including Devadas and Sādhu Sundar Singh have practised daily this kind of discipline while meditating on Christ and on his saving work. Many of the details of the seating posture, the cleanliness of body and mind and concentration of thought mentioned in the Gītā passage cited above appear also in the teachings of Devadas on prayer. Coming from this background and an understanding of yōga and meditation, a convert from Hinduism finds it a little difficult to enjoy his meditation while sitting up in rows of church pews wearing his working clothes and keeping his footwear on, in a busy, brightly lighted surrounding. He just does not get into the meditative mood.

The breath control which is associated with yōga as a means of concentration is not generally possible for an average Christian in his hurried life, but generally he tarries in silent meditation, preferably in the early hours of the day before sunrise and after sunset; when all life settles down in the night so much the more will he realise God's presence in his prayer. But many people complain that their thoughts still wander and this is a waste of time.

Indian spirituality also advocates fasting to keep the body and mind awake in prayer, and the Bible supports the idea of fasting prayer. Many times the Indian Christian is confused by the teaching of the church, which says that fasting is not necessary even if it is practised in the Bible. Thus, where there is no opportunity for this kind of prayer-life in the churches, people go into the indigenous church groups where they have all these exercises as part of their religious life.

Immanuel wisely indicates some of the possible dangers in yōga. The first and the most well known danger of course is the thinking that in yōga the soul gets lost in the Paramātman, the eternal self. The fundamental concept of the individuality of self and the important distinction between God and man is crucial in Christian faith, and Immanuel is right when he says that when this distinction is lost the fundamental purpose of prayer is lost. Subba Rao, the Hindu-Christian guru, made this mistake when he sang to Christ and said,

> When you become I, and
> I become you
> To whom shall I pray any more?
> (Prayer becomes unnecessary)[21].

Appasamy has been quoted already on this subject of adwaita (non-duality) or ātman being lost in Brahman and he said, using the words of Tagore, 'I want to eat sugar but I do not intend to become sugar'.

There are other things to guard against when we advocate yoga type of meditation. The prānāyāma, the breath control which is a part of yoga, is sometimes believed to give supernatural powers. Whether such supernatural powers are possible or not is not he question for a Christian. To him supernatural powers are not the end. To him a continuous and deep fellowship with Christ and abiding in his presence and growing in grace should be the aim. For that purpose, the yoga type of meditation has a great efficacy and power, and for that reason the church may want to encourage it.

Immanuel thinks that Indian Christian theologians hold the view that the church and the modern Western organization do not offer to the devotee advanced in higher religious experience any great help in the deep levels of Christian life.

4. Indigenization of Theological Thought

Here again much useful thinking has been done in India and much literature has been produced. Scholars like Robin Boyd have thoroughly examined the current thinking on indigenous theology. Here we shall only examine the trends of indigenization without going into the content of indigenous theology. For example, Lesslie Newbigin suggests that Christology shold be done in dialogue with the great religious cultures of the East. The formulations of the third and the fourth centuries, while being part of the tradition within which the Western churches and their missions stand, are not the last word. Newbigin has this advice to give:

> For a thousand years following the work of Augustine Christianity was the religion of a small peninsula of Asia, cut off by Islam from a real contact with the great religious cultures of the East. Now that there is again intimate contact, Christology has to be done in dialogue with these as with the other cultures of mankind. As I have

suggested, Hinduism (to speak only of one with which I have some acquaintance) provides a number of possible models within which one may try to make a provisional statement of who Jesus is. There has to be room for a great deal of experiment, for the taking of risks, and for critical reflection in ecumenical debate on the results of these experiments[22].

It is this search for new models, this willingness for experimentation, this process of risk-taking and the discipline of critical reflection we are talking about when we talk of indigenization. Although borrowing a set of words from Hindu religion and Hindu philosophy and using them to express Christian theological thought is not good enough, there is no doubt that more and more Indian vocabulary and thought forms should be brought into the service of Indian theology if the latter is to be truly indigenous. Many Indian Christian theologians, recently, have done this to the advantage of both Indian theology and the Christian church.

One primary task of Christian theology in India is that of settling sources of authority or pramānās as Appasamy reminds us[23]. Boyd, following Appasamy's argument, thinks that this primary task of settling pramanas is of fundamental importance and is especially vital in India where the possibility of syncretism is always present.

Among the three pramanas, namely śruti (that which is heard, the scripture), anubhava (experience), and yukti or anumāna (reasoning or theology), most Indian theologians give the first place to śruti, the scripture. Chenchaiah, however, thinks that anubhava is the most important because even śruti, the scripture, is someone's anumbhava, experience. But the Hindu philosophers have maintained that śruti is primary because all experience will have to be eventually validated by śruti.

Appasamy adds another pramāna and that is sabha, the church. Whether the gurus of the indigenous church groups in India will give such a big place to sabha, in the sense of an organised structure, is an open question. Some of them are arguing that Christ did not start a church but initiated the Kingdom of God.

As for the different kinds of reasoning (yukti or theology) which underlie Indian thought and which are reflected in Indian Christian theology, according to Boyd there are the following three:
> i) Reconciling the opposites
> ii) Analogical thought
> iii) Plain Aristotelian reasoning

It is possible in Hindu thought to hold simultaneously two mutually opposite ideas. This is the line of argument which makes the Hindu sometimes say that all religions are equally true. Christian theology will have to face this kind of argument in its encounter with Hinduism. According to this argument, night and day, light and darkness are both two aspects of the same reality.

On issue of Nirdwanda (non-dual) of Hindu philosophy Carl Gustav Jung says,

> How perilously fraught with meaning this Eastern reality of good and evil can be seen from the Indian aphoristic question: "Who takes longer to reach perfection, the man who loves God, or the man who hates him?" And the answer is: He who loves God takes seven reincarnations to reach perfection; the man who hates God takes only three, for he who hates God will think of Him more than he who loves him[24].

Analogical thought, on the other hand, has been used by Christian thinkers like Sādhu Sundar Singh a great deal and it goes back to Christ himself and to his parables. A useful search has also been going on for some time now to find out dynamic equivalents for theological terms in Indian languages. Words used for God and Salvation and other concepts in Indian languages are carefully studied, and debated, and new meanings are given to existing terminology wherever it is necessary.

Concerning the plain Aristotelian reasoning, Indian Christian theology has made an extensive use of it.

The question further is asked whether the redemptive work of Christ is finished or whether it is an ongoing work which finds its completion only when he conquers sin and death in our hearts. The Rethinking Christianity group headed by Chenchiah are also asking whether Christianity is only a religion of future promises and hopes or whether it is doing anything for men here and now. These are very crucial questions.

Robin Boyd regrets that the church in India today does not seem to provide the kind of framework in which a truly Indian theology can flourish. He says,

> Even today in many theological colleges the names and ideas of Barth and Brunner and Tillich and Bultmann are more familiar than Brahmabandhav or Chenchiah. The time is ripe for a new liberty, liberty to discard if so desired, the western modes of thought which have far too long been obligatory, and to move freely in the Indian universe of discourse, both classical and contemporary, building on the work of the pioneer theologians ... and forging ahead into new realms of enquiry[25].

It is also Boyd, who after dismissing the jibe that the Indian Church has so far failed to produce even heresy, rightly draws our attention to the work in the field of Indian theological terminology:

> Traces of heresy there are, perhaps but far more important, the Indian Church has demonstrated many new insights into the fundamental truths of faith, aided--as the church has never been aided since its earliest days--by a rich and flexible terminology whose resources have not hitherto been brought into the treasury of Christian theology[26].

5. Adaptation

A discussion on the subject of indigenization will not be complete without a consideration of 'adaptation', a word and a process advocated, among many others, by Roberto De Nobili, a Jesuit Missionary, as early as 1619. Ever since the days of Nobili the discussion on the question of adaptation of Hindu customs into the Christian church in India has been going on, and opinions on both sides have been expressed very convincingly. While the debate continues on the question whether adaptation is right or wrong, some kind of adaptation is all the time happening in the Indian church so that it is only adequate here to state the case briefly with the story of Roberto De Nobili of the Madura Mission.

Nobili came to South India in the early 17th century. Very soon he became a controversial figure for his missionary methods. The main source of his story briefly stated here is the work of S. Rajamanickam of the De Nobili Research Institute, in Palayamkottai, South India[27].

On the 4th of February 1619, a conference was convened by Pope Paul V and was presided over by Christopher De Sa, the Archbishop of Goa, 'to explore in general, ways and means of making things easy for the Indians to accept Christ'. This is really an investigation into the evangelistic methods then being adopted by De Nobili in the Mission at Madurai.

Nobili wrote a treatise to be presented at this conference which he called "An Exposition of the Basic Principles which Inspired the Founding of the Madurai Mission and Continue to Guide It". (The English translation is by Rajamanickam). The issue at stake was whether the new converts to Christianity from the Hindu religion could continue to practise some of the older customs from the former religion. Could they follow their practice of shaving their heads and wearing a tuft at the top of the head, for example, or that of keeping of holy thread across their bodies over the shoulder? The main concern of Nobili was to discover ways and means of making it easier for the Gentiles to come into Christianity.

Of course the question now is more than that of the sacred thread or the tuft on the head or any such insignia. The principle of adaptation is still a live issue in the churches today and the idea of making things easier for the conversion of the caste Hindus is still very much advocated, as we have seen in the writings of thinkers like B.V. Subbamma and Samuel Schmitthenner of the Lutheran Church[28]. Even if we are not talking much about the so-called adaptation as a programme of the church, in effect adaptation in some measure is going on all the time.

Nobili's thesis is that, because these insignia (thread and tuft) belong to the civil and social customs and therefore are not religious symbols, they should be allowed to continue when a person from a high caste becomes a Christian. Secondly, Nobili also held that if there are any Hindu practices from a 'profane order', they should be allowed to continue after they have been cleared of all superstition[29].

About the final results of this paper of Nobili at the Council of Goa, Rajmanickam reports:

> Not only did it convert all the Jesuit theologians to Nobili's side but it also influenced the Roman curia to judge in his favour. The <u>votum</u> written on behalf of the pontifical commission of cardinals by Archbishop Peter Lambard takes most of its arguments from this treatise and quotes it in several places[30].

How did Nobili argue his case? Of course he quotes the church authority and several instances from the church history to support his case. He supplies evidence from the Brahmins and the pundits to show that the insignia and the practices he was talking about were simply social and not religious. He also used biblical exegesis.

In India however it may be remembered that it is not easy to decide where culture ends and religion begins. Most of the religious significance of the Hindu festivals has been largely forgotten by the masses and these are considered social festivals sometimes. But it does not mean that there is no religious significance if someone takes the trouble to find out.

Nobili's argument from the scriptures is not always very convincing either. For example, in support of his view that conversion should start from the higher castes and not from the lower castes, he cites the example of Christ sending his disciples on the first mission (Matthew 10). Christ asked them not to go to the Gentiles, nor to enter the cities of the Samaritans. Why did Christ forbid the disciples from preaching to the Samaritans? Nobili asks. Surely Christ himself had stayed for two days among the Samaritans and preached to them. Nobili answers the question thus:

> The reason was at that moment, He was focussing His attention to them (Jews) alone. Had the disciples gone also to the Gentiles and the Samaritans, the Jews would consider it below their dignity to be taught by such men, would in all good faith have concluded: these men have spoken to and mixed with the Gentiles and Samaritans; therefore they are unfit to teach us. So in order not to give the Jews a chance for excusing themselves from hearing them (a mere prejudice no doubt, but one due to ignorance, and therefore enough to exonerate them from sin), the Lord Christ ordered his Apostles to shun the Gentiles and Samaritans, so that they might be well received by the Jews[31].

Nobili's exegesis is however debatable. But he concluded from this kind of thinking that it is important to convert the Brahmins and the higher castes first before the outcastes are reached. Nobili also cited the example of Paul, who, when there was the Jewish feast of Pentecost in Jerusalem, joined the Nazarenes in their ritual bath and in the celebration of the feast (Acts 24). So Nobili argues:

> Now when we see the Apostles acting in the way explained above, why should not we, in India, in imitation of the Apostles seek the conversion of the Indians, by taking up their way of life? and if we meet with an action or rite, vitiated by some superstitious end, but which they will on no account give up, why should we not allow this action or rite, after giving it a new meaning? In the course of this treatise we shall enumerate many instances in which the holy church followed a similar policy. Nor is it any use to say that such dispensations were called for at the beginning, but not so now that the faith has spread all over the world. No, in this inner land of India the faith is not yet spread; why, it has only just been born. There is therefore enough and more reason for allowing such things in this part of the world[32].

Without going any further into the details of the particular insignia or Hindu practices which Nobili was talking about, it may be useful to consider briefly the principle of 'adaptation' and its implications. As it has been indicated above, this kind of adaptation is in some measure happening in the Indian church even today. Reference has been made to the Indian custom of the bridegroom tying the yellow thread with a little gold pendant round the bride's neck as the priest in the church makes him repeat the vows. The practice of Thālipottu or mangalasūthra (literally, the holy thread) comes from the Hindu marriage ritual. But it was considered so meaningful and symbolic that it has been Christianised and no one now thinks of its Hindu origin.

In church architecture there is some adaptation happening now because the Hindu temple structure and architectural symbols are so convenient for the climate, as the Gothic structure which was imported from west has never been. In fact, the Western structure is much out of place in many ways.

Dr. John Butler, in a scholarly article on the Theology of Church Building in India[33], writes about the great experiment of Bishop Azariah and the Dornakal Cathedral, which was built with the Hindu prākāra (outer open court) and the Muslim domes. However, Butler is also conscious of the fact that hasty imitations will not, yield the desired effect. Says Dr. Butler,

> As per hybrid style, our recent experience of several types of integration warns us that, neither in society nor in architecture, do diverse traditions automatically produce a happy blend just by being placed side by side[34].

However, the Indian structure of church building with the prākāra or the outer courtyard, with gates on all four sides, the inner shrine with three sides open with pillars and cool sanctuary on the fourth side, the lotus and the lily carved on the pillars, the brass lampstands and the offering box or brass urn at

the entrance of the church--all these are much more congenial to the worship atmosphere and true to the Indian genius.

Nobili is not entirely wrong in his thinking in terms of some adaptation on the Hindu customs. Indeed he has something very important to say to the

Christian church in India today, although the process of adaptation is not without some dangers, which fact we shall consider in a later section in this chapter.

6. Agents for Indigenization

Having accepted that indigenization is necessary and important for the church, we have to consider the channels or the sources for such indigenization. In any sense true indigenization should be a natural process. It is something which happens all the time when different cultures or religions come into contact. It has happened in Africa, and it has happened in Asia. There are many examples of the influence of Graeco-Roman culture on the New Testament Church, as we have mentioned several times. What will be needed is a careful understanding of what is happening and a thoughtful interpretation and a theological assessment of the process and the results from time to time. We can also show from the New Testament that the Evangelists and St. Paul were not ashamed to indigenize the Gospel already in the first century. So we need theological thinkers to do such assessment and interpretation. We need scholars who can interpret the Gospel all the time in a way both intelligible to the non-Christians and also true to ecumenical understanding. This is what Newbigin is referring to when he talks of critical reflection in ecumenical debate on the results of these experiments[35].

a) Indian Writers and Thinkers

India has produced a galaxy of brilliant theologians, starting with people like Kēshub Chander Sēn, K.C. Banergea, Kristna Mōhun Banergea, Brhmabandhav Upādhyāy, A.S. Appasāmy, Sādhu Sundar Singh, J. Appasāmy, Chenchiah, Chakrai, and many others. Among the theologians of the present generation we may mention people like P.D. Dēvānandan, M.M.Thomas, Russell Chandran, and Stanley Samartha, to name a few. They all have made their valuable contribution to Indian theological thought[36]. As Baago says, they are part of the the history of indigenous India. Indigenous theology has thus established itself finally and India has a contribution to make to ecumenical theological thinking. In an article (mentioned above) reviewing Herwig Wagner's book, Baago pays a high tribute to Chenchiah, Chakrai and Appasamy[37] as people belonging 'to the history of indigenization in India and their thinking must be regarded as a fruit of a religious cultural and political development in India. They can not be otherwise properly understood'. Defending their theology against the Heilsgeschichte theology of Wagner, Baago says that 'what happened 1900 years ago repeats itself in the soul of Bhaktas', for the living Christ continues in the heart of men that work of salvation which the historic Jesus carried out in his earthly life.

Particularly commenting on Chakkaraih's Christology, Baago says,

> The value of Chakkaraih's theology in India is to be found in his highly original Christology: interpreting Christ as the permanent Avatār. He thereby successfully combines the Hindu mystical approach to God with the historic incarnation in Jesus Christ. Without sacrificing history he presents Christ as a living reality. The danger of over-emphasis on the historic character of revelation, so predominant in Western preaching in India, is that Christ is reagarded simply as a new Avatār who has come and gone again. It wants and needs a living Avatār who is Immanuel, God with us now. Chakkaraih's whole life was consecrated to the task of preaching that Avatār who is Christ, the only one who can lead us from the unreal to the real, from darkness to light, from death to eternal life[38].

In a different way, it is this 'Christ here and now' that Devadas also is preaching through his visions, dreams and the healing. These are examples of indigenous theology, some committed to writing, some silently practised.

But this is no place to be complacent. A whole new generation of thinkers and writers need to be encouraged to take the place of the Chenchiahs and Chakkariahs and Appasamys and Devadases. George Matthew of CISRS has recently done a content analysis of five leading theological journals in India[39] and has reported his findings. The journals he surveyed are:

1. Indian Journal of Theology, Serampore (IJT)
2. The Indian Church History Review, Jabalpur (ICHR)
3. Bangalore Theological Forum, Bangalore U. T. College (BTF)
4. Theological Research and Communications Institue Journal, Delhi (TRACI)
5. Religion and Society, Bangalore (R&S)

Among other things in this survey, a profile of the contributors to these periodicals and the authorship of book reviewed is interesting. This is a summary:

Item	IJT	ICHR	BTF	TRACI	R&S
Articles					
Number	441	130	95	90	574
By Indians	51.8%	36.9%	40.0%	47.8%	75.0%
By Westerners	48.3%	63.1%	60.0%	52.2%	25.0%
Books reviewed					
Number	656	37	26	32	246
Written by:					
Indians	14.5%	40.5%	34.6%	53.1%	62.2%
Westerners	85.5%	59.5%	65.4%	46.9%	37.8%
Reviewed by:					
Indians	43.1%	18.9%	30.8%	37.5%	65.2%
Westerners	56.9%	81.1%	69.2%	62.5%	34.8%

Of course, we realise that not all Indians produce indigenous theology and not all Westerners produce Western theology. There are clear exceptions on both sides. We have seen some excellent examples of truly indigenous theology in the works of some Westerners like De Nobili, to cite one such theologian. So this investigation of George Matthew is good only as far as it goes. One would only hope that more and more Indian theologians would find the time and the necessary discipline to make the fruit of their thinking available to the readership.

b) The New Religious Movements as Laboratories of Theology

We have already recognised the fact that real indigenous theology is happening all the time at the grass-roots level. Much of it is in the vernacular languages, as in the case of the Bible Mission, where all the 28 booklets containing the teachings of Devadas are in Telugu. Many more are not printed but are available in manuscripts with some of his followers. The theology of the Indian Christian festivals has not been analysed. New festivals are coming and some of the old ones are dying. The Gospel is becoming incarnate among the people of God. Much of this basic theology has not been tested on the anvil of the ecumenical experience. All these new trends will have to be carefully documented and interpreted. All the gurus mentioned by Hoerschelmann have something to say, but what is it that they are saying? The churches will have to hear their voices if they themselves want to become contextual. First of all, the way these new religious groups or the folk Christian religions are structured and the way in which they run their affairs and the models they use to celebrate their religion may have something to tell the churches at large. True indigenization in these groups is starting with their leadership styles, as we have seen. A simple charismatic type of leadership is accepted by their followers because of the spiritual gifts and talents of the leader and not because of considerations like their place in any authoritarian structure. They have a less complicated church management and less emphasis on constitutions and councils, which are imported ideas to a large extent. (The fact that secular India has copied these things is no excuse for a non-secular organization like the church). The decision-making process in these groups involves the whole community by collective reflection. All this helps the indigenization process.

The oral liturgical forms of these groups are to be studied carefully. The freedom of worship, the emphasis on healing and exorcism, the community concern for the sick and the needy--these too can speak to us of indigenization.

The theological models used in these new religious groups deserve careful study and interpretation. The image and the story and the parable and the analogical argument as a communication method may be very useful in the service of theology. Sadhu Sundar Singh and others have used them, as we have seen, and there are many others whose writings and teaching and preaching methods need to be studied. These thinkers and writers who are not directly related to the organised churches do not generally get a hearing, and some of the useful experimentation they are doing is lost as far as the church is concerned. If all the elements of teaching of the indigenous church groups in India are collected and if all the songs which the less-known writers and artists are producing are gathered, and if all the prayer healing stories among Hindu believers are brought in, we will have a whole treasure of indigenous theology for our use. This does not mean that everything that appears in all these sources will have to be accepted uncritically. It will have to be carefully sifted and organised and evaluated against the biblical revelation. Since these indigenous group leaders are not influenced by any systematic theological thought forms, it is hoped that what would arise out of this will be truly indigenous theology.

c) <u>Interacton with other Religions:</u>

This is another source of indigenization. Theology has always grown out of an interaction with the surrounding faiths and religions. It has tried to answer the questions which the host community is asking and it has also used the thought processes and aspirations of the host culture. But it did not confine itself to these questions. In India, for too long a time, the church had maintained a 'safe' distance between itself and the major religion Hinduism around. Christians were afraid of any contact with the Hindus in the past. It is not fair, however, to always blame the missionary for this situation. Men like Roberto Do Nobili who advocated the adaptation of Hindu customs have been severly criticised. The Protestant churches in India have adopted a puritanical attitude and the Christians have often thought that most of the Hindu religion is superstitious, idolatrous and heathen; therefore to be avoided. This feeling of 'break from all that is past' was needed in the early days of

Indian church history because it helped the Christians to keep the distinctive call of the Gospel clear. But in the process the church has mainly lost an opportunity to express its faith in truly indigenous forms and failed to speak the language of the land. The Indian Christians in their just demand to belong to the universal church became somewhat strangers to their own culture.

Very few students in the Indian theological colleges have seriously studied Hinduism, for example. The Hindu scriptures have become a closed book for many. And this has also helped to perpetuate the Brahmin monopoly on the country's wisdom for a long time. But recently a new interest in the Hindu scriptures and in the Hindu religion is fortunately appearing among church people. Again, it is not only the philosophic Hinduism that will be helpful but also the Hinduism of the masses, the popular Hinduism with its daily encounter with the gods and goddesses, with the demons and spirits, with its local medicines and the family rites, etc., so that Christian theology in that way may speak to people's concerns and their life situations and truly beome indigenous.

Useful in this process will be the art forms also, the whole wealth of painting, sculpture, drama and dance which can become powerful agents for indigenising theology. Only through such contact with Hinduism can the church's liturgical forms and practical theology become truly indigenous.

7. Some Problems of Indigenization

Finally, it must be said that the whole process of indigenization is not without its own problems, and the way to a truly indigenous church in India is not without its own risks. But the problems are worth facing and the risks are worth taking. Once the church is aware of the possible pitfalls and the great gains that could be derived, the journey is necessary to take up.

Many people talk about syncretism. Like indigenization itself the word syncretism is hard to define. It is hard to draw a line between syncretism and adaptation.

In a consultation with H. Kraemer in Madras at the time of the Tambaram Conference, Chenchiah made some important statements about syncretism[40]. He examined the view that syncretism is 'a patching up of incompatible religions, moralities, philosophies and theologies'. But he argued that this view of syncretism would not, on the other hand, make the patchwork of compatible ideas and doctrines syncretism. Compatibility to him is the test and not the patching up. He also maintains that syncretism is inevitable when varieties meet and it is a natural and inevitable process when different religions meet. The distinction between acceptable and rejectable syncretism is not in its constitution but in its behaviour. Chenchiah admits that he had not seen syncretism in India, syncretism in the sense of mixing up of religions. He may be right when he says that those who say that all religions are the same are exactly those who don't take any of them seriously (p. 180).

On the other hand, the famous Wheaton Declaration of the Evangelical Foreign Mission Association and the Interdenominational Foreign Mission Association (1966) defined syncretism as the attempt to unite or reconcile biblically revealed Christian Truth with the diverse and opposing tenets and practices of non-Christian religions or other systems of thought that deny it[41]. The Wheaton Congress holds the view that syncretism readily develops where 'the Gospel is least understood and experienced'. The Congress further made a declaration with regard to Mission and syncretism acknowledging the uniqueness and finality of Jesus Christ and pledged to 'explore the dangers of syncretism' (p. 463).

But M.M.Thomas does not find this kind of negative sense of the word syncretism very helpful[42]. In an article entitled, 'Christ-centred Syncretism'[43] Thomas examines Kraemer's thought on the subject. Kraemer defines syncretism as an 'illegitimate mingling of different religious elements' over against adaptation, which is legitimate. Thomas rightly says that the church, in trying to avoid illegitimate mixing of heterogenous elements, has gone too far and stopped legitimate interpretation which is necessary for adaptation. Thomas holds that in the post-Thambaram and post-Kraemer period any effort at indigenization of Christianity was dubbed syncretistic without being examined. Thomas says,

> Most of us in situations of pluralism know only too well in living experience that we live with elements of culture, philosophy and cult

drawn from different religions and secular ideological traditions. There is no other way of living. (p. 32). It is the nature of the central decision of Christ and the continuous effort to centre these various elements in some form of coherence around it eventually that makes us Christian.

Actually in history, all conversions are 'more or less': the perfect integration into Christ remains eschatological. The only thing we can emphasise now is that the conscious decision should be Christ-centred, and that the process of conversion be taken seriously.

On the word 'syncretism' itself, Thomas clearly says:

> I am not convinced that this continued use of the word syncretism only in the negative sense removes the hindrance to positive course to experiment among Christians. Nor do I think that it does justice to the story of the origin and development of concepts behind that word throughout the history of religions of mankind, and the reality of syncretic process in any new incarnation of Christianity in different cultures or in modern secular life. Therefore either the word should be abolished from any discussion of the theology of interfaith dialogue or should be given a neutral phenomenological connotation as in the discipline of History of Religions. No other course seems proper[44].

So there is a real place for experimentation in adaptation which should not suffer from fear of syncretism in the Christian Church. The danger is in not trying the necessary adaptation. We mentioned the Christian marriage ceremony and all the legitimate borrowing done from the Hindu marriage ritual. The little gold pendant and the yellow thread get an added meaning in the Christian marriage and the little cross which is added to the gold pendant in the Christian marriage is to symbolise the witness of Christ as sealing the wedlock as it would be the god of fire being the witness in the Hindu marriage. This would not be syncretism but a very useful adaptation. But on the other hand if Christian boys and girls bring home a clay figure of the god Vinayak along with their Hindu compatriots and worship the idol with incense and offer fruits to the idol on the day when the country celebrates the festival of the god of learning, then it would be syncretism, mixing up of incompatible things. The Christian community should be able to take this responsibility of discriminating.

Similarly, there is so much controversy about church architecture. Bishop Azariah's experiments in the Cathedral at Dornakal are really prophetic. But even then the idea did not take root on any large scale in the other parts of the country. Some people still think it is a syncretistic idea.

In the 1970's when the present writer first introduced the classical Indian dances peculiar to Andhra for the Gospel stories, some leaders of the church said it was syncretistic whereas there was unprecedented appreciation from the Hindus, who quickly identified with the medium and through the medium with the message. The Christians asked several questions. Was the Hindu dance model good enough for the Gospel? Could Hindu artistes perform the Christian story in dance even if the form is to be accepted? How much trimming and transforming (and mutilation in the process) will be needed by the art form before it is to be found good enough for the Christian use?

All these questions occupied the minds of the Christians at that time. This kind of questioning and debate is good and also necessary. This kind of discriminating was going on all through the history of the church. But at the end whatever was true to the spirit of the Gospel, whatever was 'compatible' stayed on and the others died eventually. Sometimes the things which disappeared have returned when the church understood their meaning better. An example may be the famous iconoclastic controversy. The icons have returned to some churches and their return proved a great blessing too.

It is true in India one has to be careful. Sometimes the example of Buddhism is cited to show that Hinduism as a great ocean can swallow up all the small rivers of religions. But Christianity is no small river. When the gospel comes into contact with any religion it judges the host religion. It did this to Judaism, it did this to Graeco-Roman culture, and it does this to Hinduism.

Therefore it is vitally important for the Christian church to have dialogue with Hinduism, not only at the philosophical level and intellectual level but also at the popular level, as we have suggested. This kind of encounter will enrich the Indian Church and will make it truly indigenous. The fact that the church should be truly indigenous in order to fulfil its prophetic task is now generally accepted by all thinking people.

To sum up: We have seen indigenization at three levels, namely the liturgical level, the life and witness level, and the doctrinal level and have considered the question of adaptation as a part of indigenization. We have suggested three agents of indigenization, namely the Christian thinkers and writers, the small church groups and the encounter with the non-Christian religions. Finally, we examined the problems involved in indigenization including the fear of religious syncretism.

Adinarayana rightly says that,

> Indigenization is not an academic job where experts go into Committee and draw up a list of innocuous ideas that can be 'safely' implanted in an exotic soil. It must be the result of the dynamic spirit of Christ, working through the form of Hindu thought, adapting, moulding, or transforming as the case may be. It must be the natural result of two spiritually minded groups living together as one family and sharing together their difficulties, ideas and ideologies[45].

The Woman of Samaria
(From the Author's Dance Drama -
Kim Karthavyam)

Encounter with Christ
(From the Author's Dance Drama, Kim Karthavyam)

CHAPTER XIV: Notes

1. Newbigin, Lesslie, Mission in 1980's., Occasional Bulletin of Missionary Research, Vol. 4, No. 4. October 1980, pp. 154-55.

2. Loc.cit., p. 154.

3. Lausanne Occasional Papers No. 2, The Willowbank Report - Gospel and Culture, Lausanne Committee for World Evangelism 1978, p. 7.

4. Ibid.

5. Newbigin, Lesslie, Christ and Cultures, Scottish Journal of Theology, Vol. 31, pp. 1-12., 1978.

6. Joshua, G. Kristhu Charithra, Telugu, Madras, CLS 1963. Cf., Baago, Kaj (Com) Library of Indian Christian Theology, p. 87.

7. Franklin Ewing, S.J. (Ed.) The Role of Communication Arts in the Mission Work, Fordham University Press, New York 1957, p. 43.

8. Willowbank Report, op.cit., p. 23.

9. Immanuel, R.D., The Influence of Hinduism on Indian Christians, Leonard Theological College, Jabalpur 1950.

10. Ibid., p. 85.

11. Ibid., p. 87.

12. Ibid., p. 89.

13. Asirvatham, Eddy., Christianity in Indian Crucible, p. 147.

14. I have followed Immanuel's suggestion for this summary.

15. Immanuel, op.cit., p. 99.

16. Immanuel reports of two of the Christian Ashrams in detail, see Immanuel, op.cit., pp. 103-107.

17. Cf., Immanuel, op.cit., pp. 110-14.

18. Asirvatham, Eddy., op.cit., p. 151.

19. Rawson, J.N., Katha Upanishad, Calcutta University Pub. 1937. Quoted by Immanuel op.cit., p. 50.

20. Bhagavat Gita VI: 10-15. Quoted by Immanuel op.cit., p. 51.

21. Cf. Chapter I, note 8.

22. Newbigin, Lesslie, Christ and Cultures, op.cit., p. 11.

23. Appasamy, A.J., What do We Believe - A Study of Christian Pramānas, CLS. Madras 1971.

24. Jung, C.G., Collected Works, Vo. 9, part I (Ed.) Sir Herbert Read et al., p. 36.

25. Boyd op.cit., p. 259.

26. Ibid., p. 255.

27. Rajamanickam, S., s.j., Roberto De Nobili on Adaptation, De Nobili Research Institute, St. Xavier's College, Palaymkottai, 1971. Cf. also De Nobili on Indian Customs, 1972.

28. Cf., Subbamma B.V., New Patterns for Discipling Hindus, William Carey Press, 1970.

29. Rajamanickam, Adaptation, p. ix.

30. Ibid., p. xv.

31. Ibid., p. 21.

32. Ibid., p. 29.

33. Butler, John A., Theology of the Church Building in India, Indian Journal of Theology, Vol. V, No. 2, October 1956.

34. Butler, John A., Methodist Recorder, October 7. 1971.

35. Newbigin, Lesslie, "Christ and Cultures", Scottish Journal of Theology Vol. 31, 1978, p. 11.

36. Baago, Kaj., Indian Indigenous Theology, (Review Article) International Review of Missions, Vol. LV, 1966, pp. 221-25.

37. Ibid., p. 222.

38. Ibid., p. 225.

39. Matthew, George, Content Analysis of Some Theological Journals in India, Religion and Society, Vol. XXVIII No. 4, December 1981, Bangalore, pp. 67-92.

40. Cf., Thangasamy, D.A., Theology of Chenchiah, Bangalore: CISRS 1966, pp. 173ff.

41. Wheaton Declaration Report, International Review of Missions, Vol. LV 1968, 462ff.

42. Harold Turner suggests 'Synthetist' and 'Synthetism' as useful alternatives; Cf., Turner, Harold, New Religious Movements in Primal Societies, in J.R. Honnels (ed.) The Penguin Handbook of Living Religions, Harmondsworth: Penguin Books (in Press, 1983).

43. Thomas, M.M., Christ Centred Syncretism, Religion and Society Vol. XXVI No. 1, March 1979, Bangalore, p. 26ff.

44. Ibid.

45. Adinarayana, S.P., Indian Journal of Theology, Vol. V, No. 2, 1956, p. 30.

CHAPTER XV

Where do we go from here?

The question we raise here does not intend to suggest that we have already arrived somewhere. We are still on the way as far as the search is concerned. The search goes on, the quest continues. We have asked some questions and have seen some of the trends. We have briefly studied the origin and growth of a folk Christian religion in India, the Bible Mission. With this small church group as an example, we have seen, although as from a long distance, and still as in formative stage, some trends for the future church in India. The folk Christian religions in India, like their counterparts in other parts of the world, have started a process which may have far-reaching consequences for Christianity as a whole, a process which the leaders of the mainline churches and the theologians in India, Europe and America can ignore only to their great disadvantage.

One thing seems to be certain, and that is, the church in India is not going to be what it was in the past. Christianity in India in the past became another system as burdensome as any other. It has to 'make its Easter', to use one of the expressions of Paulo Freire; it must die and rise again.

The old concepts and attitudes bequeathed by the Western Missions should give place to new concepts and new understandings. Some possible areas calling for a fresh examination could be:

a) the church's attitude to Indian culture[1];
b) its relationship to the other religions;
c) an honest re-assessment of its own understanding of the Gospel and its demands;
d) a discovery of a new vocabulary, a new language to communicate its faith[2];
e) a new dialogue with the charismatic church groups and with the folk Christian Religious forms;
f) a new and more meaningful training pattern for its ministers which is relevant to the needs of the community today[3].

It is sometimes asked what exactly the mission churches can learn from the Bible Mission and from such other groups. This may not be the most important question. There are some lessons which the mission churches can learn from these small groups and there are also lessons which the small groups can learn from the major churches. But the new indigenous church groups have probably shown a new approach, a new way of expressing their faith, and a new openness to share and learn from others. Their existence and witness, their free intermingling with non-Christians and their use of dreams, visions and charismatic gifts have raised questions which neither mission churches nor the folk churches themselves have ever seriously asked before; questions such as: how important are the Christologies of the non-Christians for a richer understanding of our own faith[4], what is the theological relevance of visions and dreams and the collective archetypes, how far can the oral mould of theology be pushed into practice of the churches, etc.

There are many ways in which the two types of churches in India can profitably cooperate with each other and benefit from each other. They can be partners in their healing campaigns, and in their song and worship festivals. A drama on the Christian faith, a festival of Christian dance, an exhibition of Christian arts, and many such meaningful activities are possible as joint ventures. In fact, these can and should provide the churches with a meaningful contact point with the non-Christians if we believe that the Spirit of God is active even outside the boundaries of the visible church.

The pastors and the leaders of the mission churches need dreams and visions, they need a new type of spirituality[5]. Above all, they need to understand the visions and dreams which are already there in their congregations. Similarly, the pastors and the preachers of the new groups need some training in preaching the word of God. Some of them treat God's word as a kind of magic. To send them to theological colleges is neither practical nor useful. So that is no solution. There should be other ways of useful communication with them and more practical ways of training. The mainline churches should be willing to share their resources and their experience in this area as well as in other areas[6].

One would also hope that the small church groups will come out of their 'cells' of seclusion and join the others in true Christian spirit, willing to learn from the experience of the others. They should not confine themselves only to the eschatological aspects in the futuristic sense but they should be more and more concerned about God's will for men here and now.

What exactly the future shape of the Church in India is going to be is hard to say. The present image of the church, however, is not quite familiar to the people of the land. The voice is familiar but the image is strange. There is much in the outward structure of the church which gives it a strange appearance, a peculiar foreign colour.

The new Christianity which I am envisaging may not even be called a 'church', much less will it be any denominaion. The new church will be more simple in its organisational patterns, more humble and more understanding. It will be willing to hear as much as it is anxious to speak. It will be slow to absolutise, and it will accept and 'baptise' for expressing its own faith several symbols, rites and institutions from its surrounding culture. It will not make demands on others which Christ himself did not make[7]. It will respect and redeem the cultures amidst which it is living rather than trying to condemn them. It will detach itself from Western influence to such an extent that the staunchest nationalist in India will not have any objection on that account to join it. It will find its death and resurrection for the sake of the countless millions of the land whom it seeks to serve for Christ's sake.

But it also will transcend the national boundaries and will commit itself to the true nature of catholic and universal koinonia[8].

The future church in India will be an organism rather than an organisation, it will be a new creation rather than an old institution. It will be a sign of the kingdom of God in India. Its creed will be self-sacrifice and not self-perpetuation. It will spend itself like a candle giving light to others, it will flow like a river quenching the thirst of a parched land rather than remaining stony and frozen like snow on the high peaks of old dogmatism.

The future church in India will speak more the language of the people, not the language of some angels which men do not understand. It will speak the language of love and not of strife. The future church in India will be not only a church looking to the future but also a church of the present, addressing itself to the present needs of the people. It will be the manifestation of the power of Christ who is living and acting through her today; it will not merely talk about a Jesus who lived and died two thousand years ago. It will seek to serve the people of the land, not as though service is its private prerogative, but taking its place with those others through whom God is willing to work out His redemptive plan for all mankind today.

The strength of the future church in India will not be in its hierarchiacal structures but it will be in its rank and file, in its ordinary members and in its humble faithful. Its leaders will be the more charismatic persons among them and not the presidents and the bishops who are elected and appointed to wield power and authority as the rulers of the world do. The future church in India will have minimal rules and adaptable constitutions and statutes to guide it, all these rules, constitutions and statutes being ever subject to the overall guidance of the Holy Spirit.

The church in India in the past was too exclusive and kept itself aloof but the future church will take its place in the life of the wider community; while being separate from the world it will yet be an integral part of mankind. It is redeemed and yet will be willing to accept God's judgement along with all the other 'institutions' and organisations of the world. It will not make its own growth, or enrolling people for church membership, its primary concern and it will recognise the followers of Christ who are outside the institutional church fold. It will respect the cultural loyalties and the social affinities of men in so far as these do not clash with the minimum claims of Jesus Christ when He confronts them to make a choice for Him. The new church in India will be a small leaven that leaveneth the whole lump without marking its own boundaries. It will permeate into the wider society and it will acknowledge that Christ came not only for the Christians but for all men. It will never find any use for military language, it will not think of its own task in terms of 'crusades', it will not believe in strategies, it will not recognise 'home bases' and 'advancing frontiers'. It will never consider its work in images of 'warfare with the heathen faiths'[9].

The future church in India will not even confine its meetings to the church buildings, it will not restrict its liturgy to printed formats, it will never limit the work of the Holy Spirit to the narrow boundaries of the 'Christian' community.

The future church in India will listen. It talked much in the past. It talked so much that it heard only its own voice and it was not prepared to hear the voices from outside. It may have missed the voice of the Holy Spirit too. The church in the past was afraid of losing itself for Christ, it was afraid that it would be converted to other faiths. But the New Testament Church did not close its ears to the voices of its times. The future church in India likewise will listen more and in listening it will itself be heard around the world.

The future church in India will cease to be another caste in the country. Its members will be a part of the total social milieu, the doors of its worship places will be open to everyone who wants to come in not only as an occasional visitor but as a partner in the heritage of its fellowship. It will not make any ritual a precondition for any man to come to Christ. Instead of sitting in judgement on people and their cultures, it will acknowledge all cultures and all people as included in the plan of God's redemption by the Gospel of Christ.

The future church will not speak in 'black and white' categories. It will not say that all those who are not for it are against it. It rather will say that all those who are not against it are for it. It will not say that all those who do not belong to it will go to hell. There must surely be other positive images to describe the joy which such people are missing. Maybe they are not even missing much outside the structures which the present church has built around itself now. But at any rate the future church will recognise that there are sheep which do not belong to this fold.

The future church in India, of course, will make a distinction between adaptation and selfish accommodation in dealing with the cultures around. It will not be interested in popularity but it will be deeply interested in people. It will not be just a display item like a tall tower of brick and mortar but it will be a functional tool in God's hands, like a little lamp with its never-ending light to call people to Christ. It will not give its own answers to people's problems but it will seek to help people to ask useful questions when confronted with the Gospel of Jesus Christ. The people of India have heard the Gospel now, and it may be that they want more to see it in action among God's people. The people of India have seen the big institutions which the

Christian missions have set up, they may want more to experience the power of God working in the church now.

The future church in India will be new, it will not be the old church any more. It will have 'made its Easter'.

CHAPTER XV: Notes

1. 'God's love descends not only on Christians but also on non-Christians. His theatre of operation is humanity, not Church' - Chenchiah. See, Chenchiah, P. Indian Christians and Cooperation with non-Christians, Indian Journal of Theology, Vol. VII, 1958, pp. 1-11.

2. On the subject of development of Indian vocabulary for theological thought, see Devanandan, P.D., Changing Context of Hindu Religious Terminology, Indian Journal of Theology, Vol. X, 1964, pp. 58-63

3. Alexander John, a leader of the Church of South India, argues for a new pattern for the training of future pastors in India. He questions the need for a full-time paid ministry in India. He suggests a need-based lay ministry with subsequent in-service training for some who are ready for such a training. There were some experiments in this regard in the Andhra Evangelical Lutheran Church in the past. See John, Alexander D., From Insularity towards a New Involvement, in: A Vision for Man: Essays on Faith, Theology and Society (ed.) Samuel Amirtham, Madras: CLS 1978, pp. 238-252.

4. A recent series of seminars in the Selly Oak Colleges on the subject of One Jesus and Many Christologies has drawn much interest and useful discussion with the members of the Centre for Islamic Studies and others who participated.

5. Morton Kelsey is right when he says that people need religious experience and not just intellectual doctrine. See, Kelsey, Morton T., The Christian and the Supernatural, p. 135.

6. An interesting experiment is now going on in such a sharing, in the Partnership Project between Black and White, in Birmingham. For a detailed account of this see Mujibuko Bongani's dissertation on Education in Mission for Pluralistic Societies: A Critical Comparative Study of Selected Approaches (Birmingham University Ph.D. Thesis, 1983).

7. Alexander John says,

> We may have to change a number of rules, like receiving of people of other faiths in the church without insisting on baptism and allowing marriages to take place between a Christian and a partner of another faith. In all these, unless we are willing to depart from the ways we have known and venture into the unknown we will be perpetuating the myth of a false security. Thus the priority is for seeking a new humanity for all Faiths and Ideologies.--John, Alexander, D, op.cit., p. 242.

8. See, Works of D.Bonhoeffer, also Visser 'T Hooft's letter to Hugh Martin concerning William Paton's Book, The Church and the New Order, Collected Works of Bonhoeffer, ed. Edwin H.Robertson, London: Collins, 1973, pp. 107ff.

9. Talking about the military terminology of Western Christianity, S.P.Adinarayana says,

> This is one aspect of indigenization which is perhaps not so often discussed or thought about as it should be. I refer to the harmful effects of certain Western ideologies on Indian Christian thought. This is particularly the case regarding the crusading spirit and the idea that the Christian is a soldier.

—Adinarayana, S.P., Indian Journal of Theology, Vol. V, Nov. 1956, p. 30.

BIBLIOGRAPHY

Airon, C.D., (Ed.), The Outpourings of My Heart, Songs of K.Subba Rao, Guntur: 1964.

---, Kalagara Subba Rao, The Mystic of Munipalle, Vijayawada n.d.

Allen, Roland, Missionary Methods, St. Paul's or Ours, World Dominion Press, 1962.

Althaus, Paul, The Ethics of Martin Luther, (Trans.) Robert C.Schultz, Philadelphia: Fortress Press, 1965.

Amirtham, Samuel, (Ed.), A Vison for Man: Essays on Faith, Theology and Society, Madras: CLS, 1978.

Appakavi, Kakunuri, (17th. C) Appakaveeyam (Telugu Grammar), Madras: Ramasway Sasthrulu and Sons, 1970.

Appasamy, A.J., The Gospel and India's Heritage, Madras: SPCK 1942.

---, Sundar Singh a Biography, Madras: CLS 1966.

---, What Shall We Believe, A Study of Christian Pramanas, Madras: CLS 1971.

Asirvatham, Eddy, Christianity in Indian Crucible, Calcutta: YMCA Publishing House, 1955.

Babin, Pierre, The Audio Visual Man (Ed.), Dayton, Ohio: Pflaum 1970.

Bago, Kaj.A., (Compiled) Library of Indian Christian Theology - A Bibliography, Madras: CLS 1969.

---, Post Colonial Crisis in Missions, International Review of Missions, Vol. LV pp. 322-32. 1966.

---, Indian Indigenous Theology, Review Article on H.Wagner's Erstgestalten einer einheimischen Theologie Sudindien, Munich 1963, in International Review of Missions Vol. LV, 1966 pp. 221-25.

---, Movement Around Subba Rao (A Hindu Christian Movement around Subba Rao of Munipalle of Andrha Pradesh) Madras: CLS 1968.

Barrett, David, World Christian Encyclopedia, Nairobi: Oxford University Press 1982.

Bennett, George, The Heart of Healing, Evesham Worcs: Arthur James Ltd., 1971.

Boyd, R.H.S., An Introduction to Indian Christian Theology, Madras: CLS 1963.

---, India and the Latin Captivity of the Church, Cambridge University Press, 1974.

Brown, Lesslie, God as Christians See Him, London: OUP 1961.

Brown, Robert McFee, My Story and The Story, Theology Today, Vol. XXXII No. 2, July 1975, pp. 166-73.

Brunner, F.D., Theology of the Holy Spirit, The Pentecostal Experience of The New Testament Witness, London: Hodder and Stoughton 1970.

Brunton, Dr. Paul, A Search in Secret India, London: Rider and Co., 1934.

Bunyan, John, Pilgrim's Progress, London: J.M.Dent and Son Ltd., 1956.

Butler, John A., The Theology of Church Building in Indai, Indian Journal of Theology, Vol. V No. 2 October 1956, pp. 1-20.

Caird, G.B., The Language and the Imagery of the Bible, Duckworth Studies in Theology, London: Gerald Duckworth, 1980.

Carey, George, The Indwelling Spirit, Theological Renewal No. 14, Feb. 1980.

Chandy, J., Healing Ministry of the Indian Church, Bangalore: CISRA (pamphlet) 1970.

Cone, James, The Story Context of Black Theology, Theology Today, Vol. XXXII No. 2, July 1975, pp. 144-50.

Davamony Mariasusai, Love of God According to Saiva Siddhanta, A Study in the mysticism and theology of Saivism, Oxford: Clarendon Press 1971.

Davies, J.G., Every Day God, London: SCM, 1973.

Devanandan, P.D., Changing Content of Hindu Religious Terminology, Indian Journal of Theology, Vol. 10, 1961, pp. 58-63.

Devasahayam, K., The Bible Mission, Religion and Society, Vol. XXIX, No. 1 March 1982, pp. 55-89.

Dolbeer, M.L. (Sr.), Andhra Evangelical Lutheran Church, A Brief History, Guntur: Lutheran Publishing House n.d.

Dolbeer, M.L. (Jr.), A History of Lutheranism in Andhra Desa 1842 - 1920, New York: Board of Foreign Missions, United Lutheran Church in America, 1959.

Douglas, Ian and Carman, Comment on Post-Colonial Crisis in Missions, International Review of Missions, Vol. LV, pp. 483-89. 1966.

Dulles, Avery, s.j., Models of the Church, Dublin: Gill and Macmillan, 1976.

Dunn, James D.G., Unity and Diversity in the New Testament, London: SCM 1977.

---, Baptism in the Holy Spirit, Studies in Biblical Theology, Second Series No. 15, London: SCM 1970.

Eagle, Robert, Alternative Medicine, London: Futura Publications, 1978.

Eliade, Mircea, Shamanism: Archaic Teachings of Ecstasy, London: Routledge and Kegan Paul, 1970.

Elwood, Douglas J. (Ed.) What Asian Christians are Thinking (A Theological Source Book) Quezon City: New Day Publications, 1978.

Estborn, Siegfried, The Church among Tamils and Telugus, National Christian Council of India, Nagpur: 1961.

Ewing, J.Franklin s.j. (Ed.), The Role of Communication Arts in Mission Work, Institute of Mission Studies, Fordham University 1957.

Farquhar, The Crown of Hinduism, Oxford: OUP 1913.

---, Gita and the Gospel, London/Madras: CLS 1946.

Fashole-Luke, Edward, et al., (Ed.), Christianity in Independent Africa, London: Rex Collins, 1978.

Fishman, A.T., Culture Change and the Underprivileged, Madras: CLS, 1941.

Foreman, Charles W., Christianity in the Non-Western World, (Global History Series) Englewood Cliffs N.J: Prentice Hall, 1967.

Forrester, Duncan B., Caste and Christianity, Attitudes and Policies of Anglo-Saxon Protestant Missions in India, London: Curzon Press, 1979.

Fox, Strangways A.H. The Music of Hidostan, Oxford: Clarendon Press, 1914.

Freire, Paulo, Pedagogy of the Oppressed, London: George Allen and Unwin Ltd., 1954/1967.

Fuchs, Stephen, Rebellious Prophets, A Study of the Messianic Movements in Indian Religions, London/Bombay: Asia Pub. House, 1965, pp. 16-43.

---, Messianic Movements in Primitive India, Asian Folklore Studies 24 (1) 1965, pp. 11-62.

Godsey, John D., Preface to Bonhoeffer the man and Two of His shorter Writings, Philadelphia: Fortress Press, 1957.

Griffiths, Bede, Vedanta and Christian Faith, Los Angeles: The Dawn Horse Press. 1973.

—, The Marriage of the East and West, Fountana, London, 1983.

—, Christian Ashrams in India, London: Longman and Todd, 1966.

Hargreaves, A.C.M., Eastern Christendom and the Miracles of Jesus, Indian Journal of Theology, Vol. 10, 1961, pp. 25-33.

Hodgson, Leonard, The Doctrine of the Trinity, London: Nisbet & Co., 1943.

Hoerschelmann, Werner H., Christlische Gurus, Frankfurt: Peter Lang, 1977.

Hoffman, Bengt R., Luther and the Mystics, Minneapolis: Augusburg Pub. House, 1976.

Hollenweger, Walter J., Conflict in Corinth, New York: Paulist Press, 1978.

—, Pentecost Between Black and White, Belfast: Christian Journals, 1974.

—, The Pentecostals, London: SCM Press, 1972.

—, Roots and Fruits of Charismatic Renewal in the Third World, Implications for Mission, Theological Renewal, No. 14, Feb. 1980. pp. 11-27.

—, The Other Exegesis, Horizons in Biblical Theology, An International Dialogue, Vol. 3, 1981, pp. 155-79.

—, Pentecostals and Charismatic Movement, (to be published) Mircea Eliade (Ed.) The Encyclopedia of Religion, New York: 1983.

Immanuel, Rajappan D., The Influence of Hinduism on Indian Christians, Jabbalpur: Leonard Theological College, 1950.

Jay, Eric G., The Church, Its Changing Image Through 20 Centuries, Vol. 2 London: SPCK 1977.

John, Alexander D., From Insularity to a New Involvement, A Vision for Man: Essays on Faith, Theology and Society (Ed.) Samuel Amirtham, Madras: CLS 1978.

Joshua, G., Kristhu Charitha (Telugu) Life of Christ in Poetry, Madras: CLS, 1963.

Jung, C.G., Dreams and Visions,

—, Four Archetypes, London: Routledge and Kegan Paul, 1972.

—, The Archetypes and the Collective Unconscious, Collected Works, Vol.IX, Part 1, (Trans) R.F.C.Hull, (Ed) Sir Herbert Read et al., London: Routledge and Kegan Paul, 1959.

Kee, Howard C., Christian Origins in Social Perspective, London: SCM, 1980.

Kelsey, Morton T. Encounter with God, Minneapolis: Bethany Fellowship Inc., 1972.

---, The Christian and the Supernatural, London: Search Press, 1977.

---, Tongue Speaking: An Experiment in Spiritual Experience, London: Hoddler and Stoughton, 1968.

---, The Other Side of Silence, A Guide to Christian Meditation, London: SPCK, 1977.

---, Healing and Christianity, London: SCM, 1973.

Kerr, Hugh T., What is the Story: Theology Today, Vol. XXXII, No. 2, July 1975. pp. 129-32.

Klostermaier, Klaus, Hindu and Christian in Vrindavan, London: SCM, 1969.

Koyama Kosuke, Waterbuffalo Theology, London: SCM, 1974.

Krailsheimer, A.J., Conversion, London: SCM, 1980.

Lambourne, R.A., Community, Church and Healing - A Study of some of the Corporate Aspects of the Church's Ministry to the Sick, London: Longman and Todd, 1963.

Luke, P.Y., and J.B.Carman, Village Christians and Hindu Culture, Rural Churches in South India, London: Lutterworth, 1968.

Lyon, David and A.D.Manuel (Ed.), Renewal for Mission, Madras: CLS, 1967.

Mackey, J.P., The Christian Experience of God as Trinity, London: SCM, 1983.

Matthai, Zacharaiah (Ed.), The Indian Church, Identity and Fulfilment, Madras/Delhi: CLS/ISPCK, 1971.

Matthew, George, Content Analysis of Theological Journals of India, Religion and Society, Vol. XXVIII No. 4, Bangalore: Dec. 1981, pp. 67-92.

McGilvray, James C., The Quest for Health and Wholeness, Tubingen: German Institute of Medical Mission, 1981.

McKenzie, John (Ed.) The Christian Task in India, Macmillan, 1929.

Moltmann, Yurgen, Theology of Hope, London: SCM Press, 1967.

Neill, Stephen, Colonialism and Christian Mission, London: Lutterworth, 1966.

Newbigin, Lesslie, The Basis, Purpose and Manner of Interfaith Dialogue, Scot. Journal of Theology, Vol. 30, pp. 253-70., 1977.

---, Christ and Culture, Scot. Journal of Theology, Vol. 31, pp. 1-12. 1978.

---, The Finality of Christ, London: SCM 1969.

---, The Healing Ministry in the Mission of the Church, The Healing Church: Tubingen Report, Geneva: WCC, 1965.

---, Mission in 1980s, Occasional Bulletin of Missionary Research, Vol. 4, No. 4, New Jersey: October 1980.

Newell, Kenneth W., (Ed.), Health by People, Geneva: WHO, 1975.

Oosterwal, Gottfried, Modern Messianic Movements as a Theological and Mission Challenge, Missionary Studies, No. 2, Institute of Mennonite Studies Elkhart 1973.

Panikkar, Raimundo, The Unknown Christ of Hinduis, London: Darton Longman and Todd, 1964.

---, The Verdic Experience Manthra Manajri, London: Darton Longman & Todd, 1979.

Paranjoti, V, An Experiment in Indigenization in Evangelism, Indian Journal of Theology, Vol. 10, 1961, pp. 108-11.

Pocock, David, Mind, Body and Wealth, Oxford: Basil Blackwell, 1973.

Popley, H.A., The Use of Indian Music in Christian Worship, Indian Journal of Theology, Vo. VI No. 1, 1957, pp. 80-88.

Rajamanickam, S., s.j., Robert De Nobili on Adaptation, Palayamkottai: De Nobili Institute, St. Xavier College, 1971.

---, Robert De Nobili on Indian Customs, De Nobili Institute, 1972.

Rajarigam, D., Theological Content in Tamil Christian Poetical Works, Indian Journal of Theology, Vol. II, 1962, p. 130ff.

Ramsey, Michael, Be Still and Know, London: Fount Publications, 1982.

Rayan, Samuel, Theology as Art, Religion and Society, Vol. XXVI, No. 2, June 1979, Bangalore, pp. 77-90.

Robinson, John A.T., Truth is Two-Eyed, London: SCM Press, 1979.

Russell, William Vincent, Christianity and Native Rites, London: Central Africa House, 1950.

Sambamurthi, P., South Indian Music, Vols. I-VI, Madras: Indian Music Pub. House, 1975 (Fourth Edition).

Scheel, Martin, Some Comments on Pre-Scientific Forms of Healing, The Healing Church: Tubingen Report, Geneva: WCC, 1965.

Schweizer, Eduard, Church Order in the New Testament, London: SCM 1961.

Segundo, Juan Luis, A Theology for Artisans of a New Humanity, 5 Vols. Mary Knoll: New York, 1974.

Stanley Jones, E., The Christ of the Indian Road, New York: Abingdon Press, 1925.

Stewart, William, India's Religious Frontier, Christian Presence amid Modern Hinduism, London: SCM Press, 1964.

Stump, Joseph, An Explanation of Luther's Small Catechism, Philadelphia: Board of Publications of General Council of Evangelical Lutheran Church in North America, 1907, Telugu Translation, Guntur n.d.

Subbamma, B.V., New Patterns for Discipling Hindus, California/South Pasadena: William Carey Press, 1970.

---, Christ Confronts India, Madras: Diocesan Press, 1973.

Sundar Rao, Mark, Concerning Indian Christianity, New Delhi: YMCA, 1973.

Swavely, C.H. (Ed.), The Lutheran Enterprise in India, Madras: Diocesan Press. 1952.

---, One Hundred Years in the Andhra Country, A History of the ULC Mission of the AELC, Madras: Diocesan Press, 1942.

Te Selle, Sallie, McFague, The Experience of Coming to Belief, Theology Today, Vol. XXXII No. 2, July 1975, pp. 159-65.

Thangasamy, D.A., The Theology of Chenchaiah: Confessing the Faith in India, Series No. 1. Bangalore: YMCA/SISRS 1966.

Thomas, M.M., Indian Christian Theology, Asian Voices in Christian Theology (Ed.) G.H.Anderson.

---, Theology of Nationalism

---, Christ Centred Syncretism, Religion and Society, Vol. XXVI No. 1 March 1979, pp. 26-35.

Thomas, V.P., The Indian Christian Theology and its Identity, Religion and Society, Vol. XXV, No. 3, September 1978, pp. 26-33.

Turner, Harold W., New Vistas: Missionary and Ecumenical, Religious Movements in Primal (or Tribal) Societies, Mission Focus, Vol 9, No. 3, September 1981. Quarterly Mennonite Board of Mission Elkhart, Indiana, pp. 45-55.

Turner, Harold W., A Further Dimension for Mission, New Religious Movements in Primal Societies, International Review of Mission, July 1973, pp. 321-37.

—, New Religious Movements in Primal Societies, J.R.Hinnells (Ed.) The Penguin Handbook of Living Religions, Harmondsworth: Penguin Books (in Press 1983).

von Akkeren, Philip, Sri and Christ, A Study of Indigenous Church in East Java, London: Lutterworth, 1970.

Weber, Hans-Ruedi, Experiments With Bible Study, Geneva: WCC 1981.

Webster, Douglas, What is Spiritual Healing? London: The Highway Press, n.d.

Wheaton Declaration, International Review of Missions, Vol. LV 1966, pp. 173ff.

Willowbank Report No. 2, Gospel and Culture.

Wilson, Michael, The Church is Healing, London: SCM Press, 1966.

—, Health is For People, London: Darton, Longman and Todd, 1975.

Year Book of India Missions 1912 (Ed.) Jones, J.P., Madras: CLS 1912.

List of Telugu Publications of the Bible Mission Consulted for this Research
(See Chapter I, pp. 18-19)

1. తెనుగుక్రైస్తవకీర్తనలు.
2. సైతానుపెదిరించుట.
3. వాగ్దానమంజరి.
4. ప్రార్థనమెట్లు.
5. ఉపవాసప్రార్థనదేశ.
6. ఉపవాసప్రార్థనప్రకరణలు.
7. సమర్పణప్రార్థన.
8. రాత్రిప్రార్థనస్తుతులు.
9.   "   రెండవభాగలు.
10. సన్నిధిసంపద.
11. God's Presence.
12. పరమతీర్థలు.
13. యెప్తాహిందుత్వ-మానసలులు.
14. Woe unto You.
15. ప్రకటనగ్రంథవివరాలు.
16. మిత్ర.
17. శ్రీస్తుసత్యమాసలు.
18. మహిమవార్తవళి.
19. అశ్వాని.
20. రక్షణపద్యలు.
21. దైవలక్షణములస్తుతి.
22. శ్రీమహాప్రభుదారు.
23. దేవుడు ఎందుకు పిలుచున్నాడు?
24. దేవసాన్నిధ్యాలు.
25. మెంజ.
26. క్రైస్తవమహిమార్థపృథ్వి పత్రిక.
27. వరబోధిని.
28. పత్రాంతరరూపణ.

Appendix I

The Chariot Wheels of God

An eschatological hymn by Srirangam Srinivasa Rao
Telugu Poet, 1940

జగన్నాథుని రథచక్రాలు ॥శ్రీ॥

పతితులార !
భ్రష్టులార !
బాధాసర్పదష్టులార !
బ్రతుకు తాని, తనిదేవ
రథచక్రపు చెరుసులలో
పడి నశినదోసులార !
హీనులార !
కూతువేని, హాతువేని,
భ్రష్టులార, పష్టులార
సములవలన పరిచ్యుతులు
పశులవలన తర్జితులు
సంఘానికి మహాష్టులు
హతాశ్రయులు
హృతారయులు
హతాశులే
ఏ తరంది !
ఏ తరంది !

మేరక్తం తలచి నసిగి
మా నాడులు తదరి తరరి
మా ప్రేక్షలు తనరి తనరి
ఏ తరంది ఏ తరంది ॥
ఒప్పరాని విస్పష్టులార
చికితావిష్టులార
పతితులార భ్రష్టులార
బాధాసర్పదష్టులార
ఏ తరంది ఏ తరంది ॥

వస్తున్నాయి యొస్తున్నాయి
జగన్నాథ జగన్నాథ
జగన్నాథ రథచక్రాల్
రథచక్రాల్
రథచక్రాల్
రథచక్రాల్ రథచాల్
ఒస్తున్నాయి
యొస్తున్నాయి ॥

పెతతులార
(స్త్రీ) పురులార
మెయు బ్బారిని
బయత్కేరిన
రథచ(క)లక
ర ధ చ (క్ర)క
బస్తున్న యెస్తున్నాయ ||

సింహాచలం తడిసింది
హిమాచలం తడిసింది
విందాస్ర చలం పశిందిది
సింహాచలం, హిమాచలం
విందాస్ర చలం, సంధ్యాచలం
మహిసగా తెగరుతున్నాయ
మహా శభం తడుచుతున్నది
చర్లసూన, ఘూర్లసూన
దొర్లసూన సిరిసి ఖురాక్
పెతతులార (స్త్రీ) పురులార
ఏదిసవకం సేసవకంది ||

~~o~~

(For a paraphrased translation see pp. 151-153)

Appendix II (i)

In Praise of Asia
(Excerpt 1, from G. Joshua, Kristhu Charithra ISPCK, CLS 1963) p. iv.

The little one of Nazareth who came in human form
to take away the sins of mankind,
The ruler of Paradise who is ever worshipped
by countless hosts of heavenly beings,
The Lord who holds in His hand
the authority to bind and to loosen
Death and Life,
The babe of Bethlehem who was born to tread
the regions of the starry heavens
Even the Lord Jesus himself
Did not choose to be born in the mighty and
glamorous lands of the earth
But he came to be born on your shores,
O, Mother Asia,
blessed are you and your prayers
are rewarded.

Appendix II (ii)

A Mother's Lamentation
(Excerpt 2, from G. Joshua, Kristhu Charithra
ISPCK, CLS 1963), p. 115.

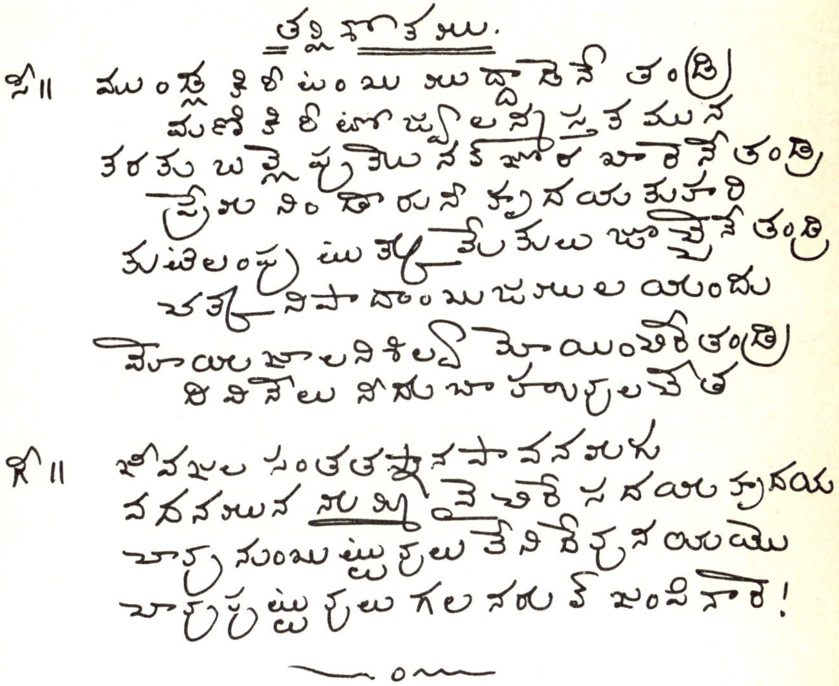

[Handwritten Telugu text]

Your brow which shines with the
brightness of a thousand diamonds
is kissed today by a crown of thorns.
Your bosom which is ever filled with eternal love
is pierced with a merciless spear.
Into your feet so tender as a lotus
are driven the cruel nails of cold steel.
Your shoulders destined to rule the universe
are laden with a heavy cross.

Upon your face they did not hesitate to spit
Men who are slaves to death and life
have killed you the very God,
the giver of eternal life.

Appendix III

Who is the Source of my Joy?

One of the well-known hymns of Devadas.
(Andhra Christian Hymnal No. 348)

(For a paraphrased translation see Chapter VIII, pp. 169-170)

Appendix IV

Notes on Poetical Structure in Telugu Language

In the Telugu language, as in Sanskrit, every syllable is a single letter. Each one of these letters is a combination of a consonant and a vowel symbol joined in one character. That is why it is cumbersome to transliterate Telugu words in Roman script. It takes more Roman letters for the corresponding number of Telugu characters. And the scanning of a poetic piece or song is done in measures of three syllables (or three letters) or their equivalents in length. These measures are called ga*n*as. There is a 'memoria technica' mentioned in Fox-Strangways, which in Telugu helps scanning of poetry. He lists all possible groups of syllables and gives the western synonyms to the names. (Fox-Strangway. op.cit., p. 196).

Yamātā	bacchic	v - -
Mātārā	molossus	- - -
Tārāja	antibacchic	- - v
Rājabhā	cretic	- v -
Jabhāna	amphibrach	v - v
Bhānasa	dactyl	- v v
Nasala	tribrach	v v v
Salagā	anapaest	v v -

The first syllable of each word in the column on the left hand side of the above list is all that is generally used. Thus these groups of syllables are rermembered as Ya-group, Ma-group, etc. The other two syllables of the word are to indicate the type of syllables that follow the first one in the composition whether they are laghu (short) or guru (long). Actually, if the first letters of the groups are written in a circle clockwise starting with Ya, we can take them three at a time in that order, starting anywhere and discern the quality of the measure thus:

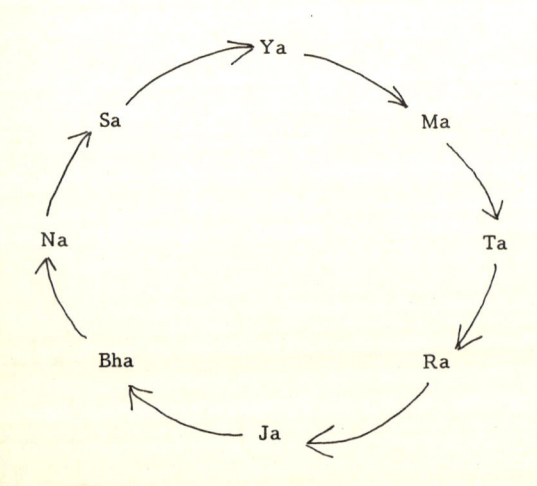

These are three-syllable ga*n*as or measures. (Fox-strangeways calls them 'feet' but it is better to call them measures to avoid confusing them with lines in a poem which are also called feet, or pādās). On the same principle, four or more measures of two syllables in each can be named and these are also used in poetic compositions. They are:

Lala	pyrrhic	v v
Laga	iambus	v -
Gala	trochee	- v
Gaga	spondee	- -

A long syllable (guru) is counted as two māthras and a short syllable (laghu) is counted as one māthra.

In music a māthra is four akshara-kālas (short-syllable counts). It means an instant or unit, what the Greeks called 'chronus protos,' the first or the smallest duration (Fox-Strangways, op.cit., p. 199).

All poetic metres (vrttas) in Telugu, such as Kanda, Seesa, Ataveladi, Tētageethi, and even those derived from Sanskrit, namely, Shārdūla, Mathēbha, Utpalamāla, Champakamāla, etc., are scanned with the help of the Ganas. (Vrtta means a circle and these poetic pieces are called vrttas because the meaning ends at the end of four lines and these four feet circles are called vrttas. In music on the other hand a vrtta or āvrtta is a musical phrase and these phrases are equal in length and they are equivalent to one cycle of the particular time measure which the song follows.)

All these poetic forms called vrttas have four pādās (feet or lines) in each stanza. Let us take one line from a Tētageethi vrtta from Appa Kavi (op.cit., p. 128, No. 6) and do the scanning:

Virathi / vishrānthi / vishrāma / - vishra/mamulu
v v v   - - v   - - v   - v v v v

The rules for Tētageethi are these:

One Sūrya Ga*n*a (solar family unit of measure)
Two Chandra Ga*n*as (lunar family units of measure)
followed by two more Sūraya Ganas again in that order.

Solar family measures are two: Gala and Na (trochee and tribach) or -v and vvv. The lunar family measures are:

Nala (Na followed by a laghu)	v v v v
Naga (Na followed by a guru)	v v v -
Sala (Sa followed by a laghu)	v v - v
Bha	- v v
Ra	- v -
Ta	- - v

Thus Tētageethi takes any one of the solar family measures and two of the lunar family measures and again two of the solar family measures in every pāda or line. Similarly all poetic species have their own structure. Before we apply these metrical rules to musical compositions of any kind, a word about the Telugu poetic rhyme also will be necessary. In Telugu poetry there are what are known as Yati and Prāsa. Yati is simply a repetition of sound at regular and prescribed intervals in the poetic line. For illustration let us see an Ātaveladi (another short four line poetic form) from Appakavi (Ibid., p. 129, No. 14):

> Uruga rāja sāyi - ūrdhwa vishtapadāyi
> Ūrjithōru keerthi - odali kārthi

Vowel groups for Yati agreement are as follows:

> a, ā, ai, au   (i)
> u, ū, o, ō   (ii)
> i, ī, e, ē, r   (iii)

So, in the above couplet, u - in uruga rhymes with ū - in ūrdhwa in line one, and similarly, ū - ūrjith rhymes with o - in odali in the second line. These are vowel sound combinations. There are also consonant sound combinations for Yati. Consonants of each Yati group with the right vowel as per the above vowel grouping agree with each other. Let us see another Ātaveladi poem from the same source (Appakavi p. 134, No. 50).

> Kandi madhya gēha - khandithāri samūha
> Khanjanābda dēha - gāna mōha

Consonant groupings for Yati are these:

> k, kh, g gh
> ch, chh, j, jh
> ṭ, ṭh, ḍ, ḍh   (hard sounds)
> t, th, d, dh   (soft sounds)

Thus in the above example, ka in kandi agrees with kh in khandi in the first line, and kh in khanja agrees with ga in gana in the second line. In addition to these separate vowel groups and consonant groups there are combined groupings. Appakavi cites 28 different kinds of Yati relationships.

A study of these relationships is important because this regularity of sound repetition is strictly prescribed for songs also.

Like Yati in poetry and song, Prāsa also is important. Prāsa concerns itself with repeating sounds in the second syllable of every line in poetry and second syllable in every musical phrase in a song. In the example given earlier the r sound in uruga and ūrdhwa is an example of this. This is ādi prāsa, or the beginning rhyme. There is an anthya prāsa also, the so-called end-rhyme. Thus in the same example, sāyi rhymes with dāyi in the first line and keerthi agrees with kārthi in the second line.

Sāmbamoorthy says that Yati and Prasa contribute a certain life, charm, regularity, symmetry and beauty to musical compositions. (See Prof. Sāmbamoorthy, op.cit., Book IV, p. 299).

One more example from Appakavi (op.cit., p. 163, No. 259) will make the prāsa principle more clear:

> Dēvakee kumāra - Gōvardha nōddhāra
> Thōyajaksha pānda - vēya paksha
> Ghana vineela gāthra - muni jana sthuthi pāthra
> Yadukulābdi soma - Kadana bheema

In each line the underlined pair of words match in sound. Dēva with gōva, thōya with vēya etc. There is an additional end-rhyme also in each of these lines: kumāra and nōddhara in the first line, Jāksha and paksha in the second line, gāthra and pāthra in the third line, and sōma and bheema in the last line.

The importance of these sound patterns in Telugu songs can never be overestimated. These alliterations provide a certain sweetness to the song, and they help the memory of people who largely belong to an oral tradition. In bhakti songs this can help involvement and provide a useful emotional satisfaction to the singers by a skillful combination of sound and meaning. That is why Telugu grammarians talk about ardhālankāra (colour of meaning) and also sabdālankāra (colour in sound).

Having said this, it is now a matter of applying these principles to one or two songs of Devadas. Song No. 47 of the Bible Mission Hymnal is a good example.

> Thanuvu nādidigō gai - konumee yō prabhuvā, nee
> Paniki prathishtinchumee
> Dinamulu kshanamulu - deesikoni yavi needu
> Vinuthin pravahimpajeyanu shakthi neeyuma

(This hymn is "Take My Life and Let It be Consecrated Lord to Thee," paraphrased by Devadas.)

In this example, the rhyming words—thanu, konu, pani, dina, kshana, vinu, yanu—all come in measured regularity like the hoof sounds of running horses and they provide an interesting pattern. The next verse of the same song has a different set of sound combinations equally musical and ever so meaningful. Devadas is talking about 'take my silver and my gold' in this verse.

> Vendi pasidi yivigō - veesa mainanu nakai
> Yundavalenani kōranu
> Nindaina neeyishta - niyamambu choppuna
> Menduga vāda pari - mithiyau gnānambidigo

vendi, yunda, nindu, mendu - these are all initial rhyming words (ādi prāsa). Ve with vee in line one, and ni with nee and ni in the third line, and me with mi in the last line are all examples of yati or alliteration at fixed musical intervals.

The same colourful arrangement is also found in another well-known hymn of Devadas (Andhra Christian Hymnal, 325; Bible Mission Hymnal, 44), his paraphrase of the prayer of the prodigal son in the words of any believer.

> Nannu diddumu chinna prāyamu
> sannuthundagu nāyana, Nivu
> Kanna thandri vanuchu nēnu
> Ninnu chērithi nāyanā

And so on, with other sounds in each of the verses that followed.

> Vāsiga nē pāpalōkapu
> Vāsuda-nō nāyana, Ni
> Dāsula-lō nokaniga nanu jesi kāvumi
> nāyanā etc.

Fox Strangways traces back many of these features in songs to the structure of Sanskrit metres. He identifies two classes of metres, viz., the syllable-fixed (varnāvrtta) and the time-unit-fixed (mātrāvrtta) (Fox-Strangways, op.cit., p. 193). The characteristic of the metres following the time-unit (mātrāvrtta) to him, 'lies in the principle of equivalence, that is in the fact which we are familiar within the hexameter, that two shorts take the time of one long'. Each foot (I would call this measure to distinguish it from the foot or line of a poetical stanza) contains four mātras and its prosodical possibilities are as follows (ibid., p. 200):

proceleusmaticus	v v v v	(1, 1, 1, 1)
amphibrach	v - v	(1, 2, 1)
dactyl	- v v	(2, 1, 1)
anapaest	v v -	(1, 1, 2)
spondee	- -	(2, 2)

Poetry, according to Fox Strangways, bases the verse on the unit of (1) the syllable (akshara), more or less fixed, and (2) the time-length (mātra) treated on the basis of equivalent combinations. Music similarly has two clearly defined stages, where time was reckoned (1) by akshara and (2) by mātra (Ibid., pp. 199-200).

An understanding of this structural arrangement is necessary to be able to recognise the time beat (tāla) in singing. The greatest difficulty in group singing in the churches in India is to see that all singers keep to time. That is why Popley says: 'the main thing is that congregations should sing the rāga (melody) correctly in correct tāla (time-beat), and if there is proper training this should not be difficult. (See Popley, R.A., op.cit., p. 80).

For a detailed discussion of Rāg or Rāgam, which means particularisation of musical mode, one can refer to Fox Strangways, p. 107. The metres of a Telugu song are mātrāvrtta, time-unit-fixed. There is a choice of syllable lengths possible within a given time unit, like two shorts in the time of one long, or a long stretched to fill a longer time within the musical phrase, etc. Groups of these mātras make an āvrtta (a cycle) or a musical phrase and the length of these phrases is fixed according to the particular tāla (time). In the hymn of Devadas which we have already seen, we can easily discern these metrical measures:

> Nannu diddumu - chinna prāyamu
> Sannuthundagu nāyana, Nīvu
> Kannathandri vanuchu nēnu
> Ninnu chērithi nāyana

This song runs in groups of 3 + 4 beats in each phrase thus:

Nannu/ diddumu/ chinna/ prāyamu
‾ v   ‾ v v   ‾ v   ‾ v v

Sannu/thundagu/ nāya/nā nivu
‾ v ‾ v v   ‾ v ‾ v v

The principle is that a short followed by a double consonant gets the value of a long (two mātras) and a single syllable followed by a nasal sound, gets similarly a double value (e.g. thun in the second line above).

In the structure of songs or bhakti hymns in Telugu and many folk Indian languages there are three units in a song. The first is the introductory part called pallavi with or without the accompanying anu-pallavi. This pallavi or pallavi anu-pallavi combination repeats at the end of the next part which is called charanam. There can be any number of charanams to a song.

Let us look at one of Devadas' hymns to see the above structure, No. 12 of the Andhra Christian Hymnal, which is a paraphrase of Ps. 103, for example.

Pallavi: Dēva samsthuthi chēyave manasā
    Srīmanthudagu ye - hōva samsthuthi chēyavē manasa
    (Bless the Lord O my soul, bless the holy name of Jehovah)

Anu-pallavi: Dēva samsthuthi chēyumā nā
    Jeevama Yēhōva dēvuni
    Pāvana nāmamu nuthimpuma
    Nā antharangamu'lō vasinchu no'samasthama
    (Bless the Lord O my soul, bless the holy name of God Jehovah, all that is within me, bless His name)

Charanam: Jīvama, Yēhōva niku - chēsina mēllanu maruvaku
    Nivu chēsina pāthakambulanu - mānninchi jabbu
    Lēviyunu lekunda chēyunu
    Aa - kāranamu che - Dēva samsthuthi chēyave manasa etc.
    (O my soul, forget not all the good the Lord has done to you. He forgives the sins you have committed and removes all the sicknesses. Therefore praise the Lord, etc.)

In this song, the dhātu (music) of the charanam is exactly like the dhātu (music) of the anupallavi. Incidentally we can also see the beautiful rhyme in the above song. Generally the anupallavi is an elaboration of the pallavi in meaning or a retelling of the same idea in different words. A song begins in pallavi (or pallavi combined with anupallavi) and ends with the same.

From among the poetical structures mentioned already, Devadas used Seesamalika, Ātaveladi and Tēta geethi. The metrical rules for these are as follows:

Seesam: 1) Any six lunar family measures (gaṇas) followed by any two solar family measures in every foot and a total of four such feet.
2) In every foot the first syllable of the first measure (gaṇa) should rhyme with the first syllable of the third measure.

3) Similarly the first syllable of the fifth measure should rhyme with the first syllable of the seventh measure.

For example, one of the invocation poems of Devadas in the Rakshana Padyamulu runs thus:

    Manaku sa/rvambu che̅/ - sina thandri/ prathi ro̅ju
    v v v -   - v -   v v - v   v v - v

    E̅mi k̅a/valasina/ - yichchu/ g̅aka
    - v -   v v v v   - v   - v

Mana rhymes with sina in the first line and the initial sounds in e̅mi and ichchu in the second line agree with each other according to yati grouping which we mentioned already.

Similarly a Te̅ta geethi of Devadas can be scannned:

Teta Geethi:
1) One solar family measure followed by two lunar family measures + 2 solar family measures again in every foot and four feet in every verse.

2) The first syllable of the first measure and the first syllable of the fourth measure should rhyme with each other in every line.

3) Pra̅sa (rhyming of the second syllable of the successive lines is not obligatory.

Example: Ni̅ru/ dra̅ksha ra/samu che̅se/ - nimusa/ mande
                - v   - - v   v v - v   v v v   - v

Meaning: In a moment He made water into wine, etc.

Appendix V

People Interviewed for the Research

Name	Subject discussed
1. Mrs. Grace Yesuratnam, follower of Devadas, writer, Lady Elder of the Bible Mission Church, Vijaywada.	Life and work of Devadas, Dreams and Visions.
2. Pastor P. Bhushanam, Bible Mission Church, Vijaywada, Editor, <u>Bible Mahima</u> (Monthly).	Bible Mission evangelistic tours, Healing work, <u>Bible Mahima</u> Periodical.
3. Pastor Charles, Bible Mission, Guntur. Earlier follower and disciple of Devadas. Healer.	Healing Missions in Kakani Gardens.
4. Ananda Rao, Preacher, Vijaywada. One of the childhood disciples of Devadas.	Some of the unpublished messages of Devadas from manuscripts.
5. Rev. P.B. Paul (deceased) Lutheran Pastor, a man who knew Devadas from the latter's Lutheran Church days. A researcher on the Bible Mission.	The birth of the Bible Mission and earlier life of Devadas.
6. Rev. V. Frederick, retired Lutheran Pastor, a student of Devadas and a man from the same village as Devadas. (Since called to rest.)	The early life of Devadas.
7. Dr. K. Devasahayam. A former President of the Lutheran Church (Convention), church historian, researcher on the Bible Mission.	Early history of the Bible Mission and the theology of Devadas.
8. Dr. J.F. Neudoerffer, son of a missionary colleague of Devadas and now the Mission Secretary, Division of World Missions, Lutheran Church in America, New York. For 30 years in charge of Southern Asia and Middle East mission work.	Mission old and new, Western missions in the Indian cultural milieu.
9. Bishop Lesslie Newbigin, former Bishop, Church of South India.	Indigenous theology and South Indian hymn tradition.

People Interviewed for the Research

10. Bishop Lakshaman Vikrama Singhe, Srilanka. (Since called to rest.) — Asian culture and Indigenization.

11. Bishop N.D. Ananda Rao Samuel, Church of South India Moderator (retired). — Mission churches and group churches, Partnership.

12. Sri Kesava Rao Choudury, Hindu businessman, disciple of Subba Rao, and healer. — Subba Rao of Munipalle and his teachings.

13. Kalagara Subba Rao of Munipalle (deceased). Founder of the Hindu-Christian movement in Andhra. — His understanding of Christian Calling and the Sacraments.

14. Rev. E.W. Gallagher, former Methodist missionary in Andhra, Telugu language examiner, at present Principal, Methodist College, Belfast, N. Ireland. (Since called to rest.) — Hymns of Devadas and their theological content.

15. Dr. B. Rajani Kantha Rao, retired Director of All India Radio, poet and writer. Presently Director of Kalabhavan (Arts Academy), Sri Venkateswara University, Andhra Pradesh. — Yaksha Ganas (Classical Hindu dance dramas of Andhra Pradesh).

16. B.V. Subbamma, Principal, Women's Bible Training School, Andhra Evangelical Lutheran Church. A Director of Christian Ashrams. — Christian Ashrams in the Andhra Lutheran Church area.

17. Pastor Samuel, President of the Bible Mission, Elur. — His boyhood training with Father Devadas.

Appendix VI

Glossary of Indian Words

āshram, āshrama: name given to the four stages of man's life in Hinduism, an institution or place of religious retreat and instruction where a <u>guru</u> lives and teaches his disciples.

adwaitha: nondualism, monism.

anubhava, (anubhav): experience, one of the <u>pramānās</u> (sources) of religious knowledge.

avathār, (avatāra): 'descent' used of the coming to earth of god, especially <u>Vishnu</u>, in human or other form.

ācharya: leader, spiritual guide.

ātaveladi: one of the prosodical structures of Telugu poetry derived from Sanskrit.

akshara-kāla: word-time length, a measure in Telugu poetry.

ardhālankāra: colour, embellishment in meaning.

anupallavi: supplement to <u>pallavi</u>, or first repetitive part of a Telugu song, appearing in some songs with <u>pallavi</u>.

archaka: worshipper or priest, hence Christian priests are sometimes called <u>archans</u>, or <u>archakas</u>.

bhajan: from the verb <u>bhaj</u> meaning to worship, religious form of worship generally in song and group chorus.

bhakta: a devotee, from the noun <u>bhakti</u>, devotion.

burrakatha: ballad type of song story with generally three people participating, the man in the middle the main story teller and the two others accompanying with small hand drums, <u>burras</u>.

Glossary of Indian Words

bhāgavatha: story of Bhagavān, God. So Bhāgavathār is a story teller telling the stories of God.

chela: disciple or friend or follower.

chakra: wheel.

charithra: story, saga.

dandakam: a long continuous poetic-prose form of writing generally in praise of gods and goddesses memorised by people and recited as a kind of oral prayer.

divāli: Hindu festival of lights originally associated with God destroying the demon of darkness but now mostly used as a social and cultural festival.

dhātu-māthu: words and music respectively in Karnatic music and song composition.

darshan: a vision, a vision of reality, thus a system of philosophy. (Shad-darshanas, the six systems of philosophy).

dānam: gift, like bhoodānam (land gift), godānam (gift of a cow, etc.).

guru: a religious teacher.

gurukul: the abode or community around the guru.

harikatha: story of Hari, God. A lyrical and prose story told by one man with musical accompaniment. Very old folk method of instruction now used for contemporary and social themes also.

janma: birth, generally referring to the cycle or births and rebirths in Hinduism.

jamindār: land-lord, or small ruler, from Arabic Jamin, land.

janaka-rāga: parent melody in Karnatic music. There are altogether 72 Janaka-rāgas or Mēlakartha rāgās as they are also called.

Glossary of Indian Words

janya-rāga:	derivative or descending melody coming from the Janaka-rāgas from some variation in the notes used.
kuśa grass:	a type of grass used for holy ceremonies in Hinduism and for making mats for worship and prayer.
kachēri:	court, or a public meeting. Thus a musical concert.
kalāpam:	name used for a certain type of muscial dance plays, e.g., Bhāmakalāpam, a musical song story of bhāma, the consort of Kristna.
karma:	fate, fruits of one's works, etc. Also, one of the three Hindu ways of salvation, karma mārga, way of works.
kulam:	caste.
lakshana:	quality, description, etc., of poetry, language, etc.
laghu:	short syllable in Telugu poetry or song as different from guru, the long syllable. e.g., in a word like Hari both syllables are laghus.
leela:	play, generally referring to the play of gods. Kristna leela, the play of Kristna.
māya:	illusion, mystery, ignorance, generally spiritual darkness.
mana(h):	Soul, mind, thought, etc.
mangalasūthra:	the auspicious thread, the yellow thread and gold pendant tied around the neck of the bride by the groom at the time of marriage. Also called thālipottu.
mahāsabha:	great gathering, a big meeting of people.
mēlakartha:	parent meolody in Indian music. There are 72 mēlakarthas possible in Karnātic music with the various combinations of the notes of the octave.

Glossary of Indian Words

māthra: measure (of time), the shortest measurable duration used in poetic construction in Telugu.

mithra: friend.

mādiga, māla: the two sections among the outcastes in India.

Mathebha: one form of poetic structure in Telugu, derived from Sanskrit. Four lines of equal length in each piece.

manthra: charm, prayer spell, etc.

makuta: crown, thus the first part of a song which comes once and repeats after every verse.

nirguna: without attribute, without form (opposite of sa-guna) without feeling or passion, generally referring to God.

nirdwanda: non-dual.

nirwikalpa samādhi: trance in prayer and meditation, undefinable state of mind and soul.

paramātman: the supreme self.

parabhrahman: the supreme self.

purusha and prakriti: the Lord and the Universe, God and Nature, personal and material parts of the universe, etc.

purāna: old legendary story, generally about gods and their actions, hence there are puranas after the names of many gods and places (sthala purānas).

pūja: worship.

prānayāma: breath control in yōga, etc.

pramāna: standard, measure.

prākāra: a wall surrounding a city, etc.

Glossary of Indian Words 373

pallavi:	the starting part of a Telugu song which states the main idea of the song and repeated after every verse. The same as <u>makuta</u>.
prāsa:	similar or related sound in poetry and song repeating at regular intervals.
prabōdha:	instruction, edification, proclamation.
prathyaksha:	appearing to the eye, thus apparition or vision of God.
pandāl, pendāl:	leaf shelter or temporary structure put up for festivals, marriages, etc.
prabhu:	Lord, Kurios.
rāgabhāva:	embellishment (colour) in musical melody.
sannidhi:	presence, nearness, fellowship, etc. (generally of God).
sampada:	treasure, blessing, boon, etc.
shārdh:	anniversary of death, observed as a solemn day every year by the descendants of the dead.
Shārdūla:	a type of poetic structure in Telugu derived from Sanskript.
sabdālankāra:	sound embellishment in literary pieces as different from <u>ardhālankāra</u>, the sense embellishment.
seesam:	a type of pure Telugu poetic structure famous for its flow and popularity among the writers. One of the few which do not come from Sanskrit.
sādhu:	a mendicant, a holy man.
sanyāsi:	one who has renounced the world, a mendicant.
satyam:	truth.

Glossary of Indian Words

sankrānthi: Hindu festival coming at the end of winter, also observed as the harvest festival in Andhra.

sáthakam: a kind of literary style containing 100 poems in Telugu.

sŕuthi: that which is heard, one of the three pramānas, sources of knowledge in Hindu philosophy. Vedas are considered as sŕuthis.

sabha: gathering of people, a meeting, especially for religious purposes or social functions.

sthala mahāthya: the glory or powerfulness of a place, generally referring to literary works describing such.

sáshti-poorthi: completion of sixty (years of age) of a man, generally observed as a function to honour people arriving at that age, a social and family function.

tāla: time beat in Indian music, the cymbals used to mark such time audibly.

Tētagīthi: a form of poetic structure in Telugu, derived from Sanskrit.

Utpalamāla: a form of Telugu poetry derived from Sanskrit.

ugādi: Telugu New Year's day festival which comes in March.

varṇa: letter of the alphabet, or colour, hence also Hindu caste to which a person belongs.

vishtnu: Hindu god, one of the Hindu triad.

viñāyak: a minor god of Hinduism, the elephant headed god, promoter of learning and wisdom.

vāggēyakāra: composer of music and words, one who is talented to write both words and music of a song.

veedhi naatakam:	street drama, a folk dramatic form which is very old in Telugu tradition.
vāc:	word, voice.
yōga:	mental, physical exercise, contemplative meditation, union, a method of achieving union with God.
yukti:	reason, inference, theology.
yaksha-gāna:	a type of old dance drama in Telugu.

STUDIEN ZUR INTERKULTURELLEN GESCHICHTE DES CHRISTENTUMS
ETUDES D'HISTOIRE INTERCULTURELLE DU CHRISTIANISME
STUDIES IN THE INTERCULTURAL HISTORY OF CHRISTIANITY

Begründet von/fondé par/founded by
Hans Jochen Margull †, Hamburg

Herausgegeben von/edité par/edited by

Richard Friedli	Walter J. Hollenweger	Theo Sundermeier
Université de Fribourg	University of Birmingham	Universität Heidelberg

Band 1 Wolfram Weiße: Südafrika und das Antirassismusprogramm. Kirchen im Spannungsfeld einer Rassengesellschaft.

Band 2 Ingo Lembke: Christentum unter den Bedingungen Lateinamerikas. Die katholische Kirche vor den Problemen der Abhängigkeit und Unterentwicklung.

Band 3 Gerd Uwe Kliewer: Das neue Volk der Pfingstler. Religion, Unterentwicklung und sozialer Wandel in Lateinamerika.

Band 4 Joachim Wietzke: Theologie im modernen Indien - Paul David Devanandan.

Band 5 Werner Ustorf: Afrikanische Initiative. Das aktive Leiden des Propheten Simon Kimbangu.

Band 6 Erhard Kamphausen: Anfänge der kirchlichen Unabhängigkeitsbewegung in Südafrika. Geschichte und Theologie der äthiopischen Bewegung. 1880-1910.

Band 7 Lothar Engel: Kolonialismus und Nationalismus im deutschen Protestantismus in Namibia 1907-1945. Beiträge zur Geschichte der deutschen evangelischen Mission und Kirche im ehemaligen Kolonial- und Mandatsgebiet Südwestafrika.

Band 8 Pamela M. Binyon: The Concepts of „Spirit" and „Demon". A Study in the use of different languages describing the same phenomena.

Band 9 Neville Richardson: The World Council of Churches and Race Relations: 1960 to 1969.

Band 10 Jörg Müller: Uppsala II. Erneuerung in der Mission. Eine redaktionsgeschichtliche Studie und Dokumentation zu Sektion II der 4. Vollversammlung des Ökumenischen Rates der Kirchen, Uppsala 1968.

Band 11 Hans Schoepfer: Theologie der Gesellschaft. Interdisziplinäre Grundlagenbibliographie zur Einführung in die befreiungs- und polittheologische Problematik: 1960-1975.

Band 12 Werner Hoerschelmann: Christliche Gurus. Darstellung von Selbstverständnis und Funktion indigenen Christseins durch unabhängige charismatisch geführte Gruppen in Südindien.

Band 13 Claude Schaller: L'Eglise en quête de dialogue.

Band 14 Theo Tschuy: Hundert Jahre kubanischer Protestantismus (1868-1961). Versuch einer kirchengeschichtlichen Darstellung.

Band 15 Werner Korte: Wir sind die Kirchen der unteren Klassen. Entstehung, Organisation und gesellschaftliche Funktionen unabhängiger Kirchen in Afrika.

Band 16 Arnold Bittlinger: Papst und Pfingstler. Der römisch katholisch - pfingstliche Dialog und seine ökumenische Relevanz.

Band 17 Ingemar Lindén: The Last Trump. An historico-genetical study of some important chapters in the making and development of the Seventh-day Adventist Church.

Band 18 Zwinglio Dias: Krisen und Aufgaben im brasilianischen Protestantismus. Eine Studie zu den sozialgeschichtlichen Bedingungen und volkspädagogischen Möglichkeiten der Evangelisation.

Band 19 Mary Hall: A quest for the liberated Christian, Examined on the basis of a mission, a man and a movement as agents of liberation.
Band 20 Arturo Blatezky: Sprache des Glaubens in Lateinamerika. Eine Studie zu Selbstverständnis und Methode der ›Theologie der Befreiung‹.
Band 21 Anthony Mookenthottam: Indian Theological Tendencies. Approaches and problems for further research as seen in the works of some leading Indian theologians.
Band 22 George Thomas: Christian Indians and Indian Nationalism 1885—1950. An Interpretation in Historical and Theological Perspectives.
Band 23 Essiben Madiba: Evangélisation et Colonisation en Afrique: L'Héritage scolaire du Cameroun (1885—1965).
Band 24 Katsumi Takizawa: Reflexionen über die universale Grundlage von Buddhismus und Christentum.
Band 25 S.W. Sykes (editor): England and Germany. Studies in theological diplomacy.
Band 26 James Haire: The Character and Theological Struggle of the Church in Halmahera, Indonesia, 1941—1979.
Band 27 David Ford: Barth and God's Story. Biblical Narrative and the Theological Method of Karl Barth in the *Church Dogmatics*.
Band 28 Kortright Davis: Mission For Caribbean Change. Caribbean Development As Theological Enterprise.
Band 29 Origen V. Jathanna: The Decisiveness of the Christ-Event and the Universality of Christianity in a world of Religious Plurality. With Special Reference to Hendrik Kraemer and Alfred George Hagg as well as to William Ernest Hocking and Pandipeddi Chenchiah.
Band 30 Joyce V. Thurman: New Wineskins. A Study of the House Church Movement.
Band 31 John May: Meaning Consensus and Dialogue in Buddist-Christian-Communication.
Band 32 Friedhelm Voges: Das Denken von Thomas Chalmers im kirchen- und sozialgeschichtlichen Kontext.
Band 33 George MacDonald Mulrain: Theology in Folk Culture. The Theological Significance of Haitian Folk Religion.
Band 34 Alan Ford: The Protestant Reformation in Ireland, 1590—1641.
Band 35 Harold Tonks: Faith, Hope and Decision-Making. The Kingdom of God and Social Policy-Making. The Work of Arthur Rich of Zürich.
Band 36 Bingham Tembe: Integrationismus und Afrikanismus. Zur Rolle der kirchlichen Unabhängigkeitsbewegung in der Auseinandersetzung um die Landfrage und die Bildung der Afrikaner in Südafrika, 1880—1960.
Band 37 Kingsley Lewis: The Moravian Mission in Barbados 1816-1886. A Study of the Historical Context and Theological Significance of a Minority Church Among an Oppressed People.
Band 38 Ulrich M. Dehn: Indische Christen in der gesellschaftlichen Verantwortung. Eine theologische und religionssoziologische Untersuchung politischer Theologie im gegenwärtigen Indien.
Band 39 Walter J. Hollenweger (Ed.): Pentecostal Research in Europe: Problems, Promises and People. Proceedings from the Pentecostal Research Conference at the University of Birmingham (England) April 26th to 29th 1984.
Band 40 P. Solomon Raj: A Christian Folk-Religion in India. A Study of the Small Church Movement in Andhra Pradesh, with a Special Reference to the Bible Mission of Devadas.

Haire, James
THE CHARACTER AND THEOLOGICAL STRUGGLE OF THE CHURCH IN HALMAHERA, INDONESIA, 1941-1979
Frankfurt/M., Berne, Las Vegas, 1981. XII, 382 pp.
Studies in the Intercultural History of Christianity. Bd. 26
ISBN 3-8204-5888-3   pb. sFr. 74.–

This study looks at the expression of Christianity in the Eastern Indonesian Island of Halmahera in the years 1941 to 1979. Against the historical, theological and missiological backgrounds, it examines the interactions between pre-literary religion, Islam and Christianity. From this it tries to evaluate the nature of the Gospel in relation to its cultural expressions, and the implications for the Church.
Contents: Halmahera Church Independence Movements, 1941-47 – Church Development, 1947-79 – Historical Background – Dutch Theological Antecedents – Missionary Experience, 1865-1941 – Pre-Literary Religious Beliefs, and interactions of these, Islam and Christianity – Gospel and Cultures.

Davis, Kortright
MISSION FOR CARIBBEAN CHANGE
Caribbean Development As Theological Enterprise
Frankfurt/M., Berne, 1982. 259 pp.
Studies in the intercultural History of Christianity. Vol. 28
ISBN 3-8204-5732-1   pb. sFr. 61.–

Caribbean society has constantly been characterized by poverty, dependence, and alienation. The Caribbean Conference of Churches, during the 1970's, promoted extensive development programmes to meet these challenges. Was this development activity recognizable as theological praxis? This study provides a framework for such a recognition by exploring a theological hermeneutic appropriate to the Caribbean, and by suggesting a theologically illuminating way of understanding why liberation praxis and Church proclamation are inseparable for Christian witness in the Caribbean.
Contents: Poverty, Dependence and Alienation in the Caribbean – Ecumenical Action For Caribbean Development – For Full Human Development – Theology For Change – Theological Paths For The Caribbean – Caribbean Theological Explorations – The Caribbean Conference of Churches And Theological Praxis – Towards Greater Christian Maturity – Appendices, Bibliography.

Verlag Peter Lang Bern · Frankfurt a.M. · New York
Auslieferung: Verlag Peter Lang AG, Jupiterstr. 15, CH-3000 Bern 15
Telefon (0041/31) 32 11 22, Telex verl ch 32 420

This work is an attempt to critically assess the life and the theology of the small churches in India especially in the Telugu-speaking land of Andhra Pradesh in the South. For a close examination the author chose the Bible Mission which started as a break-away group from his own church, the Andhra Evangelical Lutheran Church. The relationship of these small groups to the mission churches and their appeal to the non-Christians has been a much discussed subject in India in recent times.

P. Solomon Raj (born 1921) is an ordained minister in the Andhra Evangelical Lutheran Church, South India. He holds several degrees from various universities including a Ph.D in Theology from Birmingham University. He had teaching experience in Selly Oak Colleges, Birmingham, England from 1978 to 1983 in the field of Cross-Cultural Communications. Later he taught for a short time in the U.S.A. His interest in the small church movement started in 1950's when he was working as a pastor in his church in India. He conducted research in the subject under the guidance of Professor Walter J. Hollenweger.